Acknowledgments

This book has been a collaborative effort, not only between the authors, but also among the many people who make up our physical computing community. The material included here is a collection of what we consider to be the most useful material that's come out of our work and that of our friends, colleagues, and students over the past ten or twelve years.

Red Burns is the godmother of physical computing and of this book. Through the Interactive Telecommunications Program at the Tisch School of the Arts at NYU, she has championed physical computing from the start, indulged us in many outlandish requests, and pushed us always to make the subject inclusive and empowering to those who would otherwise fear technology. Red has seen to it that physical computing is not a subject for technophiles only, but for everyone.

Geoff Smith is the godfather. His thoughts on everything from interaction design to microcontrollers to electronics to software have aided and inspired us over the years. We wouldn't have written this book without him.

Daniel Rozin has been a valuable collaborator and advisor to both of us. His ideas are reflected heavily in this book, and in our work, research, and teaching.

Individuals had to be brave to support some of the unscientific approaches to research sometimes seen at ITP. Among our brave funders, past and present, are Sergio Canetti at NYNEX, Joy Mountford and Mike Mills and Linda Stone at Apple Computer, Joy Mountford (again) and Bob Adams at Interval Research, Sharleen Smith at USA Networks and Oxygen, Dana Plautz at Intel, Lili Cheng and Linda Stone (again) at Microsoft Research.

The physical computing faculty and staff (past and present) at ITP has played a major role in the shaping of this book. Gary Schober, together with Rolf Levenbach, gave us much advice on electronics over the years, and bridges the gap between the worlds of physical computing and professional electronics engineering for the students at ITP. Jeff Feddersen, Todd Holoubek, Greg Shakar, and Michael Luck Schneider, as faculty and research fellows, have kept our students and us going through the writing of this book and have contributed to many of the examples herein. Jody Culkin, Cynthia Lawson, Jen Lewin, Andrew Milmoe, Camille Norment, Will Pickering, Joe Rosen, Ben Rubin, Joey Stein, Camille Utterback, and Steve Weiss have collectively taught the material to hundreds of students. Many others from the ITP community have contributed their specific expertise, including Luke Dubois, Dan Palkowski, Amit Pitaru, Eric Singer, Leo Villareal, and Jaime Villarreal. James Tu made a contribution in many of the roles mentioned above, and as our technical editor.

The faculty and staff of ITP as a whole have also made this possible. Faculty members such as Pat O'Hara, Marianne Petit, and John Thompson have supported the physical computing curriculum, offered valuable advice, and helped us make it grow. Staff members (past and present) George Agudow, Edward Gordon, Midori Yasuda, Robert Ryan, Nancy Lewis, Marlon Evans, Ben Gonzalez, Gilles Bersier, and Michael Wright have indulged our fantasies and those of many students over the years, and helped to make those fantasies into realities.

We have also drawn from work done at sister institutions, including the MIT Media Lab, The Royal College of Art, KTH and The Swedish Interactive Institute, The IVREA Interactive Design Institute, and UCLA Design and Media Arts. In particular, Ben Fry and Casey Reas helped us include examples of their Processing programming environment in this book.

Ultimately it is the students in the physical computing classes at ITP who push the program forward. Many of them contributed (sometimes unwittingly) to the ideas in this book. We have learned from hundreds of students over the years; thank you all for making this a better book. Current and recent students Jamie Allen, Mark Argo, Jason Babcock, John Bergren, Jonah Brucker-Cohen, Eric Forman, Sasha Harris-Cronin, Daniel Hirschmann, Rania Ho, Daniel Howe, Tetsu Kondo, Takuro Lippitt, Kari Martin, Dan Mikesell, Jin-Yo Mok, Josh Nimoy, Kentaro Okuda, Billy Taylor, Michael Sharon, Ahmi Wolf, Scott Wolynski, and many others have directly contributed ideas, additions, and corrections, that appear in the chapters that follow.

Thanks also to our editors at Thomson: Stacy Hiquet, Dan Foster, Danielle Foster, Kim Benbow, Michael Tanamachi, and our agent, Laura Lewin, at Studio B. We are especially thankful for the insight and provocative feedback of our technical editor, James Tu, who had to check examples of an absurd variety of technologies across many platforms.

Of course, this book would not have been possible were it not for the support, patience, and inspiration of our families and partners. Thanks and love to Kate, Lily, Terri, and our parents, brother, and sisters.

To those we've overlooked, we apologize, and thank for their unsung support.

Physical Computing

Sensing and
Controlling the
Physical World
with Computers

Dan O'Sullivan and Tom Igoe

...OGY

Australia • Brazil • Japan • K...   ...nited Kingdom • United States

COURSE TECHNOLOGY
CENGAGE Learning

Physical Computing: Sensing and Controlling the Physical World with Computers
Dan O'Sullivan and Tom Igoe

SVP, Course Technology PTR:
Andy Shafran

Publisher: Stacy L. Hiquet

Senior Marketing Manager: Sarah O'Donnell

Marketing Manager: Heather Hurley

Manager of Editorial Services: Heather Talbot

Associate Marketing Managers:
Kristin Eisenzopf and Sarah Dubois

Project Editor: Dan Foster, Scribe Tribe

Technical Reviewer: James Tu

Course Technology PTR Market Coordinator:
Amanda Weaver

Copy Editor: Kim Benbow

Interior Layout Tech: Danielle Foster,
Scribe Tribe

Cover Designer and Interior Illustrator:
Mike Tanamachi

Front Cover Illustrators: Merce Dunningham,
Paul Kaiser, and Shelley Eshkar. Still from
Hand-drawn Spaces (1998)

Indexer: Kelly Talbot

Proofreader: Estelle Manticas

Library of Congress Control Number: 2004101322

ISBN-13: 978-1-59200-346-4

ISBN-10: 1-59200-346-X

Course Technology
5191 Natorp Boulevard
Mason, OH 45040
USA

Cengage Learning is a leading provider of customized learning solutions with office locations around the globe, including Singapore, the United Kingdom, Australia, Mexico, Brazil, and Japan. Locate your local office at **international.cengage.com/region**

Cengage Learning products are represented in Canada by Nelson Education, Ltd.

To learn more about Course Technology, visit
www.cengage.com/coursetechnology

Purchase any of our products at your local college store or at our preferred online store **www.ichapters.com**

Printed in the United States of America
6 7 8 9 10   21 20 19 18 17

Contents at a Glance

Contents

Introduction

We believe that the computer revolution has left most of you behind. Steve Jobs had similar thoughts when he founded Apple Computer and set out to build "computers for the rest of us." The idea was to enable people who were not computer experts—like artists, educators, and children—to take advantage of the power of computing. The graphical user interface (GUI) popularized by Apple was wildly successful, widely copied, and is now the standard interface of almost all personal computers. Thanks to this interface, people from all walks of life use computers.

Now we need to make "computers for the rest of *you*." We need computers that respond to the rest of your body and the rest of your world. GUI technology allows you to drag and drop, but it won't notice if you twist and shout. It's made it easy to open a folder and start a program, but we'd like a computer to be able to open a door or start a car. Personal computers have evolved in an office environment in which you sit on your butt, moving only your fingers, entering and receiving information censored by your conscious mind. That is not your whole life, and probably not even the best part. We need to think about computers that sense more of your body, serve you in more places, and convey physical expression in addition to information.

In more than a decade of teaching physical computing at New York University's Tisch School of the Arts, we have found people from very diverse backgrounds looking to bridge this gap between the physical and the virtual. Perhaps you are a sculptor who would like different sounds or videos to play depending on where a person touches your sculpture, or a dancer who wants a knee bend to cause bells to ring. Maybe you are a sociologist who needs to automatically log how many people pass a street corner. Maybe you're a teacher who wants to make tools for children to understand the world by doing rather than just reading. Or maybe you just want your window blinds to be lowered automatically in the afternoon if it's hot outside. Regardless of your background or technical experience, this book is designed to help you make a more interesting connection between the physical world and the computer world.

How We See the Computer

When asked to draw a computer, most people will draw the same elements: screen, keyboard, and mouse. When we think "computer," this is the image that comes to mind. In order to fully explore the possibilities of computing, you have to get away from that stereotype of computers. You have to think about *computing* rather than *computers*. Computers should take whatever physical form suits our needs for computing. So what is computing good for?

One common reply is that computing is like human thinking. The area of Artificial Intelligence (AI), using computers to imitate, and maybe someday replace, human beings, has been an important part of computer science since its beginning. Robotics is the physical equivalent to AI. The technology you will learn in this book is very similar to what you'd learn in a book on robotics, but our typical applications are different. In robotics, people generally build robots—things that try to imitate the autonomy of human beings. We have nothing against robots, but we find the best robots much less interesting than even the dullest people (for now). Our approach comes out of a different area of computing called Intelligence Amplification (IA). This approach looks to people to supply the spark of interest and computers to capture and convey a person's expression. Rather than trying to imitate the autonomy of human beings, we want to support it. IA treats the computer as a medium of communication between people.

So what does computing offer as a medium? It can store sounds and images, but so could previous media like magnetic tape and movie film. With film and magnetic tape, information and images must be called up sequentially, according to their physical location on the tape or film as it rolls along. Ideas can only be directly linked with the previous and next idea in the sequence. Because of this, these are called *linear media*. Computers offer a break from linearity. With *random access media*, non-sequential parts of a computer's memory can be called up as if they were next to each other. This allows any idea recorded in memory to appear as if it's next to any other idea. When you combine random access with networked communication, you can display information and images stored on different continents as if they were stored next to each other. Reordering and making multiple versions are all made much easier, as anyone who has used a computer's copy and paste functions understands. Computers reduce the barriers of time and space when playing with and rearranging ideas. As a result, they better depict the changing and manifold relationships between ideas in human thought, and they can be more egalitarian in giving voice to multiple versions of those relationships.

Even if you're not out to save the world by annihilating time and space, computational media offer some concrete advantages. Without a computer, you can connect a button being pressed to a light turning on. With a computer, you can make the relationship between the button and the light more complex. For example, you can make the light's turning on dependent on the number of times the button was pressed, for how long it was pressed, or whether it was pressed in conjunction with other buttons in other rooms or on other continents. You can change the relationships on the fly; for example, you can make the light come on after two button presses during the day, and after only one button press at night. To get the computer to make these relationships between events it senses and events it causes, you write computer programs. The intelligence amplification approach counts on human beings to make the most interesting relationships, so your programs for physical computing are often relatively simple.

How the Computer Sees Us

If you want to put the computer in a role that supports people (rather than the other way around), you need to look at the person and her environment to determine what needs to be supported. So what does a person look like to a computer? Ask this question, and you're likely to get a bunch of blank stares. Why should we care? A computer's image of human beings is reflected by its input and output devices. In the case of most desktop computers, this means a mouse, a keyboard, a monitor, and speakers. To such a computer, we might look like a hand with one finger, one eye, and two ears (see Figure I.1). To change how the computer reacts to us, we have to change how it sees us.

Figure I.1
How the computer
sees us.

The human being as seen through the computer's input devices is a sad creature. Kurt Vonnegut's Tralfamadorians from *The Sirens of Titan* look much like this, and their perspective is as alien to ours as this poor creature's. It can't walk, dance, or jump; it can't sing or scream. It can't make grand sweeping gestures. And it has only one direction in which to look.

Before we invent new forms for the computer, we need to decide why it needs to take new forms. We need to take a better look at ourselves to see our full range of expression. This includes everything from the spontaneous expression on your face to the more deliberate expression of a trained artist. Just in the act of standing up, a person effortlessly reveals important details through hundreds of subtle and unconscious adjustments every second. Even though these expressions come and go very quickly, humans have amazing abilities for reading into this body language the interior state of another person. To make the computer a medium for expression, you need to describe the conversation you want to have with (or better yet, through) the computer. For example, in a Web chat room, should the *context* of the expression—that is, the posture of the user—accompany the *text* of the chat? You also need to examine your environment. Does life continue when you leave the swivel chair? Should the computer be able to interpret this action? Do people prefer to vote with their feet? How do you record their vote? Once you've taken these steps, you'll be able to realize more of the physical potential of computers, and also that of human beings.

The Concepts

There are a few key concepts that come up repeatedly throughout this book, so it's worthwhile to introduce them briefly here. Physical computing is about creating a conversation between the physical world and the virtual world of the computer. The process of *transduction*, or the conversion of one form of energy into another, is what enables this flow. Your job is to find, and learn to use, *transducers* to convert between the physical energy appropriate for your project and the electrical energy used by the computer. To cut this task down to size, it helps first to identify the direction of the energy flows as *input* or *output*, and then treat each flow as a separate problem. You will learn that the signals in these energy flows can be viewed as *digital* or *analog*. Identifying how you want to view the flow will help both to clarify the interaction you are creating and to further narrow your search for transducers. Being able to identify how events in the flow occur over time, whether they happen *serially* or in *parallel*, will help determine how best to plan the interaction.

Interaction: Input, Output, and Processing

When people talk about computers, they often say that computers are useful because they make things interactive. "Interactive" is a fuzzy term, and often misused for all kinds of ridiculous purposes. Author and game programmer Chris Crawford has a great definition for it: *interaction* is "an iterative process of listening, thinking, and speaking between two or more actors." Most physical computing projects (and most computer applications in general) can be broken down into these same three stages: listening, thinking, and speaking—or, in computer terms: input, processing, and output. Breaking down your project along these lines will enable you to better focus on your particular challenges and possibly to skip entire sections of this book. In Chapter 8, "Physical Interaction Design, or Techniques for Polite Conversation," we will return to this three-part cycle of events to create interactions that balance them in a satisfying way, like a good conversation.

Input

For many people, input is all they want to learn from physical computing. They are already happy with their ability to express themselves on a computer, either through the screen or through the speakers, but feel constrained by the input of a mouse and keyboard. Input is usually easier than output because it takes less energy to sense activity than to move things.

Output

The most provocative physical computing projects are ones that don't just sense the world; they also change it. In general, physical output can be more difficult than input because it often requires electrical (as opposed to electronic) and often mechanical skills. There are a couple of devices for light, sound, and movement that are very easy to use, which we will cover in Part I of this book. You can also get fairly far rather easily by connecting your physical input to a desktop computer, which has great capabilities for sound and video output. In Part II, we will meet the challenge of output in depth, using motors and other devices to move things in the physical world.

Processing

Input and output are the physical parts of physical computing. The third part requires a computer to read the input, make decisions based on the changes it reads, and activate outputs or send messages to other computers. This is where programming comes in.

Transduction

One of the main principles behind physical computing is *transduction*, or the conversion of one form of energy into another. A microphone is a classic transducer because it changes sound pressure waves in the air to a changing electrical voltage. Speakers convert the same energy in the opposite direction. Transducers are the eyes, ears, hands, legs, and mouth of any physical computing system.

Much of the challenge of physical computing is converting various forms of energy, such as light, heat, or pressure, into the electronic energy that a computer can understand. Sometimes it's easy to find the right transducer for the job; at other times, you will contrive the interaction to fit a transducer that you know how to use.

Input transducers (sensors), such as switches and variable resistors, convert heat, light, motion, and sound into electrical energy. Output transducers (actuators), such as motors and buzzers, convert electrical energy into the various forms of energy that the body can sense.

Digital and Analog

When describing an activity, begin by breaking it down in terms of how many possible outcomes there are. Sometimes we view events in the world along a continuous range of possible states. At other times, we only care about the difference between two possible states. When two states will suffice, we'll call it *digital*. When a continuous range of multiple states is considered, we'll call it *analog*. For example, as you get dressed in the morning you might prefer to know the actual outdoor temperature (analog) rather than just hearing that it's hot or cold (digital).[1] On the other hand, when deciding to bring your umbrella, you only want to know whether it is raining or not (digital); you don't care how hard it's raining (analog). In general, digital input and output (I/O) are easier than analog I/O because computers use a two-state, or binary system, but analog I/O can be more fun and interesting.

The language you use to describe the project will tip you off to whether your I/O requirements are analog or digital. For example, if you can use the words "whether or not," or the word "either," in describing the input or output, then you're probably talking about a digital input or output. If you can use words like "how much" for input or superlative adjectives like "stronger," "faster," "brighter," then you're probably talking about an analog input or output. For example, a digital output would work to *either* turn a light on or off; an analog output would be required to determine whether the light is *brighter* or *dimmer*.

Parallel and Serial

The terms digital and analog make it possible for us to be clear about what we're listening to (our input) or what we're saying (our output). We also need to be clear about how we're speaking or listening. Sometimes we present ideas simply, one after another, in discrete chunks. For example, a simple melody played on a solo instrument lets us focus on the structure of the melody, and how its changes affect our emotions. At other times, we present many ideas all at once so that they complement each other. For example, a symphony's power comes from the experience of hearing many instruments playing different harmonies all at once; each individual instrument's melody line is important, but the combined effect of all of them presented at once is what we take away from the experience.

To describe the order in which events happen, we can talk about them happening either one after another in time or all at once, simultaneously. For our purposes, we'll refer

---

[1] The truth is that analog and digital may not be the most accurate terms. Terms like multi-state versus two-state or continuous versus binary might be better. But digital and analog are commonly used terms among the manufacturers of the tools we will be using.

to events that happen one at a time as *serial* events, and when several events happen simultaneously, we'll refer to them as *parallel* events.

While we're using these terms in a broad sense, to talk about how events are organized in time, we'll also use them to refer to more technical aspects of the work as well. You'll see how electrical energy can flow through components serially (one after another) or in parallel (through several components at the same time), and we'll talk about how computers can exchange bits of information serially or in parallel as well.

The Practice

Physical computing is best understood by doing it rather than talking about it, so in this book we focus primarily on how to do it. Following are a few general guidelines that will help you keep your wits about you in the midst of all the technical information that follows later in this book. If you find yourself getting lost in the details, come back to this section and use it as a guide to regain an overview of your whole project.

Getting Started: Describing What Happens

The first step in a physical computing project is to describe what you want to happen. If you can't first describe what happens in plain language, it will be difficult to write the programs and build the circuits to make it happen. Describe the whole environment of the project from the point of view of the person experiencing what you're making. Describe what she sees, hears, and feels and what she can do to change the environment. Describe the experience as it unfolds, what changes as the person takes various actions, and how her attention and actions are focused by the changes. Describe why this is engaging to the person and how the sequence of events should work to keep her engaged. You'll revise this description several times as you realize the project, so don't worry if some details are missing. On the other hand, don't let the process of implementation distract you from filling in the missing details as you go.

Focus your description on *what* happens, not *how* it happens. Avoid describing the specific technologies involved or the tools used to make things happen. These details will prejudice your thinking and possibly cripple your concept. Frequently, we've had students skip to the technology, coming to ask how to implement some esoteric and difficult-to-use sensor. Our first question is always, "What are you using this to do?" Quite often, once they describe what they want to happen without describing the technology, a simpler solution can be found.

For example, say you want to announce guests at a party in a big way. When a person walks into the room, a theatrical curtain opens, a bright spotlight hits the person, and loud applause is heard. This description tells you nothing about the technologies that make it work, but it gives you enough description to start to plan how to make it a reality. You know you need a curtain, a spotlight, and applause, and you know you need to be able to sense when a person enters the room.

After you've described the project and iterated your concept a few times in plain language, without thinking about the technology, you should break the project down into the stages of input, output, and processing. For example, the input in the example above would be the person walking into the room, the output would be the spotlight and the applause, and the processing would be turning on the light and playing the applause *if* a person walks in.

Next, identify your input and output as digital or analog and begin your search for the perfect transducers. Again, in the example above, if you wanted the volume of the applause to depend on *how far* the person walked into the room, you would need an analog input and output. If you wanted the applause to either be on or off, depending on whether or not the person was in the room, you would need digital input and output. It will help you to focus in on the most relevant parts of this book if you can break your project description into parts that fit into the categories shown in Figure I.2. Use this or a similar worksheet to fill in the input/output needs of your project.

Figure I.2
Categorize your physical computing challenges.

DIGITAL INPUT	ANALOG INPUT	PROCESSING	DIGITAL OUTPUT	ANALOG OUTPUT

In addition, you should describe the sequence of events. Does the light happen before the applause? Or do they happen at the same time? In the former case, they'd be *serial* events, and in the latter, they'd be *parallel* events.

Refer to the chart in Figure I.3 to help figure out how complex your project is, and what needs to be done.

Figure I.3
Mapping your project: analog and digital, serial and parallel.

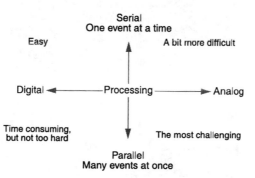

Level of Abstraction (and Distraction)

With any technical practice, you inevitably have to make strategic decisions about the level of abstraction between you and your tools. Higher-level tools place you at a higher level of abstraction from the details of the technology.[2] As a result, they are easier to use but don't

---

[2] This way of thinking of high levels and low levels may seem counterintuitive if you're used to thinking of "higher level" meaning more advanced technologically. Instead, think of "lower level" meaning a lower level of padding between you and the metal of the computer. We think a little padding goes a long way.

always allow you to do everything you would like. Our approach starts at the highest level that still gets the job done and works down when necessary. With high-level tools, you can quickly try a new idea, and if it doesn't work, you can move on before you get too invested technically and emotionally. In technology, tools change rapidly enough that a high-level approach works in your favor: tomorrow's high-level tool will have the power of today's low-level tool.

In practice, though, it's never that clear. There are temptations in lower-level tools to lead you astray. For example, if you are a food lover, you might be attracted to cooking from scratch, regardless of whether it tastes better, because you enjoy the process. Be aware that you may be indulging a technical machismo that will be distracting, time-consuming, and will probably yield a less impressive result. Just because you made your crème brûlée from scratch doesn't mean your guests are going to like it (especially if you've never cooked it before). On the other hand, when you know something about cooking, it's difficult to make a signature dish using only pre-prepared foods. If you are attempting something very specific and unusual, there will come a time when it's easier to do it yourself than to find, cobble together, and then work around a bunch of mix-and-match prepared solutions. A combination of working at the highest level, knowing what's available at lower levels, and knowing when to switch up or down, will yield the best results (see Table I.1).

Table I.1
Levels of Abstraction

SOFTWARE	FOOD	MICROCONTROLLERS
Higher Level ("Hello World!")	Higher Level ("Hello, may I take your order?")	Higher Level ("Hello World!")
MAX	Ordering out	Teleo
LINGO/ACTIONSCRIPT	TV dinners	BASIC STAMP 2
PROCESSING	Hamburger Helper	BX-24
JAVA	Using the deli counter at the supermarket.	Basic Atom Pro24
C	Using produce and the butcher at the supermarket.	PIC
ASSEMBLY	Growing your own foods, harvesting them, and preparing them from scratch.	SX
Lower Level ("1001001 0110110")	Lower Level ("Henry, go kill me a chicken, and we'll have some pot pie tonight.")	Lower Level ("1001001 0110110")

The Tools

We will give examples at different levels, but our inclination will be toward tools in the middle to high level. To make the connection between the physical world and the digital, you'll learn to assemble circuits, connect them to computers, write software for the computers, and enable computers to communicate with each other (see Figure I.4).

Figure I.4
The parts of a physical computing system.

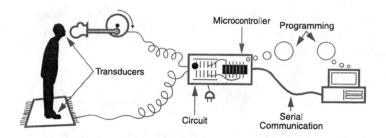

Circuits

You will have to build a little circuitry as the glue between the transducers you use to sense and control the world and the computers you use to interpret what's going on. For the majority of common transducers, you will copy one of four or five basic circuits we'll lay out in the early chapters. Building these circuits is fairly simple. It amounts to connecting a few wires and an electronic component or two.

While it will help to have some feeling for how electricity behaves, we're aiming to make you do the least amount of work to get information from the physical world through sensors into the computer. We'll cover the basics needed to understand the circuits we're using, and point to other sources for more detail. In a sense, the computer is the mother of all general circuits, and you can finesse the connection between input and output further in software. You can get far in physical computing with the most basic understanding of electricity.

Circuits are usually described in a diagram called a *schematic* that shows the electrical components and how they are connected to each other. You will need to know enough about schematics to be able to read them, but to get started you need not be able to draw schematics or design circuits.

As you get more adventurous with your transducers, the translations of energy will get a little more involved. Then you will need to learn more about the behavior of electricity and how to build circuits, particularly when dealing with more powerful output devices like motors.

Computers

The word "computing" might seem at odds with the word "physical." One of the main strengths of computer technology is transcending the time and space of the physical world. Yet physical computing is all about recognizing that people are still 99 percent monkeys who really enjoy the pleasures and constraints of the physical world. In physical computing, we want it both ways: we want the liberation that computers allow situated in the sensual world that humans enjoy. To do this, we'll use a variety of computers, but always do our best to put them in the background so that we can focus on the experience between humans in the foreground.

Microcontrollers

The main computer we'll use in physical computing is the microcontroller. This is a very small, very simple computer that's good at three things: receiving information from sensors, controlling basic motors and other devices that create physical change, and sending information to computers and other devices. They act as gateways between the physical world and the computing world. Microcontrollers are often at the heart of complex electronic devices, so understanding how they work will give you new insight into electronic devices that you already own

Figure I.5
The four microcontrollers discussed in this book. These simple computers are at the heart of many physical computing applications.

Microcontrollers are small and cheap. This allows you to explore location-specific projects that embed computers in the most unlikely places, like shrubbery and sneakers, or to develop projects where the actions of many simple devices add up to a more interesting whole.

Microcontrollers are found in everything from washing machines to light switches. You benefit from this ubiquity, as it has brought down the cost and improved the ease of use of microcontrollers.

Multimedia Computers

To some degree multimedia computers (desktop and laptop computers) are what we are working against in physical computing. These computers presume that the person using them will be relatively inactive, except for her fingers and hands, and that her eyes and ears will be focused in one direction. These computers may be multimedia-capable on the output side, but they are not so on the input side. One of our main objectives is to get people to picture a computer as something other than a couple of big beige plastic boxes on a desk and to picture their interaction with computers as something other than typing and clicking. The problem with our zeal to stretch your concept of computers beyond multimedia computers is that they are so useful, particularly for tasks such as generating sounds and graphics and sensing physical activity through cameras and microphones. Many projects combine the interesting input and output possibilities of microcontrollers with the multimedia output capability of multimedia computers. On the other hand, if your project does not involve any multimedia, such as playing sounds or videos, you may not need the complication and expense of a multimedia computer at all. Connecting back to multimedia computers is one of the things that separates this book from books about robotics. Robotics books tend to insist on having the microcontroller stand alone. We're not so swift to dismiss the multimedia computer's output capabilities when it's useful for communicating with people or between people. Multimedia computers are also useful for prototyping part of a project that ideally will be small and portable, but is not easy to miniaturize quickly. For the purposes of a demonstration of a futuristic project you might prefer to just say "Pay no attention to that huge computer behind the curtain."

Intermediate Computers

There is a wide range of computers between multimedia computers and microcontrollers. For example, notebook computers, tablet computers, single-board computers, palmtop computers, and mobile phones are all types of computers that might fit perfectly into your particular physical setup. Most of these intermediate platforms use operating systems and development environments that resemble the multimedia computer's, so our material on making a connection between the microcontroller and the multimedia computers will give you a leg up with these platforms.

Programming

This will send many readers running for the doors because they've tried and failed in the past to learn programming. In fact, physical computing is an excellent environment to learn computer programming. Abstract programming concepts like bits and bytes are embodied by tangible things like switches. In addition, the programs for microcontrollers tend to be very small and simple. There are only a few things you might want to do on a microcontroller: read sensors, turn things on or off, and send messages to other computers. Often it only takes a few lines of code, and much of that code can be borrowed from others and modified to suit your purposes.

You have a choice of many languages and microcontrollers, but we will be giving our examples for programming microcontrollers in one of the friendliest languages, BASIC. The process of programming microcontrollers involves typing out the programs on a multimedia computer and downloading them into the microcontroller. Chapter 5, "Programming," is geared toward someone who has little programming experience. If you are an experienced programmer, you can probably just skim the examples to get the syntax.

Programming multimedia computers, on the other hand, is a big subject. The topic of programming is too broad to be covered in one book, so our focus will be on how to get computers to communicate basic information with each other. If you already have some experience programming in Director/Lingo, Max/MSP, Processing, or Java, you are in perfect shape for this book because we will show you how to communicate between the microcontroller and the multimedia computer in these languages. Beyond communicating with the microcontroller, programming multimedia computers for the multimedia needs of your project is too idiosyncratic for us to cover properly here. If you are new to programming in general, you will need to pick a multimedia programming environment and learn it. We recommend those mentioned above, and we will provide a few examples using them to get information from a microcontroller into a multimedia computer.

Communicating between Computers

We rarely talk about computers anymore without talking about a network of computers. Even if you are not sending messages across the Internet, you might need to communicate between two different types of local computers. For example, your microcontroller is good at listening to switches, but not so good at more advanced multimedia tasks. It might send messages to your multimedia computer, which is better at playing sounds or videos. There are many different ways to communicate between computers. We'll be introducing a method called *serial communication* that offers the most flexibility for the least amount of work. We will also talk about more specialized versions of this method, such as MIDI and Internet protocols.

Your Concept: Don't Lose It

This book is about working backward from your project idea to the specific techniques you need to know to realize it. The journey from the concept of the project to realization is seldom one-way. The technical skills you develop along the way will inform and change the concept. After you develop some fluency with the tools, ideas often come concurrently with the making of the project, not necessarily before. But if this is your first experience with these technologies, it's easy to lose your way.

There are two big traps along the journey into physical computing. The first and more pleasant of the two traps is technological seduction. It's possible to get so pleased with your new technical powers that you dig into unnecessary technical detail or start growing weird new limbs for your project. In practice it's hard to tell the difference between when technical obsession will result in a very subtle and unexpected project and when it will just lead to lonely mutterings to yourself. It's a good idea to check your work with a potential audience as you go. If your audience doesn't notice any improvement in a project as a result of a particular technical change, you might want to re-evaluate how necessary the change is.

The second trap is spinning your wheels for so long, trying to get something to work, that you give up on the entire project in frustration over one part of it. Here again, sometimes sidestepping a technical problem will require ingenuity that may totally jumpstart and liberate your project; other times it will leave a glaring compromise in the final product.

There are four things that can keep you focused as you implement your ideas. First, keep a journal of the journey. Write down your ideas as you go, as well as the questions you have, the problems you encounter, and the solutions you come up with. This helps you to remember where you were going before you got discouraged by a technical or conceptual problem. In fact, your best entry may be the one you make right at this moment, recording what got you going down this road before you lost your technical innocence (assuming you had any to begin with). A healthy process is one in which you take frequent breaks from the details of realization to look at the overall idea, so don't wait until you're discouraged to revisit your journal. Better yet, make it a public Web log so other people can benefit from your progress.

Second, work fast and at a high level. Whenever possible use prefabricated technical solutions to at least test things. Don't spend your time perfecting endless details until you have proven the overall concept. The longer you spend implementing something, the more invested you will become in it and the less objective you become about its actual value to the project.

Third, don't become paralyzed by planning. Unless you're psychic, it's better to just try something and see how it works out. If the first solution doesn't work, try another. Each variation will give you new ideas on what's good about your project and what's not.

Furthermore, being less invested in any one solution at the beginning will make it easier to find a workaround or a different solution when you hit an obstacle later in the process.

Fourth, collaborate with other people. Explaining yourself, particularly to people who do not think like you, will keep you honest. When you have checked everything a hundred times and still can't imagine what could be causing the problem, a fresh set of eyes is the best solution.

Finally, take frequent showers and work on many parts of the projects at once. A lot of solutions will appear in your peripheral vision, so taking frequent breaks or switching tasks will help.

Part I
The Basics

IN THIS SECTION, we'll explain the major technical concepts underlying physical computing, define the terms used to describe them, and give working examples to illustrate the concepts. We tried to keep it lean, including only the things you need to know to pull off some basic physical computing projects and leaving out more advanced things about electronics that you don't need to know right now. If you read the chapters in order, you will get a general background to launch many types of physical computing projects.

On the other hand, if you're really impatient to get going on a project, you might skip directly to Chapter 6 to find which types of transducers, circuits, and programs you will need for your project. This will probably give you more questions than answers, but then you can skim through the rest of the chapters to fill in the gaps.

1

Electricity

Transduction: Electrical Basics

Transduction, the conversion of one form of energy into another, is an important part of physical computing. Looking at it from a high level, you're converting the intentions of the participant into action. At a lower level, you're converting the physical energy he or she exerts into electrical energy so that a computer can sense it. In the other direction, you are converting the electrical energy of the computer's output into movement, light, heat, or some other form of energy. At the center of all this transduction is electrical energy, so it's necessary to understand how electricity works in order to make things happen.

All electrical and electronic devices exploit the fact that electrons have a tendency to go from a point of greater electrical energy to a point of lesser electrical energy. You provide a positive connection (greater energy, or *power*), a negative connection (lower energy, or *ground*), and a *conductor* through which the electrons flow. When you've done that, the electrons will travel from power to ground. Along the way, you insert various electrical devices to divert the electrons to do your bidding.

Electrical energy always follows the path of least resistance to ground. The better the conductor, the easier it is for the electrons to flow. The point of lowest electrical energy is the earth itself, which is where we get the term "ground." If you build up enough electrical energy, electrons will flow through any conductor, even air. Lightning is just electrical energy that's built up in the clouds flowing through air to the ground.

A *circuit* is a closed loop containing a source of electrical energy (a battery) and a load (a light bulb). Figure 1.1 shows a simple circuit. Electrical energy flows from the positive terminal of the battery through the wires to the light bulb, and from the light bulb back to the negative terminal of the battery. The light bulb resists the flow of that energy, converting it into heat and light. In a well-designed circuit, all the electrical energy gets converted into some other form of energy by devices like light bulbs, heaters, and so on. In the example in Figure 1.1, the battery converts chemical energy from chemicals mixing inside it to electrical energy, and the light bulb converts electrical energy into light and heat energy.

Figure 1.1
A basic electrical
circuit.

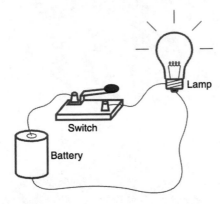

We're interested in using electrical energy to convert human action into other forms of energy, though, so we'll introduce that into the circuit by adding a switch. A *switch* is a break in the circuit that stops the electrons from flowing. By closing the switch, you close the break in the circuit and allow the electrons to flow again.

Every component you put into your circuit has certain electrical characteristics. The battery can provide a certain amount of electrical energy, and the light bulb can resist a certain amount of electrical energy. If you don't provide enough energy, the wire inside the light bulb won't heat up and provide light. If you provide too much electrical energy, the wire inside the light bulb will melt, breaking the circuit.[1]

In order to prevent this, you need to know how much energy the light bulb needs to light up, how much energy it can take before it breaks, and how much the battery can provide.

There are three basic electrical characteristics that come into play in every circuit. The relative level of electrical energy between any two points in the circuit (for example, between power and ground) is called the *voltage*. Voltage is measured in *volts*. The amount of electrical energy passing through any point in the circuit is the *current*. Current is measured in *amperes*, or *amps* for short. The amount that any component in the circuit resists the flow of current is called the *resistance* of the component. Resistance is measured in *ohms*. Voltage, current, and resistance are all related, and they all affect each other in a circuit (see sidebar).

Electrical devices resist the flow of current, converting it into other forms of energy in the process. A circuit without enough resistance in its load is the *dreaded short circuit* and should be avoided at all costs. As previously mentioned, a circuit is a closed loop, so all the energy that comes in from the battery has to get used up somehow by the resistance of your load. If your circuit does not use enough energy, it will just go right back into the battery, heating it up, and eventually blowing it up. Any time you find a component in your circuit heating up, you know it's getting electrical energy. Most electrical components can handle a certain amount of abuse, taking a little more voltage or current than they're rated for. However, if a component feels drastically hotter than usual or it starts to smell like it is burning, it's getting too much electrical energy and you have a problem.

---

[1] Initially, you will be working with small DC voltages, so you don't have to worry too much about things heating up. But even when you use AC voltage, there will be fuses to protect against burning down the house.

The combination of current and voltage is called *electrical power*, or *wattage*. It's measured in *watts*. The relationship is straightforward: *watts = volts × amps* (likewise, amps = watts/volts or volts = watts/amps). For example, a 120-watt light bulb would need 1 amp at 120 volts.[2]

The amount of wattage you supply to a circuit determines how much work it can do. The more work you need to do, the more power you need. So turning a motor to lift weight, for example, would take more power than turning on a small light like an LED.

Although you may never need to use Ohm's Law, you will probably at least need to match a power supply to your load. When you buy an electrical device or component, you should look in the packaging or documentation to see how much voltage it can take and how much current it needs. Some documentation may only specify volts and watts, in which case you would have to use the formula above to learn how many amps are required (amps = watts/volts). You can supply more than enough current (amps), and a load will use what it needs. On the other hand, you should be careful to match the voltage as closely as possible to the device's rating.

Electricity versus Electronics

You've already used your first sensor to sense human activity: the switch in our circuit is the most basic sensor there is. At present, it can only turn the light bulb on or off. The pattern of turning the switch on and off can convey some meaning, if you observe it over time. In this case, you're using the change in electrical energy to pass a message or a signal. For our purposes, this is the distinction between *electricity* and *electronics*. Think of electronics as a subset of electrical circuits that is used to convey information.

How Voltage, Current, and Resistance Are Related

One way to ensure that you balance the resistance of your load with the energy in your supply and avoid the dreaded short circuit is to restrict yourself to the circuits that we show you. If you will be making your own circuits or if you are just curious, there's an equation that relates these three electrical characteristics: *Voltage = Current × Resistance* (likewise, Current = Voltage/Resistance and Resistance = Voltage/Current). This is known as Ohm's Law. But it's easier to understand by using an analogy. The flow of water through a hose is like the flow of electricity through a circuit. Turning the faucet increases the amount of water coming through the hose, or increases the current (amps).

The diameter of the hose offers resistance to the current, determining how much water can flow. The speed of the water is equivalent to voltage. When you put your thumb over the end of the hose, you reduce the diameter of the pathway of the water. In other words, the resistance goes up. The current (that is, how much water is flowing) doesn't change, however, so the speed of the water, or voltage, has to go up so that all the water can escape. If it doesn't, the hose explodes, just like a fuse melts in a short circuit. When we change how the water travels through the hose, the total amount of water used is still the same, but the way it moves through the conductor changes (that is, it comes out of the hose faster).

[2] An ordinary household circuit in the U.S. will supply 15 amps of current at 120 volts.

Generally speaking, electronic circuits don't need a lot of electrical power. They just need enough power to register a message in a brain or in another computer by turning on small things like an LED or a *transistor* (an electrical component that can act like an electrically controlled switch; we'll discuss them in more depth later in the book). On the other hand, when you use electrical energy to do physical work, such as turning on motors, you need much more electrical power. For this reason, you'll find that the input components of your projects will generally need less power than the output components. On the input side, you're listening to the world; on the output side, you're attempting to change it.

There are two ways in which electrical power is usually supplied: direct current and alternating current. A *direct current (DC) source* supplies current on one wire and ground on another, and the voltage between them is constant with the supply wire always at a higher voltage. An *alternating current (AC) source* alternates the voltage on the two wires. It's easier to supply electrical energy over very long wires using AC, which is why commercial electrical power is AC. The power coming out of your electrical socket is typically 120 volts AC in the United States and 220 volts AC in Europe and Asia. Electronic components generally operate using DC, however, and at a much lower voltage, typically around 5 volts. They generally need very little amperage as well (less than one amp for most of the circuits you'll build), so we use AC-to-DC converters and transformers to change alternating current to direct current. The large, blocky power supplies that come with most electronic devices are AC-to-DC converters/transformers that convert the 120/ 220 volts AC to around 5 to 12 volts DC.

Batteries supply DC, usually in the range needed for electronic circuits. A 9-volt battery is an ideal source of power for many physical computing projects. We don't recommend using batteries while you're debugging your systems, however, because having them run out is just one more thing for you to worry about.

How Electricity Flows

There are two basic properties of electrical energy that will be useful to you in all of the circuits you build. These will help you to understand why a circuit works. They'll also help you avoid the dreaded short circuit and help you to troubleshoot your circuit when it's not working.

Electricity always favors the path of least resistance to ground.

This means that anytime electricity has two possible paths to take, it'll take the one that offers less resistance. In other words, if you connect power and ground with a wire (which offers very little resistance), electricity will follow that path instead of through the rest of your circuit; thus it will create the dreaded short circuit.

All the electrical energy in a circuit must be used.

This means that the components in your circuit have to consume all of the energy that you put into the circuit. Any extra energy will get converted to heat by your components. If there's too much energy, the components will overheat and stop working. This is a slightly less dangerous version of the dreaded short circuit. It won't kill you, but it will kill your components.

To illustrate these two ideas, take a look at the simple circuit back in Figure 1.1. There's only one path for the electricity to take: from the battery's positive terminal through the switch, then through the light bulb, then to ground. All of the electricity follows this path because it's the only path. In this circuit, the light bulb, which is the only component that uses electrical energy, has to consume all of the electrical energy. In this circuit, the battery, the switch, and light bulb are all in *series* with each other, meaning that they are all on the same electrical path. When components in a circuit are in series, the current is the same for each of them, but the voltage decreases as each component uses some of it up.

Now take a look at another circuit. In the circuit in Figure 1.2, we connect a second light bulb. The second light bulb is smaller. It uses less electrical energy, and offers less resistance than the big light bulb.

Figure 1.2
Two light bulbs in
parallel.

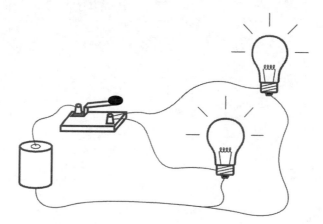

Since the smaller light bulb offers a path of less resistance, some of the current goes through it and some goes through the big light bulb, so both bulbs are a bit dimmer than they would be if they were alone in the circuit. These light bulbs are in *parallel* with each other, meaning that they are on two different electrical paths in the circuit. When components are in parallel, the current is split between them, depending on their relative resistances. The more resistance a component has, the less current goes through it. The voltage across them is the same, though.

Take a look at one more circuit. In this one, we've added a bare wire in parallel with the two light bulbs, as shown in Figure 1.3. Since the bare wire has almost no resistance, almost all of the current goes through it. This is the dreaded short circuit.

When you start to build circuits, you'll see examples of components in series with each other and in parallel, and you'll see how all of the energy gets used up.

Initially, you'll be following very limited recipes for your circuits. For these recipes, you really only need to know the most basic ingredients and their characteristics. The definitions we've laid out here will stand you in good stead to do that. In Chapter 3, "Building Circuits," and in the advanced section of this book, we will go into more detail about electrical relationships. Now that you've got an idea how electricity works, it's time to go shopping.

Figure 1.3
Two light bulbs in
parallel with the
dreaded short circuit.

2
Shopping

Unless you've made electrical or mechanical devices before, you'll need to do some shopping for electronic parts and tools. We'll end this chapter with a shopping list. Sometimes we might recommend one part number (usually the least expensive) where several others would work. For other items, we will present a couple of part numbers where you only need one. In the rest of the chapter, we will describe why these items are useful and what varieties are available to help you make your own purchasing decisions. We will talk more about how to actually use these items in later chapters.

All the parts are easily bought from catalogs or from online sources. Among the online vendors, we recommend Jameco Electronics and Digi-Key Corporation. Jameco is handy because they have pictures of their parts on the Web site, but Digi-Key carries a wider range of parts and materials. We'll list many others throughout the book and in Appendix A.

If you can't wait for a shipment, or if you just like to touch things before you buy them, most of these things can be purchased at a local electronics store such as Radio Shack. Radio Shack has been moving away from supporting the hobbyist market in recent years, and their sales staff aren't always very knowledgeable about the components they sell, so it's best to learn to navigate the electronics section on your own. Hopefully, you'll start to find your own local resources for physical computing, to the point where you slow down when passing promising dumpsters and start asking the people you meet at Radio Shack out for coffee.

Following is a description of parts you'll need to get started. At the end of the chapter you'll find the shopping list with part numbers.

Solderless Breadboard

The breadboard will be the foundation of all your circuits. These are also called experimenter's boards or prototyping boards. A *breadboard* is a tool for holding the components of your circuit and connecting them together. It's got holes that are a good size for hookup wires and the pins of most components, so you can push wires and components in and pull them out without much trouble. When you need to change something, you just pull the wire out. This saves a lot of time that you'd otherwise have to spend using solder to connect wires.

You could buy a short 3" breadboard if you are sure that your needs are simple. We recommend the more standard 6" models that will give you room to grow. Breadboards typically have long lines of holes on the sides that are used to provide power and ground to your circuit. Breadboards with two long lines on each side are a great convenience because you can have both power and ground on both sides. These lines are sometimes referred to as *bus rows*. Picture them as mass transit for the happy little electrons, and you've got the idea. You will also see big breadboards with screw terminals for power and ground, but these may not be worth the extra money.

Microcontrollers

Microcontrollers will be at the heart of most of your projects and at the center of the work in this book. Microcontrollers are available at many different levels. We recommend that you start with mid-level microcontroller modules, such as the Basic Stamp, BX-24, or Basic Atom Pro24. The majority of examples in this book were created with these chips in mind. To give you a broader picture of the possibilities, we will go through some of the trade-offs of moving up or down to better meet your needs and experience (see Appendix A for more details).

Microcontroller Features (in Order of Priority)

There are several features to consider when picking which microcontroller you plan to use. We're recommending several microcontrollers, but you'll have to make your own choices. These notes will help you to decide, based on your own personality and capabilities.

Programming Environment

If your time and sanity are worth anything, then a simple and easy programming environment should be your first priority. The inconveniences of low-level programming languages and of too many steps in transferring the program to the chip may seem small to an expert. But it only takes a single obscure detail at the start to stall your project for several days. Even a few extra steps can wear you down as you iterate and debug your program many times.

What programming language (or languages) is used to program the microcontroller? All of the ones we recommend can be programmed in a variant of the BASIC programming language. However, the BasicX BASIC (for the BX-24) is both more complex and at times more powerful than the other BASICs used here. In addition, the PIC microcontroller can also be programmed in C, a lower-level and more complex and powerful language. Everything we are doing can be done in all the versions of BASIC used below. However, if you're already comfortable in C, you could consider the PIC and C, or if you're comfortable with Microsoft Visual Basic, you will find the BasicX BASIC very familiar.

Do you need extra hardware to program the microcontroller? The PIC is the only microcontroller recommended here that needs a hardware programmer.

Can you change the program while the chip is in your circuit? This is possible for all of our microcontrollers, but is a little more difficult with the PIC.

NOTE

Currently, all the microcontrollers we'll discuss are mainly programmed from a PC running some variation of Windows. While Macintosh users can *use* a microcontroller in connection with their machine, the options for *programming* it from their machines are limited. You don't need a very fancy machine for programming, so many Macintosh users get used and outdated PCs from a thrift store just for programming the microcontroller.

Analog Input

Does your microcontroller have analog-to-digital converters for reading analog voltages in? How many does it have? The Basic Stamp 2 is the only microcontroller we're recommending that has no analog inputs, but you can fake it as long as all your sensors are variable resistors. The Basic Atom Pro24 has only four analog inputs. The BX-24 and the PIC 18F452 have eight analog inputs each.

Digital Input and Output

How many digital input and output pins does your microcontroller have? All of the microcontrollers we're recommending have sixteen digital I/O pins, except for the PIC 18F452, which has 33.

Analog Output

Can your microcontroller provide dedicated pulse width modulation (which will be explained in Chapter 6, "The Big Four: Schematics, Programs, and Transducers"), so that it can provide continuous analog output without interrupting the rest of your program? The PIC 18F452 is the only microcontroller we're recommending that can truly do this, though the BX-24 and the Basic Atom Pro24 can come very close.

Speed of Execution

How many instructions per second can your microcontroller execute? Is the program interpreted, as on the Basic Stamp 2, or compiled before running, as on all of the other microcontrollers we're recommending? For our purposes, it's less important to know the actual number of instructions per second than to know that the PIC is the fastest of the four recommended, the Basic Atom Pro24 is second, the BX-24 is third, and the Basic Stamp 2 is the slowest. All of them will operate fast enough to do the tasks explained in this book, faster than human perception.

Another speed factor to consider is the maximum baud rate the chip can use for serial communication. If you need to communicate with a device that has a particular baud rate (for example, MIDI devices communicate at 31,250 bits per second), then you need to make sure your microprocessor can operate at that speed.

Price

How expensive is the microprocessor itself? How expensive is the development environment? Of the microprocessors recommended, the PIC 18F452 is the cheapest (about one quarter the price of the others), but its development environment is the most expensive (the others are all free). This means that you need to use a number of PICs for a number of projects before you've paid off the cost of the development environment relative to the others. On the other hand, once you've done a few dozen projects, you save money using PICs.

Amount of Memory

How much memory your microprocessor has affects how big your program can be. For the four microcontrollers we're using, this is seldom a significant factor, as they're all in the same general range in terms of memory.

Power

How much power does your microcontroller consume? Can it run on batteries? For how long? Of the microcontrollers we're recommending, the PIC is the most power-efficient, but the difference is negligible when you add in external devices like motors and sound devices.

High-Level Microcontroller Modules

Examples: Making Things' Teleo system, Infusion Systems' I- Cubed, Electrovoce's MIDITools, Ezio

You can buy boxes that can do the most popular physical computing tasks, such as digital and analog I/O and serial communication, but hide most of the wiring and electrical components from you. They have simple connectors for everything from power and serial ports to switches, potentiometers, and motors. They are much more expensive than lower-level solutions, but they will save you a lot of time if you know that your needs are clear and simple. We don't usually recommend beginning at this level, however. As long as you're going through the trouble to learn any wiring at all, you should go the few extra steps to learn about mid-level microcontroller modules. The level of complexity is not that much greater, but the amount of flexibility gained and money saved can be significant. Although our examples will be more detailed than you need for the high-level devices, the major concepts we cover will still apply.

Mid-Level Microcontroller Modules

Examples: Parallax's Basic Stamp 2, NetMedia's BX-24, Basic Micro's Basic Atom Pro 24.

The Basic Stamp, and later the Basic Stamp 2 (BS-2), made by Parallax, was one of the first to fill the need for cheap mid-level microcontrollers. Other brands have since come along with improved features and more speed or memory. Because the Basic Stamp 2 is so popular, many of the later competitors have copied the BS-2's physical pin layout in order to make their products compatible. Circuits designed for the Basic Stamp 2 will generally work with the competitors' modules as well. We will refer to all of these as "stamp-like" modules.

These modules are like training wheels for the lower-level microcontroller contained within them. The modules themselves are more expensive than lower-level processors because they contain all the extra wiring necessary to turn on the microcontroller. Often these modules run slower than the lower-level processors because the programming languages for them sacrifice efficiency for ease of use. The software environments for programming mid-level modules are simple and can usually be downloaded for free. You can program and reprogram the chips in a friendly language like BASIC, and you get feedback very quickly.

The companies who make mid-level modules will sell you a development environment that usually consists of the manual and the programming software on a CD. The nicely printed manual is handy, but generally both the manual and the software can be downloaded for free. Other accessories such as carrier boards or demo boards make these seem very much like the higher-level boxes. They're nice if you have the money and are in a hurry, but they mostly just save you from doing a little wiring that you're better off learning to do for yourself. With the carrier board and the manual, an average mid-level module will cost around $100. If you buy the module alone, it's usually $50 or less. We recommend the latter option.

Low-Level Solutions
Examples: PIC chips, SX chips, Atmel (AVR) chips

At the heart of the high-level and mid-level modules are the microprocessors themselves. It is possible to work with them directly and assemble all of the circuitry on the module yourself. The initial learning curve to do this is the steepest of all three approaches, and the initial expense is the highest. The tradeoff is that once you've mastered the skills and bought the tools, the processors themselves are much cheaper (as low as $1 per chip) than the high- and mid-level modules. This book will cover the basics at this level and give some examples for their use, but we really don't recommend this approach if you're just getting started. Compared to working with mid-level chips, working with the processors themselves requires you to build more circuitry just to turn them on. In addition, you'll have to understand the electronics a bit more in depth to keep them running smoothly. You'll also need an additional piece of hardware between your desktop computer and the processor in order to program them.

There are compilers that will convert programs written in friendly languages like BASIC (or C, which is more friendly to experienced programmers) into instructions the chip can understand, but you won't find all the tools in one piece of software. You'll have to cobble together a few different software packages in order to write your programs and download them to the processor. While there are free programming tools available, the more useful ones are not free. The one we recommend is about $250; they range in price from $100 to more than $1000.

Getting the program from the multimedia computer into the low-level processors involves an added piece of hardware called a chip programmer. These range in price from $7 to $300; you can get a good one for around $60. Most chip programmers require you to remove the processor from your circuit in order to program it, but some offer the option of in-circuit programming, using a cable adapted for the job. This is a handy way to go.

Common Components
The following are a handful of common components and their schematic symbols. This covers the components you will use in most circuits. In the next chapter, you will be referring to these schematic symbols when you combine these components into circuits using schematic diagrams (see Appendix C for a more complete list of schematic symbols).

Switches

Figure 2.1
Schematic symbol for a switch and a variety of switches.

Switches pass or interrupt the flow of electricity. A simple switch, like those shown in Figure 2.1, has two interchangeable leads. The leads are attached to two contacts inside the switch that can put them in contact with each other or be separated by the action of the switch. Many switches are simple mechanical devices that move the contacts, but there are some interesting variants. Magnetic switches, for example, usually have two very thin metal leaves inside, and when a magnet is brought near the body of the switch, the leaves touch and conduct current. Ball switches or tilt switches have a metal ball that is brought into contact with the two leads by tilting the switch.

Switches are rated by the maximum voltage and current that they can conduct. A switch can generally be used to control any voltage or current less than the maximum, so a switch rated for 120 volts, for example, will work fine in a 5-volt circuit. If you're using a switch as an input to a microcontroller, you'll be passing a very small amount of current through it, so you should feel free to make your own switches from any mechanical devices that cause metal things to either touch or not.

There are a large variety of switches available, and it's useful to have a few in your toolbox at all times for various purposes. There are a few characteristics of switches to know about:

Switches are either *normally open (N.O.)* or *normally closed (N.C.)*. A normally open switch will conduct only when you activate it, and a normally closed switch will conduct only when not activated.

Switches can be *momentary* or *toggle* switches. Momentary switches (or pushbuttons) spring back to their normal position after you release them. Toggle switches stay in the last position to which they were set. Remote control buttons and keyboard keys are momentary switches, whereas household light switches are toggle switches.

We keep a few momentary switches and a few toggle switches on hand at all times.

Resistors

Figure 2.2
Schematic symbol for a resistor and a pile of resistors.

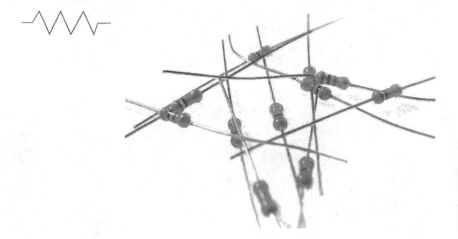

Resistors give electricity something to do: they convert electrical energy to heat. Thus, they prevent the dreaded short circuit. Resistors have two leads with no polarity (no positive and negative side) so the leads are interchangeable (see Figure 2.2). Resistors are rated in ohms, indicating how much resistance they offer in a circuit, and in watts, indicating the maximum power that they can take. The value of a resistor will be written right next to its schematic symbol. The value of an actual resistor can be identified by

1. The package
2. Decoding the stripes from a chart (see Appendix C)
3. Checking it using a multimeter set to measure resistance.

For most of the circuits you'll be building, you'll put very little power through the resistors, so a low power rating (1/4 watt or 1/8 watt, for example) will be fine.

You'll need a variety of different values of resistors. One-quarter watt or 1/8 watt resistors will work for most electronic applications. Resistance values of 220 ohms, 1000 ohms (1K ohm), 10K ohms, and 22K ohms are the ones you'll need the most for the applications in this book. If you keep them in their packages until you use them, it will save you having to learn how to decode the colored bands on the side. However, the color code can be found in Appendix C.

Variable Resistors

Variable resistors resist the flow of electricity to varying degrees. Figure 2.3 shows a variety of variable resistors. As you will see later in the book, these are very common transducers for analog input. *Thermistors* convert a change in heat to a change in resistance. *Photocells* or *photoresistors* change their resistance in response to changing light levels. *Force-sensitive resistors* respond to a changing force exerted on them. *Flex sensors* change their resistance when they are bent to varying angles. All of these are variable resistors. Like fixed resistors, all of these will have two non-polarized (interchangeable) leads.

Figure 2.3
Variable Resistors.
Schematics from
left to right: generic
variable resistor,
photocell, thermistor,
potentiometer. Images
from left to right:
photocell, thermistor,
potentiometer, flex
sensor, force-sensitive
resistor (FSR).

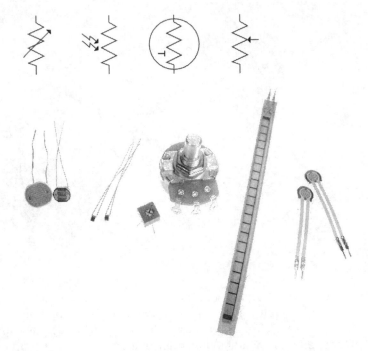

The most common of all variable resistors is called a *potentiometer,* or *pot* for short.
This is what is behind every volume knob. Pots are a little different than most variable
resistors because they have three leads. If you pop open a pot, you would see that the
middle lead is connected to a wiper that moves along a band of conductive metal. The two
outside contacts are the ends of the band. As the wiper moves closer to an end contact,
the resistance between the wiper and that contact goes down while the resistance to the
opposite contact goes up. Some schematics will show two connections to the potentiometer,
in which case you would use the center wiper and either of the end contacts.

Variable resistors are great fun to use in physical computing projects, so buy any that you
find interesting. Definitely buy the most common variable resistor, a potentiometer. A 1/2-
watt potentiometer that ranges from 0–10K ohms will be sufficient. Try to get a "linear
taper," which gives you an even distribution of resistance instead of an "audio taper,"
which has a logarithmic curve to its distribution of resistance and is used specifically for
sound volume. Photocells (light-sensitive resistors) and thermistors are easy to find and
find unique applications for.

Capacitors

A *capacitor* is a bit like a savings account. When times are good and electricity is flowing
into a capacitor, it stores up the charge. When the current is removed, the capacitor releases
its charge until it's got no charge left. Just like a bank, there is a delay between the time the
charge is put into a capacitor and when it's released. Unlike a bank, you can use this to your
advantage. For example, capacitors can serve to smooth out erratic electrical flow, releasing
charge when the current dips, and store excess charge when the current spikes. Capacitors
are rated by how much charge they store, which is called their *capacitance*. Capacitance is

Figure 2.4
Capacitors in
schematic (unpolarized
and polarized) and
actual capacitors (left
to right: ceramic,
tanatlum, electrolytic
capacitors).

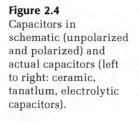
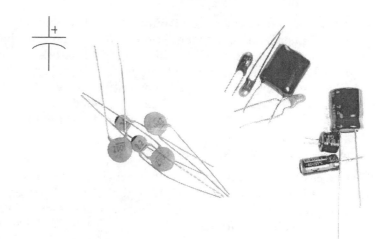

measured in farads (F). A farad is really a lot of charge, so most of the capacitors you'll use
will be measured in microfarads (mF or µF), picofarads (pF), or nanofarads (nF). Capacitors
all have two leads. Some capacitors are unpolarized, meaning that it doesn't matter which
side you connect to where. Figure 2.4 shows a variety of capacitors, both polarized and
unpolarized. If you are using a polarized capacitor, a + or – sign should be printed on the
outside of the capacitor itself. The + side of the capacitor goes toward the higher voltage in
your circuit, and the – side goes toward lower voltage.

Capacitors come in lots of different shapes and are made of different materials (for
example, ceramic, tantalum, or electrolytic), but they all do pretty much the same thing.
Tantalum and electrolytic capacitors are higher quality and last longer. Pay attention to
your schematic diagrams; if a polarized capacitor is called for, make sure to use one. The
most common values you'll need for this book are 22pF, 0.01µF, and 0.1 µF ceramic or
electrolytic capacitors, and 1µF and 10µF electrolytic capacitors.

Diodes

Figure 2.5
Diode schematic
and general-purpose
diodes.

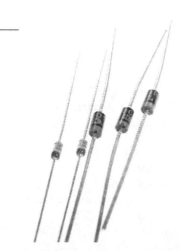

A *diode* is like a one-way street: it only allows electricity to flow in one direction and not the other. This means that by definition diodes are polarized, meaning that they can only be placed in a circuit in one direction. Figure 2.5 shows two different types of diodes. the burly-looking ones on the right can carry more current. The two sides are called the cathode (−) and the anode (+). You may have to consult the packaging or look for + or − signs on the outside of the diode itself to tell one lead from another. Diodes have a band on one end that indicates the cathode and the forward current direction. Current will pass when it's flowing toward the band from the other end of the diode and will block current in the other direction.

You'll use two types of diodes in this book: general-purpose diodes, such as the 1N4002, shown in Figure 2.5, and light-emitting diodes. An *LED (Light-Emitting Diode)* is a diode that also emits light in the process. Figure 2.6 shows a number of LEDs in different colors. The shorter leg is the cathode (−), and the longer leg is the anode (+).

Figure 2.6
LED schematic and
LEDs.

LEDs are the most common form of output from most microcontrollers because they take very little power to turn on. The first program you will write on a microcontroller will light an LED. The cheapest LEDs are not very bright, but it's possible to get LEDs bright enough to read by. They're used in outdoor video displays, stoplights, and many other places because they can offer a lot of light for relatively little power. There are also infrared LEDs that are invisible to human eyes, but work very well for wireless signaling. These are the main component in most remote controls. Though it's tempting to get super bright LEDs for every application, the cost can add up. It's best to keep a handful of the cheapest LED's in your toolbox to use whenever you need an indicator light. LEDs rated at or below 5 volts and 20 milliamps or with a forward voltage rating between 2.5 and 5 volts will work for most microcontroller applications. Avoid the flashing LEDs.

Transistors and Relays

Transistors and *relays* are switching devices. Normal switches can be thrown by your finger, but these can be thrown by an electronic signal from your microcontroller. Think of them as small switches that activate larger switches. When you put a small amount of current through the small switch (the base in a transistor, or the coil in a relay), it activates the large switch, letting a large amount of current flow through it. Transistors are actually

Figure 2.7
Transistor and relay
schematics, and
transistors.

capable of more than that, but you'll start by using them as electronic switches. We'll explain them in more depth in later chapters.

There are two types of transistors you'll use in the examples in this book. The first type you will use is the very common 2N2222 transistor. In the advanced section, you will use a TIP120 Darlington transistor, which you'll use for switching devices that use a large amount of current. It looks identical to the 5-volt voltage regulator mentioned below but performs a very different function, so be sure not to confuse them. The transistors themselves will usually have some markings to indicate their type. Keep the packaging for distinguishing between the three leads. Figure 2.7 shows the two types of transistor in this book on the left, and the two most common relays on the right.

The best relay to start with is a 5-volt reed relay. It can be switched with 5 volts at 20 milliamps (coil power), which is just right for the output of a typical microcontroller, and can then turn on a 120 volt, 0.5 amp load such as a 60-watt light bulb. Reed relays usually look like little tubes that barely fit in your breadboard. You can get reed relays from Digi-Key that come in a standard chip shape that connect to your board more easily. The part numbers are listed at the end of the chapter. You will find other relays that can switch larger loads, but many of them will require more power to be switched (coil power) than your microcontroller can provide without additional circuitry. Solid State relays are really great because they can usually be operated by your microcontroller and switch much bigger loads. They are more expensive than mechanical relays, however.

Wires

Figure 2.8
Wires of various types.

The wire used to connect components comes in a wide range of sizes and types, but there are a few rules of thumb you need to remember. Thicker wire can carry more current. The American Wire Gauge (AWG) rating is the system we use. In that system, the bigger the number, the thinner the wire. The number indicates fractions of an inch, for example, 22-guage wire is 1/22 of an inch in diameter. Most household wiring is 12- or 14-gauge, for example, but since you won't need to carry that much current, you'll typically use 22-gauge wire.

Wire comes in two varieties, solid core and stranded. Figure 2.8 shows both types of wire. Solid core wire is stiffer and better for building circuits because it fits more easily into solderless breadboard (more on that later). 22-gauge solid-core wire, sometimes called hook-up wire, is what we'll use most often. If cutting and stripping wire is not your cup of tea, you can get jumper kits that contain various common lengths of wire already cut and stripped.

Solid hook-up wire gets unwieldy when you need to run multiple wires over longer distances. Stranded wire has many fine strands of wire inside the insulator and is more flexible and better for longer runs. You can also get multi-conductor wire, which contains multiple wires in one insulating jacket, like ribbon cable or telephone cord. Stranded wire is too soft to insert into the holes of your breadboard, however. You'll need to solder (see the "Tools" section below) a stiff post called a *header* to the end of your stranded wire in order to connect it to a breadboard.

Power Supply

Figure 2.9
A typical DC power
supply.

All of the circuits in this book will use DC power (like a battery) as opposed to AC power (like a wall socket). You could use a 9-volt battery for all of your projects, but exhausting it while you're building the project will just add to the list of things that could go wrong. You are better off with an AC/DC converter. You might have one of those "wall warts" from an old piece of electronics in your closet, like the one shown in Figure 2.9. There are two important statistics you need to know about your DC power supplies: the voltage and the amperage they can supply. The projects in this book will mostly need +5 DC volt power. However, you should use a power supply that's between 8 and 15 DC volts because most of the microcontrollers have a built in voltage regulator, which can convert that higher voltage into 5 volts. When considering the amperage of your supply, the more amperage the better. You will need about 300 milliamps for most projects, but when you start adding motors and other actuators that create heat or motion, you'll need more amperage. It's best to get a power supply that can supply one amp (1000 milliamps).

Power Connector

Figure 2.10
A coaxial power
connector.

If you are anxious to get going, you can clip the connector off of any power supply and plug the wires directly into the breadboard. Never do this with the power supply plugged in— that can lead to sparks and short circuits if you're not careful, and it means you can never use your power supply for anything else again. It's useful to be able to re-use your power supply, and it's safer to have a connector you can plug and unplug. Nine-volt battery snaps are common and will work nicely for portable projects with a 9-volt battery, but it's easy to reverse the terminals on them, with bad effects. Coaxial connectors are safer. It's necessary to match the inner and outer diameters of the jack to the power connector you want to use. The model we recommend has a 2.1mm inner diameter, and a 5.5mm outer diameter that will match most common AC/DC power adaptors. It's shown in Figure 2.10.

Voltage Regulator

Figure 2.11
A voltage regulator.

Voltage regulators are components that convert a varying range of voltages to a fixed voltage. You'll use them to convert the 8 to 15 volts coming from our AC/DC power converter to the 5 volts you'll need for your projects. Most stamp-like modules have a voltage regulator built in, but they tend to be cheap. We usually recommend adding an external voltage regulator in case you destroy the one on the chip. The ones you'll use are model 7805 voltage regulators. like the one shown in Figure 2.11.

RC Servomotor

RC servomotors (servo, for short) are easy to control from a microcontroller and offer a wide range of possibilities for controlled movement. Radio Shack does not sell servomotors,

Figure 2.12
An RC servomotor.

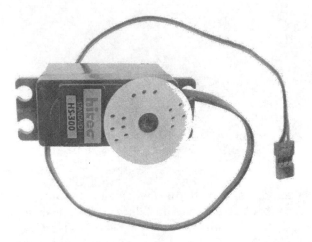

but most hobby shops do, and our online suppliers do as well. The bigger ones might be too much for your power supply, but if you buy the cheapest one they sell, you'll be fine. The Hobbico cs-61 is a common small servo that's readily available and relatively inexpensive. It's functionally identical to the Hitec HS-300 model shown in Figure 2.12. If you start using a number of these, you should look into dedicated servo controllers and external power supplies.

Serial Connector

Figure 2.13
A DB9 serial connector.

Serial connectors like the one in Figure 2.13 are the connectors that allow you to connect your serial cable to your breadboard. The ones needed for the projects in this book are DB9 female connectors with solder terminals (also called solder lugs) on the back. You'll need a serial connector for downloading your programs to the microcontroller and for communication between the microcontroller and the multimedia computer, so it's good to have two connectors for the sake of convenience.

Serial Cable

Serial cables are used to communicate between multimedia computers and microcontrollers. They're used both to download new programs into the microcontroller and to send messages between the microcontroller's program and the multimedia computer's program. Look for a DB9 male to DB9 female cable like the one shown in Figure 2.14. Don't get a null modem serial cable, as those have two important wires crossed inside

Figure 2.14
A serial cable with DB9
connectors.

the cable. Although you could use one cable and switch it between the programming and communication, it is worthwhile to buy two dedicated cables.

Clock Crystals

These are the timekeepers for low-level processors. You'll only need clock crystals if you are planning to use a low-level processor instead of a mid-level module. If you're using a BX-24, Basic Stamp, or Basic Atom 24, then you can skip this component. They come at a variety of speeds, but 4 MHz is the best place to start for the processors we'll reference.

Headers

Figure 2.15
Headers.

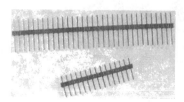

Headers are small metal posts to which you can solder the wires of various components in order to make a good, stiff connection to the breadboard. Figure 2.15 shows a typical row of headers. They come in rows attached together on 0.1-inch spacings, and are easy to break apart for individual use. You'll use a lot of these, and they're cheap, so get at least 100 to start. Radio Shack does not carry these, but you can improvise with stiff wire.

Project Box

This is the home for your breadboard. Theoretically, when you're done with your project you make your circuitry safe from the world by enclosing your breadboard in a box. Even during development, it's nice to anchor long wires to the box so they don't accidentally get ripped out of your breadboard. Any old box you have lying around would do, but the project boxes made for this purpose are cheap and they're easy to make holes in. Typically you attach the breadboard to the top of the box to allow for maximum access. Get a box that's big enough to hold your breadboard with room on all four sides and a few inches of space above it.

Cable Ties

Figure 2.16
Cable ties.

These are useful for strapping your wires down so they don't escape your breadboard. Once you get started with cable ties, it's easy to become addicted to them as a general construction tool. Figure 2.16 shows the type that we use all the time.

USB-to-Serial Adaptor

Figure 2.17
A USB-to-serial
adaptor.

The microcontrollers you'll be using communicate with multimedia computers via serial communication. If your computer only has a USB port, you'll need a USB-to-serial adaptor. Though USB is a serial communications protocol, it's much more complicated than the form of serial communication you'll be using. Apple computers and some new laptop PCs have abandoned the old type of 9-pin RS-232 serial ports in favor of USB ports. Check the back of your computer for a connection with 9 pins, usually with markings like 0|0|0| or "COM1." That's a 9-pin serial port. If you don't have it, you'll need one of these adaptors. On Windows PCs, just about any USB-to-serial adaptor will do the job; if you're a Macintosh user, you'll need to get one that's got software drivers that work with your machine. We recommend the Keyspan USA19HS because it's compatible with every Macintosh1 operating system through OSX 10.3, and it's got a DB-9-style serial connector like most PCs. It also works on PCs. It's the model shown in Figure 2.17.

Tools

There are only a few tools you'll use all the time when building electronic projects. Like with any hobby, you might develop tool lust, and start buying all kinds of esoteric tools that you don't necessarily need at first. Feel free to indulge your lust in the future, but for now, stick with these staples. Your pocketbook will thank you.

Figure 2.18
An array of the tools you'll use all the time. Left to right: diagonal cutters, screwdriver, wire stripper, needle-nose pliers.

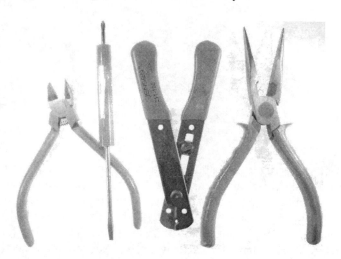

Soldering Iron

Even if you use a breadboard, you will need a soldering iron for your more permanent connections. Get a soldering iron with a stand and a sponge. Since the iron gets very hot when you use it, a stand gives you a safe place to put it down without starting a fire. A sponge allows you to clean the tip, which makes for much faster and reliable soldering. Get an iron with a narrow point tip in order to do fine soldering; 1/32" tips will do you well.

Solder

Get rosin core solder, 22 AWG or higher. Solder is measured using the same standard as wire, so higher numbers mean thinner solder. Anything thicker than 22AWG tends to be awkward for electronics work. Get lead-free solder if you can, as it's safer for you.

Needle-Nose Pliers

Breadboards get cramped, and it's often difficult to get your fingers on one wire or component without disturbing the others. Needle-nose pliers are essential for solving this problem.

---

[1] It is not common to program these microcontrollers on a Macintosh, as we mentioned previously, but after you finish programming you may want to reuse the USB-to-serial adaptor to talk to your own software. That software might be running on a Macintosh, so it's useful to have an adaptor that works on both platforms.

Wire Strippers

There are lots of different types of wire strippers. Their purpose is to take the plastic insulation off without cutting the wire inside. Get whichever you like, as long as the ones you get can strip the insulation from the standard 22 AWG hookup wire.

Wire Cutter

Many pliers and strippers already have a cutting edge in them, but a separate pair of diagonal cutters is useful for making clean cuts.

Mini-Vise or Helping Hands

Figure 2.19
A Mini-vise (left) and
helping hands (right).

The trickiest part of soldering is that you need to hold four items: the two components or wires to be soldered, the solder, and the soldering iron. Unfortunately, we only have two hands. A vise or a pair of clamps to act as a spare set of hands helps. Some vises have clamps or vacuum seals on the bottom to hold them to the table, but for soldering, your vise does not have to be very strong or secure, as long as it stays put on the table. "Third hands" are another alternative. These have two alligator clips mounted on swivel bearings to hold the two components to be soldered. They allow more flexibility than a vise, but are more delicate. If you have cash to spare, it's often useful to have both, as shown in Figure 2.19.

Small Screwdrivers

Precision drivers in both Philips and slotted heads always come in handy.

Drill and Drill Bits

If you have a handheld drill, you'll use it frequently. A few common bit sizes you might use are 7/64", 1/8", 5/16", and 1/4".

Multimeter

A multimeter is a device used to test various electrical properties of a component or in a circuit. It's one of the most important debugging tools you can have when you're building circuits. Make sure your meter can measure voltage, resistance, and continuity. Many meters can measure more than this, but these are the most common properties you'll measure with a meter. The meter in Figure 2.20 is basic, but functional for everything you'll do in this book. Chapter 3, "Building Circuits," explains a bit more about what a meter is used for, if you'd like to know more before you buy.

Figure 2.20
A basic multimeter.

Hot Glue Gun

A hot glue gun like the one in Figure 2.21 comes in handy for a multitude of reasons in physical computing. Hot glue makes a decent insulator on some wires, and it holds the universe together.

Figure 2.21
A hot glue gun.

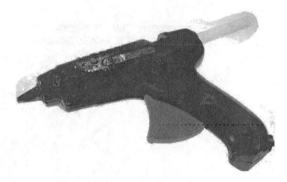

Toolbox

You don't need a big heavy metal toolbox, but it's handy to have somewhere to put all your stuff. Fishing tackle boxes work well because the tiny compartments work great for holding components, but a Tupperware container or shoebox would work fine as well.

Shopping List

Microcontroller Options

Item	Notes	Manufacturer URL
Parallax Basic Stamp 2 (BS-2)	The earliest of the mid-level modules. Very common, but lacking some features of some of the others	http://www.parallax.com
NetMedia BX-24	Mid-level module. Slightly more complex programming environment and language; many good features	http://www.basicx.com
Basic Micro Basic Atom Pro 24	New to the mid-level market, but simple programming environment with some nice new features	http://www.basicmicro.com
Microchip PIC 18F452	Low-level microcontroller. Not recommended as a starting place, but good if you're doing lots of projects	http://www.microchip.com

Component Shopping List

Priority	Item	Jameco Part No.	Radio Shack Part No.	Notes
1	Breadboard	20722 (2 bus rows per side)	276-174 (1 bus row per side)	6" board
1	DC power supply	170245 (12V, 1000mA)	273-1667 (3-12V, 800mA)	5-9V DC and 700-1500mA
2	Power supply connector	159610	274-1577	2.1mm x 5.5mm male
2	5V DC voltage regulator (7805 regulator)	51262	276-1770A	There are many variations on the 7805 regulator: 7805A, 7805T, 78HCT05, and more. For your purposes, any of them will do the job.
2	LEDs, Green	34761	n/a	
1	LEDs, Red	94511	276-307	
2	LEDs, Yellow	34825	276-351	
1	220 Ohm resistors, 1/4 watt	30470	271-1313	
1	1K Ohm resistors, 1/4 watt	29663	271-1321	

Component Shopping List (continued)

Priority	Item	Jameco Part No.	Radio Shack Part No.	Notes
1	10K Ohm resistors, 1/4 watt	29911	271-1335	
1	22K Ohm resistors, 1/4 watt	30453	271-1128	
1	Capacitors, 0.1uF	15270	272-1053	
1	Capacitors, 1uF	94160	272-1434	
2	Capacitors, 10uF	29891	272-1025 (this is polarized)	
1	Switch	187805 (lever)	275-017 (roller)	Any store-bought or homemade switch.
1	Switch	164081	980-0820	Alternative switch: magnetic.
1	Switch	106112	275-1549	Another alternative switch: pushbutton.
1	Switch	106067	275-324	More alternatives: toggle switches.
1	Potentiometer	29081	271-1715	Always good to have one of these handy, in addition to other variable resistors.
1	Variable resistors: Photoresistor	120299	276-1657	Look for ones that vary anywhere from 0 to 100 K.
	Flex sensor, 10–100K	150551	n/a	
	Thermistor , 10–100K	207036	271-0110	
1	Servomotor, Hobbico cs-61	157067	n/a	
1	Serial cable, 9-pin	208581	260-0117	Do not get a Null modem serial cable. Make sure your cable has a female adaptor on one end and a male on the other.
1	9-pin D-sub female connector	15771	276-1538	Should mate with serial cable, above.

Shopping List

Component Shopping List (continued)

Priority	Item	Jameco Part No.	Radio Shack Part No.	Notes
1	USB-to-serial adaptor	Keyspan USA19HS	26-183	If your computer doesn't have a serial port, you'll need one of these. The best one we've used comes from Keyspan (http://www.keyspan.com), the USA-19HS, listed here. It works on both Macs and Windows computers. The Radio Shack model listed here is fine for Windows, but doesn't work on Macs.
2	Transistors— TIP120 Darlington	32993	276-2068	
1	NPN Transistors, type 2N2222	38236	276-2009	
1	Relays	Digi-Key* 306-1034-ND	275-232	120V AC reed relays or solid state relays.
1	Clock crystals, 4Mhz	14592	n/a	This is for PIC users only. This is the clock that runs your PIC microprocessor.
2	Headers	103376	n/a	They come in rows of 10–20.
2	Project box	18905	270-1809	You'll use this to enclose your project board.
2	Standoffs	133604	276-195	For mounting your board to your box.
2	Screws for standoffs, size #4-40, 1/2"	106809	276-195	

*Where Jameco part numbers were not available, Digi-Key Corporation part numbers were substituted. We like both vendors, and often go to one when the other doesn't have what we need.

Tool Shopping List

Item	Jameco Part No.	Radio Shack Part No.	Notes
Soldering iron	146595	64-2802 or 64-2184	For example, Weller model WLC 100. We prefer the ones with a stand, but get the one that feels right for you. Make sure to get one with a fine-pointed tip.
Solder	141794 Digi-Key KE1351-ND (Jameco doesn't carry lead-free solder)	640-0013	Use lead-free when possible.
Multimeter	220812	22-810	There are many models to choose from. If you get an inexpensive one that can read voltage, resistance, and continuity, you'll be in good shape.
Wire, 22AWG	Black: 36791 Blue: 36767 Green: 36821 Red: 36855 Yellow: 36919	Red: 278-1215 Mixed: 276-173	Solid core hook-up wire; get several colors.
Flat needle-nose pliers	35473	64-2803/A	This Radio Shack kit includes a soldering iron, pliers, diagonal cutters, and screwdrivers. It will serve you well for all these tools, so we've listed it for all of them. Or, check your hardware store.
Wire stripper	159290	64-2803/A	To strip 22-30 AWG.
Diagonal wire cutter	161411	64-2803/A	Get a reasonably small one.
Mini-vise	127167	n/a	One option for holding parts to solder.
Helping Hands	26690	n/a	Another option for holding parts to solder.
Miniature Philips/flathead screwdriver	127271	64-2803	Check your hardware store for alternatives, too.
Drill and drill bits, 7/64", 1/8", 5/16" , 1/4"	n/a	n/a	These sizes are the ones you'll need most often for wood, plastic, and thin metal. Most hardware stores will carry them for less than a dollar each.
Hot glue gun	72696 and 78633	n/a	
Toolbox	n/a	n/a	
Cable ties	145701	278-1720	
Electrical tape	n/a	64-2375	
Alligator clips	107422	278-1157	

Shopping List

Bringing It All Back Home

Once you've got all of your parts, tools, and components, make sure you keep them organized. Many electronic components look alike, and with no labels, it's difficult to tell one from another. Hang on to the labels for your components and stick them on whatever boxes, compartments, or bins that you store the components in. You may be tempted to tear everything open at once and start building, but a little organization at the beginning will make your life much easier later on. One of the more irritating problems you'll hit later on is getting the wrong resistor value because you grabbed from a miscellaneous pile without looking.

Once you've got all of your parts in a row, you're ready to start building. We'll add more components in later chapters for various advanced techniques, but keep this chapter bookmarked for replenishing your staple supplies in the future.

3
Building Circuits

Once the parts are at hand, you can begin combining them into circuits. We will keep the circuitry to a minimum, just enough to get a transducer's signal into the microcontroller. Once the signal is in the microcontroller, you can do in software a lot of the logical work that used to be done in circuitry. This chapter outlines some of the methods and tools you'll need to build these small circuits.

The best way to learn these things is to do them, so you'll work through some examples as you go along.

Schematics

You will get far in physical computing using other people's recipes for circuits. However, you must learn to read the schematic diagrams used for these recipes.

Figure 3.1
A schematic of a circuit versus a drawing of a circuit.

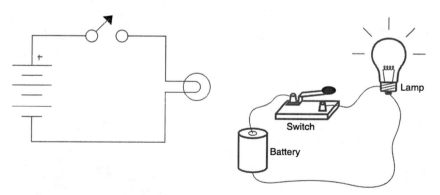

Figure 3.1 shows a drawing of the actual circuit and the schematic diagram. The schematic is more abstract than the drawing, which gives you minimal information about each component. The first step in reading a schematic is to decode the schematic symbols. You saw many of these symbols for the most basic components in Chapter 2, "Shopping." Now you will discover a few more symbols for showing connections between components for power and ground. In Appendix C, you'll find a glossary of more schematic symbols.

Connection Symbols

Here's a guide to the connection lines that connect components.

Connected wires are drawn like the one shown in Figure 3.2.

Figure 3.2
Connected wires in a
schematic diagram.

When there is a dot at the joint in the diagram, the two wires should be physically connected. These are called *junctions*.

Unconnected wires look like the ones shown in Figure 3.3.

Figure 3.3
Unconnected wires in
a schematic diagram.

Different schematics will use one of these three styles. We'll mainly use the leftmost style in this book. When two lines skip over each other, or have no dot connecting them, the wires they represent should not touch. They cross only for convenience in laying out the diagram.

Power Symbols

There are a number of possible power source symbols in a schematic. For example, the circuit might be powered by a DC power adaptor, a battery, or even an AC source. Figure 3.4 shows the schematic symbols for these three sources.

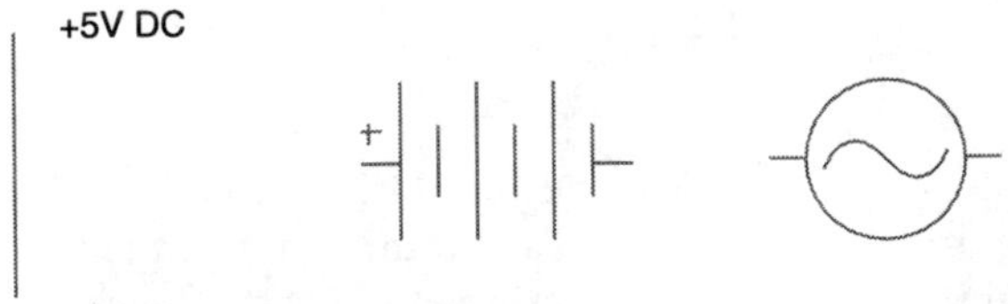

Figure 3.4
Power supply
schematic symbols.
Left to right: generic
DC source (+5 volts in
this example), battery,
and AC power source.

Each power source has its own symbol. The positive side of your power supply is indicated by one of the symbols in Figure 3.4. In pin diagrams for chips, this is often labeled "Vcc" or "Vdd." In our diagrams this will almost always refer to the +5 volts (though occasionally we will use a higher voltage). Some circuits might involve two separate power supplies, in which case the voltage should be indicated.

Figure 3.5
Ground schematic
symbols.

Just as power is always labeled on a schematic, so is ground. Figure 3.5 shows two typical options for the ground symbol in a schematic. Many circuits that use two separate power supplies will join the negative side of the supplies into a common ground.

Finding Schematics

In the chapters that follow, we'll introduce and discuss a number of circuits that serve as the foundation for a large number of physical computing applications. It's possible that these circuits and a few variations will serve your needs for most of your projects. However, if you're using a device that will not work with these circuits, then you can usually find the appropriate circuit in the application notes or instructions for that device. In addition, there are thousands of sensor and actuator circuits available online produced by other microcontroller hobbyists and professionals. You may be tempted to use a schematic or a kit for a standalone device, such as a lie detector or a light organ. These circuits are more complicated than you need because they rely on a lot of circuitry to route, transform, and perform logic on the signals. We suggest you stick to circuits that are designed to take advantage of the microcontroller.

Breadboards

Breadboards are the fastest way to build circuits, but until you get used to them, they can be confusing. It's important to understand where the holes are connected and where they're not connected.

The pattern of holes varies from model to model; some breadboards have only one strip down each side, and others have multiple side rows. The basic model, with many horizontal rows separated by a central divider and one or two long side rows, called bus rows, is the type that we'll focus on.

Figure 3.6 shows a two-bus row breadboard. On each side of the board are two long rows of holes, sometimes with a colored line next to each row. All the holes in each of these lines are connected together with a strip of metal in the back. These long strips are generally reserved for the two most popular junctions in your circuits, 5 volts and ground.

In the center are several short rows of holes separated by a central divider. All of the holes in each row in the center are connected with a metal strip underneath the holes. This allows you to use the holes in any given row to form a junction connecting components together.

The reason for the center divider is so that you can mount *integrated circuit chips*, such as microprocessors, on the breadboard. IC chips typically have two rows of pins that you need

Figure 3.6
A breadboard.
The overlaid lines
show the connections
that are being made
beneath the surface.

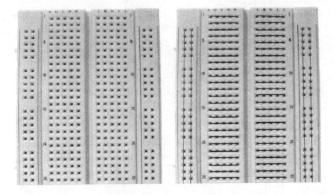

to connect other components to. The center row isolates the two rows from each other and gives you several holes connected to each pin so you can connect other components.

CAUTION
When you start to put components on your breadboard, avoid adding, removing, or changing components whenever the board is powered. You risk damaging your components by accidentally pushing two wires together and causing a short circuit. Later, if you have AC power, or larger DC power, running through your circuit you could also seriously shock yourself.

Where Does the Microcontroller Fit In?

Some microcontrollers are enclosed in boxes with screw terminals for connections. Most come as chips to be plugged into a breadboard or printed circuit board, as in see Figure 3.7.

Figure 3.7
The microcontroller on
a breadboard.

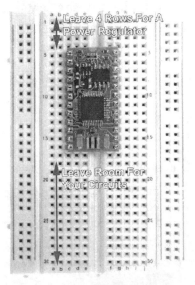

The vendors also sell "carrier boards," "demo boards, " or activity boards that act as readymade breadboards. These extra boards will save you from making your own power and programming connections, which are necessary if you're making the microcontroller circuit yourself on your own breadboard. Unless you are making a very limited experiment with this stuff, you will eventually end up needing a breadboard anyway. We suggest that you avoid the demo boards; just buy the chip itself and use it in your own breadboard.

Push the pins of your microcontroller into the holes of the breadboard. The chip should straddle the center divide of the board so that none of the legs are initially connected to each other. The top of the chip is usually marked with a rounded notch or a square metal pad around the first pin or hole.

It's best to place your chip toward the top. Generally the lower pins get to do most of the work, and it's good to have some extra breadboard real estate near them. Make sure that that the legs actually make their way into the hole and don't get caught on the edge, bending up behind the chip. If you have to take the chip back out, pry it gently from both ends using a flat bladed screwdriver. The pins are easily bent, and the more you bend them, the more likely they are to snap off.

Translating Schematics into Circuits

In every schematic, the connection lines indicate how components should be connected physically. Wherever there is a junction in your schematic, you must join all the components connected to that junction. The most common problems arise when you treat the schematic as a geographic map of what the circuit should look like. The schematic indicates how components are connected electrically. The spatial arrangement of the components in the circuit may not match the spatial arrangement in the schematic, but all of the connections must match up. Follow the connections from one component to the next, and make sure that they match the schematic's connections. Pay attention to the connected and unconnected wires as well. Connecting wires where there is no real connection is another common source of error, and will lead to short circuits.

Figure 3.8
Schematic and two
possible arrangements
of the same circuit.

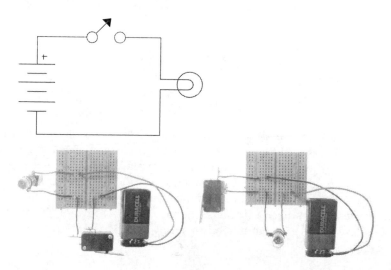

The simple schematic and the circuit shown in Figure 3.8 are identical. Notice how the two very different arrangements follow the same schematic. Although the components are not in the same place in each, the connections between them are the same. For example, peek ahead to what will be your first circuit for digital output in Figure 3.9.

Figure 3.9
Digital output
schematic.

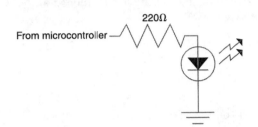

Don't worry; there will be more explanation of this circuit later. For now, just use it to practice translating from a schematic to a circuit in a breadboard. Before you look at Figure 3.10, see if you can make the circuit shown in Figure 3.9.

Figure 3.10
Correct wiring
of digital output
schematic (left) versus
incorrect wiring
(right).

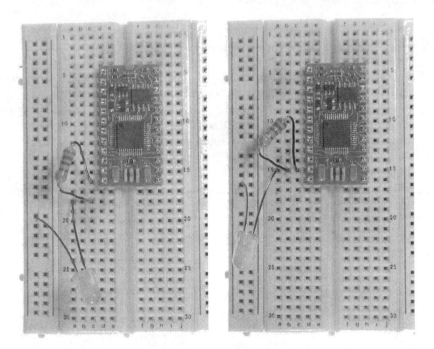

Attach one leg of an LED to a ground and the other leg via a resistor to a pin on the microcontroller. You should be able to tell that something is wrong with the way the resistor is connected on the right just from our explanation of how a breadboard works. The resistor is connected to itself because both ends are in the same row. You know that electricity follows the path of least resistance, so the resistor is rendered useless, and you potentially have a short circuit if the LED does not provide enough resistance by itself. Instead, the components are connected in series by first connecting one end of one resistor to the same row as the microcontroller's output pin. Then use any unused row to serve as a junction for the other end of the resistor and the long lead of the LED. Finally, put the short lead of the LED into one of the long rows on side of the breadboard (this will be ground). Remember, because the LED is a diode, it will only conduct electricity in one direction, from the long lead (the anode) to the cathode (short lead).

Using a Multimeter

Multimeters can act as your X-ray vision to see the flow of electricity through your circuit and components. You can debug your circuit by checking that the voltage between any two points in a circuit, or the current flowing past a certain point, is what you expect it to be. Oscilloscopes can look at changes in these properties over time, but they are much more expensive and more than you need to get started. Multimeters are also used to measure the electrical characteristics of a component, such as the resistance or capacitance. There are color codes and letter codes to identify the value of all components, but the surest way to know the value of a component is to measure it directly.

There are a few different kinds of meters to know about. *Analog meters* have a needle that moves along a dial to indicate the result of your test. These are usually more sensitive, but harder to read than *digital meters*, such as the one shown in Figure 3.11, which give you the result on an LCD screen. Digital meters also come in two flavors: normal and auto-ranging meters. *Auto-ranging meters* will automatically adjust if the component you're measuring has a much higher or lower value than you anticipated. Normal meters will have a range of magnitudes for each characteristic you can measure. You'll need to set your meter to the magnitude that you think is appropriate, take a measure, and change the magnitude if you don't get the result you expected. Auto-ranging meters are more expensive, but often more convenient. Unfortunately, different manufacturers use different icons to mark the multiple functions of a multimeter.

Figure 3.11
A digital multimeter.

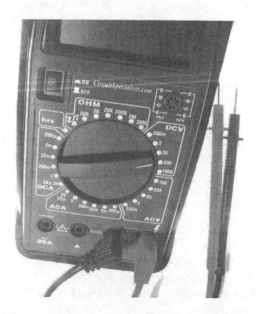

Voltage readings are like blood pressure readings: blood pressure is the first thing a doctor checks, regardless of what may be wrong with you. Likewise, you should check the voltage between power and ground first, regardless of what you think the problem is. Voltage measurements are taken with the circuit intact and powered. It is important to distinguish DC volts (sometimes symbolized by a solid line over a dashed line) from AC volts (sometimes symbolized by a tilde). To see the voltage between two points in your circuit (the most common place is between power and ground), touch the black lead of your multimeter to a ground connection in your circuit and the red lead to the place where you expect to see voltage. Try this now by touching the positive lead of your multimeter to one lead of the power supply that you bought and the black lead to the other lead, as shown in Figure 3.12.

Figure 3.12
Measuring voltage.

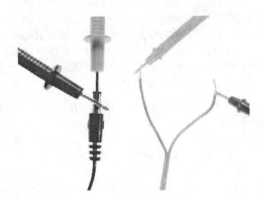

Your multimeter might read something like "12.3V" (which is close enough for you to call 12 volts). If you have an analog readout, the needle should go half way (on a 0–24 scale). If you get a negative reading, then you have the positive and negative leads reversed. There is no harm done to the multimeter when you reverse positive and negative. In fact, this is often how you figure out which wire on your power supply is positive and which is negative. This is known as the *polarity* of the circuit. Be aware that many other components (in particular your microcontroller) may not be as forgiving if you reverse the polarity like this. If you reverse the power and ground connections on your microcontroller, you're likely to destroy it. So use a meter to check that you've got the connections right before you add the microcontroller to your circuit!

Checking for continuity allows you to see that things you think are connected really are connected. Many meters have an audible continuity check, which beeps so you don't have to take your eyes off your circuit to look at the multimeter's display. Continuity check is usually the same setting as diode check. When you touch the probes of the meter together, it should beep. In the continuity setting, the two leads of the multimeter are interchangeable. To test a switch, as shown in Figure 3.13, you touch the two ends of a switch and see that you get continuity (and the meter will beep) when the switch is on and not when it is off.

There are a few common tasks that a meter gets used for all the time. *Resistance* of a fixed or variable resistor is measured by setting the meter to measure ohms (the usual symbol is Ω). We can check which poles of a switch are connected using the *continuity check* or *diode check* (sometimes symbolized by a musical note, a set of waves, or sometimes by a diode). We can check the direction of a diode using the diode check as well. To do these tests, remove the component

Figure 3.13
Testing a switch for
continuity.

from the circuit and touch its leads to the meter's probes. Try measuring a few resistors by setting your meter to measure ohms and see if their value is what you expected. Try a diode with the meter set to diode check. Try reversing the leads on your diode to see how the result differs.

Soldering

In the spirit of high-level rapid prototyping, you should solder only when there is no other way to make the connection. We love the solderless breadboard for this reason, but you will encounter components or wires that don't fit into the breadboard. You might also have to solder longer wires on a switch or a sensor that needs to be distant from the breadboard. When you're happy with the design of your project, you may want to make it more robust by redoing all the connections on a soldered board, also called a *printed circuit board (PCB)*.

The trickiest part of soldering is holding four items steady: the two components being soldered, the solder, and the iron. It's useful to have a small vise or a pair of clamps (helping hands) to hold the two things being soldered, freeing your hands for the iron and the solder, as in Figure 3.14.

Before you start soldering, let the soldering iron get hot, wipe the tip on a damp sponge quickly, and then melt some solder directly onto the tip. Coat the tip smoothly; you don't want a glob of solder on the end. If you get a glob, tap the iron gently on the edge of a metal tin can to get the glob off. You should have a nice, smooth coating remaining. This is called *tinning* the iron, and it makes the solder flow more smoothly when you work.

The first rule of soldering is to heat the joint, not the solder. This means that the solder should not touch the iron directly. Instead, put the two components being soldered together so that their metal parts are touching. Then touch the solder to their joint from the other side. This lets the heat travel through the components to the solder, melting it. This ensures that solder can ooze between all the crevices of the joint, and everything will cool at the same rate. It is very tempting to heat the solder directly and drip it over the joint. You might get a joint that will look fine, and even work for a long time (right up until you need to show the project). But that joint will be brittle because the metal of the solder and the components heated at a different rate. The joint will break right at the wrong moment.

Following the first rule of soldering is difficult when the tip of your iron is not clean. The heat of the iron does not transfer as well to the joint—it takes a long time for the heat to reach

Figure 3.14
Holding components
for soldering.

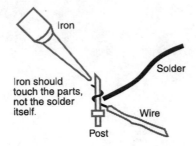

the solder, and you become impatient and just touch the solder directly to the iron. Don't do this. Wipe the tip and tin it again frequently. You'll make better solder joints and make your soldering iron tip last a lot longer.

Try not to overdo it with the solder. Big fat solder joints have more opportunity to accidentally rub up against another joint to form the dreaded short circuit.

Needless to say, you should be careful where you lay the hot iron and how you pick it up. The fumes from the solder are another safety issue because some solder contains lead. Make sure the room is well ventilated. Use a fan to send the fumes out the window instead of up your nose, which will keep you from breathing it in and becoming progressively dumber as the lead kills your brain cells. Don't forget to turn off the iron when you are done.

You can also undo a solder joint. You can remove the solder using suction (you will need to buy a de-soldering tool) or absorption (you will need to buy a solder wick).

There are two components you'll need from the beginning that require soldering, so this will be your first solder project. First, you need to solder wires onto a power connector. Second, you need to solder headers onto a serial connector. See the following exercise, "Soldering Exercise: Serial Connector," in which we describe how to solder the serial connector.

Powering the Breadboard

We will discuss a couple of ways to connect power to your board. For all of them, however, you will have to be able to identify the positive and negative leads of your power supply. This process was described in the previous section, "Using a Multimeter." Mark the leads with tape or a marker so that you clearly remember which is positive and which is negative. After you have established which wire is which, unplug the power supply again before you start connecting it to your board.

Connecting the Quick and Dirty Way

You could put the bare ends of your connector directly into the breadboard now, plug the connector into your AC/DC power supply, and you'd have power to your board. However, for extra safety, we recommend soldering two headers onto the ends of the wires, as shown on the far left in Figure 3.15.

To insulate the headers, you can cover them with hot glue, as shown in the middle of Figure 3.15.

Figure 3.15
Methods for connecting power to the board. Soldering headers onto the bare ends of a DC power connector (1) is quickest and least safe. Soldering to two connected headers is safer (2). Insulating the connection is safer still (3). Using a battery terminal connector is even safer (4), and using a coaxial power connector is safest and most convenient (5).

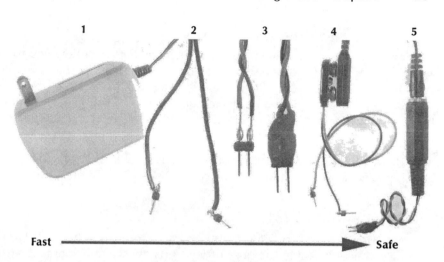

Fast ➤ Safe

SOLDERING EXERCISE: SERIAL CONNECTOR

You'll need a serial connector that can plug into your breadboard in order to program the microcontroller. This requires soldering, so there's no time like the present to do it. Once you've soldered one job, the rest are easier.

The serial connector we're using has nine solder terminals on the back. You'll be soldering four headers to four of the connectors. Specifically, you'll use connectors 2, 3, 4, and 5. The numbers are hard to read, so compare your connector to the one in Figure 3.16.

Figure 3.16
A serial connector, front and back.

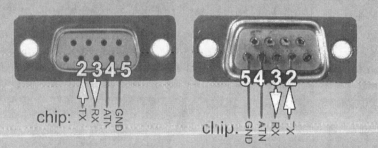

To make this connector, break four headers off a row together. Use your vise or helping hands to hold the pins next to the four appropriate solder terminals. Make sure all four headers are held securely at once. The soldering iron tends to soften the plastic that holds them, which can loosen the pins if you hold the iron on them for too long. Tin your iron and touch it to the top of each solder terminal while holding the solder to the bottom (where the terminal meets the pin). Be careful not to get too much solder on each connection. If the connections touch, you've got too much solder. When you're done, check each header and its corresponding hole with a continuity meter. Check each header with the other headers as well. You should *not* have continuity between headers. Each one should be connected only to its hole.

Once you've made a serial connector, you'll not only have a grasp on how to solder, you'll also be ready to start working with the microcontroller.

Connecting the Professional Way

If you want a more professional power connector that will allow you to disconnect your power adapter safely and reuse it for other projects, then build a power connector for your circuit. The easiest type of connector is a 9-volt battery snap, as shown in Figure 3.16 (fourth from left). Battery snaps attach nicely to 9-volt batteries but not very well to standard power adapters. It is also easy to accidentally reverse the polarity with battery snaps, which can fry a voltage regulator.

Instead, we recommend a coaxial connector, as shown on the far right in Figure 3.16. See the following exercise, "Soldering Exercise: Power Connector," for details on how to do it.

Voltage Regulators

In this section you will be using a voltage regulator to supply ground and 5-volt power to the long strips of holes on the sides of your breadboard. Some breadboards have power on one side and ground on the other, but it is more convenient to have both power and ground on both sides. We will show you both styles of breadboard here. For the rest of the book we will use the boards with two long rows on each side.

Built-In Voltage Regulators

Most of the circuits you'll build on a breadboard, even the ones with no microcontroller, are likely to work at 5 volts. It's so common, in fact, that most high- and mid-level microcontrollers (for example, Basic Stamp, BX-24, and Basic Atom Pro24) come with a 5-volt voltage regulator built in. These regulators allow you a little bit of latitude in the voltage you supply (from 8 to 15 volts DC), converting whatever you input to 5 volts DC. Next, you distribute the 5 volts and ground to the side rows of your breadboard.

The quickest way to get going is to use the built-in 5-volt voltage regulator of your microcontroller, as in Figure 3.17. Connect the positive side of your power supply (5 to 15 volts) to the top-right pin and ground to the next pin down. Your microcontroller will then give an even 5 volts out of the fourth pin down. The ground for the 5 volts will be the same as the big power supply. Run wires to distribute ground and 5 volts to the side rows for future circuits.

Figure 3.17
A microcontroller with a built-in regulator, powered directly from a DC power supply.

Single Power Strip Board

Double Power Strip Board

SOLDERING EXERCISE: POWER CONNECTOR

Coaxial power connectors mate with the connectors on most DC power supplies. Usually, the center of your power supply connector is connected to voltage, and the outside is connected to ground. When you measured for voltage in the section above on using a multimeter, you saw this in action. If you got a positive number when the red lead was in the center of the connector and the black was on the outside, then the center was indeed connected to power. In this exercise, you'll solder a connector to mate with that kind of *center-positive* power supply.

A coaxial power connector has a plastic sleeve that screws off to uncover the guts of the connector. Inside, you'll find two tabs with holes in them. Set your multimeter to continuity check (or diode check), touching one probe to the center pin of the connector and the other to one of the tabs. When you get continuity, you know which tab is connected to the pin and which is connected to the outer ring. Do a continuity check on the outer ring and the other tab just to be sure. The inner pin will have the power wire connected to it, and the outer ring will have the ground wire attached to it.

Be sure to put the cable through the plastic sleeve now, because you will not be able to fit it over the ends of the cable after you have soldered it. Cut two lengths of wire about 6 to 8 inches long, one red and one black. Strip about 1/2 inch of insulation from either end. Bend one bare end into a hook. Hook the red wire onto the tab that's connected to the center pin, and the black wire onto the tab that's connected to the outer ring. Use a vise or helping hands to hold the wires and the connector. Use needle nose pliers to squeeze the hook ends of your wires tight to the tabs. Now you're ready to solder. Tin your iron and touch it to either tab, as close to the hole as possible. Touch the solder to the other side. When the solder flows over the joint and you have a small bead of it surrounding the wire and the hole, remove the solder and the iron and let it cool (15 to 30 seconds is plenty of time). Repeat the procedure on the other tab and wire. When you're done, the wires should not move on the tabs. If they do, re-solder until they're secure. Your connector should look like the one in Figure 3.18.

Figure 3.18
A properly soldered
power connector.

Check for continuity between the other end of the red wire and the center pin. If you get it, your solder joint is good! Do the same for the black wire and the outer ring. Now slip the plastic sleeve over both wires and screw it back onto the connector. It's also convenient to twist the wires together so they move as one and don't get tangled.

Now, on the other end, solder two headers, as shown third in Figure 3.16, and insulate them with hot glue, as shown fourth in Figure 3.16. Screw the connector back together and you're done! Connect it to your power supply, plug in the power supply, and check the header pins for voltage. If you get a positive voltage with the red lead on the red wire's header and the black lead on the black wire's header, you got it right.

Powering the Breadboard

The voltage regulators that come with the microcontrollers are easily fried by a brief short circuit or reversed polarities. If this happens, putting in an external voltage regulator will probably revive your microcontroller. Better yet, skip this drama and use an external voltage regulator from the start.

7805 5-Volt Regulator

Figure 3.19
A 7805 5-volt voltage regulator.

8–15V Input   **5V Output**

Ground For Both

If you are using a lower-level chip (for example, a PIC) or if you are like us and don't trust the built-in regulators on the Stamp-like microcontrollers, then you will build a default power supply circuit onto every board. The 7805 regulator is used to take a varying range of voltage (from 8 to 15 volts DC) and convert it to 5 volts DC. It can supply almost 1000 milliamps of current (1 amp) at 5 volts, assuming the power supply that's feeding it can supply up to an amp as well. The pins of the regulator are numbered from left to right as you look at the front of it (the side with the label), as shown in Figure 3.19. Pin 1 is the input pin, which you connect to the 8 to 15 volts of the power supply. Pin 2 is the ground, which you connect to the ground of the power supply and to the ground of your circuit. (The metal top of the regulator is also a ground. This will be helpful later when you are looking for a ground connection to touch with your multimeter probe.) Pin 3 is the output pin. This outputs 5 volts. Connect this pin to the voltage side of your circuit.

Place a 7805 5-volt voltage regulator in the top three rows of the board with the front of the regulator (the side with the label) facing to the left, as shown in Figure 3.20. This will place the voltage regulator's input pin in the top hole, its ground in the second hole, and its output pin in the third hole. First, you'll connect the output side of the regulator to the long rows on the board. Run a red wire to connect the regulator's third pin (the output pin) to the 5V power strip(s) on your breadboard. Next, connect a black wire from the ground (center) pin of the regulator to the ground strip(s) on your breadboard. On the input side of the regulator, connect the black (ground) wire of your power connector (which you soldered above) to the regulator's ground (center) pin as well. The ground pin is shared by both the input and output. Then connect the red (power) wire of your power connector to the row holding pin 1 of the regulator (the input pin).

When you're sure you've wired it right, plug the power connector into your DC power supply, and connect it to the wall. Set your multimeter to read DC voltage, and put the leads on the metal ends of the wires in the red and blue rows. If you wired it correctly, you should read 5 volts. If you wired it incorrectly, your regulator probably overheated and produced a puff of smoke. It is normal for a voltage regulator to get a little hot if it operating at the high end of its range. That is why it has that metal fin on top to dissipate the heat. If you have the dreaded short circuit your regulator could heat up to the point where it burns you when you touch it. Let it cool down, throw it out, and try again with another regulator.

Figure 3.20
A 7805 voltage regulator powering a stamp-like microcontroller on a breadboard.

 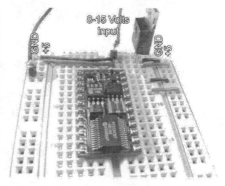

Single Power Strip Board   **Double Power Strip Board**

The long side rows will be used to connect many of the components in your circuit to power or ground. From now on, we'll refer to them as the power bus (the row connected to 5 volts) and the ground bus (the row connected to ground).

If you've done everything right, your microprocessor is now running. If it's already got a program on it (the BX-24 ships with a program on it already), you may see blinking LEDs. If not, you have a bit more work to do to get the LED blinking.

Be Neat

Keeping your circuits neat will make debugging much easier. When possible, shorten the leads on components so there is no bare metal sticking up from the breadboard. Make sure the exposed parts of wires can't lean against each other. This is the biggest source of short circuits on a breadboard. Use consistent colors of wires when possible; for example, use black for ground connections, red for power connections, yellow, white, or blue for data connections, and so forth. Use cable ties to anchor your power connector (and any future wire connecting to the outside world) to something stationary on your board. This *strain relief* will make it less likely that your circuit will be disconnected accidentally when your power cord inevitably gets tugged as you connect and disconnect your project. Figure 3.21 shows the right way and the wrong way to wire a board.

Once you've assembled this circuit on your board, keep it together; you'll use it again in the next chapter.

Figure 3.21
Examples of a messy
board (top), and a neat
board (bottom). Strive
to make your board
look like the one on the
bottom.

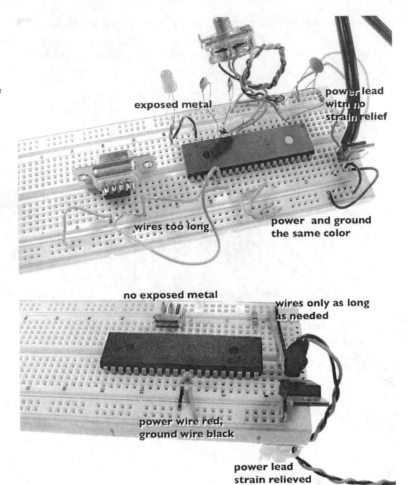

4

The Microcontroller

"Hello World!" Is the Hard Part

Anybody who has learned how to use a couple of different computer systems or programming languages will tell you that the hardest part is getting a computer to do anything at all. It usually involves learning an arbitrary and proprietary development environment where many obscure files have to be located in many obscure places. After you've mastered the environment well enough to accomplish something trivial, implementing the intricate particulars of your project is comparatively easy and definitely more fun. In software, it's traditional to prove your mastery of any environment by getting your program to say "Hello World!" The "Hello World!" message of the microcontroller is a blinking LED. Once you get the microcontroller to blink an LED, it's all downhill from there.

In the last chapter, you should have inserted your microcontroller into a breadboard and applied power. You might even have a built-in program with a blinking LED. In this chapter, you'll walk through the basics of the microcontroller and its environment, culminating in you running a program of your own to blink the LED. Most people find this immensely satisfying. We'll explain how to do this on a few different microprocessors. You can skip the sections that don't apply to your processor. We'll do the same in subsequent chapters as well.

Where Does the Microcontroller Fit In?

So far your basic circuit in Figure 4.1 doesn't have a lot of possibilities for interaction. On the input side you have a switch, and on the output side you have a light.

The interaction is like a one-line joke: you close the switch and the light goes on. There are no surprises (assuming the light bulb is good). When you introduce a computer, in the form of a microcontroller, you start to see some rich possibilities for interaction.

Figure 4.1
The simple circuit.

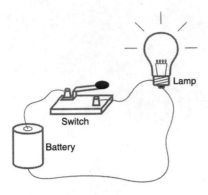

Input

When you replace the load in your circuit with the microcontroller, as in Figure 4.2, you could count how many times a person presses the switch.

Figure 4.2
The microcontroller
reading input.

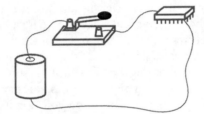

Or you could have multiple switches and have the microcontroller consider them together before it takes action, as would happen on a combination lock. Or you could have the same switch do two different jobs, depending on the context, as happens all too often on the interfaces to your personal electronics. Or maybe you are interested not only in whether a person is pressing the button, but also for how long and how hard.

Output

When you replace the switch in your circuit with a microcontroller, you can automate when the load is turned on according to commands in your software (see Figure 4.3).

Figure 4.3
The microcontroller
controlling output.

You can then turn on multiple devices in concert or in sequence. You can turn on a device for a particular duration or turn it on by degrees. For example, you can turn on a whole row of light bulbs all at once, or you can flash them on and off in a sequence, or you can dim them individually or as a group.

Routing Inputs to Outputs

Best of all, you can cause a variety of different output actions to happen based on various input actions. For example, you could have a burglar alarm switch that sends a signal to the microcontroller when someone walks in the room. The microcontroller might then turn on an alarm, call the police department on the telephone, and flash the lights. If that is too easy, you can program it so the person has to dance around in a circle three times before the microcontroller flashes the lights to the beat and calls the police. That's not too boring at all.

Identifying the Pins of the Microcontroller

In your microcontroller's documentation, you'll find a diagram and chart describing the different jobs that each pin does. Every component's documentation will have a similar diagram, known as the *pin diagram*. We refer to this diagram so often that we usually photocopy it and put it on the wall. Every microcontroller will have pins for connecting to power and ground, pins dedicated to programming the chip, and general input and output (I/O) pins. Some microcontrollers will have additional special function pins, some of which we discuss below. Depending on your microcontroller, your I/O pins will have a number of different possible functions. In software, you will set which task you want a pin to do. The most basic functions are digital input and output. Almost all pins are capable of digital I/O. In addition, some pins are capable of analog input as well. The various functions of each pin are marked on the pin diagram, and explained more fully in the rest of the processor's documentation.

NOTE

Stamp-like brands covered in this book are the NetMedia's BasicX BX-24 chip, Parallax's BASIC Stamp 2, and Basic Micro's Basic Atom Pro24. These follow the layout of the original BASIC Stamp 2. We will also show examples using Microchip's PIC 18F452, which has an entirely different physical layout.

Figures 4.4 and 4.5 are simplified pin diagrams for a typical Stamp-like processor and for the PIC 18F452.

On any chip with this basic form (two rows of pins, called a DIP package), the pin numbering starts at the top-left corner and moves in a U shape around the chip. All of the Stamp-like modules have 24 pins. The PICs have a varying number of pins; the 18F452 is typical of those PICs that have 40 pins.

On the Stamp-like modules, the first four pins on the left are used for programming the chip, the first four on the right are used for powering and resetting the chip, and the bottom 16

Figure 4.4
A basic pin diagram for
Stamp-like modules.

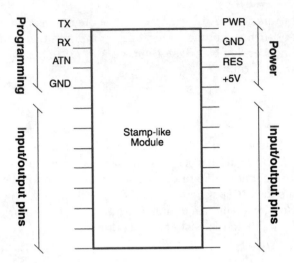

Figure 4.5
A basic pin diagram for
the PIC 18F452.

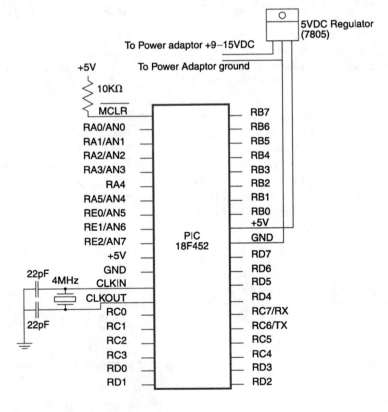

pins are used for general I/O. The BASIC Stamp 2, the BX-24, and the Basic Atom Pro24 are all alike in this layout. The I/O pins all function as digital inputs and outputs on all three modules, though some of them have additional functions that differ from module to module.

On the PIC, the power and ground pins are near the center of the chip, and the I/O pins spread outward from the center. Some of the I/O pins also function as programming pins.

In addition, there are two pins, CLKIN and CLKOUT, for an external crystal that functions as the PIC's timing clock. On the Stamp-like modules, the clock is built into the module.

Lower-Level Microcontrollers: External Clock

Every microprocessor needs a regular voltage pulse by which to clock its operations. If you are using a Stamp-like module, you can skip this section; your module has a clock built into it. Typically, these clocks pulse several million times a second. One of the inconveniences of using lower-level chips like the PIC is that you have to supply a separate clock. You can use an external crystal for a clock or use a resistor/capacitor circuit that's built into the chip. The R/C circuit that's built in is not very accurate, however, and we don't recommend it. We recommend using an external crystal instead.

A crystal is designed to pulse at a specific speed when given power. It has two pins, which are interchangeable. When connected to the PIC's CLKIN and CLKOUT pins, and connected to ground through 22-pF capacitors, the crystal will vibrate at its given frequency and give the PIC a clock. Figure 4.6 shows the clock circuit for the PIC.

Figure 4.6
Clock circuit for PIC
18F452.

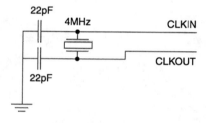

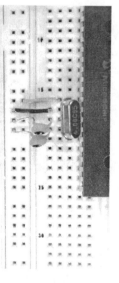

Your First Microcontroller-Based Circuit

Before you program the microcontroller, you need to build your first output circuit. You'll need to connect an LED to a pin of the microprocessor. You may already have it connected because this is the example circuit we used in the previous chapter. We will visit this circuit yet again in the section on digital output in Chapter 6, "The Big Four: Schematics, Programs, and Transducers." Just to review, connect a 220-ohm resistor to the same row as the bottom-left pin of your microprocessor. Connect the other end to an empty row. Connect the positive lead (usually the long lead) of an LED to that same row. Connect the negative lead (usually the short lead) of the LED to the ground row. Figure 4.7 illustrates what you should have wired.

Figure 4.7
LED connected to pin
of the microcontroller
as a digital output.

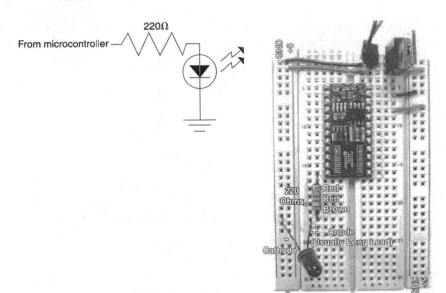

NOTE

Make sure to note which pin you used for your LED circuit. You might encounter two
numbering systems for the pins. One set of numbers is for all the physical pins on
the chip. The system you really care about is the numbers used by software to refer to
the I/O pins. Each manufacturer labels the pins slightly differently for programming
purposes. Most start counting with the number 0, which takes some getting used to.
Make an "x" on Figure 4.8 next to the pin used in your circuit. On the BASIC Stamp
2, the I/O pins, which are physically pin numbers 5 through 20, if you count from
the top left of the module, are referred to as pins 0 through 15. On the BX-24, they're
labeled pins 5 through 20, the same as their physical numbers. On the Basic Atom
Pro24, they're labeled 0 through 15, or P0 through P15.

Figure 4.8
Pin diagrams for the
BX-24, BASIC Stamp 2,
and Basic Atom Pro24.

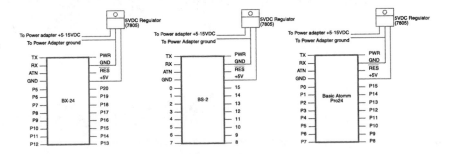

Getting Your Program to the Chip

The microcontrollers that we're discussing can be reprogrammed repeatedly. Not all
microprocessors are like this. Some are *one-time programmable*, meaning that you program
them once and they're programmed for life. One-time programmable chips are much
cheaper, but are used for mass production after you have figured everything out, not for
individual projects or for developing new devices. The process for putting a program

into a microcontroller will vary between brands, but there are two components that are common to all of them: a hardware connection between the multimedia computer and the microprocessor, and a suite of software programs on the multimedia computer for programming and compiling your program and downloading it to the microprocessor. The software suite will include a text editor for writing your program; a compiler, which converts your text into a binary file containing instructions that the microprocessor and read and interpret; and a downloader, which is used to transfer the binary file to the microprocessor. Most environments will also include a debugger for sending messages to and from your microprocessor while it's running. Each time you transfer a program to your chip, the previous program is erased from the chip's memory and the new program takes its place. The downloader starts the program running on the microprocessor once the transfer is complete. Figure 4.9 lays out the steps for getting your program running on the chip.

Figure 4.9
Writing, compiling, and downloading.

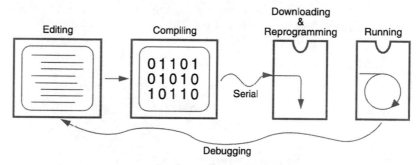

Transferring the program to the microprocessor is a one-way journey. It's not possible to get it back from the chip to the multimedia computer in human-readable form. Make sure you keep track of the text files that you create on your multimedia computer because they will be your only copy of your program.

NOTE

The software for programming all of the microprocessors we're discussing exists for Windows PCs only (though there is a Macintosh-based programming environment for the BASIC Stamp 2). Once you've programmed the computer, you can communicate with a Macintosh computer from your microcontroller, however. It is possible to use VirtualPC to run for the programming software for all of these microcontrollers on a Mac, but there are a number of technical difficulties to overcome to make that happen. The programming environment does not require a very powerful computer, so some Mac users prefer to just pick up an old PC from a junk store or eBay and use that just for programming their microcontrollers.

Programming Stamp-Like Modules

For Stamp-like modules the editor, compiler, downloader, and debugger are combined in one application, which is free to download from the manufacturer. They use a simple programming language, BASIC (though the three Stamp-like modules we're discussing use three different variants of BASIC). Once you've made the serial connector in Chapter 3, connect it to the serial port on your PC with a normal serial cable.

> **NOTE**
> Make sure your serial cable is a standard one, not a "null modem" cable.

Stamp-Like Programming Hardware Connection

The first four pins of Stamp-like modules form a serial port that connects to the RS-232 serial port of your multimedia computer. Connect the serial connector from Chapter 3 to these four pins, as shown in Figure 4.10.

Figure 4.10
Connecting the serial cable to the Stamp-like module.

The Stamp-like module connects via a serial cable to the serial port on your multimedia computer. Look for a port on the back of your computer with a 9-pin male connector (DB9) labeled |o|o|o 1, not |o|o|1. On very old machines, the connector has 25 pins. Nowadays many machines (Mac and PC) are only equipped with a USB serial port. For those, you'll have to get a USB-to-RS-232 adapter.

Stamp-Like Programming Software Environments

In this section, we will talk about where to write this code; in the next chapter, we'll talk about what to write. If you bought only the chip itself, as we recommended, and not the whole development environment, you will have to go to the manufacturer's Web site to download the programming software and the manual. See Appendix B for URLs of the manufacturers of the modules we're discussing. The instructions that follow assume you've installed the application and run it. You'll write the same program on all three environments. When it's run, it will make an LED attached to pin 12 of the module (the bottom-left pin) blink on and off every half second.

Following is the text you'll enter. We'll explain it in more depth in Chapter 5, "Programming." This is just enough code to make the chip do something you can see. If you're using the BASIC Stamp 2, you'll be using the pBasic variant of BASIC. On the Basic Atom Pro24, you'll use mBasic, and on the BX-24, you'll use BX BASIC.

(PBASIC)

(MBasic)

```
Main:
        High 7
        Pause 50
        Low 7
        Pause 500
Goto main
```

(BX-Basic)

```
Sub Main()
        Do
                Call putPin(12, 1)
                Call delay(0.5)
                Call putPin(12, 0)
                Call delay(0.5)
        Loop
End sub
```

Connect your module to the COM1 serial port of the PC via the serial connector and serial cable, and give it power. Open the programming environment and you're ready to begin.

In the BASIC Stamp programming environment, you type in a program, then choose the version of the BASIC Stamp you're using by clicking the BS-2 stamp mode icon on the toolbar. Then choose the version of the programming language you're using by clicking the pBasic language version icon for 2.5 in the toolbar. Then click the Program button. Figure 4.11 shows the programming environment. The application then compiles your program and sends it to the microcontroller. Disconnect your serial cable and the program will start running. When you save your program, the BASIC Stamp application produces a single text file containing your BASIC commands. This is also the file that gets downloaded to the module. It's compiled on the microprocessor itself as it runs.

Figure 4.11
The BASIC Stamp programming environment.

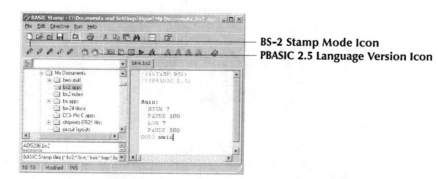

— BS-2 Stamp Mode Icon
— PBASIC 2.5 Language Version Icon

Programming Stamp-Like Modules

The Basic Atom Pro environment is similar to the BASIC Stamp environment, except that you don't need to pick the version of the chip or the version of the programming language. Figure 4.12 shows the Basic Atom Integrated Development Environment (IDE). To start a new program, click the New icon on the toolbar or select New from the File menu, as with most text editing environments. Once you've entered your code, click the Program button and the program is compiled and downloaded. Disconnect your serial cable and the program will start running. When you save your program, the Basic Atom Pro application produces a text file containing your BASIC commands and a binary file (with a .bin extension) containing the machine code that's downloaded to the module.

Figure 4.12
The Basic Atom
programming
environment.

The application for the BasicX has two parts, a downloader/debugger window and an editor window. The Editor window is shown in Figure 4.13. When you open the program only the downloader/debugger window will appear. Click on the Open Editor icon to bring up the Editor window. Once it's open, click the New Project button to begin a new project. Give the project and the module the same name, for simplicity's sake. The environment will automatically enter some text to begin with; select all and delete it, then enter your own text. To run your program, click the Compile and Run button. The application will compile and download your program to the module and run it. When you look in the directory where you saved the program, you'll see that for a single program the BX programming

Figure 4.13
The BasicX
programming
environment (editor
window only).

environment creates several files grouped together as a project. They all start with the same name, the name of the project, but have different file extensions. The file with the .bas extension contains the text of your program, and the one with the .bxb extension is the binary file that gets downloaded to the module.

Programming Lower-Level Chips

In order to program on the PIC or another lower-level processor, there's more work to do before you get the LED to blink. First, there are some extra components you need to add to the circuit in order to get it to run. Second, there is an additional piece of hardware you need in order to transfer the program to your chip. Third, there are several pieces of software that you must install and configure in order to write, compile, and download your program. Some of the software is free, and some of it is not.

As we mentioned before, the disadvantages of working with lower-level processors are counterbalanced by their speed and cost. PICs cost anywhere from one-third to one-tenth as much as the Stamp-like modules, so the expense that you suffer in buying the development tools is offset by the fact that the chips are so cheap. We don't recommend the lower-level approach for the absolute beginner, but we include it here for those with some electronics or programming background, as well as for those who want more after they've worked with the mid-level modules.

If you're working with a PIC, you should already have added the external clock circuit to your board as shown earlier in this chapter. You should also add a 10 kilohm (kΩ) resistor to the MCLR pin of the processor and connect the other end of the resistor to ground. Now you're ready to begin programming.

The Hardware Programmer

The biggest change from mid-level modules to lower-level chips is the addition of a hardware programmer. This device connects to the parallel port or the serial port of your PC and loads the program into the PIC. There are several models on the market. Some require you to remove the PIC from its circuit and place it in the programmer. Others connect directly to the PIC's circuit board. They range in price from $7 to over $100. Our examples use the EPIC Plus Programmer from microEngineering Labs. It costs about $60, and connects to the parallel (printer) port of your PC. There's also a serial version of this programmer available for a bit more money. Check Appendix A for recommendations and notes on other hardware programmers.

Lower-Level Programming Software Environments

As we mentioned previously, lower-level microprocessor programming requires three different pieces of software: a text editor, a compiler, and a downloader. Some text editors are specially designed for programming, have formatting features to make reading your program easier, and include tools to automatically run the compiler and open the downloader. Our examples in this chapter and following will use MicroCode Studio Lite as the editor, PicBasic Pro as the compiler, and the EPIC Plus software as the downloader. You'll also need an additional compiler, cryptically named MPASMWIN, from Microchip. This is freeware, and can be downloaded from http://www.microchip.com (there's also a link to it from http://www.melabs.com). MPASMWIN takes the partially compiled code from PicBasic Pro and assembles it into a final binary file for download to the PIC. Of these, only MicroCode Studio is free (available from http://www.mecanique.co.uk). PicBasic Pro can be purchased from microEngineering Labs. EPIC Plus software comes with the EPIC Plus Programmer.

We'll assume in the following example that you've installed MicroCode Studio, PicBasic Pro, and the EPIC Plus software already, and configured them. MicroEngineering Labs distributes another editor, CoDesigner Lite, with PicBasic Pro, but you don't have to use it. If you install PicBasic Pro and the EPIC software first, then MicroCode Studio will automatically search for them as has programmer and downloader when you install it.

You'll build the same blinking LED example on the PIC that you built on the Stamp-like processors. Using the circuit in Figure 4.14, attach a 220-ohm resistor to the bottom-left pin of the PIC (pin 20, or RD1 on a PIC 18F452), then attach the resistor to an empty row of the breadboard. Attach the long lead of the LED to the same row, and attach the short lead of the LED to ground. What it will look like is shown in Figure 4.14.

Figure 4.14
PIC 18F452 with an
LED and resistor on
Pin RD1.

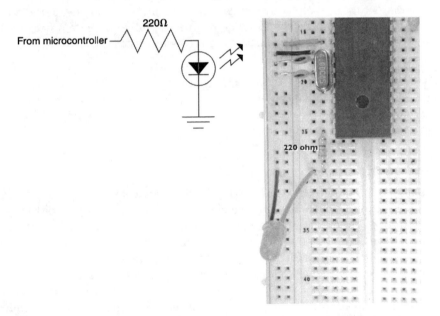

Following is the code you'll enter. Notice that it's very similar to the BASIC Stamp and Basic Atom code. PicBasic Pro and mBasic, the Basic Atom BASIC, are both based on BASIC Stamp's BASIC, pBasic.

```
Main:
     High portd.1
     Pause 500
     Low portd.1
     Pause 500
Goto main
```

Attach the EPIC Plus Programmer to the parallel port of the PC, and make sure it's powered. Open MicroCode studio, and enter the code above. Figure 4.15 shows the MicroCode Studio editor. Click the Compile and Program button and MicroCode Studio will call PicBasic Pro and MPASMWIN to compile the program. The compiler will produce a number of files, all with the same name and different extensions, like the BasicX software did for the BX-24. The file with the extension .bas contains your text and the file with the extension .hex is the one that will be downloaded to the chip.

If MicroCode Studio can't find MPASMWIN or the EPIC programming software, you might have to configure it yourself. Click the View menu, then choose PicBasic Options. Select the Assembler Tab, and check the Microchip MPASM check box. Then click the Find Automatically button. MicroCode Studio should now be able to find the MPASMWIN assembler. The procedure for configuring MicroCode Studio to find the EPIC programmer is similar. Click the View Menu, then choose PicBasic Options. Select the Programmer Tab, and add a new programmer. Select the MicroEngineering Labs EPIC programmer and you should be all set.

Figure 4.15
The MicroCode Studio environment.

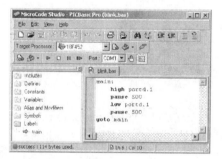

Once the compiling is done, MicroCode Studio will open the EPIC Plus software to prepare for download. It's up to you to complete the download.

First, attach the 40-pin ZIF adaptor to the EPIC Programmer like in Figure 4.16.

Figure 4.16
The EPIC Programmer.

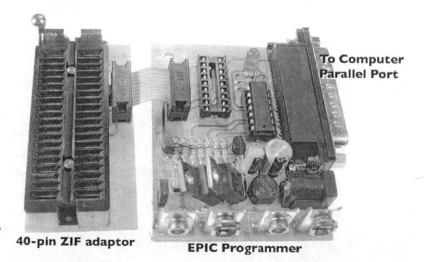

To Computer Parallel Port

40-pin ZIF adaptor   **EPIC Programmer**

Next, insert the PIC into the socket with the top next to the lever. Press the lever down to hold the PIC in the socket.

Figure 4.17
The EPIC Plus environment.

Figure 4.18
Configuration Window of EPIC Plus environment.

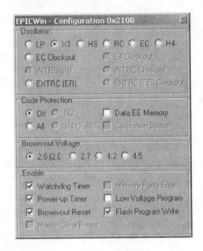

Figure 4.17 shows the main window of the EPIC Plus environment. Click on the View menu of the EPIC software and choose Configuration. This menu (see Figure 4.18) allows you to set various characteristics of the PIC, such as the type of clock crystal you are using, which timers in the PIC are turned on or off, and so forth. For this example, set the clock to XT and leave the rest alone. Then click the Program button and the software will download your program to the PIC. Put the PIC back into its circuit, power it up, and your LED should blink.

Debugging

In programming or electronics, nothing ever works right the first time. Learning how to program is really about learning how to debug. The first step is to come up with an idea about what might not be working. Then, replace what you think isn't working with something that should work to see if that's the problem. When troubleshooting, try to change only one element of the system at a time. If the element that you changed was not the problem, then put the original element back and try another. Being systematic like this is the key not only to solving the problem, but also to knowing how you solved it once it works again.

Here are some common sources of error in the examples above, and how to fix them.

> ► *Is the circuit powered?* Check to see that it's got power and ground. Because it's necessary to unplug the circuit any time you make a change, this is the most common source of error. Take a multimeter to the power and ground pins of the chip to see that it's getting 5 volts.

▶ *Is the pin mentioned in the software the one used in the circuit?* Look at the pin diagram for your microcontroller to be sure your circuit and your software are referring to the same pin.

▶ *Does the LED work?* Disconnect the end of the resistor that's attached to the pin of the chip and connect it directly to 5 volts. If the LED doesn't light up, then try another LED.

▶ *Is the resistor the right value?* If the new LED doesn't light up either, remove the resistor from the circuit and check its value by setting your multimeter to ohms and measuring it. If it's not 220 ohms, get one that is.

▶ *Is the circuit connected to the serial port correctly?* If you have more than one serial port on your computer, you may have attached the serial cable to the wrong port. Check to see that you're in the right port.

▶ *Is the software configured to use the right serial port?* Each environment has a menu item that allows you to set the serial port. In the BASIC Stamp environment, select Port from the Directive menu. In the Basic Atom environment, it's on the General tab under Preferences in the Tools menu. In the BasicX environment, it's in the I/O Ports menu of the debugger window. Choose Download Port from the I/O Ports menu. In the EPIC Plus software, select EPIC Port from the File menu. Be sure that the port selected is the one that your serial cable or parallel cable is attached to.

▶ *Does another application have control of the serial port?* If the programming environment can't open the serial port, perhaps another application has control of it. If you have a PDA that syncs through the serial port, this might be the problem. Disabling the PDA software or picking another port should solve the problem.

When all else fails, question your most basic assumptions. The most persistent problems usually hide in the areas about which you're most confident. If you're sure the power is good, check it. If you're sure the serial cable is connected, check it. If you're sure the chip is in the circuit correctly, check it. The less you assume, the better you get at debugging. You'll need this skill frequently in the chapters ahead, so get in the habit of being systematic and questioning your assumptions now, in order to save you heartache later.

If you have managed to get the LED to blink, you should marvel at your new skills as master of both bits and atoms. It is traditional at this point to do the hokey-pokey and turn yourself around!

Debugging

5
Programming

Your microcontroller earns its keep by doing processing in software between its inputs and its outputs. In the last chapter you saw how to put your software program onto the microcontroller. Now you have to make the program specific to your project. This chapter is written to accommodate beginning programmers. You will learn about programming languages in general and about programming on a microcontroller in particular. If you are an experienced programmer, you can safely skip this chapter and pick the syntax of your microcontroller's language from examples in other chapters.

The Good News

If you don't have any experience with computer programming, you'll be glad to know that programming for microcontrollers is much simpler than programming for desktop computers. It will also relieve you to know that for any kind of programming there are only four main tools that programmers use: loops, if statements, variables, and routines. Most everything else you do when programming is a combination of these tools. In fact, most of the things you'll want to do will be small variations of the programs you'll see here. Until you get the hang of writing your own programs, you should copy, paste, and use the routines in the following chapters. Just as it's easier to learn a foreign language when you need it to get by in a foreign country, you'll find programming concepts easier to learn when you need them to realize your project.

Flow Control: How a Computer "Reads" a Program

The microcontroller "reads" your program in the order that you write it, starting from the top and working its way down, executing instructions line by line until there are no more instructions to execute. There are certain words that it knows innately (sometimes called *keywords* or *reserved* words), and other words that you define for it. Keywords, like Goto or Gosub, tell the computer to skip to a particular place in the program. When it gets there, it keeps reading down the program until it gets an instruction to return to its previous place in the program or to skip to somewhere else in the program. When the computer gets to the end of a program, it simply stops.[1]

Programs are organized much like everyday writing. They're broken into sensible sections so you can understand them one piece at a time. While everyday writing is broken into sentences and paragraphs, programs are broken into statements and blocks. We'll give names to certain blocks of code so that we can come back to them frequently. These blocks are called *routines*.

NOTE

We will give examples in four different forms of the BASIC language. At first glance this makes the code samples seem more complicated than they are. It will all look simpler after you get used to skipping directly to the example in your language. Because the differences in these languages are generally syntactical and superficial, our explanations in the main text will apply to all four. This general approach will help you in the future, when newer, faster, cheaper competitors to these processors are released. Similarly, when you look on the Web for examples you will be able to translate examples from other brands of microcontrollers to work for yours.

BX-Basic is different enough from the others that we will occasionally have to point out exceptions, which you can ignore if you're not using the BX-24.

The following table shows you the languages we're using and how they're related to each other and to other forms of BASIC.

Microcontroller BASICs

MICROCONTROLLER	LANGUAGE	RELATIVES
Basic Stamp 2	PBASIC	PBASIC (the original)
Basic Atom	MBasic	PBASIC
PIC	PicBasic Pro	PBASIC
Bx24	BX-Basic	Visual Basic

Loops

Many of your programs will only have one block of code, called the *main routine*. Usually you don't want a program to stop when it reaches the end of the main routine. You want it to keep going over and over until you turn it off. To keep the program going, you put in a loop. You tell it, "When you have reached the end of your routine, go back to the beginning and do it all again." The main loop is the heartbeat of your program. It is also called the *event loop*.

---

[1] This easy-to-follow code, usually contained within a single file, is one reason why microcontrollers are an excellent platform for learning programming. Object-oriented languages and languages with many separate event handlers tend to decentralize your code into many different places. This is great for complicated projects, but it makes program flow a little hard to follow for first-time programmers.

Here are examples of a main loop in all of our versions of Basic:

PBASIC
MBasic
PicBasic Pro

```
Main:
        Statement1
        Statement2
Goto main
```

BX-Basic

```
Sub main()
    Do
            Statement1
            Statement2
    Loop
End sub
```

In PBASIC, MBasic, and PicBasic Pro, you create a routine just by labeling it. Any word that the programming environment doesn't already know can be used as a label. Just type it in your program, put a colon after it, and you've labeled a routine. A label does not actually do anything except give the routine a name. Goto is a command (one of the keywords) that sends the flow of the program to a label. In the example above, Statement1 and Statement2 would happen over and over and over again for as long as your microcontroller is running. Your program could easily outlive you as long as the microcontroller has power.

In BX-Basic, you do things a little differently. Every routine starts with the keyword Sub followed by its name and a pair of parentheses (we'll get to those later), and ends with the statement End sub. Loops start with the keyword Do and end with the keyword Loop.

If Statements

If statements, also called *conditional statements*, are used to make decisions based on various conditions that may occur during the running of a program. If a particular condition is true, then the computer will execute the statements that follow the conditional statement. If not, then it will skip those statements.

The most common form of the if statement looks like this:

PBASIC
MBasic
PicBasic Pro

```
If In6 = 1 then
        Statement1
Endif
Statement2
```

If Statements

```
BX-Basic    If getPin(6) = 1 then
                   Statement1
            End if
            Statement2
```

In the example above, you are testing an input pin of the microcontroller (we will talk more about how to do that later). If the sensor attached to that pin is activated, then Statement1 will get executed. If not, then the computer will skip Statement1 and go on to execute Statement2 and anything else that follows it.

An if statement starts with the keyword if, followed by a condition that it has to evaluate (In6 = 1, in the example above), followed by the keyword then. Any statements that you want to happen if the condition is true come after that, followed by the statement End if. Note that in PBASIC, MBasic, and PicBasic Pro, end if gets squashed together into one keyword, endif. This isn't the case in BX-Basic.

Before version 2.5, PBASIC had a less convenient form for its if statement. There was no endif. You had to put the commands you wanted to happen into a routine and point to the routine from the if statement. The new form allows you to put the commands you want to happen right under the if statement. The new way is much better. You might see the old style used in older examples and application notes on the Web. All of our examples are written in PBASIC 2.5, so you should always insert the following line at the beginning of your programs:

```
'{$PBASIC 2.5]
```

Variables

Variability of computer memory is at the heart of what makes computational media different from traditional media. *Variables* are places in computer memory for storing or changing information. We use variables to keep records for our program, such as whether the user has pushed a button or not, how many times they've pushed the button, how many times the computer has flashed a light, how much time has passed since the last button push, and so forth.

Think of computer memory as a bunch of coffee cups that you can put labels onto the outside and store things on the inside. Variables allow you to put your own names on the outside of the coffee cup and put things you want to remember inside of it. Your if statements and loops can then find the coffee cups by name and take different actions, depending on what they find inside. The real power comes not from the fact that you can place things in the cup, but that you can replace them or "vary" them easily. That's why they are called variables and not memorables.

Before you use a variable in BASIC, you need to give it a name. This is generally done at the very beginning of your program or at the beginning of a routine. This is called *declaring the variable*.

Use a name that describes what you're using the variable to remember because it will make your code much more readable. We often add "Var" to the ends of our variable names as well so they're easy to distinguish from reserved words when reading the code. You can use any name you want for your variable as long as it does not start with a number, has no spaces, and isn't a keyword. When you try to run your program, the compiler will let you know if your variable name isn't allowed.

To store a value in a variable, you put the name of the variable on the left side of an equation and the value you want to remember on the right, like so:

```
DateVar = 12
ticketValueVar = 250
FareVar = 125
```

In higher-level languages, like Lingo in Macromedia Director MX or ActionScript in Macromedia Flash MX, you can put all kinds of information into your variables: strings of text, integers, fractional numbers, and more. The type of data you will store in that variable will automatically be interpreted from the context in which you use the variable, and the variable will be given more space in memory dynamically on an as-needed basis. In contrast, microcontroller operating systems are a little more bare bones and memory space is a little tighter. As a result, when you declare your variables, you also have to specify how to interpret the data you plan to store and how much storage space you need. Variables are declared in your program like this:

PBASIC	
MBasic	`SensorVar var byte`
	`TicketVar var byte`
PicBasic Pro	`BiggerVar var word`

BX-Basic	`Dim sensorVar as byte`
	`Dim ticketVar as byte`
	`Dim biggerVar as integer`

The size of your variable and the way it's interpreted is called the *data type* of the variable, and it's largely determined by how big a number you need to store. For example, if you plan to put one of only two values (0 or 1) into your variable, it will fit in the smallest unit of memory space, called a *bit*. A number between 0 and 255 will require 8 bits of memory, which is called a *byte*. If you imagine each of the 8 bits in a byte as a switch, like the ones in Figure 5.1, then you can imagine that the numbers you can store in the byte depend on which way the switches are set.

Figure 5.1
A physical byte of memory.

Variables

In one direction each switch holds a 0, and in the other it holds a 1. With 8 switches, you have 2^8, or 256 possible combinations of switch settings. That's how you can fit numbers between 0 and 255 in a byte.

You'll need even more space if the ranges of values you are storing need to be interpreted as fractions or with negative numbers. Beginners' programs rarely run short on memory space[2], so when in doubt, use big data types. It's important that you understand types of variables so that you're able to use them with the microcontroller's built-in functions, which we will discuss below. Often, you'll be supplying variables as parameters for these built-in functions, or having them return information by placing it in variables. You have to match the variable types that you use to those that the built-in functions expect. For example, the rctime function on the Basic Stamp expects a word-sized variable, and the Pulseout() function on the BX expects to be supplied with a type called a *single*.[3] The type of variable expected by a function is usually the first item specified in the documentation for a given function. Sometimes you'll need to use the same variable with two functions that have conflicting types, in which case you'll have to convert the variable to another type using a type-conversion function.

Various forms of BASIC use different data types and different names for the same types. Listed below are the types for each language, how much space they take in memory, and what the range of possible values are.

PBasic

TYPE	NUMBER OF BITS	RANGE OF VALUES
Bit	1	1 or 0
Nib	4	0 to 15
Byte	8	0 to 255
Word	16	0 to 65535

MBasic

TYPE	NUMBER OF BITS	RANGE OF VALUES
Bit	1	1 or 0
Nib	4	0 to 15
Byte	8	0 to 255
SByte	8	–127 to +128
Word	16	0 to 65535
SWord	16	–32,767 to +32,768

---

[2] For example, BX-24 has room for 400 byte-sized variables, so it will be a while before you run out.
[3] A single is a single-precision floating point number, meaning that it's got a fractional part, and the fractional part can be up to six places after the decimal point. The decimal point "floats" in the number.

PicBasic Pro

Type	Number of Bits	Range of Values
Bit	1	1 or 0
Byte	8	0 to 255
Word	16	0 to 65535

BX-Basic

Type	Number of Bits	Range of Values
Boolean	8	True or false
Byte	8	0 to 255
Integer	16	−32,768 to 32,767
Long	32	−2,147,483,648 to 2,147,483,647
Single	32	−3.402823E+38 to 3.402823E+38
String	Varies	0 to 64 bytes

Not all of the microcontrollers we're showing allow you to use negative numbers or fractional numbers. You might think about whether you need this when choosing one. Those that can store negative numbers use one of the bits to store the sign of the number. In MBasic, for example, they refer to the data types that can store negative numbers as sWord and sByte, short for "signed word" and "signed byte." BX-Basic is the only environment we're discussing that can store fractional numbers in its single type.

Here's an example routine using variables:

PBASIC
MBasic
PicBasic Pro

```
ticketsSubmitted var byte
ticketSensor var byte

main;
    If (ticketSensor = 1) then
    ticketsSubmitted = ticketsSubmitted + 1
    Endif
    If (ticketsSubmitted = 3) then
        Gosub OpenGate
        TicketsSubmitted = 0
    Endif
Goto main
```

BX-Basic

```
Dim ticketsSubmitted as byte
Dim ticketSensor as byte

Sub main()
```

Variables

```
          Do
              If (ticketSensor = 1) then
                  ticketsSubmitted = ticketsSubmitted + 1
              End If
              If (ticketsSubmitted = 3) then
                  Call OpenGate()
                  TicketsSubmitted = 0
              End if
          Loop
      End sub
```

In this example, you need three tickets before you can pass through the gate. You'll use a variable called ticketSensor to keep track of the sensor that counts tickets, and a variable called ticketsSubmitted to keep track of how many tickets have been submitted. Notice you must add 1 to what was already in ticketsSubmitted (ticketsSubmitted = ticketsSubmitted + 1), and you have to reset ticketsSumitted to 0 after you open the gate. You could make the cost of the train vary by making the number of tickets required, fixed in the example at 3, into another variable.

Built-In Routines: Subroutines and Functions

In any programming language, there are a number of built-in routines for accomplishing the most common tasks. The number and variety of these built-in routines is a major selling point for a microcontroller's language. For example, all microcontrollers will allow you to sense the state of an input pin or set the state of an output pin. In BX-Basic, there are routines for this: putPin() and getPin(). In pBasic, MBasic, and PicBasic Pro, there are equivalent routines. Most routines will need some additional parameters that follow the name of the routine, separated by commas. For example, if you wanted to output voltage on pin 6, you would call putPin(), giving the pin number and the desired state as parameters.

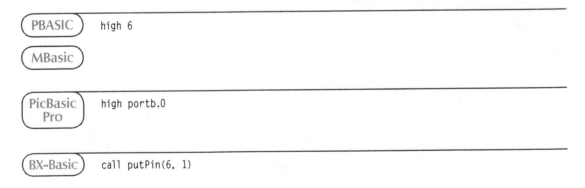

```
( PBASIC )    high 6

( MBasic )


( PicBasic   high portb.0
   Pro )


( BX-Basic )  call putPin(6, 1)
```

The above would set the desired pin to 5 volts. The following code would set it to 0 volts.

PBASIC

```
low 6
```

MBasic

PicBasic Pro

```
low portb.0
```

BX-Basic

```
call putPin(6, 0)
```

Notice on the BX-Basic you use the word call before the name of any routine.

CONSTANTS

In addition to variables, every programming language also includes constants, which are simply variables that don't vary once the program starts running. Use them to label numbers that get used repeatedly within your program. You can make changes to all the places where the constant is used by making a change in just one place: where you defined the constant. This makes your code more reusable across different applications. For example, in Chapter 6, "The Big Four Schematics, Programs, and Transducers," you'll see an example program that runs a servo motor. Servo motors have a minimum and maximum pulsewidth that doesn't change, although each servo brand's minimum and maximum might be somewhat different. When you buy a different brand of servo, you make these values constants, so you only have to change them in one place, rather than change every occurrence in the program.

Because constants don't change, you set their values when you declare them, all in one step at the beginning of the program. In PBASIC, MBasic, and PicBasic Pro, constants are declared at the beginning of your program, like so:

```
MinPulse con 100
```

Then you can refer to them in the program just as you do variables, like so:

```
PulseWidth = minPulse + angleVar
```

In BX-Basic, you also have to declare the type of the constant, like so:

```
Const minPulse as single = 0.001
```

You don't have to use constants in your programs, but they're handy to know about, and you will encounter them in other people's programs.

Routines or functions that just take action without giving back any information are sometimes called *commands*. If the routine returns a value, it's called a *function*.

If you wanted to get the state of pin 5 and store it in a byte variable named pinStateVar, you would write:

| PBASIC
MBasic | `input 5`
`pinStateVar = in5` |

| PicBasic
Pro | `input portb.1`
`pinStateVar = portb.1` |

| BX-Basic | `pinStateVar = getPin(5)` |

NOTE

In pBasic, MBasic, and PicBasic Pro, you have to declare the desired pin as an input first before you can get its state. That's what the `input` command does above.

The most common way of getting a value back from a function is by setting a variable equal to the function, as you saw in the example above (pinStateVar = getPin(5)). You don't always need to use a function to get information back from the microcontroller. For example, in the PBASIC and MBasic examples above, in5 is not really a function but a built-in variable that's always equal to the input state of pin 5.

Some functions use yet another way to get values into your variables. You provide the variable that you want to receive the value as an input to the function. For instance, in the examples below, the rctime command will store its results in a variable called sensorVar.

| PBASIC
MBasic | `sensorVar var word`
`rctime 5, 1, sensorVar` |

| PicBasic
Pro | `sensorVar var word`
`rctime portb.1, 1, sensorVar` |

| BX-Basic | `dim sensorVar as integer`
`sensorVar = Rctime(5,1)` |

Every microcontroller has a large number of commands, and the section of your microcontroller's manual that contains the command library will be the section you use most frequently. Look in the manual for the command that you have already used in Chapter 4, to make your LED blink. Browse through some of the others to get a sense of what your microcontroller is capable of. After you figure out what the routine does, pay special attention to the parameters needed and the data types of those parameters. If it's a function (that is, if it returns a value), the data type of the value it returns will be listed as well. Declare your variable to match the data types of the parameters that the routine is expecting.

Homemade Routines

Sometimes you'll find a particular combination of code that you use over and over. Instead of writing out the same combination of lines in several places in your program, you can write it once in a routine and call that routine from those several places. The routine is then referred to as a *subroutine*. This makes your code much better organized and easier to modify. It's possible that your microcontroller program will only be a few lines long and will not require much organization or maintenance, and thus no subroutines. Nevertheless, it's common to have at least one or two subroutines, even in the simplest program.

Like variables, you can name your routines anything that doesn't start with a number and doesn't contain spaces. However, as with variables, it's wise to give your subroutines names that describe what they do. You've already written one routine, called main, or sub main().

In pBasic, MBasic, and PicBasic Pro, a routine is delimited by a label name and a colon. To call a subroutine, you use the keyword gosub followed by the label of the subroutine. Subroutines end with the keyword return. When the processor reaches the return keyword, it returns to the line after the gosub command that called the subroutine.

For example, suppose you are developing a very polite program. It should have a subroutine to thank people:

PBASIC

MBasic

PicBasic Pro

```
Main:
        If (theySneezeOnYou) then
            gosub myThankYouRoutine
        EndIf
        If (theyKickYou) then
            gosub myThankYouRoutine
        Endif
        If (burnDownYourHouse) then
            gosub myThankYouRoutine
        endif
Goto main

MyThankYouRoutine:
        High 0 'turn on the thank you light
        Pause 1000
        Low 0 'turn off the thank you light
        Pause 1000
Return
```

As we mentioned before, in BX-Basic, a routine is delimited by the word sub and the name of your routine at the beginning and the words end sub at the end. When you want the code inside a routine to happen, you "call" the routine, just as with built-in routines.

(BX–Basic)

```
Sub main()
        Do
                If (theySneezeOnYou) then
                        Call myThankYouRoutine ()
                End If
                If (theyKickYou) then
                        Call myThankYouRoutine ()
                End if
                If (burnDownYourHouse) then
                        Call myThankYouRoutine ()
                end if
        Loop
End sub

Sub myThankYouRoutine ()
        Call PutPin(5,1) 'turn on the thank you light
        Call Delay (1.0)
        Call PutPin(5,0) 'turn off the thank you light
        Call Delay (1.0)
End sub
```

No matter where in the main routine you call MyThankYouRoutine from, it always executes the same code and then returns to the line following the one that called it. The big win here is that if you ever want to change the action for a thank you, you only have to change it in one well-labeled place.

Advanced Loops: While-Wend and For-Next

So far, you've seen only one type of loop, one that runs forever. This kind of loop is called an *infinite loop*, or an *event loop*. Anything that the microcontroller must listen for constantly (for example, input from a button push) should be in the main loop. Likewise, anything that the microcontroller must constantly control (for example, the state of a blinking LED) must also be in that loop.

(PBASIC)

(MBasic)

(PicBasic Pro)

```
main:
        ' stuff to do over and over
Goto main
```

```
BX-Basic    Sub main()
                Do
                    ' Stuff to do over and over
                    Loop
            End sub
```

In a simple program, there is a good chance this will be the only loop you need. However, there are some shorter-term loops, like the *for-next*, *while-wend*, and *do-while* loops that can really make coding easier.

While-Wend or Do-While

Sometimes you'll want the duration of the loop determined by some condition. For instance, you may want something to happen while a button is held down. You can then use a while-wend or do-while loop to repeat a series of actions while the pin connected to that switch is getting 5 volts (logic true), returning a true value. Here's an example:

```
MBasic      Input 5

            While in5 = 0
                High 1
                Pause 250
                Low 1
                Pause 250
            wend
```

```
PicBasic    Input portb.5
Pro
            While portb.5= 0
                High portb.0
                Pause 250
                Low portb.0
                Pause 250
            wend
```

```
BX-Basic    Do while getPin(5) = 0
                Call PutPin(6,1)
                Call delay(0.25)
                Call putPin(6,0)
                Call delay(0.25)
            Loop
```

If the while statement is not true, the program jumps to the next line after the loop. If there's nothing after the loop, the program stops.

Advanced Loops

NOTE
PBASIC doesn't have the while-wend structure. The alternative is to use a pair of if-then statements and a label, like this:

PBASIC
```
Input 5
WendLabel:
if in5 = 0 then
  High 1
  Pause 250
  Low 1
  Pause 250
Endif
If in5 = 0 then wendLabel
```

For-Next

The for-next loop is used when you want to do something a specific number of times and then move on. For example, you have sixteen possible output pins on the Stamp-like controllers. Say you had an LED attached to each one of them, as in the example in Chapter 4. If you wanted to light each LED in sequence, with a pause between each one, you could write a line of code for each one, like this:

PBASIC
MBasic
```
High 0
Pause 1000
High 1
Pause 1000
High 2
Pause 1000
```

Etc.

BX-Basic
```
Call putPin(5, 1)
Call delay(1.0)
Call putPin(6, 1)
Call delay(1.0)
Call putPin(7, 1)
Call delay(1.0)
```

This is okay for three lights, but if you have 16, your code gets ugly. Instead, you could count from the lowest pin to the highest pin and use a variable to hold the number of the current pin. A for-next loop is a special loop for doing this kind of counting. The syntax of a for-next loop is the same in all forms of Basic we're discussing. It looks like this:

```
' declare yourVariable and its data type at the beginning of the program

For yourVariable = intialNumber to limitNumber
     Statement 1
     Statement 2
Next
```

PBASIC

MBasic

```
counterVar var byte
For counterVar = 0 to 15
     High counterVar
     Pause 1000
Next
```

PicBasic Pro

```
' PicBasic Pro doesn't let you address the pin names as variables
' in a for-next loop, so you need to use a little trickery.
' in this example, you're using the DECODE function (DCD)
' to turn on the 8 pins of PORTB (RB0 through RB7).
' For the details of DCD, see the PicBasic Pro manual.
counterVar var byte
' make all the pins of PORTB outputs:
TRISB = %000000000
For counterVar = 0 to 7
     PORTB = DCD counterVar
     Pause 1000
Next
```

BX-Basic

```
Dim counterVar as byte
For counterVar = 0 to 15
     ' add 5 to the counter, because pin numbers start with 5:
     Call putPin(counterVar + 5, 1)
     Call delay(1.0)
Next
```

Advanced Loops

When the processor encounters the For line, it sets the variable that you supply (in this case counterVar) equal to its initial number (in this case 0) and then starts executing the statements in the body of the loop. When it encounters the Next keyword, it adds 1 to the variable and goes back up to the For line. It's as if there's an invisible line saying "counterVar = counterVar + 1" at the bottom of the loop. If counterVar is less than or equal to limitNumber (in this case 15), it executes the statements again. If counterVar is greater than limitNumber, it skips to the line after the Next line and continues the program from there. CounterVar is a variable, so it must be declared before you use it in a for-next loop.

NOTE

In BX-Basic, you must declare any variables that you use for loop counters inside the subroutine that contains the loop.

This takes much less typing for the same effect! We use for-next loops frequently in our code because they're a convenient way to check or change the state of several things that follow each other in a sequence.

Pseudocode

Following the code here is fairly easy, but facing a blank screen before writing your own can be daunting. It usually helps to use *pseudocode* to ease the transition from your idea to your code. First, break down what you want the computer to do into steps described in plain language. This is called an *algorithm*. It helps to imagine your numbers as physical objects that you are moving around like marbles between the coffee cups that are your variables[4]. Next, write this plain language description in a more formal style called pseudocode. Pseudocode restates the steps you described in plain language, using the structure of a program, but not the actual words of the particular programming language. Once you get used to the flow of programming, your plain language description is almost identical to your pseudocode.

Sometimes the plain language will tip you off to the best programming tool. Whenever you hear yourself saying the words "each," "every," "any," or "always," you'll probably need a loop. If statements are easily identified because the same word, "if," or sometimes "when," shows up in plain language descriptions. The words "store," "record," "remember," or "keep track of" might tip you off that you need a variable. The truth is that variables can be a little more difficult to identify. Work backwards. After you have your loops and if statements, look inside the loops for quantities that will vary, taking these as opportunities to use variables. It doesn't hurt to cheat and try to work in the words "if" "for each," and "vary" in your plain language description. Following is an example.

Plain language:

Every time a passenger goes through the turnstile of a subway train, they have to slide their fare card through the slot. If they have enough money on their card, the amount on their card is decreased and the turnstile turns.

Pseudocode:

```
Check for passenger:
    Read card in slot
    If the amount on card is greater than the fare, then

    Subtract the fare from what's on the card
```

---

4. Physical computing is a nice pedagogical tool for teaching general programming concepts because it naturally causes people to imagine the program's tasks in physical terms.

```
                    Blink the "GO" light three times
                    Open the turnstile so they can go thorough
              Go back to check for passenger again
```

You can see from this example that you have a clear loop (continually check for passengers), a sensor-reading function (read card in slot) and an if statement (if the amount on the card is enough to pay for the fare). You could use a variable to keep track of the fare so you can change it, perhaps making it higher during rush hour. You would use another variable to keep track of the amount the customer has on the card. You could use a for-next loop to make the "GO" light blink. The command to open the turnstile might take several steps, which you could put into separate routine so that you could call it elsewhere in the program (for example, if a station manager needed to manually open the gate).

After you have the general plan of attack in pseudocode, it's time to start writing actual code for your particular microcontroller. In some cases, you may find that your pseudocode is replaced with specific commands for the microcontroller, line for line. In other cases, you will need to translate a particular intention in your pseudocode into a series of statements in actual code.

In terms of the timing of your program, it helps to remember that *when* something happens is determined by *where* it is placed in the code. For instance, things that you want to happen once *at the start* of the program should be placed before the main loop. Things that you want to happen *repeatedly* should be placed within the main loop or in a subroutine called from the main loop. Things that you want to *sometimes* happen should be placed inside if statements within your main loop.

Don't try to be clever or elegant at the beginning. You may have a long page of commands or if statements that could be reduced to a single statement with a variable or a repeat loop. Do it the long way first to understand what you're doing, then look for an opportunity to simplify it with a well-placed variable or repeat loop. Because programs on the microcontroller are often short and simple by nature, you may not need to optimize them.

Comments

Theoretically, BASIC code is supposed to be close enough to everyday language to be read by anyone. In practice, it isn't. Often, you will want to place some plain language comments in your code to note what a particular block of code is doing, or to note for yourself where you still need to add a routine. You can do this by starting your comments with a single quote. BASIC considers anything after a single quote on a given line to be a comment and ignores it.

Commenting is a useful way to think out loud and to take notes as you program. For example:

```
' This line is a comment. The next line starts the main loop:
Do
      If ticketValueVar > 0 then ' checks the user's ticket value
          Call takeFare()
      End if
Loop
```

Comments are also useful for isolating parts of your program for debugging. Often, you will disable all but one part of your code to be sure you have that part just right before reintegrating it with the rest. Commenting out lines is a way to store code that may not be necessary, but might be useful in the future.

Comment early and often. This is particularly important if other people will be reading your code, but even if you are working alone, you'll be surprised how quickly you forget what you're doing in some parts of your BASIC code.

Debugging

Pseudocode helps you form a plan for your program, but it seldom survives intact for very long when you actually try to run it. Your final programs seldom follow the exact logic of your pseudocode. You will spend much of your time finding out why a plan that makes perfect sense to you does not make sense to the microcontroller. You start by forming a hypothesis about where the misunderstanding might be. Avoid hypotheses that are out of your control, such as looking for bugs in the microcontroller compiler.

The most common problem is that it's sometimes difficult to adopt the literal thinking style of a computer. To help you eavesdrop on your microcontroller's thinking, most programming languages have a debug command. This command causes the processor to send a message to be printed out in a window of the programming environment, intended purely for the programmer's eyes.

The most basic thing you'll use the debug command for is to see if a particular line of code is being executed. Once your program has a few if statements, for-next loops, and subroutines, you may lose track of how the program flows. Place a debug statement right before or after a line that does not seem to be working. If the line is being executed, the debug statement will print a message to the screen for you. If it's not getting to the line of code in question, you'll get no message.

The debug command can also be used to find out the value of a given variable at a given time. For example, say your microcontroller is storing sensor readings into a variable, and you want to see the range of values that comes from the sensor. You could place a debug statement after the sensor is read, to see the value of the sensor as you change the physical conditions around the sensor. Or maybe you have a for-next loop that is repeating five times when you want it to repeat 10 times. You can have the microcontroller report back the value of the loop counter variable so that you can see when it stops corresponding to your expectations. All the messages sent back to the computer are formatted as text strings, so you may have to convert some variables from numeric types into text strings to see their values.

These various forms of BASIC all have a debug command with a slightly different format to each:

(PBASIC)
```
Debug "hello world", 10, 13
Debug "start of routine", 10, 13
' don't forget to declare your variables first!
Debug "fareVar = ", DEC fareVar, 10, 13
```

NOTE

Sometimes you may find that your program on the BS-2 doesn't run when you keep your programming cable connected. This is because it's in debug mode. Either add a debug statement and recompile or remove the programming cable and your program will work.

MBasic

```
Debug ["hello world", 10, 13]
Debug ["start of routine", 10, 13]
' don't forget to declare your variables first!
Debug ["fareVar = ", DEC fareVar, 10, 13]
```

NOTE

To see debug statements in MBasic, you have to use debug mode. To do this, click the Debug button on the toolbar when you've written your code. This will open debug mode. Then choose Run from the debugger menu and your code will run, showing you the debug messages in the debug pane at the bottom of the screen. When you're done debugging, program your chip by clicking the Program button on the toolbar, then disconnect your programming cable from the breadboard and the program will run.

PicBasic Pro

```
' in PicBasic Pro, you need these lines at the top of your program
' to set the pin that you're debugging on and the baud rate at which
' to send debug messages:
INCLUDE "modedefs.bas"
DEFINE DEBUG_REG PORTC
DEFINE DEBUG_BIT 6
DEFINE DEBUG_BAUD 9600
DEFINE DEBUG_MODE 1

' these are the actual debug statements:
Debug "hello world", 10, 13
Debug "beginning of main routine", 10, 13
' don't forget to declare your variables first!
Debug "fareVar = ", DEC fareVar, 10, 13
```

BX-Basic

```
Debug.print "Hello world"
Debug.print "Start of routine"
' don't forget to declare your variables first!
Debug.print "fareVar = " ; cstr(fareVar)
```

Debugging

To print two items on the same line in pBasic, MBasic, and PicBasic Pro, separate them with a comma. The DEC in front of fareVar tells the computer to print out fareVar as a decimal number for you to read. The numbers 10 and 13 are special codes that tell the computer to move the cursor down a line. They act like the line feed and carriage return on an old typewriter.

In BX-Basic, separate items on the same line with a semicolon. The line feed and carriage return codes aren't needed in BX-Basic. The cstr() function is similar to the DEC function in the other BASIC variants; it converts the variable fareVar into a decimal number for you to read.

Debug statements are useful when you're not sure where the program flow is going. Make sure to comment them out once your program is running properly because they slow the microcontroller down.

Good Debugging Habits

Besides liberal use of debug statements (which you should remove once your code works), there are a few general guidelines that make debugging go faster:

▶ *Keep your programs small.* It's often easier to prove a device works by writing a one- or two-line program than it is to add those one or two lines to an existing program. Even when you build complex programs, keep these short programs around for retesting when things go wrong. It's easy to temporarily replace a big program in a microcontroller with a small one that proves one thing, and it saves you loads of time.

▶ *Save many versions.* Whenever you make changes, save the program as a new version. It's easier to find your changes if you have a record of your changes. Add a comment at the top of each version of a program explaining the changes in that version.

▶ *Know every line.* If your program gets too complex and you're not sure how it works, go through it line by line and make comments on what you think happens. This will force you to make sense of every line of your program, and often leads to an epiphany in which you realize that one particular line or routine is the problem.

▶ *Look at all of your variables.* Try debugging all of your variable values, not just the one that you think is giving you problems. Sometimes the problem is not where you think it is, and seeing all of your variables can sometimes reveal where the problem really is.

DEBUGGING CONNECTIONS FOR THE PIC

In PicBasic Pro, you must define the I/O port, pin number, and the baud rate that you plan to send debug messages on at the top of your program. The DEFINE statements in the previous code example set these properties. You also need to connect a serial connector to the debug pins, as shown in Figure 5.2.

Figure 5.2
Serial out connection from a PIC.

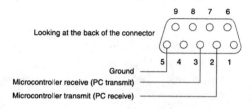

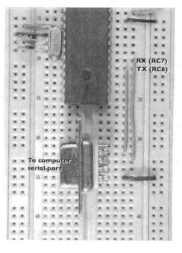

Once you've done this, connect the serial connector to one of the COM ports on your PC. You'll need a program to read your debug statements. We usually use HyperTerminal, which comes with the Windows operating systems and reads the serial port. To open HyperTerminal, choose Start, Accessories, Communications, HyperTerminal. Or you can open HyperTerminal by choosing Run from the Start menu, typing hypertrm, and pressing Enter.

HyperTerminal will first ask you to open a file, or if you've never run it, to set up your connections settings. Cancel out of this dialog box, click on the File menu, and choose File, Properties. Choose the com port you want to use from the Connect Using drop-down menu in the Properties dialog box, then click Configure. Configure the connection for 9600 bits per second, 8 data bits, no parity, 1 stop bit, and no flow control. This will match all of our debug examples and serial communication examples. When you've finished configuring, save your settings as a file so you can just open that file the next time you open HyperTerminal. To open the serial port, click the Call button (phone on hook), and to close the serial port, click the Disconnect button (phone off hook).

Once you've configured HyperTerminal, opened the serial port, and connected your PIC's serial port to the appropriate serial port on your PC, any debug statements in your PIC program will print out to the HyperTerminal window.

Good Debugging Habits

The Bad News

Like many things, no one can teach you how to program well. You just have to practice it. But we can help you put yourself in a position to understand it. In the chapters that follow, we'll give many examples of full programs, as well as subroutines that can be added to existing programs with little effort. These, and other programs you find online, are your best first resource. Try to reverse-engineer the logic of these programs before you set out on your own. As you go over them, pay attention to the flow of each program first, by following the if statements and loops. Try to get the general ideas behind the program before you get down to the syntax of the individual commands. Start with pseudocode and grow your project slowly, testing out the parts separately. The truth is that the time you spend programming is usually one-tenth designing and nine-tenths debugging. To cope with this, it's important to know the difference between persistence and endurance. Take breaks, work on other problems, and talk to other people about your work. Be prepared to start again from a high-level description when you lose track of what your code is doing. When you hit problems, always ask yourself how important the solution is to your overall application. Know when to abandon those problems that you don't need to solve. It is worth the effort because knowledge of programming will increase your understanding and mastery of all of the programmed and programmable devices in your everyday life.

6

The "Big Four" Schematics, Programs, and Transducers

Now that you've got the basics of programming in hand, it's time to start talking about where the computing meets the physical. As we mentioned in the Introduction, one of the key aspects of physical computing is *transduction*, or the conversion of one form of energy into another. Recognizing which form of energy you can sense as input and which form of energy you need to generate as output will determine which transducers you will use. Choosing your transducers is often the biggest challenge in designing and implementing a physical computing project. This chapter presents transducers organized by the categories discussed in the Introduction: input (sensing actions) and output (controlling actions). Both of these categories are further broken down into analog or digital. Digital control or sensing methods result in only two possible outcomes: on or off, in or out, up or down, left or right, and so forth. Analog methods provide for a range of possible outcomes: dark, dim, brighter, and blinding; far away, closer, much closer, and "Get outta my face!"

In this chapter, we'll introduce some transducers, circuits, and programming for what we call the "Big Four:" digital input, digital output, analog input, and analog output. Almost everything you make in physical computing will fall fairly neatly into one of these categories and will use some variation of the transducers, circuits, and programs we present here.

Digital Input

Digital inputs are the simplest transducers. There are only two possible states for a digital input: on or off. At its most basic, a digital input is just two conductors that can be touched together to complete a circuit or moved apart to break the circuit. The switch is the most common example.

Transducers: Switches

Suppose you want to know when a cat is on a mat. You could put a small switch under the mat so that the weight of the cat would press the switch, completing the circuit containing the switch. It may seem a bit grand to call something so simple a transducer, but it is converting the mechanical energy exerted by the cat's body weight into electrical energy in the circuit.

There are a few terms that are useful when choosing switches.

Normally open means that the switch's contacts are not touching when the switch isn't pressed, so the circuit is not complete. These switches make the most intuitive sense. In *normally closed* switches, the contacts are touching when the switch is not pressed, so that the circuit is complete.

Momentary switches have a spring in them so that they snap back to their normal position after you stop applying pressure. The switch that controls your refrigerator light is usually a momentary switch. *Toggle* switches don't have a spring, and will stay in whatever position they're left in. Most wall light switches are toggle switches.

A switch has a certain number of *poles*. Each pole can connect (or disconnect) two wires. In other words, each pole can control a separate circuit. For example, for stereo speakers you might need a double-pole switch to switch both speaker circuits at once. A switch's *throw* describes how many possible closed positions it has. For example, a double-throw switch will actually have three positions: a center position (in which the switch is open), a left position, and a right position. You'll see these two characteristics, pole and throw, listed together frequently and abbreviated as SPST (single-pole, single-throw, the most common and most basic switch), DPDT (double-pole, double-throw), SPDT (single-pole, double-throw), and so forth. For now we'll keep it simple and use single-pole, single-throw switches (SPST). Figure 6.1 shows a DPDT knife switch.

Figure 6.1
A double-pole,
double-throw switch.

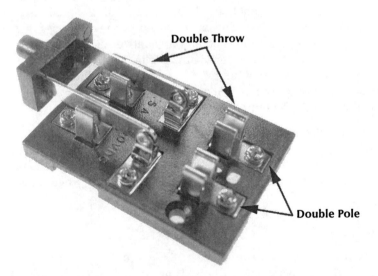

Double Throw

Double Pole

Switches are normally rated by the maximum voltage and amperage that they can carry. For example, most household light switches will be rated to carry 250 volts AC, and 15 to 20 amps of current. You can always put less current or amperage through a switch than it's rated for. This means that if you wanted to use the aforementioned household switch as an input to your microcontroller, you could, even though it would only be carrying 5 volts DC and a few milliamps.

If your switch is meant to be seen and intentionally pressed by the user, you can go to any hardware store and buy a wall switch or doorbell push button. Radio Shack and the various online vendors listed in Appendix B also have a wide variety of regular switches. You can get some really fun switches from arcade game vendors, like Happ Controls (http//:www.happcontrols.com).

In many cases you will want the user to throw a switch without knowing it; for example, the cat on the mat shouldn't have to intentionally press the switch. His normal behavior, that is, sitting on the mat, should activate the switch. In these cases, you will need to build the switch in such a way that the user triggers it in the course of their normal action. This requires building the switch into some object that they'll touch. A switch is really just two pieces of metal that touch or don't touch. If you can engineer a way for two contacts to touch or not touch, depending on the user's actions, you have made a switch. For example, if you take a thin slice of foam rubber with holes in it, sandwich it between two metal plates, and attach a lead from each plate to your circuit, then you have a switch. If someone steps on the metal plates, the foam rubber will compress and the plates will touch where there are holes in the foam rubber.

When building switches for microcontrollers to read, the voltage and amperage going through the switch's contacts will usually be so small that a person touching the bare metal wouldn't get hurt. However, you should get in the habit of building your switches in such a way that the person throwing the switch never comes in contact with any of the bare metal carrying electric current.

In addition to building your own switches, there are many types of interesting switches to know about. See Figure 6.2 for a few examples.

Figure 6.2
A variety of switches.

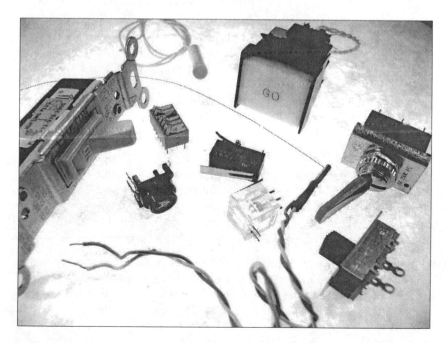

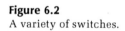
Digital Input

▶ *Foot switch.* These are usually rugged toggle or momentary switches designed to take a hard stomp from a person's foot. The H&R Catalog [(215) 788-5583] has many nice foot switches.

▶ *Tape switches or mat switches.* These are similar to the cat mat switch described above; they are simply two metal strips separated by thin foam encased in a mat. Most security stores sell these, as does http://www.tapeswitch.com.

▶ *Roller switch.* This is a momentary switch that requires very light pressure to close it. It has a ball or wheel at the end of the switch to reduce the friction of whatever is pushing the switch. Roller switches are useful for detecting closing doors, closing box lids, or objects sliding over a surface. You can get them from Radio Shack or any online electronics vendor.

▶ *Hair trigger switches or whisker switches.* These are momentary switches, similar to roller switches, only more sensitive. They're usually a spring with a fixed post in the center. When the spring moves, it contacts the post and closes the circuit. They can detect the slightest contact. Solarbotics (http://www.solarbotics.com) sells some very sensitive whisker switches.

▶ *Mercury switches or tilt switches.* These open or close depending on how they are oriented. They have a drop of mercury, which is both a liquid and a good conductor, in a glass tube with two contacts at the end. When the mercury rolls to one end of the tube, the mercury conducts current between the leads and the switch closes. When the tube is tilted the other way, the contacts are not connected. Mercury is very poisonous, so these switches are becoming less common. A similar switch, made with a ball bearing in the tube instead of mercury, is a safer replacement and very common.

▶ *Magnetic switches.* These switches close when a magnet passes over them. There are two very thin metal contacts inside that are pulled together by a magnetic field. They are common in cheap burglar alarm installations. They're handy when you need a moving object to throw a switch. The object only needs to have a magnet in it so it can be free of encumbering wires. You can pick these up at Radio Shack, where they are called *reed switches*.

Digital Input Circuit

To connect a digital input to a microcontroller, you need three connections: a connection to power on one side of the switch, a connection to your microcontroller on the other side of the switch, and a connection to ground. From the schematic in Figure 6.3, you can see that if the switch is closed, the microcontroller's input is connected to +5 volts, and if the switch is open, it's not. So why do you need the resistor?

When a microcontroller pin is in input mode, it's waiting for any voltage to affect it. When the switch is connected to 5 volts, it's clear what the voltage affecting it is, and the input on the microcontroller reads as high. When it's not connected to 5 volts, however, any stray voltage can affect it: static electricity, voltage generated by radio waves, and so forth. By connecting it to ground through a resistor, we have a way for those stray voltages to get to ground instead of affecting the input.

Figure 6.3
Digital input to a
microcontroller.

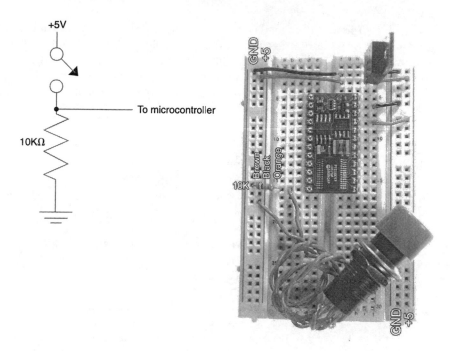

Great, you're saying, so why not just use a wire to connect to ground without the resistor? Remember: electrical current follows the path of least resistance to ground. If you just had a wire connecting the switch and the pin to ground, then, when you closed the switch, the path of least resistance would be through that wire, and you'd have a short circuit. The easiest path for the current is through the closed switch. When the switch is open, the resistor offers the only path and the current goes through it.

Programming

Here's the pseudocode describing what we're going to do in our program to make the microcontroller read the switch:

```
Put a pin into input mode
Loop
    Check if the pin is 0 or 5 volts
    If the pin has 5 volts
        Do something
    End if
End Loop
```

Since a microcontroller's I/O pins can be either inputs or outputs, you have to put a pin into input mode before you can use it as an input. On some microprocessors, the command to read the pin as an input automatically makes it an input. On others, you have to give a command to make it an input first. The input command is the easiest way to do this in PBASIC, MBasic, and PicBasic Pro. In BX-Basic, the command for reading the pin, getPin(), also sets the pin to input mode.

Digital Input

When the microcontroller reads a pin, it is sensing the voltage at that pin. It can sense the difference between no voltage (0 volts) or full voltage (5 volts), but nothing in between.[1] Software represents those voltages as true or false, 1 or 0. If it's reading 5 volts, this will be read as the value 1 (true). If it's reading 0 volts, it will be read as the value 0 (false). The following program reads a digital input and prints out the state of the input continuously:

PBASIC

MBasic

```
' declare a variable called X:
X var byte
' make pin 7 an input pin:
Input 7
Main:
      ' read the value of pin 7 into the variable X:
      X = in7
      ' for Pbasic, remove the square brackets below:
      Debug ["X = ", DEC X, 10, 13]
Goto main
```

PicBasic
Pro

```
' in PicBasic Pro, we need these lines at the top of our program
' to set the pin that we're debugging on, and the baud rate at which
' to send debug messages:
INCLUDE "modedefs.bas"
DEFINE DEBUG_REG PORTC
DEFINE DEBUG_BIT 6
DEFINE DEBUG_BAUD 9600
DEFINE DEBUG_MODE 1

' declare a variable called X:
X var byte
' make pin B0 an input pin:
Input portb.0
Main:
      ' read the value of pin B0 into the variable X:
      X = portB.0
      Debug "X = ", DEC X, 10, 13
Goto main
```

---

[1] In fact, a digital input on a microcontroller changes from 0 to 1 at a certain threshold between 0 and 5 volts. The threshold varies from processor to processor, but if you assume the threshold is about halfway between 0 and full voltage, you're usually safe.

NOTE

On the PIC 18F452 if you try to use the pins RA0 through RA5 or RE0 through RE2 as digital inputs, you may have some difficulty. These pins are set as analog inputs by default (see below for more on analog inputs). To set all these pins as digital inputs, add the following lines of code to the top of your program:

```
ADCON1 = %10000110
TRISA = %11111111
TRISE = %00000111
```

This sets the pins of PORTA and PORTE to digital input.

BX-Basic

```
' declare a variable called X:
dim x as byte

sub main()
    do
        ' getPin command sets the I/O mode and reads
        ' the value of the pin into the variable X:
        X = getPin(12)
        Debug.print "X = "; cstr(X)
    Loop
End sub
```

You put the input commands outside the main loop because once you tell a pin that it is being used as input, it stays that way, so you don't need to repeat the command. There are methods for setting the mode of multiple pins with one command, and for reading multiple pins with one command, that you will see later in Chapter 14, "Managing Multiple Inputs and Outputs."

When you ran the program above, you noticed that the microcontroller printed out X = 1 over and over whenever you pressed the switch, and X = 0 over and over whenever you didn't. This is because the microcontroller hasn't been told to make any decisions, just to report the state of the switch. Once you know the state of a digital input, you have to decide what to do with it. You might output something immediately on another pin of your microcontroller; for example, you might turn on an LED. But if all you're doing is turning something on when the switch is thrown, you don't need a microcontroller. The microcontroller's value lies in the fact that it lets you make more complex choices. You can use the if statement to turn something on only if a particular combination of switches is thrown, or only if the switches are thrown in a particular sequence. You can use the microcontroller to control the duration of your response to the switch, or to delay your response to the switch. Or you can use it to send messages to other devices in response to the switch. It makes possible a more complex response to, and a more detailed message from, the input.

In the following example, there are three switches attached to a microcontroller. We've also attached digital outputs (see the next section) to a few pins of the microcontroller in the form of an LED. If all three switches are not on, an LED attached to pin 8 comes on. When all three switches are pressed simultaneously, another LED attached to pin 7 flashes twice.

Digital Input

PBASIC

MBasic

```
' Put pins into input mode:
input 2
input 4
input 6
MyLoop:
    ' turn off the "switches off" LED:
    low 8
    'if all the switches are on then turn off the "switches off" LED
    ' and go to the flash routine:
    if in2 = 1 and in4 =1 and in6 = 1 then
        ' Turn on the flashing LED, and turn off the "switches off" LED:
        High 7
        Low 8
        Pause 100
        flash the flashing LED:
        Low 7
        Pause 100
        High 7
        Pause 100
        Low 7
    Else
        ' if any one of the switches is not on, turn on the "Switches off"
LED:
        High 8
        ' turn off flashing LED:
        Low 7
    Endif
Goto MyLoop
```

PicBasic
Pro

```
' Put pins into input mode:
input portB.0
input portB.1
input portB.2

MyLoop:
    ' turn off the "switches off" LED:
    Low portC.1
    'if all the switches are on then turn off the "switches off" LED
    ' and go to the flash routine:
    if portb.0 = 1 and portb.1 =1 and portb.2 = 1 then
        ' Turn on the flashing LED, and turn off the "switches off" LED:
        High portC.2
        Low portc.1
        Pause 100
        ' flash the flashing LED:
```

```
            Low portC.2
            Pause 100
            High portC.2
            Pause 100
            Low portC.2
        else
            ' if any switches are not on, turn on the "Switches off" LED:
            High portC.1
            ' turn off flashing LED:
            Low portC.2
        endif
    Goto MyLoop
```

<hr>

BX-Basic

```
' no need to declare pins as inputs: putPin() command does this automatically later on.
Sub main()
    do
            ' turn off the "switches off" LED:
        call putPin (11,0)

        'if all the switches are on then turn off the "switches off" LED
        ' and go to the flash routine:
        if (getPin(14) = 1) and (getPin(16) = 1) and (getPin(18) = 1) then
            ' Turn on the flashing LED, turn off "switches off" LED:
            call putPin(12,1)
            call putPin(11,0)
            call delay(0.1)

            ' flash the flashing LED:
            call putPin(12,0)
            call delay(0.1)
            call putPin(12,1)
            call delay(0.1)
            call putPin(12,0)
        else
            ' if any one of the switches is not on,
            ' turn on the "Switches off" LED:
            call putPin(11, 1)
            ' turn off flashing LED:
            call putPin(12, 0)
        end if
    loop
End Sub
```

Digital Input

Digital Output

There are countless types of digital output transducers. Anything that can be turned on or off—for example, a fan, a radio, or a car—is a potential digital output transducer. The challenge in interfacing output devices to the microcontroller lies in figuring out how those devices can be turned on or off using the 5 volts and approximately 10 to 20 milliamps that a microcontroller's output pin supplies.

Transducers

The simplest digital output transducers are those that can connect directly to the microcontroller. You've already used one, the LED, back in Chapter 4. LEDs are staples of physical computing applications because they're so easy to power. They're an ideal way to give a simple indication as to whether something's working or not. It's good to keep a handful around if just to use as indicators and debugging tools. The BX-24 even has two LEDs built into the module. Try this bit of code to see them.

```
(BX-Basic)    Sub main()
                  do
                          Call putPin(25, 0)
                          Call putPin(26,1)
                          Call delay(0.2)
                          Call putPin(25, 1)
                          Call putPin(26,0)
                          Call delay(0.2)
                  Loop
              End sub
```

Notice that the LEDs mounted on the BX-24 are turned on by taking the pin low, and off by taking it high. Extra credit if you figure out why (hint: what happens if the LED's direction is reversed, and the LED and resistor are connected to 5 volts instead of ground?).

Besides the everyday LEDs, there are a variety of other LEDs that can be useful. Superbright LEDs (usually rated to output 1000 millicandela or more, where a candela is a unit of brightness) come in a range of colors, and, at their brightest, are enough to read by. Red and yellow ones tend to be cheapest, followed by green, blue, and white. In addition to being used as digital outputs, LEDs can also be used as analog outputs by dimming them. We'll get to how that's done later on.

In addition to LEDs, any piezo buzzer that operates at 5 volts or less, and 10 to 20 milliamps (mA) or less can connect to the microcontroller. Connect the buzzer's other end to ground, and it'll buzz when you put the output pin high.

Most other digital output devices, from motors to solenoids to light bulbs to coffee grinders, will need more voltage and amperage than a microcontroller's outputs can supply. For these, you'll need an intermediary. The two most common devices you'll use to control devices that need higher current are the relay and the transistor. Digital output techniques using transistors and relays can be used to control anything that can be switched on and off—too many to list completely here. A standard relay is simply an electronically thrown switch that can control anything controllable by a normal switch. That includes DC power or AC power and audio, video, or data signals. In our work, we've seen CD players, remote control cars, talking teddy bears, food blenders, and more, all interfaced to microcontrollers by simply substituting an existing switch with a relay. Transistors are fast and cheap but can only work for DC loads. DC motors are very easy to interface to transistors, and are good for creating rotary motion (we'll discuss those in more depth in Chapter 10, "Making Movement"). Solenoids can be used to create linear motion (also discussed in Chapter 10). Fans, which are just applications of motors, are good for air movement and temperature regulation. Incandescent light bulbs can create light and heat, and they have a gentler fade than LEDs. Peltier junctions can create a cooling effect; heaters of many varieties can do the reverse. Rather than going on about what you can possibly turn on and off, we will go into some depth on the intermediary devices, the relay, and the transistor that will be used for almost all of them.

Relays

Relays are switches that are thrown by an electromagnet instead of the mechanical action of your finger. There are two types, electromechanical relays and solid state relays.

Electromechanical Relays are devices that use electrical energy to control a mechanical switch. When the microcontroller sends current through the electromagnet, the electromagnet pulls a conductor across two contacts inside the relay. These two contacts being moved by the electromagnet are in turn attached to a separate circuit, called the *load circuit*, carrying enough power to control the device you want to control. You can actually hear the click of the conductor hitting the contacts. Figure 6.4 illustrates this idea. Some electromechanical relays are called *reed relays* because the contacts for the switch look like thin metal reeds.

Figure 6.4
Electromechanical
relay.

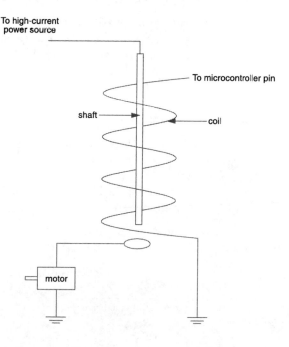

To high-current
power source

To microcontroller pin

shaft

coil

motor

Digital Output

Solid state relays function similarly to electromechanical relays, but there are no moving parts. As a result, they are slightly faster than electromechanical relays. They are also more expensive.

Relays are rated by the current and voltage required to control the electromagnet, or "coil," and by the current and voltage that can pass through the bigger load circuit. In order to use a relay to control a device from your microcontroller, you must first find a relay with a coil that can be thrown by the digital output power (5 volts, 10 to 20 milliamps) of your microcontroller. 5-volt reed relays and most solid state relays will work well with the power from a microcontroller's output pin. When you've found a relay whose coil can be controlled from the microcontroller, check that your relay will carry the load of the device you are trying to turn on and off. The capacity of your relay will be specified in volts and amps, but your load might be described in watts. You can go back to a formula from Chapter 3 to figure this out: *watts = volts x amps*. For example, a typical reed relay's load circuit can carry 0.5 amps at 120 volts, enough to control a 60-watt light bulb.

Sometimes the electromagnet in your relay will require more current or voltage than the microcontroller can output. This is particularly true of electromechanical relays that can switch very high current loads, because they need to move large conductors across the contacts. Solid state relays, on the other hand, can usually switch a larger load with a relatively small control voltage and current, because they have no moving parts.[2]

Transistors

Transistors are electronic devices that control a large current from a smaller current, much like relays. Transistors are very versatile devices, and there are many varieties and uses for them that we won't go into here. For our purposes, they work well as electronic switches, and function much faster than relays and are less expensive. Unlike relays, however, transistors are strictly DC components. They cannot switch alternating current.

There are several types of transistors. They come in two major classes: *bipolar transistors*, and *field-effect transistors* (FETs). For our purposes, we'll be talking only about bipolar transistors. All transistors have some properties in common. They all have three connections, referred to as the *base*, the *collector*, and the *emitter* (on FET transistors, the three connections are the gate, the source, and the drain). By putting a small voltage and current on the base of a transistor, you allow a larger current to flow from the collector to the emitter. In this way they function as amplifiers.

Among bipolar transistors, there are two types: NPN transistors, and PNP transistors. To use the nomenclature from switches, the NPN is equivalent to a normally open switch and PNP is equivalent to normally closed switch. You'll use NPN transistors in the examples here, specifically a very robust transistor called a Darlington transistor. This type of transistor is designed to switch high-current loads.

Keep the packaging for your transistors because it should have a key for telling which leg is the base, the collector, and the emitter. If not, you will need to look up the transistor's data

---

[2] If you can't find a relay that will match both your microcontroller and your load, match the load and put in a transistor circuit as another intermediary to power the relay.

sheet on the Internet. We recommend http://www.findchips.com for this; you can enter any electronic part number and find a reseller and a data sheet. Alternately, type the part number into any search engine and you'll often get the data sheet as one of the first links.

Circuit

To turn almost any device on or off, you interrupt one of two wires running from its power supply and place a microcontroller, relay, or transistor in that path. In most cases, you will just be snipping one of the wires in the power cable of the device. If you are hacking into an existing device, like a teddy bear or a remote control car, you will be replacing an existing switch, which already interrupts the circuit. Whether you use just a microcontroller, a relay, or a transistor to interrupt the circuit will be determined mostly by the amount of current and voltage that your device requires.

The simplest digital output circuit is one you've already seen that only needs the microcontroller to interrupt power to the device. It's the one used to turn on an LED, shown in Figure 6.5.

Figure 6.5
The simplest digital output: an LED, and its schematic.

Digital Output

If you have a buzzer or another device that can operate on 5 volts and 10 to 20 mA or less, you can replace the LED and resistor with the buzzer in this circuit and it will turn on when you take the output high. For any other device, you'll need a transistor or relay.

For small battery powered (DC) devices, a transistor will work well. For example, DC motors work well when controlled by a Darlington transistor. The circuit looks like the one shown in Figure 6.6.

Figure 6.6
A microcontroller controlling a DC motor through a transistor. For more on the capacitors in this circuit, see the sidebar below on decoupling capacitors.

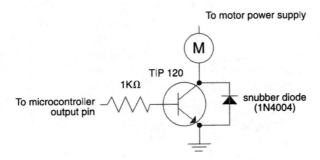

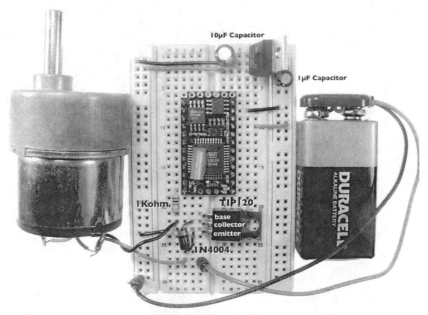

Note that the ground of the motor's supply circuit and the ground of the microcontroller must be common. You need to combine these grounds for the circuit to work. The diode across the motor in this case is used to control *blowback voltage*. When a motor is spinning, it induces an electrical current in the wires wound inside it in the opposite direction of the current that's powering it. The diode across the motor stops this back electricity from affecting the rest of the circuit. We'll talk more about this in the chapter on motors, Chapter 10.

If you want to control a device that uses AC current from a wall socket, the simplest way is to use a relay. Relays can switch AC or DC power and video or audio signals as well. See the circuit in Figure 6.7.

Figure 6.7

A 120V AC relay circuit

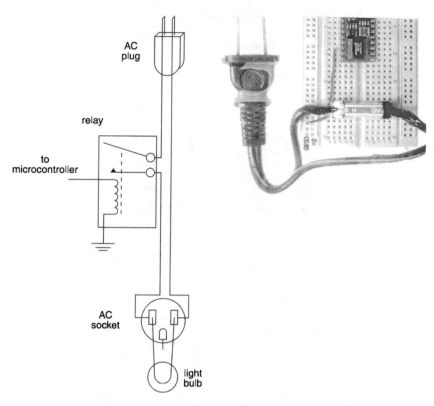

CAUTION

This circuit gives you the capacity to put AC voltage in your circuits. This power can kill you, not to mention your microcontroller. Get the DC side of the circuit correct before you plug in the AC side of it. Before attaching the AC or the load, use a multimeter to test the resistance on the switch side of the relay (continuity check will not work on solid state relays). Make sure the AC power connects to the two contacts on the switch of the relay and never touches anything else that leads back to the microcontroller. Insulate all AC contacts with rubber or electrical tape before powering the circuit. Only cut one of the two AC wires to connect the relay. Be clear headed when wiring AC circuits. Make sure the AC cables are securely fastened and will not get detached while the circuit is plugged in. Note that in the AC control circuit, there is no connection between the microcontroller ground and the AC ground. If possible, get a person more experienced with electricity to look over your circuit before plugging it in.

Digital Output

Programming

The programming for digital output is very simple, and you have already used it to control an LED. Simply take the output pin high to turn on the device, and low to turn it off. Here's a simple program to turn a device on and off every third of a second. Once you have this program working with an LED, try it with a transistor or relay controlling a motor or another more exciting device.

PBASIC

MBasic

```
main:
        ' turn the device on:
        High 0
        ' wait 1/3 of a second:
        pause 300
        'turn the device off:
        Low 0
        ' wait 1/3 of a second:
        pause 300
Goto main
```

PicBasic
Pro

```
main:
        ' turn the device on:
        High portb.1
        ' wait 1/3 of a second:
        pause 300
        'turn the device off:
        low portb.1
        ' wait 1/3 of a second:
        pause 300
Goto main
```

BX-Basic

```
Sub main()
        do
                ' turn the device on:
                Call putPin(5,1)
                ' wait 1/3 of a second:
                Call delay(0.3)
                'turn the device off:
                Call putPin(5,0)
                ' wait 1/3 of a second:
                Call delay(0.3)
        Loop
End sub
```

Analog Input

If you are after more information about a person's actions than can be supplied by a digital input, you will need an analog input. For example, let's return to our cat on the mat. Perhaps you want to know how fat the cat on the mat is. In order to determine this, you'll need a way to measure the varying range of force exerted on the mat. An analog sensor like a force-sensing resistor (discussed below) would let you measure not only the presence or absence of force exerted by the cat's weight, but also how much force is exerted.

Transducers

A few different kinds of transducers will read an analog input. Some are very simple to work with, and others require a significant amount of extra circuitry to use. For this chapter, we'll concentrate on the simple ones: variable resistors.

Variable Resistors

The most common class of transducers for analog input are variable resistors. *Variable resistors* convert a change in mechanical, light, heat, and other forms of energy into a change in resistance. The most common variable resistor is a *potentiometer*, or pot for short. Pots are used in many everyday devices. Volume knobs are pots, varying the resistance and therefore the signal strength that reaches the speakers. Pots are great in situations where you need a simple variable control that's hand-operated, but that's not always what you need in physical computing projects. Fortunately, there are many other types of variable resistors.

Thermistors are variable resistors whose resistance changes with the ambient temperature. A photocell's resistance varies with the intensity of the light hitting it. *Force-sensing resistors*, or *FSRs*, have a

INDUCTIVE VERSUS RESISTIVE LOADS

There are two general classes of devices you might control from a microcontroller: inductive loads and resistive loads. *Inductive loads* are devices that work by inducing a current in a wire using the current in another wire or by passing the wire through a magnetic field. Motors and solenoids are examples of inductive loads. Inductive loads produce blowback voltage. They should have a diode placed in parallel with them, or with the transistor controlling them, as in the motor circuit in Figure 6.6, to lessen the effects of the back voltage. You'll deal with them in depth in Chapter 10. *Resistive loads* are devices that work by resisting electrical current and converting it to some other form of energy. Light bulbs and heaters are resistive loads. Resistive loads don't create a blowback voltage, so no diode protection is necessary. A good rule of thumb is that if it creates motion of any sort, it's probably an inductive load.

variable resistance that depends on the amount of force exerted on the sensor. *Flex sensors* offer a varying resistance depending on how sharply they are bent. It may be that one of these is perfect for your needs. For example, a flex sensor could determine how much a person is bending her finger, or a force-sensitive resistor could measure how hard she is squeezing a ball. You may have to creatively contrive the situation so that the information you're after alters the energy on a transducer you want to use. For example, you might use a thermistor to sense how hard a person is blowing (because a person's breath will change the ambient temperature) or use a photocell to determine the distance of an object from the sensor (objects closer to the photocell will block more light, if the object is between the light source and the photocell).

Because microcontrollers are binary in nature, they can only read a high voltage or a low voltage. In order to read a changing voltage, certain accommodations are necessary. Many microcontrollers come with built in analog-to-digital converters. An *analog-to-digital converter* measures a range of voltages and converts the value of the voltage at any given moment to a digital value to be stored in the microcontroller's memory. Some microcontrollers, such as the BS-2 and certain PIC models, do not have built-in ADCs.

Analog Input

For those microcontrollers, you use a resistor-capacitor circuit to "fake" an analog-to-digital conversion.

Variable Voltage Analog Input Transducers

Besides the simple analog transducers we've already mentioned, there are several more complex analog transducers that can be very useful. Many of these operate on 5-volt DC power already, making them convenient to interface with a microcontroller. Usually, complex analog transducers operate on a given power supply (for example, 5 volts) and produce a variable voltage as output. For example, the Sharp infrared proximity ranger (Sharp GP2D12) operates on 5-volt DC, and outputs a variable voltage between 0 and 5 volts depending on the proximity of an object in its field of view. The GP2D12 can sense objects in a range from about 10 to 80 cm. Other models in the same family can detect objects in different ranges. We'll discuss these more in depth in Chapter 9, "Sensing Things."

There are some devices that produce a varying voltage that's not in the 0 to 5 volt range of a microcontroller's ADCs. For example, microphones produce a varying voltage, but one that varies only by a few microvolts. In order to use microphones and other devices that produce microvolt changes, it's necessary to use a circuit to amplify the voltage to the range that the microcontroller can read. One simple way to do this with a microphone is to pass the microphone's signal to an audio amplifier, which raises the voltages to levels that are readable by a microcontroller. We'll detail this in Chapter 13, "Controlling Sound and Light."

Circuit

There are two basic circuits for reading an analog voltage on a microcontroller: the voltage divider and the resistor-capacitor circuit. Voltage divider circuits work only on microcontrollers that have analog-to-digital converters. R-C circuits work on all the microcontrollers we're writing about.

Voltage Divider

Even microcontrollers that support analog to digital conversion usually only do so on select pins. Before you get started with this circuit, you should identify the ADC-capable pins on your microcontroller. On the Basic Atom Pro24, they're pins 0 through 4. On the BX-24, they're pins 13 through 20. On the PIC 18F452, they're pins RA0 through RA3, RA5, and RE0 through RE2. The BS-2 does not have any ADC pins.

You use variable resistors by passing a current through them and reading the voltage that comes out of them to determine how much they are resisting that current. In Figure 6.8, we connected a variable resistor (in this case, a flex sensor) from +5 volts to the microcontroller pin and a fixed resistor from the pin to ground. Use a fixed resistor that's in the general range of the variable resistor's range. For example, if your variable resistor varies from 10K to 100K, a 10K fixed resistor will suffice.

This is called a *voltage divider circuit* because the variable resistor and the fixed resistor divide the voltage into two parts. The variable resistor feeds a varying voltage to the microcontroller pin. The fixed resistor provides a path to ground. The voltage at the point where the resistors meet (namely, the pin) will vary with the ratio of the resistors' values. For example, when the resistors are equal, the voltage on the pin will be exactly half of the supplied voltage, or 2.5 volts.

Figure 6.8
Analog input: a flex
sensor.

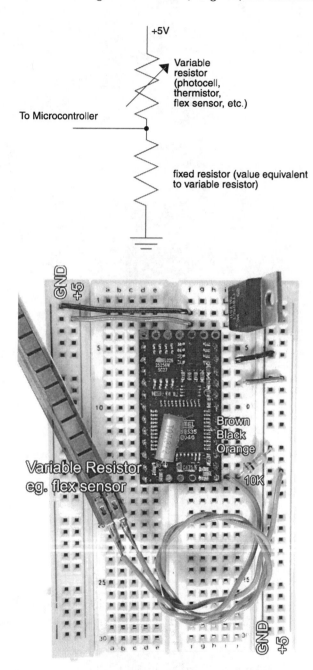

+5V

Variable
resistor
(photocell,
thermistor,
flex sensor, etc.)

To Microcontroller

fixed resistor (value equivalent
to variable resistor)

GND
+5

Brown
Black
Orange

Variable Resistor
eg. flex sensor

10K

GND
+5

Analog Input

In the circuit seen in Figure 6.9, we used a potentiometer instead of the two resistors from
the previous circuit. If you break open a potentiometer, you'll find a center slider touching
into a single resistive strip. This makes the resistance of the two sides of the potentiometer
perfectly complementary, and so it's perfect to replace the two resistors in our voltage
divider circuit. If you connect one side of the pot to ground, the other to 5 volts, and the

center to the microcontroller ADC pin, you will get a range of numbers from 0 to the maximum that the ADC can return.

Figure 6.9
Analog input:
a potentiometer.

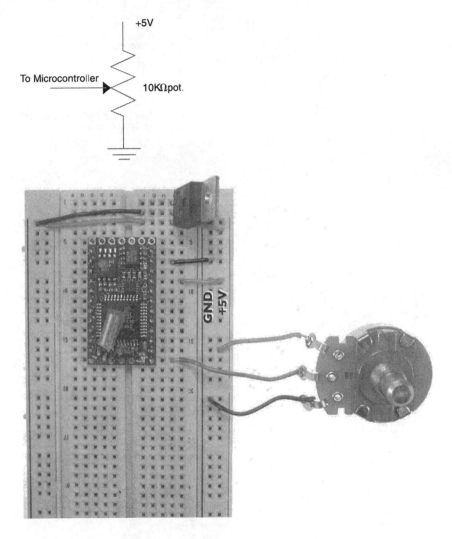

If you build these circuits as-is, place your multimeter leads at the point that would go to the microcontroller and at ground, and measure for voltage, you will see a changing voltage value.

RC Circuit

If your microcontroller doesn't have any ADC pins on it, or not enough of them, there is another method you can use to measure a varying resistance using a capacitor. The method you'll be using is called rctime. The circuit for it looks like the one shown in Figure 6.10.

Here's what happens when you use the rctime command. Capacitors store charge when they're fed electricity, and release it when the feed is turned off. First, you take the input pin high. This lets all the charge out of the capacitor (since both sides of it are high). Then the microcontroller sets the voltage on the input pin low, causing the capacitor to start

Figure 6.10
Analog input:
RC circuit.

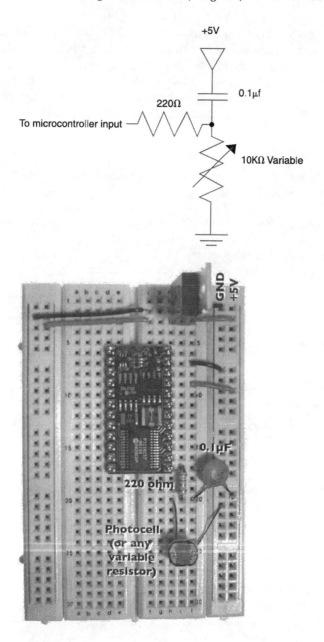

building up a charge. The microcontroller starts counting time, waiting for the capacitor to recharge. The charging happens in a matter of microseconds, but a microcontroller is fast enough to measure that time. The more resistance from the variable resistor, the longer it will take to charge. Once all the capacitor is charged, the microcontroller returns a value. The higher our variable resistor's resistance, the higher the value the rctime command returns. `rctime` is somewhat slower than using an ADC but it's handy when you don't have an ADC to use. For most variable resistor sensors, it will do the job just fine. You may also be able to use the `rctime` command with a sensor that produces an analog voltage in the 0 to 5 volt range, like the Sharp IR rangers mentioned above. Remove the resistor from the RC Circuit and attach the sensor's voltage output to the microcontroller pin. Leave the capacitor in your circuit, between the microcontroller pin and ground.

Programming

Here's the pseudocode describing what we're going to do in our program to make the microcontroller read an analog input:

```
Make a variable big enough to store the analog value that you'll be taking in.
Loop
        Read the analog value coming in
        Output the number
End loop
```

Analog-to-Digital Converters

Here's the code for reading an analog-to-digital converter.

NOTE

Because the BS-2 does not have ADCs, no PBasic is shown below.

MBasic
```
' note: the Basic ATOM Pro24 has 4 ADC inputs, pins 0 through 3.
' this example uses pin 0.

ADCVar var word
OutputVar var byte
Main:
    ' read the ADC on pin 0:
    ADIN 0, ADCVar
    ' debug the raw value:
    debug ["ADCVar: ", DEC ADCVar, 10,13]
goto main
```

NOTE

With the PIC, you have to set up a number of special function registers before you can use the ADCs.

PicBasic
Pro

```
' Set Debug pin port
DEFINE DEBUG_REG PORTC
' Set Debug pin BIT
DEFINE DEBUG_BIT 6
' Set Debug baud rate
DEFINE DEBUG_BAUD 9600
' Set Debug mode: 0 = true, 1 = inverted
DEFINE DEBUG_MODE 1

' Define ADCIN parameters
DEFINE ADC_BITS 10          ' Set number of bits in result
DEFINE ADC_CLOCK 3    ' Set clock source (3=rc)
DEFINE ADC_SAMPLEUS 20     ' Set sampling time in uS

' declare a variable to hold the result:
ADCVar var word

TRISA = %11111111       ' Set PORTA to all input
ADCON1 = %10000010     ' Set PORTA analog and right justify result
Pause 500          ' Wait .5 second

main:
    ' read ADC channel 0:
    adcin 0, ADCVar
    ' debug the raw value (the value 13 makes the return):
    debug "ADCVar: ", DEC ADCVar, 13, 10
GoTo main
```

BX-Basic

```
' Note: the BX-24 has 8 analog inputs, on pins 13 - 20.
' This example uses pin 13

' set up a variable to hold the result:
dim ADCVar as integer

Sub main()
    call delay(0.5) ' start program with a half-second delay

    do
        ADCvar = getADC(13)
        debug.print "ADCVar = " ; cstr(ADCVar)
        loop

end sub
```

Analog Input

RCTime

Since the BS-2 has no analog-to-digital converters, you must use the `rctime` command to read analog inputs on it. It is also possible to use an RC circuit as analog in on the other microcontrollers, as all of our environments have an `rctime` command. Here's the example code.

PBASIC

```
' since RCTime doesn't depend on an ADC, we can use any pin.
' This example uses pin 0:

' set up a variable to hold the result:
RCVar var word

Main:
    ' Take pin 0 high to discharge capacitor:
    high 0
    ' hold 1 millisecond to make sure capacitor is discharged
    pause 1
    ' Measure time it takes to charge again.
    rctime 0,1,RCVar
    ' debug the result:
    debug "RCVar: ", DEC RCVar, 10, 13
goto main
```

MBasic

```
' since RCTime doesn't depend on an ADC, we can use any pin.
' This example uses pin 0:

' set up a variable to hold the result:
RCVar var word

Main:
    ' Take pin 0 high to discharge capacitor:
    high 0
    ' hold 1 millisecond to make sure capacitor is discharged
    pause 1
    ' Measure time it takes to charge again.
    rctime 0,0,RCVar
    ' debug the result:
    debug ["RCVar: ", DEC RCVar, 10, 13]
goto main
```

PicBasic Pro

```
' since RCTime doesn't depend on an ADC, we can use any pin.
' This example uses pin B0:

' Set Debug pin port
```

```
DEFINE DEBUG_REG PORTB
' Set Debug pin BIT
DEFINE DEBUG_BIT 6
' Set Debug baud rate
DEFINE DEBUG_BAUD 9600
' Set Debug mode: 0 = true, 1 = inverted
DEFINE DEBUG_MODE 1


' set up a variable to hold the result:
RCVar var word

Main:
    ' Take pin 0 high to discharge capacitor:
    high portB.0
    ' hold 1 millisecond to make sure capacitor is discharged
    pause 1
    ' Measure time it takes to charge again.
    Rctime portB.0,1,RCVar
    ' debug the result:
    debug "RCVar: ", DEC RCVar, 10, 13
goto main
```

BX-Basic

```
' since RCTime doesn't depend on an ADC, we can use any pin.
' This example uses pin 5:

' set up a variable to hold the result:
dim RCVar as integer

sub main()
    do
        ' Take pin 0 high to discharge capacitor:
        call putPin(5, 1)
        ' hold 1 millisecond to make sure capacitor is discharged:
        call delay(0.001)
        ' Measure time it takes to charge again:
        RCVar = Rctime(5,1)
        ' debug the result:
        debug.print "RCVar: "; cstr(RCVar)
    loop
end sub
```

Analog Input

Pulsewidth Modulation for Input

Pulsewidth modulation (PWM) is another common method for getting an analog input. With PWM, the analog value is not derived from the amount of voltage, as it is with ADC, but from duration of a digital pulse of voltage. PWM is the main technique for powering transducers for analog output, but it can also be used for analog input. All of the microcontrollers we're discussing have a command to read an analog value from a device that produces a varying pulsewidth. On the BX-24, it's called PulseIn. In pBasic, mBasic, and PicBasic Pro, it's called Pulsin. When you call the command, it waits until the pin changes from high to low or low to high, then counts the time until the pin changes back to the previous state. The result is a pulsewidth that represents the intensity of the energy that the sensor measures. On the input side, PWM is not really used directly with transducers but instead mostly as a form of communication protocol with advanced sensor modules. There are two good examples using this technique, both with an infrared sensor and an accelerometer, in Chapter 9, "Sensing Movement."

Analog Output

There are times when you want to do more than simply turn a device on or off. Instead of wanting the microcontroller to turn a light on or off, for example, you might want to control how bright a lamp gets, or open a curtain halfway, or change the pitch of a sound. In these cases, you will use analog output techniques.

As you saw in digital output, the small power output of a microcontroller limits the devices that you can directly power to LEDs, piezo buzzers, and other low-current devices. With analog output, you gain one very useful device, the hobbyist servo motor. You won't be powering it directly from the microcontroller, but you will be controlling it using the signal available from an I/O pin. You'll be using a method to control it that's based on pulsewidth modulation PWM, described above. For anything other than these transducers, you'll need some additional components and circuitry between the microcontroller and the final output device, just as you needed a relay or a transistor to control a higher current load for digital output. Quite often, you'll handle analog output by using other devices with their own microcontrollers, such as lighting dimmers, synthesizers, and motor controllers. In those cases, you'll talk to the devices using serial communication, which we'll cover in Chapter 7, "Communicating between Computers" and Chapter 12, "More Communication between Devices."

Pulsewidth Modulation for Output

Microcontrollers also can't produce a varying voltage, they can only produce a high voltage (in our case 5 volts) or low (in our case 0 volts). So to create a varying output voltage, you "fake" an analog voltage by using pulsewidth modulation.

The pulsewidth is usually a very small time, a few microseconds or milliseconds at most. Just as your mind can create the illusion of motion when images are flashed in front of it rapidly (for example, at the movies, where 24 still frames a second makes a movie), it will fill in the dark and light moments of a flashing LED so that the LED appears to be somewhere between fully bright and off. The resulting average voltage is sometimes called a *pseudo-analog voltage*.

In the graph in Figure 6.11, we pulse our pin high for the same length of time we pulse it low. The time the pin is high (called the *pulsewidth*) is about half the total time it takes to go from low to high to low again. This ratio is called the *duty cycle*. The duty cycle is 50 percent and the average voltage is about half the total voltage.

Figure 6.11
Pulsewidth modulation
with a duty cycle of
50 percent.

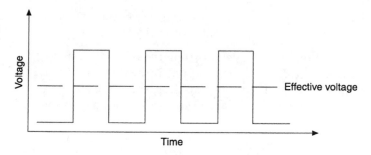

If you make the duty cycle less than 50 percent by pulsing for a shorter amount of time than you pause, you get a lower pseudo-analog voltage (see Figure 6.12).

Figure 6.12
Pulsewidth modulation
with a duty cycle of
20 percent.

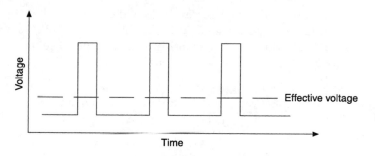

The Pulsout command is the main tool for analog output. In pBasic, mBasic, and PicBasic Pro, it looks like this:

```
Pulsout pin, time
```

▶ *Pin* is the output pin you want to send a pulse on.

▶ *Time* is the pulsewidth. On the BS-2, it's in increments of 2 microseconds, on the Basic Atom Pro24, it's in increments of 1 microsecond, and on the PIC it varies with the clock speed, 10 microseconds for a 4 MHz clock and 2 microseconds for a 20 MHz clock.

On the BX-24, the pulseOut does the same thing with a different syntax:

```
Call pulseOut(pin, time, state)
```

▶ *Pin* (a byte variable) refers to the pin you're going to pulse.

▶ *Time* (a single variable) is the length of time each pulse takes, in seconds. It's in increments of 1.085 microseconds.

▶ *State* (a byte variable) is the state that the pin will be in when pulsed. If state = 1, the pin will normally be low, and pulse high. If state = 0, the pin will normally be high and the pulse low.

While Pulsout (or Pulseout) is executing, nothing else can happen. The microcontroller will do nothing else but pulse the output pin for the time of the pulsewidth. So if you give a very long pulsewidth value, you might see the microprocessor stop all other functions, like reading sensors or controlling other outputs, at that time.

In the following section, we will demonstrate the basic circuits and programs for analog output by dimming an LED, and then by controlling the speed of a regular DC motor. We'll go on to show how to vary the tone of a speaker and the position (as opposed to speed) of a servo motor. The circuits and programming for these are fairly specialized, so we will treat them individually.

LED Dimming

The easiest way to see PWM in action is to attach an LED to the pin that you're pulsing. You'll use the same digital output circuit for the LED that you used above.

We recommend that you try this just so you get the idea of PWM. It's not a very satisfying display for your projects for two reasons: it has visible blinks, and it is not very powerful. To solve the first problem you'll add a smoothing circuit, and to solve the second you will add a transistor circuit and replace the LED with a motor.

Normal LEDs respond to the changing voltage very quickly. As the pulsewidth gets greater, you will actually see the LED going on and off rather than dimming. This is because your eye can detect the changes if they're slow enough. Adding a low-pass filter circuit will smooth this somewhat.

Smoothing circuits or low-pass filter circuits use a combination of a capacitor and a resistor to average out the pulses so the time when the LED is off between pulses is not so pronounced (see Figure 6.12). The capacitor stores up a charge during a pulse and releases it between pulses.

This circuit doesn't smooth all the pulses. It's called a "low-pass filter" because it allows pulses below a certain threshold frequency to pass through without smoothing them, and smoothes out those above the threshold frequency into an even pseudo-analog voltage. The range of frequencies filtered out is determined by the ratio of the resistor's value to that of the capacitor. The formulas are more complex than we want to delve into here. If you're dimming an LED, start with a 10µF capacitor and a 220-ohm resistor, then experiment with different values from there to see what works best.

DC Motor Speed Control

You can use PWM to dim an LED, and you can also use it to control higher-current devices too, by using a transistor, just as you did in the digital output section above. Below, you'll use it to vary the speed of a DC motor.

You use the same transistor circuit as we did in Figure 6.6 to turn the motor completely on or off, but instead of putting the output pin of the microcontroller high or low, you use the pulseout command to turn it both on and off thousands of times per second. The range of the required pulseout varies depending on the motor and the transistor used, but a range from 200 microseconds to 20 milliseconds is a good starting range. The varying pseudo-analog voltage on the base of the transistor creates a corresponding variation of the current

Figure 6.13
Smoothing circuit
for an LED (low-pass
filter).

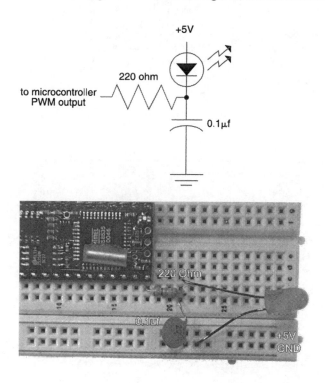

flowing through the motor, and the motor spins at a variable rate. The motor has built-in smoothing because it takes a while to speed up and slow down, so it will probably not need a smoothing circuit. We'll discuss this in more depth in Chapter 10.

Programming

Programming for DC Motor speed control is similar enough to dimming an LED that you can use the same code for both. Here's the basic idea, in pseudocode:

```
Loop
        'The ratio of the high pulse to the pause
        ' determines the value of the pseudo-analog voltage:
        Pulse the motor or LED high
        Pause with it low. End loop
```

Following is a simple program to dim an LED or control the speed of a motor. You can see that the values for pulsing differ from one microcontroller to the next. Remember, the pseudo-analog voltage is the ratio of the on time to the off time (that is, the pulse to the pause). Try changing the values of the pulse range and the pause to see what happens.

| PBASIC |
| MBasic |

```
' The LED to be dimmed is on pin 7
period VAR Word
OUTPUT 7


main:
```

```
                FOR period = 10 TO 10000 STEP 10
                    ' pulsout 1 = 2 microseconds on the BS-2
                    ' pulsout 1 = 0.5 microseconds on the ATOM:
                    PULSOUT 7, period
                    PAUSE 1
                NEXT
            GOTO main
```

PicBasic
Pro

```
    ' the LED to be dimmed on pin RC3.
    period var byte
    output portc.3

    main:
        for period = 0 to 255
                ' pulse LED (pulsout 1 = 2 microseconds)
            pulsout portc.3, period
            ' pause in microseconds;
            ' pause time gets longer as pulse gets shorter
            ' pauseus pauses for microseconds, not milliseconds:
            pauseus 2*(255 - period)
        next
    goto main
```

BX-Basic

```
    ' the LED to be dimmed is on pin 12
    dim period as single

    Sub Main()
        ' because the period of the pulseout() command is
        ' data type single, we can't use a for-next loop
        ' to change its value:
        do
            if period < 0.01 then
                period = period + 0.0001
            else
                period = 0.0001
            end if
            call pulseout(12, period, 1)
            call delay(0.01 - period)
        loop
    End Sub
```

Pulsing an output like this works fine when that's the only thing your program is doing. But when you add code to read inputs or control other outputs, you'll see that the pulse output gets choppy. There are other commands that you can use for pulsewidth modulation (PWM). The PWM commands in Mbasic and PicBasic Pro and the PutDAC() and DACPin()

commands on the BX-24 output a train of several pulses at a time, and allow you to set the duty cycle of the pulses. Additionally, all of the microcontrollers except the BS-2 have hardware built in that can produce a *hardware PWM* signal, which runs continuously. Look into the HPWM commands in Mbasic and PicBasic Pro, and the multitasking commands on the BX-24 for more on this.

Generating Tones

The output from a pin of the microcontroller is just barely strong enough to drive a small speaker. You won't hear these devices used on stage at Carnegie Hall, but they are useful as a tool for user interface. They also further illustrate the idea of using digital pulses over time to create analog signals.

Circuit

You can connect a speaker with a couple of capacitors and resistors, as shown in Figure 6.14.

Figure 6.14
Analog output to a speaker.

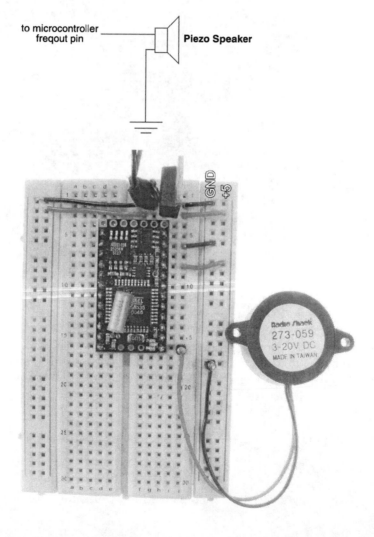

The tones from the microcontroller are not amplified, however, so you may have difficulty hearing them. For better sound, wire your microcontroller to an audio jack so you can connect its output to the input of an amplifier. Figure 6.15 shows the circuit you need.

Figure 6.15
Connecting an audio jack for sound output. This circuit can also be used with a speaker.

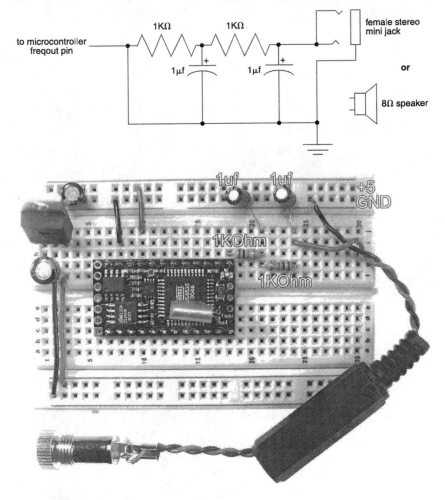

Programming

The microcontrollers you're working with have a command, freqout, which allows you to generate a tone from any of the I/O pins. When a speaker or amplifier is connected properly to the pins, the tone can be heard. In pBasic, mBasic, and PicBasic Pro, the syntax is as follows:

```
Freqout pin, duration, Freq1, freq2
```

On the BX-24, the syntax is different, but the parameters are the same:

```
Call FreqOut(Pin, Freq1, Freq2, Duration)
```

▶ *Pin* is a byte variable, the pin on which you want to generate the tone.

▶ *Freq1* and *Freq2* are the frequencies you want to generate. Units are in cycles per second, or Hertz (Hz). Human hearing extends from 20 to 20,000 Hz, so with an integer (whose values can be as high as 32,767), you can generate tones higher than the human ear can hear. Two tones can be generated at the same time. To generate a single tone, use the same tone for both frequency parameters or make the second frequency double the first. In pBasic, mBasic, and PicBasic Pro, these parameters take a word variable in milliseconds. In BX-Basic, they're integers.

▶ *Duration* is the duration of the tone. In pBasic, mBasic, and PicBasic Pro, it's a word variable in milliseconds. In BX-Basic, it's a single precision floating point. It can range from 1 millisecond to about 2.56 seconds. Your program will not do anything else for that period of time.

Programming for `freqout` is very simple. Simply call the `freqout` command as written above. This example takes input from an analog input and plays a variable pitch sound.

This example also uses a new variable construct called an array. An *array* is just a variable with many numbered compartments. The useful thing about arrays is that the values in these compartments can be pulled out by the number of the compartment they're stored in. For example, you might store a list of 5 bytes in a byte array called `myList`. To see the second byte, use the following syntax:

```
SecondByte = myList(1)
```

Confused? Remember when we said that a byte variable could range from 0 to 255? Just as variable values start with 0, most programming languages start array values from 0 as well. So the first element in your array is `myList(0)`. Of all of the versions of BASIC shown here, only BX-Basic will let you start numbering arrays from a number other than 0. It takes some getting used to when you've been raised to count from one, so be careful when using arrays. You can also use another variable to determine which element of an array you want to access, like so:

```
myList(whichCompartment)
```

This makes an array into a sort of super-variable. Because arrays are lists of numbered things, they are quite often used in connection with for-next loops, which do things multiple times while automatically incrementing an index variable. Just like regular variables, arrays have a type and a size and must be declared. See the following examples for details.

PBASIC

MBasic

```
' declare an array of 10 word variables:
pitch var word(10)

' declare other variables:
note var byte

' the 10 elements of the array called pitch are 10 notes of a scale.
' The BS-2 doesn't have enough memory for all 12 notes:
pitch(0) = 262    ' middle C
```

Analog Output

```
            pitch(1) = 277     ' C#
            pitch(2) = 294     ' D
            pitch(3) = 311     ' D#
            pitch(4) = 330     ' E
            pitch(5) = 349     ' F
            pitch(6) = 370     ' F#
            pitch(7) = 392     ' G
            pitch(8) = 415     ' G#
            pitch(9) = 440     ' A


        main:
            For note = 0 to 9
                    freqout 7, 1000, pitch(note), pitch(note)
            next
        goto main
```

PicBasic
Pro

```
' declare an array of 12 word variables:
pitch var word(12)


' declare other variables:
note var byte
thisNote var word


' the 12 elements of the array called pitch are the 12 notes of a scale:
pitch(0) = 262     ' middle C
pitch(1) = 277     ' C#
pitch(2) = 294     ' D
pitch(3) = 311     ' D#
pitch(4) = 330     ' E
pitch(5) = 349     ' F
pitch(6) = 370     ' F#
pitch(7) = 392     ' G
pitch(8) = 415     ' G#
pitch(9) = 440     ' A
pitch(10) = 466    ' A#
pitch(11) = 494    ' B


main:
    For note = 0 to 11
        ' so we put the pitch into a normal word variable:
        thisNote = pitch(note)
        ' play note:
        freqout portc.4, 1000, thisNote, thisNote
    next
goto main
```

```
(BX-Basic)    ' declare an array of 12 integer variables:
              dim pitch (0 to 11) as integer


              Sub Main()
                  ' note is a variable you're using
                  ' as a for-next loop counter, so it has to be
                  ' declared inside the main subroutine:
                  dim note as byte

                  ' the 12 elements of the array called pitch are the 12 notes of a scale:
                  pitch(0) = 262      ' middle C
                  pitch(1) = 277      ' C#
                  pitch(2) = 294      ' D
                  pitch(3) = 311      ' D#
                  pitch(4) = 330      ' E
                  pitch(5) = 349      ' F
                  pitch(6) = 370      ' F#
                  pitch(7) = 392      ' G
                  pitch(8) = 415      ' G#
                  pitch(9) = 440      ' A
                  pitch(10) = 466     ' A#
                  pitch(11) = 494     ' B

                  do
                      For note = 0 to 11
                          call freqout(13, pitch(note), pitch(note), 300)
                      next
                  loop
              End Sub
```

There are a few factors to consider in working with freqout.

First, when the freqout command is being executed, nothing else happens. In other words, if you give freqout a duration of one second, then the microcontroller won't read your sensors for that full second. The shorter you play the sound, though, the worse it will sound. So it's up to you to balance the quality of sound with the speed of reaction to sensors.

Second, if you're intending to make musical sounds, you must play frequencies that match the musical pitch of the notes you want to play.

RC Servo Motors

Perhaps the most exciting thing you can do as analog output is to control the movement of something. With ordinary DC motors, you can control whether or not they are on or off, and the speed, but controlling the direction or position takes more work and more components. RC servo motors have built into them the components needed to control the motor's position.

Analog Output

Inside the servo is a combination of gears and a potentiometer with some circuitry that allows you to set its position fairly quickly and precisely and within a 180-degree range of travel. RC servos are also relatively strong, considering that they can be powered by the same +5 volts power supply that drives your microcontroller. Although the motion is basically circular, you can add mechanical linkages to create linear motion as well. These motors are most commonly used to control the flaps of radio-controlled planes and boats, but for us, they are the first choice for moving almost anything small in physical computing.

Figure 6.16
RC servo motor.

Circuit

RC servos are very easy to control. They have three wires: power (+4 to 6 volts, 150 to 200 milliamps), ground, and control. Connect the +5 volt directly to a 5 volt power source that can supply at least one amp of current. Don't use the 5 volt output pin of your microcontroller; it hasn't got enough power. Connecting it to the same power feed before it reaches your microcontroller will work as long as that source is in the 4 to 6 volt range and can supply up to 200 milliamps of current. If you need a separate power supply for the servo motor, join the grounds of the two power supplies. Finally, attach the control pin to a pin on the microcontroller.

Programming

To set the angle of the motor, the microcontroller will send pulses on the pin attached to the motor's control wire. The servo expects a 5-volt positive pulse between 1 and 2

Figure 6.17
RC servo motor
connected to a
microcontroller.

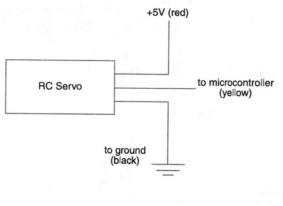

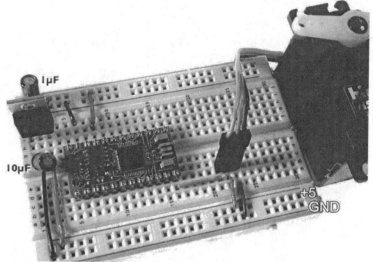

milliseconds (ms) long, repeated about 50 times per second (every 20 milliseconds). The duration of the pulse corresponds to a given angle of the motor. Different servos will vary, but for most servos 1-ms pulses will take them to one extreme of their travel, 1.5-ms pulses will take them to the center, and 2-ms pulses will take them to the other extreme. You have to send a given pulse to the motor every 20 milliseconds repeatedly, even if you don't want it to move, to keep it in one position. You'll find that with each servo, the minimum and maximum pulsewidths change a few microseconds. When you get a new servo, test its range with a simple program like the ones below, and adjust the pulsewidths as needed. Here's the pseudocode:

```
Set the increment in pulse width for movement of one degree
Set the minimum pulse width for beginning of the travel
Loop:
    Loop between positions 0- 180
    calculate the pulsewidth that corresponds to that position
    Send that pulse to the servo
    Delay until servo needs another pulse
End loop
```

Decoupling Capacitors: Stabilizing Your Voltage Regulator

Servo motors, like other motors, are inductive loads (see the "Inductive versus Resistive Loads" sidebar, earlier in this chapter), and their blowback voltage will affect your voltage regulator. One way to help minimize this problem is to put capacitors between power and ground on either side of the regulator. These are called *decoupling capacitors*. They smooth out the power, as the motor will cause spikes and dips when it turns on and off. Put a 1-microfarad capacitor between the +5 volt output and ground, and a 10-microfarad capacitor between the input and ground. It should look like Figure 6.18.

Figure 6.18
7805 voltage regulator with decoupling capacitors.

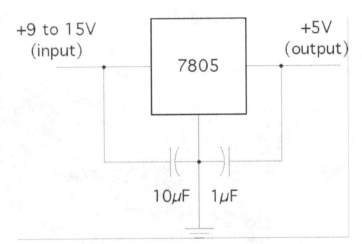

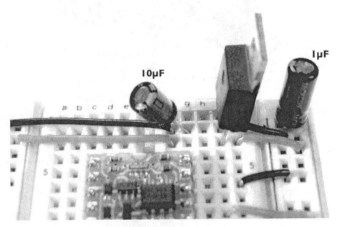

The data sheets for the 7805 voltage regulator actually calls for decoupling capacitors to be used always. We've been using them for microcontrollers for years without the decoupling capacitors without many problems, but if you've got them at hand, it can't hurt and it might help your application, particularly if it involves an inductive load such as a motor or solenoid (more on those in Chapter 9).

And here's the code. Each microprocessor has a different minimum pulsout time, so the code is different for each one. Try modifying the minAngle and maxAngle constants to see how it affects your servo's range:

PBASIC

```
' the servo is on pin 7.

angleVar var word

' set up constants with the minimum and maximum pulse widths
minAngle con 250
maxAngle con 1250

' set up a constant with the time between pulses:
refreshPeriod con 20

' set an initial pulsewidth:
angleVar = minAngle

main:
    'take the output pin low so we can pulse it high
    Low 7
    ' pulse the pin
    PulsOut 7, angleVar
    ' pause for as long as needed:
    pause refreshPeriod

    ' change the angle for the next time around:
    if angleVar > maxAngle Then
        angleVar = minAngle
    else
        angleVar = angleVar + 1
    endif
GoTo main
```

MBasic

```
' the servo is on pin 7.

angleVar var word

' set up constants with the minimum and maximum pulse widths
minAngle con 1200
maxAngle con 5000

' set up a constant with the time between pulses:
refreshPeriod con 20

' set an initial pulsewidth:
```

```
        angleVar = minAngle

main:
        'take the output pin low so we can pulse it high
        Low 7
        ' pulse the pin
        PulsOut 7, angleVar
        ' pause for as long as needed:
        pause refreshPeriod

        ' change the angle for the next time around:
        if angleVar > maxAngle Then
            angleVar = minAngle
        else
            angleVar = angleVar + 1
        endif
GoTo main
```

PicBasic Pro

```
' the servo is on pin C3

' note: if you use a crystal other than 4MHZ,
' it changes the pulsewidth of pulsout.
' For a 20MHZ crystal, for example, pulsout is five times as
' fast, so you'd need to multiply the pulse widths by 5
' with a 20 Mhz crystal.

DEFINE OSC 4
angleVar VAR word

' set up constants with the minimum and maximum pulse widths
minAngle con 50
maxAngle con 250

' set up a constant with the time between pulses:
refreshPeriod con 20

' set an initial pulsewidth:
angleVar = minAngle

main:
        'take the output pin low so we can pulse it high
        Low portc.3
        ' pulse the pin
        PulsOut portc.3, angleVar
        ' pause for as long as needed:
```

```
        pause refreshPeriod

        ' change the angle for the next time around:
        if angleVar > maxAngle Then
            angleVar = minAngle
        else
            angleVar = angleVar + 1
        endif
GoTo main
```

BX-Basic

```
' the servo is on pin 12.

Const minPulse as single = 0.0006 ' the minimum pulseWidth
Const maxPulse as single = 0.0023 ' the maximum pulseWidth
Const refreshPeriod as single = 0.02 ' the time between pulses

dim pulseWidth as single ' the servo's pulsewidth

Sub main()
    pulseWidth = minPulse
    do
        ' pulse the servo:
        call pulseOut(12, pulseWidth, 1)

        ' increase the pulsewidth for the next pulse:
        if pulseWidth <= maxPulse then
            pulseWidth = pulseWidth + 0.00001
        else
            pulseWidth = minPulse
        end if

        ' wait 20 milliseconds before pulsing again
        call delay(refreshPeriod)
    loop
End Sub
```

From Analog In to Analog Out: Scaling Functions

In converting the range of an analog input to an analog output, it's necessary to know the maximum and minimum values of each range so that a ranging function can be made up. Some ranging functions are very simple multiplications, and some take a little more work.

Ultimately your analog inputs will return an idiosyncratic range of numbers. The range will vary depending on many factors, such as the brand of transducer, the values of the resistors and capacitors in your circuit, quality of your microcontroller and the time of day. To use these numbers you will have to know the range your output device needs and convert the input range into that range. Usually this just requires some simple math. The first step is to empirically find the input range and the output range.

To learn the range of an analog input sensor you have to run the simple program shown above in the analog input section that just prints the input value out using a debug statement.

Adjust the transducer, trying to run it through its full range. Try to account for future changes in ambient conditions; for example, with a photocell, more light will come in the window during the day than at night. Study the incoming numbers to find the maximum and minimum.

The output range is quite often dictated first by the parameters that a function call can take. For example, a `freqout` command might expect numbers between 20 to 20,000. If we're sending information using serial communication, we try to stay within a range from 0 to 255, because we like sending data one byte at a time. The particular device you are talking to might require an even more specific range. To learn the output range of a servo, for example, you can use trial and error, starting with the standard 1 and 2 millisecond endpoints and adjusting the extremes of the pulsewidth until the motor doesn't move as expected. Servos being pulsed outside their range will typically move to the end of the range and shudder. Reduce the extreme end of the range until the shuddering stops.

Once you know the input range of your sensor and your desired output range, you can often use a fairly simple formula to convert from one to the other. For example, if your sensor ranges from 500 to 1500 and your output needs a range from 0 to 500, you subtract 500 and divide by 2.

What you've just done is to create a formula called a *scaling function* or *ranging function*. Let's take a slightly more difficult case and make a general formula for what you're doing. In this example, your input is a variable resistor, and your output is a servo. Let's say we get an input range from 30 to 500. You know that if you look at the two ranges side by side, you want to match them up, like this:

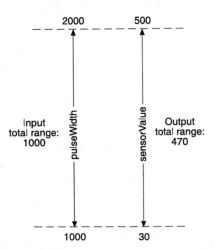

So we know that

$$\frac{(\text{PulseWidth} - \text{min. pulse})}{\text{pulseRange}} = \frac{(\text{SensorValue} - \text{min. sensor value})}{\text{sensorRange}}$$

You can rearrange this to get the pulsewidth. First, multiply both sides by `pulseRange`:

$$(\text{PulseWidth} - \text{min. pulse}) = \frac{(\text{SensorValue} - \text{min. sensor value}) \times \text{pulseRange}}{\text{sensorRange}}$$

Then add the minimum pulse to both sides, like so:

$$\text{PulseWidth} = \frac{(\text{SensorValue} - \text{min. sensor value}) \times \text{pulseRange}}{\text{sensorRange}} + \text{min. pulse}$$

That's it. It seems a bit more complex than the first example, but it's the same thing, only more generalized.

There are a couple of things to keep in mind about math on a microcontroller. Most microcontrollers can only deal with integer division. This can create rounding problems. For example, if your output range is 1 to 100 and your input range is 1 to 75, you would ideally like to scale your inputs by 100/75 or multiply them by 1.3. In systems that only do integer division, like all of our microcontrollers except the BX-24, 100/75 returns 1, not 1.3. You could either accept the 1 to 75 range, or multiply by 13 and then divide by 10. If you do the latter, you'd need to use a word or integer size variable because you'll be handling numbers greater than 255 (for example, $75 \times 13 = 975$ before you divide by 10 to get 97.5, which gets truncated to 97).

Even if you are very careful determining your input ranges, there is often a fluke reading now and again that falls outside the observed range (unless the range is the full range of the ADC). After determining the expected range, you should ensure that the incoming values never fall outside that range, by using `if` statements or `min`/`max` statements. If you don't, you'll see that bytes do not respond gracefully to being given values above 255 or below 0. They roll over, so that 256 becomes 0, 257 becomes 1, and so forth. Likewise, –1 becomes 255, –2 becomes 254, and so forth. Had you used a byte variable in the example above, 75×13 would equal 207! Why? 975 is $(3 \times 256) + 207$. The byte variable rolled over four times and ended at 207.

When you use division to scale down a number, you are losing resolution. Sometimes this is desirable for smoothing erratic readings, but other times it makes your application feel chunky. On the other hand, multiplying to increase the range does not really increase the resolution. When possible, try to find ways to avoid scaling, or scale as smoothly as possible using an accurate ranging function.

When you're building the input circuit yourself from one of the examples above, you can simplify these functions by choosing the right components. For example, if you're using the `rctime` function, try using a smaller capacitor and resistor, because the capacitor will charge and discharge faster, meaning you get a lower range of numbers. In the PBasic and MBasic examples below, the resistor and capacitor values are listed. Try different ones to see what happens. If you're using an ADC circuit with a variable resistor, try a different base resistor. In the PicBasic Pro and BX Basic examples below, changing the base resistor gave a much easier range to work with.

Below is a typical use of ranging functions. The input is a flex sensor, and the output is a servo motor. Flexing the sensor through its range moves the servo through its range. You know you can change the flex sensor's range by changing the components around it, but the servo motor has a fixed range. First, get the flex sensor's readings as an analog input and try different resistor and/or capacitor values until you get a range that's easy to work with. Then apply the formula. Here's the pseudocode:

```
Loop:
    Read sensor
    Convert its value to a value in the range of the servo
    Pulse the servo
End loop
```

And here's the actual code:

PBASIC

```
' This example uses pin 0 for the analog input (flex sensor)
' the servo is on pin 2.

' set up constants with the minimum and maximum values you get from the sensor.
' Before you can set these constants, you will have to
' determine what they are by experimentation
' In this example, a flex sensor (50 - 100K) was used with
' a 0.01 capacitor and a 10-Ohm resistor:
minSensorReading CON 5
maxSensorReading CON 130
' a variable to hold the range:
sensorRange VAR Word
SensorRange = maxSensorReading - minSensorReading

' set up constants with the minimum and maximum pulse widths
minAngle CON 250
maxAngle CON 1250
' a variable to hold the range:
angleRange var word
angleRange = maxAngle - minAngle

' set up a constant with the time between pulses:
refreshPeriod CON 20

RCVar VAR Word       ' the raw sensor value
scalerVar VAR Word       ' the scaling factor
angleVar VAR Word     ' the servo's pulsewidth
```

```
    pause 500         ' wait 0.5 seconds

Main:
    HIGH 0
    PAUSE 1
    RCTIME 0,1,RCVar
    ' this is a good place to debug your sensor value for testing:
    ' DEBUG "RCVar: ", DEC RCVar, 10, 13


    ' here is the application of the scaling function.
    scalerVar = (angleRange / sensorRange)
    angleVar = (RCVar - minSensorReading) * scalerVar
    AngleVar = angleVar + minAngle


    ' this is a good place to debug your angle value for testing:
    ' DEBUG "AngleVar: ", DEC angleVar, 10,13

    'min and max limits in case an input value strays from the range
    IF angleVar > maxAngle THEN
        angleVar = maxAngle
    ENDIF
    IF angleVar < minAngle THEN
        angleVar = minAngle
    ENDIF

    ' pulse the servo:
    LOW 0
    PULSOUT 2, angleVar
    ' wait 20 milliseconds:
    PAUSE refreshPeriod
GOTO main
```

MBasic

```
' This example uses pin 0 for the analog input (flex sensor)
' the servo is on pin 2.


' set up constants with the minimum and maximum values you get from the sensor.
' Before you can set these constants, you will have to
' determine what they are by experimentation
' In this example, a flex sensor (50 - 100K) was used with
' a 0.01 capacitor and a 10-Ohm resistor:
minSensorReading CON 5
maxSensorReading CON 130
' a variable to hold the range:
sensorRange VAR Word
```

Scaling Functions

```
            SensorRange = maxSensorReading - minSensorReading

            ' set up constants with the minimum and maximum pulse widths
            minAngle CON 1200
            maxAngle CON 5000
            ' a variable to hold the range:
            angleRange var word
            angleRange = maxAngle - minAngle

            ' set up a constant with the time between pulses:
            refreshPeriod CON 20

            RCVar VAR Word        ' the raw sensor value
            scalerVar VAR Word       ' the scaling factor
            angleVar VAR Word ' the servo's pulsewidth
            pause 500          ' wait 0.5 seconds

        Main:
             HIGH 0
             PAUSE 1
             RCTIME 0,0,RCVar
             ' this is a good place to debug your sensor value for testing:
             ' DEBUG "RCVar: ", DEC RCVar, 10, 13

             ' here is the application of the scaling function.
             scalerVar = (angleRange / sensorRange)
             angleVar = (RCVar - minSensorReading) * scalerVar
             AngleVar = angleVar + minAngle

             ' this is a good place to debug your angle value for testing:
             ' DEBUG "AngleVar: ", DEC angleVar, 10,13

             'min and max limits in case an input value strays from the range
             IF angleVar > maxAngle THEN
                 angleVar = maxAngle
             ENDIF
             IF angleVar < minAngle THEN
                 angleVar = minAngle
             ENDIF

             ' pulse the servo:
             LOW 0
             PULSOUT 2, angleVar
             ' wait 20 milliseconds:
             PAUSE refreshPeriod
        GOTO main
```

PicBasic
Pro

```
' the servo is on pin RC3
' the sensor is on pin RA0
DEFINE OSC 4

' Set Debug pin port
DEFINE DEBUG_REG PORTC
' Set Debug pin BIT
DEFINE DEBUG_BIT 6
' Set Debug baud rate
DEFINE DEBUG_BAUD 9600
' Set Debug mode: 0 = true, 1 = inverted
DEFINE DEBUG_MODE 1

' Define ADCIN parameters
DEFINE ADC_BITS 10          ' Set number of bits in result
DEFINE ADC_CLOCK 3      ' Set clock source (3=rc)
DEFINE ADC_SAMPLEUS 20      ' Set sampling time in uS

ADCVar var word         ' the raw sensor value
angleVar var word ' the servo's pulsewidth
scalerVar var word        ' the scaling factor

' set up constants with the minimum and maximum values you get from the sensor
' before you can set these constants, you will have to
' determine what they are by experimentation.
' read the sensor as an analog input, then change the base
' resistor until you get a range you like.
' In this example, a flex sensor (50 - 100K) was used with
' a 1K base resistor:
minSensorReading con 5
maxSensorReading con 110

' a variable to hold the range:
SensorRange var word
SensorRange = maxSensorreading - minSensorReading

' set up constants with the minimum and maximum pulse widths.
' test your servo alone to see if these ranges work best for you.
minAngle con 50
maxAngle con 250
' a variable to hold the range:
angleRange var word
angleRange = maxAngle - minAngle

' set up a constant with the time between pulses:
```

```
refreshPeriod con 20

TRISA = %11111111      ' Set PORTA to all input
ADCON1 = %10000010     ' Set PORTA analog and right justify result
Pause 500          ' Wait .5 second

main:
    ' read ADC channel 0:
    adcin 0, ADCVar
    ' this is a good place to debug your sensor value for testing:
    'debug "ADCVar: ", DEC ADCVar, 13,10

    'here is the application of the scaling function:

    angleVar = ((ADCVar - minSensorReading)* angleRange)
    angleVar = angleVar / sensorRange
    angleVar = AngleVar + minAngle
    ' this is a good place to debug your angle value for testing:
    ' debug "AngleVar", DEC angleVar, 13, 10

    'apply max and min limits in case an input value strays from the range
    if angleVar > maxAngle then
        angleVar = maxAngle
    endif
    if angleVar < minAngle then
        angleVar = minAngle
    endif

    ' pulse the servo:

    Low portc.3
    PulsOut portc.3, angleVar

    ' wait 20 milliseconds before pulsing again:
    pause refreshPeriod
GoTo main
```

(BX-Basic)

```
' This example uses pin 13 for the analog input
' the servo is on pin 12.

' set up constants with the minimum and maximum values you get from the sensor
' before you can set these constants, you will have to
' determine what they are by experimentation.
' read the sensor as an analog input, then change the base
' resistor until you get a range you like.
```

```
' In this example, a flex sensor (50 - 100K) was used with
' a 1K base resistor:
Const minSensorReading as integer = 5
Const maxSensorReading as integer = 110
' a variable to hold the range from min to max:
Dim sensorRange as integer


' set up constants with the minimum and maximum pulse widths.
' test your servo alone to see if these ranges work best for you first:
Const minAngle as single = 0.0006
Const maxAngle as single = 0.0023
' a variable to hold the range from min to max:
Dim angleRange as single


Const refreshPeriod as single = 0.02 ' the time between pulses



dim angleVar as single ' the servo's pulsewidth
dim ScalerVar as single ' the scaling factor
dim ADCVar as integer ' for the raw sensor reading

Sub main()
    ' set the angle range and sensor range from the constants:
    angleRange = maxAngle - minAngle
    sensorRange = maxSensorReading - minSensorReading

    call delay(0.5) ' start program with a half-second delay
    do
        ADCvar = getADC(13)
        ' this is a good place to debug your sensor value for testing:
        'debug.print "ADCVar = " ; cstr(ADCVar)

        'here is the application of the scaling function:
        scalerVar = angleRange/csng(sensorRange)
        angleVar = csng(ADCVar - minSensorReading) * scalerVar + minAngle

        ' this is a good place to debug your angle value for testing:
        'debug.print "AngleVar = " ; cstr(angleVar)

        ' apply max and min limits in case
        'an input value strays from the range
        if angleVar > maxAngle then
            angleVar = maxAngle
        end if
        if angleVar < minAngle then
            angleVar = minAngle
```

```
            end if

            ' pulse the servo:
            call pulseOut(12, angleVar, 1)

            ' wait 20 milliseconds before pulsing again
            call delay(refreshPeriod)
        loop
    End Sub
```

Conclusion

Nearly every physical computing project will use some combination of analog inputs or outputs. Your first step should be to identify the input and output needs of your project, and then categorize them as analog or digital. Use this section first to get all your inputs and outputs to work on their own, and then integrate them using ranging functions. Once you've worked out the scaling function, keep the program that does it on hand as a separate, small program for debugging purposes, and copy the code from it into your larger program as needed.

7
Communicating between Computers

While it's possible to realize many physical computing projects with only a microprocessor running the whole show, it's more common to use a couple of computers, each a specialist for a different part of your project. One of the most common configurations for physical computing systems is to have a microcontroller read a sensor, and then send the value of the sensor to a multimedia computer. The multimedia computer then changes the playback of a video or the pitch of a sound, or activates some other multimedia response. The reverse of this configuration is also common. For example, a multimedia computer sends the coordinates of the mouse to the microcontroller to position a motor. In some cases, the microprocessor may be controlling a video or audio mixer, a servo motor controller board, a MIDI synthesizer, or some other specialized device. In any application where it's necessary to make one computer talk to another, the most common (and usually the easiest) method is to use *serial communication*.

In serial communication you send digital pulses one after another back and forth between computers. There has to be agreement on both sides regarding the physical connections over which the pulses travel. There also has to be agreement about the rate, the voltage, and the grouping of these pulses. A *protocol* is the set of parameters that the two devices agree upon in order to send information. There are many different protocols for serial communication, each suited to a different application.

One of the most common serial protocols is the *RS-232 serial protocol*. An RS-232 serial port is found on most multimedia computers because prior to USB (Universal Serial Bus, another more complicated serial protocol), most personal computers used RS-232 to communicate with modems, printers, and other devices. Even if your multimedia computer doesn't have an RS-232 serial port, it can be outfitted with one by using a USB-to-serial adaptor.

Another protocol, called *TTL serial*, is used to talk directly between microcontrollers. These two protocols, RS-232 and TTL, are similar enough (see the "Electrical Agreement" section below) to make communication between microcontrollers and multimedia computers relatively easy. This chapter will cover everything you need to know to make this connection happen so the sensors on your microcontroller can control your multimedia machine and vice versa.

There are other things besides a multimedia computer that you might want your microcontroller to talk to: for example, a video switcher, a sound synthesizer, a video camera, a DVD player, a distant multimedia computer, or another IC chip. There are also many different protocols for these applications: Midi, DMX-512, X10, USB, RS-485, UDP/IP, TCP/IP, and so on, We will cover some of these other communications methods in the second part of this book. For now the RS-232 and TTL protocols are going to give you the ability to communicate between more computers sooner than any of these others.

Physical Agreement

The first step in mastering serial communication is making the physical connection between the two computers. The easiest way to do this is to use a 9-pin serial cable, like the one you used to program the computer, and a serial connector like the one you built in Chapter 3.

NOTE

What about wireless?

In Chapter 12, "More Communication between Devices," we'll discuss options for creating wireless connections between computers, but we strongly recommend that you get your application working first with a wired connection, and only then get into wireless solutions. It's much easier to troubleshoot a wireless connection when you know you've gotten all the other details correct using a wired connection.

When you connected the microcontroller to the multimedia computer to program it, you used the multimedia computer's serial port. If your computer doesn't have a serial port, you probably used a USB-to-serial adaptor. In either case, you're already familiar with the physical connection to your multimedia computer. If you have two serial ports on your multimedia computer, you can continue to use one for programming and use the second for serial communication by getting a second cable and making a second serial connector.

NOTE

Macintosh users, this is the part of the book you've been waiting for. Though programming a microcontroller is an activity limited to the Windows platform, serial communication can occur between microcontrollers and Windows PCs, Macs, Linux machines, or any other multimedia computer with a serial port. Unless your Mac was made before 1999, you'll need a serial-to-USB adaptor (we recommend the Keyspan USA19HS); but once you've got one, your Mac and your microcontroller can begin chatting away.

Serial cables appear to have lots of wires and pins, but you'll only use three of them: one wire for sending electrical pulses, another for receiving the electrical pulses, and a third for a common ground so each device has a reference point for the voltage level at which the other is sending data. Which pin does which job is the first of the agreements that has to be made in order to facilitate serial communication. See Figure 7.1 for the pinouts of a typical DB-9 style serial port.

Figure 7.1
A DB9-style serial connector, showing the pin numbers for serial communication.

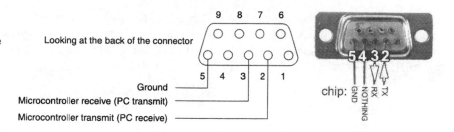

The extra pin on your serial connector, pin 4 in Figure 7.1, is used by the programming environment only, as a way to get the microcontroller's attention during programming. It's not used for what we're doing in this chapter. Nevertheless, you can use a serial connector just like the one you built for programming a Stamp-like module for serial communication and just leave that pin unattached.

The next step is to decide which of the microcontroller's I/O pins will be used for serial communication. If you look at a diagram of a Stamp-like microcontroller, you might be tempted to use the pins in the upper left that are labeled TX, RX, and GND. These labels stand for *transmit, receive,* and *ground.* This is a serial port, and it's already set up to speak the RS-232 protocol, but it's most convenient to reserve this port for programming the chip. You can arbitrarily pick any I/O pins and assign them in software as the RX pin (where the microcontroller receives data) or the TX pin (where it sends data to the multimedia computer). You can connect the ground wire to the ground strip on the side of your prototyping board.

Write down which pins you assign for RX and TX because you'll need to know it when you write software for serial communication. The biggest mistake that people make at this point is to connect their TX pin of the multimedia computer to their TX pin of their microcontroller and the RX to the RX. This does not make for a very good conversation. The TX pin of the microcontroller should be connected to the RX pin of the multimedia computer, and vice versa.

PICs and other lower-level microcontrollers may have I/O pins noted in their pin diagrams as RX and TX. This means that they've got a built-in serial receiver-transmitter assigned to those pins. If you were programming the PIC in its low-level assembly language, this would make your life much easier. When you're using our programming examples in PicBasic Pro, this doesn't make a significant difference, and you can use any pins that you wish. However, it's good form to use them anyway, which we'll do in our examples.

Timing Agreement

The next level of agreement is the timing of the pulses. This has to be set regardless of what serial protocol you're using. To be able to count the pulses, there has to be agreement about how fast they are coming. You will be using *asynchronous serial communication,* in which both devices have their own separate clock to keep track of time[1]. The sender sends pulses representing the data being transmitted at an agreed-upon data rate, and the receiver

---

[1] *Synchronous serial communication* dedicates another connection between the two devices to send pulses that set the rate of data transfer. Synchronous serial communication is common when talking to other IC chips. Only the controlling device has a clock in synchronous serial communication. We will cover it in Chapter 12, "More Communication between Devices."

listens for pulses at that same rate. The timing of the pulses is called the *data rate* or the *baud rate*. You'll usually use a data rate of 9600 pulses per second. Typically you group 8 pulses together. This means that you could send one group of 8 pulses (also called a *byte*) per millisecond, which is faster than human perception.

Electrical Agreement

After you make the physical connection, you have to agree on the voltage levels of the electrical pulses you will be sending over them. As mentioned earlier, most of our microcontrollers are using the TTL protocol, where pulses are either 5 volts or 0 volts. But RS-232 uses –12 volts and 12 volts. The good news is that we have never encountered a multimedia computer that could not understand the TTL voltage levels. However, the voltage coming from a proper RS-232 port might be too much for your microcontroller. If so, you should place a 22-kilohm resistor in the connection between the TX of the multimedia computer and the RX of your microcontroller. All of the microcontrollers discussed in this book should work fine without it, though.

After you decide on the voltage level of a pulse, you have to agree on the *logic*. With *inverted* logic, a positive pulse signifies a 0 or false. With *true* logic, a positive pulse signifies a 1 or true. This is another way that RS-232 and TTL differ. RS-232 uses inverted logic: –12 volts = true, +12 volts = false. TTL uses true logic: 5 volts = true, 0 volts = false. This is rarely an issue because your microcontroller's serial commands can adjust the logic for you most of the time.

There are a few other, lesser details to the agreement. You have to decide on whether there will be an extra pulse before or after the message (referred to as *start bits* or *stop bits*), whether you will sacrifice one of the 8 pulses for parity error checking, and whether the 8 pulses are coming highest value first or lowest value first. The most common configuration is 9600 bits per second, 8 data bits, 1 stop bit, no parity. You'll use this as your default. The 9600 bits per second rate is generally the only parameter that varies from this configuration.

Package Size

Finally, there has to be some agreement as to how the sequence of pulses is interpreted. By interpreting them in groups of 8 (a byte), you can send numbers between 0 and 255. The byte is the standard number of bits for storing data in a computer, so you'll see it a lot. See the "Variables" section of Chapter 5 to review this idea.

Serial data is passed byte by byte from one device to another. It's up to the programmer to decide how each device (computer or microcontroller) should interpret those bytes: when the beginning of a message is, when the end is, and what to do with the bytes in between.

If you're only sending one changing number (perhaps the value received from an analog sensor), and that number is less than 255, you know it can fit in a byte. This kind of message is easy. Just send the same byte over and over, and the computer can pick it up at any time. If you're sending more than that (and you usually are), things are a little more complicated. The receiving computer has to know when the message starts and when it ends.

Different serial devices will use different codes to perform different actions. If a device, like a tape deck or laser disk player, is serially controllable, there will usually be a section in its manual outlining the messages it expects to receive and at what baud rates it expects to receive them.

Numbers or Letters: Using ASCII

Every grouping of pulses can be interpreted as a particular value by a computer and stored using a series of 0s and 1s, as we explained in the "Variables" section in Chapter 5. This is fine for communication between machines. If the machines ultimately have to communicate with people, you will often want to represent the values of these bytes using readable text instead of numbers. You need a way for the bits and bytes to be converted into alphanumeric characters that people can read.

Fortunately, there is a standard system, called the ASCII[2] code, that assigns each text character (letter, number, or punctuation mark) a specific value from 0 to 255. For example, capital A is ASCII value 65. This chart can be found in many computer manuals' indexes and all over the Web. Table 7.1 lays it out for you.

Table 7.1
ASCII Chart

0	NUL	16	DLE	32	SP	48	0	64	@	80	P	96	`	112	p
1	SOH	17	DC1	33	!	49	1	65	A	81	Q	97	a	113	q
2	STX	18	DC2	34	"	50	2	66	B	82	R	98	b	114	r
3	ETX	19	DC3	35	#	51	3	67	C	83	S	99	c	115	s
4	EOT	20	DC4	36	$	52	4	68	D	84	T	100	d	116	t
5	ENQ	21	NAK	37	%	53	5	69	E	85	U	101	e	117	u
6	ACK	22	SYN	38	&	54	6	70	F	86	V	102	f	118	v
7	BEL	23	ETB	39	'	55	7	71	G	87	W	103	g	119	w
8	BS	24	CAN	40	(	56	8	72	H	88	X	104	h	120	x
9	HT	25	EM	41	)	57	9	73	I	89	Y	105	i	121	y
10	LF	26	SUB	42	*	58	:	74	J	90	Z	106	j	122	z
11	VT	27	ESC	43	+	59	;	75	K	91	[	107	k	123	{
12	FF	28	FS	44	,	60	<	76	L	92	\	108	l	124	|
13	CR	29	GS	45	-	61	=	77	M	93	]	109	m	125	}
14	SO	30	RS	46	.	62	>	78	N	94	^	110	n	126	~
15	SI	31	US	47	/	63	?	79	O	95	_	111	o	127	DEL

[2] ASCII (American Standard Code for Information Interchange) is very common and used by many devices as part of their serial protocol. As you can tell by the name, ASCII is biased toward English alphanumeric communication. It's convenient in that any ASCII symbol can be represented in one byte, but it's also limited. Other alphanumeric systems with more characters than the limited number in the Latin (English) alphabet are not represented in ASCII. Other schemes will take more than a byte to represent one character. An expanded code called Unicode, a superset of ASCII, is used to represent most of these character sets.

Confusion sometimes pops up here because there are two ways to send numbers between computers. For example, if you get a sensor reading of 12, you can send a byte with a value of 12. This is sometimes called the *raw value*, meaning that it's not encoded using ASCII or any other code. Or you can send a string of two bytes of ASCII-encoded text, "1" and "2" or "12." You can send the reading either way. All that really matters is that you are consistent in your interpretation on the receiving end. However, if you send the text string as ASCII characters ("12") and then interpret it as a raw value on the receiving side, you might think you had received two sensor readings, 49 and 50, when you really received one: the ASCII codes for "1" and "2." In general, sending things as a raw value rather than as a text string is more efficient. A single byte can contain any number between 0 and 255. But when you send things as text, it takes as many bytes as there are digits. For example, "2" would still only take one byte, but "22" would take two bytes and "222" would take three bytes. At the standard baud rate (9600, or one character per millisecond) you are unlikely to feel this inefficiency for just a couple of numbers.

Another point of confusion stems from the fact that the first 32 entries in the ASCII table are *control characters*, which are invisible when interpreted as text characters. Some of these invisible characters, like the "carriage return" (ASCII 13) and "line feed" (ASCII 10), are familiar to you from word processing. Some of them, like "bell" (ASCII 7), are left over from the old teletype days. Sending these numbers can cause confusion in environments that can only interpret text characters (see "Testing with Terminal Software" below) because either nothing shows up, or you get a bunch of garbage characters (squares, smiley faces, and other dingbat characters).

HEXADECIMAL NOTATION

There is yet another system for sending a number between 0 and 255. Numbers can be converted to base 16, also called *hexadecimal*, as opposed to the decimal system, which is the normal base 10 counting system. In hexadecimal, you have 16 digits. You use the ten digits from base 10 (0 through 9), and then use the letters A through F for a total of sixteen possible values per digit. The hexadecimal system uses two bytes to transmit a number between 0 and 255 instead of the three you'd need if you represent the number in base 10. For example, the decimal number 14 is represented by the character E in hexadecimal. The decimal number 156 is 9C in hexadecimal (9 groups of 16, and 12 ones, represented by the letter C). Counting in hexadecimal, you can send the values from 0 to 255 with only two ASCII characters (0 to FF) instead of the three you'd need in decimal (0 to 255). See Charles Petzold's excellent book *Code: The Hidden Language of Computer Hardware and Software* (Microsoft Press, 2000) for a good explanation of hexadecimal and other counting systems used in programming computers.

Software for the Microcontroller

Before you can do anything else, you need to be able to send and receive a byte. The commands and syntax for doing this will be different for each microcontroller and each different programming environment on a multimedia computer. The basic steps will be the same on each platform, though, so we've outlined them in pseudocode below. You'll start by sending serial, then move on to receiving serial.

Serial Output from a Microcontroller

Here's the pseudocode for the basic steps you'll take:

```
Set up a place to store incoming serial data
Set up a place to store outgoing serial data
Define which I/O pins are to be used for serial TX and RX
Set the baud rate and other serial protocol parameters
Open the serial port

Loop:
Read sensors
    Send data out
End loop
```

NOTE

There's a significant difference between the programming steps for BX-Basic and the rest of the languages we're using, so we'll start by explaining serial output for pBasic, mBasic, and PicBasic Pro, then revisit the ideas to explain in BX-Basic.

For all of our serial examples, you'll use the same pins. Remember, on the Stamp-like modules the same physical pins have different names, depending on the platform. See Figure 7.2 for how the serial connector connects to each.

Figure 7.2
Serial connections for a Stamp-like module and for a PIC 18F452.

Pins Used for Serial Examples

MICROCONTROLLER	TX	RX
Basic Stamp 2	6	7
Basic Atom Pro24	6	7
PIC	portC.6	portC.7
BX-24	11	12

PBASIC, MBasic, PicBasic Pro

In PBASIC, MBasic, and PicBasic Pro, many of the serial steps are included in one of two commands: serin or serout. To set up a place for incoming data, you simply declare a variable. To set up a place for outgoing data, you can declare another variable, or you can send the literal data out. The I/O pins, baud rate, and serial protocols are set each time you send or receive, in one command. The example below sends the message "Hello World" out the serial port over and over.

PBASIC
```
Main:
        Serout 6, 16468, ["Hello World!", 10, 13]
    Goto main
```

MBasic
```
Main:
        Serout 6, N9600, ["Hello World!", 10, 13]
    Goto main
```

PicBasic Pro
```
Main:
        Serout2 portC.6, 16468, ["Hello World!", 10, 13]
    Goto main
```

NOTE
PIC users: there are several serial in and out options in PicBasic Pro. We'll be using serout2 and serin2, which we've found to be the most compatible with pBasic, and the most stable. Wherever we refer to serin or serout in the general text, use serin2 and serout2.

The serout command (serout2 on the PIC) has three parameters: the I/O pin, the serial configuration, and the data to be sent. The number 16468 is the serial communications mode parameter. In MBasic, it's replaced by a constant defined by the compiler. This particular value sets the serial protocol for 9600 baud, 8 data bits, 1 stop bit, no parity, inverted logic. For details on how to decode this number, see the manual for your microcontroller. You'll find the details and some other common serial settings listed under the serout command.

The brackets hold the actual data to be sent. Items to be sent out are separated by commas. By putting the literal message in quotes, you tell the microcontroller to send each letter's ASCII value. Fourteen bytes are sent by the example above, one for each letter or punctuation mark, and two for the numbers following the quoted phrase. Because those numbers aren't in quotes, the actual values 10 and 13 are sent in the last two bytes. If you look up these values in the ASCII chart in Table 7.1, you'll see that the number 10 represents a line feed (LF) and the number 13 represents a carriage return.

If you want to send information from a sensor, put that information in a variable:

(PBASIC)
```
' TX is connected to pin 6; switch is connected to pin 0
switchVar var byte
input 0


Main:
    SwitchVar = in0
    Serout 6, 16468, ["Hello World!", DEC switchVar, 10, 13]
Goto main
```

(MBasic)
```
' TX is connected to pin 6; switch is connected to pin 0
switchVar var byte
input 0
Main:
    SwitchVar = in0
    Serout 6, N9600, ["Hello World!", DEC switchVar, 10, 13]
Goto main
```

(PicBasic Pro)
```
' TX is connected to pin C6; switch is connected to pin B0
switchVar var byte
input portb.0


Main:
    SwitchVar = portb.0
    Serout2 portC.6, 16468, ["Hello World!", DEC switchVar, 10, 13]
Goto main
```

The instruction DEC in front of the switchVar variable in the serout command tells the microprocessor to convert the variable's actual value (which will be a 0 or a 1, since it's coming from the switch) to its ASCII representation ("0" or "1"). You might want to send a message only if the switch is closed:

(PBASIC)
```
' TX is connected to pin 6; switch is connected to pin 0
switchVar var byte
input 0
Main:
```

Serial Output from a Microcontroller

```
        SwitchVar = in0
        If switchVar = 1 then
            Serout 6, 16468, ["Hello World!", DEC switchVar, 10, 13]
        endif
    Goto main
```

MBasic
```
' TX is connected to pin 6; switch is connected to pin 0
switchVar var byte
input 0

Main:
    SwitchVar = in0
    If switchVar = 1 then
        Serout 6, N9600, ["Hello World!", DEC switchVar, 10, 13]
    endif
Goto main
```

PicBasic Pro
```
' TX is connected to pin C6; switch is connected to pin B0

switchVar var byte
input portb.0

Main:
    SwitchVar = portb.0
    If switchVar = 1 then
        Serout2 portC.6, 16468, ["Hello World!", DEC switchVar, 10, 13]
    endif
Goto main
```

BX-Basic

The BX-24's serial commands are slightly more complex than our other microcontrollers. The place that you store incoming and outgoing data isn't a simple variable, but a data structure called a *queue*. Queues are very similar to arrays, which were discussed in Chapter 6. BX-Basic also separates the serial configuration step from the sending step. This means that there's more code to write before your main loop.

The reason for this is that the BX-24 serial is *buffered*. This means that in a complex program, you can have serial data coming in and going out while other things are going on. This is not possible on the other microcontroller environments shown here. The two queues are the input buffer and the output buffer. To imagine how they work, think of peas rolling through a straw: the first byte in the queue is the first byte out the other end. You put bytes in a particular sequence and receive them out the other end in the same sequence. This is called *first-in, first-out*, and you'll often see it abbreviated as FIFO. All multimedia computers have FIFO buffers as well, so that they can keep the operating system running while using the serial ports. A queue in BX-Basic is an array that's been set up as an FIFO buffer.

In order to keep track of the order of the bytes in a queue, BX-Basic uses some of the bytes (9, to be precise) assigned to the queue. So to define a queue, you give it an array of bytes that's 9 bytes longer than you want the queue to be. To get a 1-byte queue, you give it a 10-byte array.

First you define two arrays that will be the input and output queues. Your input queue in the example below is 9 bytes long and your output queue is 40 bytes long (the corresponding queues will be 1 and 31 bytes long, respectively). They can be longer, if you want them to be, but you'll find it easier if they're at least this long.

Once you've set up your buffers, you define which pins you'll use for serial communication and the communication parameters. The defineCom3() command defines a serial port on the BX. It has three parameters: the RX pin, the TX pin, and the serial mode. The serial mode defines the start bits, stop bits, parity setting, and logic, but not the data rate. The data rate is set when you actually open the serial port using the openCom() command.

OpenCom() has four parameters: the first is the serial port you're opening the BX has two serial ports, called COM1 and COM3 for arcane reasons. COM1 is always pins 1 and 2 of the chip, and you'll seldom use it. See the section on MIDI in Chapter 12 for details. The second parameter is the data rate. The third and fourth parameters are the queues to use for the input buffer and output buffer, respectively.

There are two commands you'll use for sending serial data out, putQueue() and putQueueStr(). You'll start with putQueueStr(). The putQueueStr() command has two parameters: the queue you're putting the string in, and the string you're putting in it. Here's a "Hello world!" example:

(BX-Basic)

```
' TX is connected to pin 11

Dim InputVar(1 To 10) As Byte
Dim OutputVar(1 To 40) As Byte
Dim outputString as String

Sub main()
    ' turn the arrays into queues:
    Call openQueue(InputVar, 10)
    Call openQueue(OutputVar, 40)

    ' define the TX and RX pins and the serial parameters
    ' (except for baud rate):
    Call defineCom3(12, 11, bx1000_1000)

    ' open the serial port for sending and receiving at 9600 baud:
    Call openCom(3, 9600, InputVar, OutputVar)

    ' make a message to send
```

Serial Output from a Microcontroller

```
            OutputString = "Hello World!" & chr(10) & chr(13)

        do
             ' put a string in the output queue to send:
             Call putQueueStr(outputVar, outputString)
        Loop
    End sub
```

Sending a number variable is similar. However, instead of the putQueueStr() command, use the putQueue() command. The putQueue() command has three parameters: the queue, the variable you're putting in the queue, and the size of the variable. Note that since switchVar is a byte variable, and the values 10 and 13 both fit within a byte, you're sending one byte at a time.

 NOTE
You cannot supply the putQueue() function with a literal like "3" or 3. You have to put the data you want to send into a variable before giving it to the putQueue() function.

BX-Basic

```
' TX is connected to pin 11.

Dim InputVar(1 To 10) As Byte
Dim OutputVar(1 To 40) As Byte
Dim switchVar as byte

Sub main()
    ' turn the arrays into queues:
    Call openQueue(InputVar, 10)
    Call openQueue(OutputVar, 40)

    ' define the TX and RX pins and the serial parameters
    ' (except for baud rate):
    Call defineCom3(12, 11, bx1000_1000)

    ' open the serial port for sending and receiving at 9600 baud:
    Call openCom(3, 9600, InputVar, OutputVar)

    ' make a message to send

    do
        switchVar = getPin(12) + 48
        ' send it out the serial port:
        call putQueue(OutputBuffer, thisByte, 1)
        switchVar = 10
        call putQueue(OutputBuffer, thisByte, 1)
```

```
                    switchVar = 13
                    call putQueue(OutputBuffer, thisByte, 1)
                                        Loop
        End sub
```

TIP

Why did you add 48 to `switchVar` before you sent it out? It's a quick way to convert between a raw value and an ASCII interpretation for single-digit numbers. You know that the `getPin()` command will give you a 0 or a 1. Because you're printing this out to a terminal program that only interprets bytes as ASCII characters (more on this to come), you want to see the text 0 or 1, not the raw values 0 or 1, which are invisible control characters discussed in the section above, "Numbers or Letters: Using ASCII." You know that the character 0 is ASCII value 48, and 1 is ASCII 49, so by adding 48 to the values that you get from `getPin()`, you get the characters 0 and 1. Another reason is that the 0 character is reserved by some software (like Flash's XMLSocket) as an end of transmission character. If it is this easy to avoid using it, you should do so.

Testing with an LED

At the electrical level, serial communication consists of a series of timed pulses of voltage coming from the TX line of one computer to the RX line of the other. As a result, the most basic test you can do to see that your microcontroller is sending serial data out is to put an LED from the TX line to ground. If the LED lights up and appears to be blinking very slightly, then you know you're sending serial data out. The blinking is very slight because it's so fast; the LED is going on and off as fast as 9600 times per second. Once you've done this test, be sure to remove the LED before moving on to the next step.

Testing with Terminal Software

Serial communication is harder to debug than anything you have done so far because the problem could be in many different places: your microcontroller software or circuit, the multimedia computer software or hardware, or the conduit between the two. Before writing any custom software on the multimedia computer, it's worth stopping now to test your physical connection and the software on your microcontroller. You can do this by using terminal software on your multimedia computer. Terminal software prints onto the screen anything that comes in from the serial port and sends anything you type on the keyboard out the serial port. There are many free or shareware versions of this software. Zterm is our favorite on the Mac; it's downloadable from many sites on the net (http://www.shareware.com is a good place to start). HyperTerminal comes with the Windows operating systems; it's usually found by clicking the Start menu, then choosing Start, Programs, Accessories, Communications, HyperTerminal. You can also open it by clicking on the Start menu, choosing Start, Run, then typing **hypertrm** (sic). In every terminal program you'll find a menu option for settings, properties, or preferences where you can specify which serial port you want to use (for example, Direct to COM1 in HyperTerminal) and with what configuration (9600, 1 stop bit, no parity, 8 data bits, no flow control).

NOTE
One important fact to note about serial ports: A multimedia computer's serial port can only be controlled by one program at a time. If you have only one serial port and your microcontroller program is running, then your terminal program may not be able to use the serial port and will probably give you an error message. If this is the case, quit both programs and open the terminal program again. It should now be able to gain control of the serial port. Make sure that background programs that use the serial port, such as modem software, PDA connection software (such as Palm's HotSync), and so forth, are not using the serial port either.

Run the examples above on your microcontroller. Connect the microcontroller's serial output to the serial port on the multimedia computer. Run the terminal program, and you should see the output messages filling up the screen. This would be a good time for a celebratory hokeypokey before moving on to serial input.

The main shortcoming of terminal programs is that they can only interpret bytes as ASCII characters. If you are expecting your messages to be interpreted as numbers—for example, if you're sending a number between 0 and 255 for a light sensor—it will appear as gibberish. The values 0 to 31 may not appear at all because they are control characters in ASCII used for screen formatting. Even gibberish, if it is consistent, can be reassuring at this point. It means that your data is getting through but is not being displayed by the terminal program as you want it to be displayed. You will fix that when you replace the terminal software with your own software for the multimedia computer.

Serial Input to a Microcontroller

In pBasic, mBasic, and PicBasic Pro, the command to receive serial data from another computer is called serin (serin2 in PicBasic Pro). As you can see from the examples below, it's very similar to serout. The parameters are the RX pin number, the baud mode, and the variable into which you want to receive the data.

Run this program on your microcontroller. Each time you type a character into the terminal program on your multimedia computer, you should see it appear in your microcontroller's debug window. In the other direction, the "A" being sent by your microcontroller should appear in your terminal software's window.

NOTE
This example requires that you have two serial ports, one for programming and one for connecting your serial line. If you don't have two ports, then close your programming software and move the serial connection from your programming pins to your serial pins once you've programmed the chip. You won't see the debug messages, but you will see the "A."

NOTE

PIC users: since the `serout2` command is so simple, and since you can't use the same pins of your microcontroller for both `serout2` and `debug`, you'll use `serout2` for all debugging messages from here on out, instead of the `debug` command.

(PBASIC)

```
' TX is connected to pin 6. RX is connected to pin 7.

inFromSerialVar var byte

main:
      SEROUT 6, 16468, ["A"]
      SERIN 7, 16468, [inFromSerialVar]
      DEBUG ? inFromSerialVar
GOTO main
```

(MBasic)

```
' TX is on pin 6; RX is on pin 7

inFromSerialVar var byte

main:
      SEROUT 6, I9600, ["A"]
      SERIN 7, N9600, [inFromSerialVar]
      DEBUG [inFromSerialVar]
GOTO main
```

(PicBasic Pro)

```
' TX is connected to pin C6. RX is connected to pin C7.

inFromSerialVar var byte

main:
      SEROUT2 portc.6, 16468, ["A"]
      SERIN2 portc.7, 16468, [inFromSerialVar]
      SEROUT2 portc.6, 16468, ["I got: ", inFromSerialVar, 10, 13]
GOTO main
```

In BX-Basic, serial in is a bit more complex because of the serial buffers. It's similar to serial out in that you set up an input queue and get the data in from that queue. The serial in commands are `statusQueue()` and `getQueue()`. StatusQueue() takes one parameter, the name of the input queue. It returns true if there are bytes in the input queue. GetQueue() takes two parameters, the name of the input queue and the number of bytes you want to get. It plucks the first available byte off the queue and returns it. GetQueue() will not work if there are no bytes available in the queue, so you put it inside an If statement that checks `statusQueue()`. This program will do the same as the above examples for the other microcontrollers. Each

Serial Input to a Microcontroller

time you type in a character on your multimedia computer's keyboard, you should see it appear in your microcontroller's debug window. An "A" should appear in your terminal software's window as well.

BX-Basic

```
' TX is on pin 11; RX is on pin 12

Dim InputVar(1 To 10) As Byte
Dim OutputVar(1 To 40) As Byte
dim inData As byte

Sub main()
    Call openQueue(InputVar, 10)
    Call openQueue(OutputVar, 40)
    Call defineCom3(12, 11, bx1000_1000)
    Call openCom(3, 9600, InputVar, OutputVar)
    outData = 65

    do
        Call putQueue(OutputVar, outData, 1)
        Call getQueue(InputVar, inData, 1)
        ' check to see if there is a byte in the input buffer;
        ' if there is, get it with getQueue()
        If statusQueue(inputBuffer) = true then
            call getQueue(inputBuffer, inData, 1)
            Call putQueue(outputBuffer, inData, 1)
            Debug.print cstr(inData)
        End if
    Loop
End Sub
```

If this test works, then you've proven that your cable works and your microcontroller software is running correctly. The hokeypokey may again be called for. Before testing any of your own software that you write on the multimedia computer, you should always do this simple test. The following could be the leading causes of failure at this point:

▶ The pin numbers for TX or RX in the software are wrong.

▶ You soldered to the wrong terminals of the serial connector.

▶ Your connections on your serial connector are not soldered well, causing a bad connection.

▶ Your TX of one side is connected to the TX (instead of the RX) of the other side.

▶ You are plugged into the wrong port on your multimedia computer.

▶ You have the settings wrong on the multimedia computer.

Serial Freeze and Blocking Functions

Because you are using asynchronous serial communication (meaning that either device can send data whenever it wants to), you never know exactly when data is going to arrive. In order not to miss an incoming message, a microcontroller will usually have to dedicate its undivided attention to the input pin. As a result, when a microcontroller is given a command to receive serial data, it stops all other action until the requested amount of data bytes are received. This is called a *blocking function,* meaning that all other action is blocked until it's done. It can be very useful for keeping your microcontroller and multimedia computer synchronized. For example, if you are sending sensor readings to a multimedia computer and you want to make sure it has processed the last set of readings before you send a new set, you could send a set of readings and then wait with the blocking function until you receive a byte back from the multimedia computer signifying that it is ready for another (see the "Call and Response" section below).

Sometimes blocking functions are a problem, however, and you need the microcontroller to keep running its program if no data comes in. You can do this using a *timeout*, which is an option in the serial in command that says, "If you get no data in a certain time, go on to something else."

Here's a variation on the serial testing code that uses a timeout. In this example, if no data is received, the microcontroller sends back a period character ("."), and if data is received, the microcontroller sends back an "Λ".

Note the extra parameters in the serin function below (10, noData). These parameters tell the microcontroller that if it gets no serial data in after 10 milliseconds, then it should go to the label noData. When it gets there, it sends back a period and goes back to the main label. The serout command that sends the A is never run unless serin gets data.

PBASIC
```
' TX is on pin 6; RX is on pin 7
inFromSerialVar var byte

main:
    serin 7, 16468, 10, noData, [inFromSerialVar]
    serout 6, 16468, ["A"]
    debug ?inFromSerialVar
goto main

NoData:
    Serout 6, 16468, ["."]
Goto main
```

MBasic
```
' TX is on pin 6; RX is on pin 7
inFromSerialVar var byte

main:
    serin 7, N9600, 10, noData, [inFromSerialVar]
```

```
            serout 6, N9600, ["A"]
            debug [inFromSerialVar]
        goto main


        NoData:
            Serout 6, N9600, ["."]
        Goto main
```

PicBasic Pro

```
        ' TX is on pin C6; RX is on pin C7
        inFromSerialVar var byte

        main:
            serin portc.7, 16468, 10, noData, [inFromSerialVar]
            serout2 portc.6, 16468, ["A"]
            serout2 portc.6, 16468, ["I got: ", inFromSerialVar, 10, 13]
        goto main


        NoData:
            serout2 portc.6, 16468, ["."]
        Goto main
```

BX-Basic

```
        Dim InputVar(1 To 10) As Byte
        Dim OutputVar(1 To 40) As Byte
        dim outData As byte
        dim inData As byte


        Sub main()
            Call openQueue(InputVar, 10)
            Call openQueue(OutputVar, 40)
            Call defineCom3(12, 11, bx1000_1000)
            Call openCom(3, 9600, InputVar, OutputVar)

            do
                If statusQueue(inputVar) = true then
                    Call getQueue(InputVar, inData, 1)
                    OutData = 65 ' ASCII value for "A"
                    Debug.print cstr(inData)
                Else
                    OutData = 46 ' ASCII value for "."
                End if
                Call putQueue(OutputVar, outData, 1)
            Loop
        End Sub
```

Timeouts are particularly useful when the microcontroller has multiple time-dependent tasks to perform. For example, let's say you have the microcontroller running a servo motor that's moving your window blinds. The microcontroller gets a serial command from a multimedia computer, and it repositions the blinds. But keep in mind, as you learned in Chapter 6, servo motors need a pulse every 20 milliseconds, even if they're not moving. You could have the microcontroller listen for serial data in for 18 milliseconds, then if it gets nothing, pulse the servo motor again and go back to listening for serial input again.

Your Private Protocol

The RS-232 protocol specifies many things, but the content of the message and the formatting of that content are not dictated. Assuming you are sending more than one byte of information, you will need a scheme for ordering your bytes. If one end of the conversation is out of your hands (for instance, if you are talking to a motor control board), you will have to study the documentation to learn and conform to their scheme for formatting messages. If you control both sides of the conversation (for example, when your microcontroller is talking to your software on a multimedia computer), you can invent any scheme you like for formatting your messages, as long as you are consistent. We will talk about two techniques, *punctuation* and *call and response*.

Punctuation

Imagine you're sending the values of three sensors from the microcontroller to the multimedia computer; call them sensor A, B, and C. You're sending three bytes of data over and over, like so:

```
Loop
     Read sensor A
     Read sensor B
     Read sensor B
     Send serial string of bytes: A, B, C
End loop
```

The multimedia computer has a serial buffer, so it stores all the bytes there until it's ready to do something with them. To the multimedia computer, the incoming data looks like this:

```
ABCABCABCABCABCABCABCABCABC
```

However, if the microcontroller starts sending before the multimedia computer starts listening, the string of data might look like this:

```
CABCABCABCABCABCABCABCABCAB
```

Your Private Protocol

The multimedia computer has no way of knowing which byte corresponds to which sensor. It would be great if you could add a character to delimit the beginning of each new set of readings, like this:

C.ABC.ABC.ABC.ABC.ABC.ABC.ABC.AB

Each time you get a period, you know the next three bytes make up a full set of values for the switches in the right order.

In order for this method to work, you have to use an end-of-transmission character that will never be found in the message itself. That is easy enough to do when you send your messages as an ASCII text string, where only a small range of characters are commonly used (32 to 127), leaving lots of candidates for message delimiters. Carriage returns (ASCII 13), commas, or just spaces are commonly used. For example, you could send the reading from each sensor separated by a space, and every set of readings separated by a comma. It might come out looking like 210 200 44, 200 20 44, 150 30 44. 44 is the ASCII value for a comma.

Finding a good delimiter when you send your readings as raw values is a little more difficult. If the A, B, and C bytes can all range from 0 to 255, what can you use as a unique delimiter? You can get around this by limiting the range of the other three bytes to a range from 0 to 254, then using 255 as your punctuation.

Below are some code snippets for punctuating your transmissions. These assume that you have put readings from either switches or analog sensors into three different variables.

PBASIC

```
 send the numbers with a 255 character at the end
serout 6, 16468, [AVar, BVar, CVar, 255]
' OR
' send as a text strings separated by spaces with a comma at the end
serout 6, 16468, [DEC AVar,32,DEC BVar,32,DEC CVar, 44]
```

MBasic

```
'send the raw values with a 255 character at the end
serout 6, N9600, [AVar, BVar, CVar, 255]
OR
' send as ASCII text strings separated by spaces with a comma at the end
serout 6, N9600, [DEC AVar,32,DEC BVar,32,DEC CVar, 44]
```

PicBasic Pro

```
'send the raw values with a 255 character at the end
Serout2 portc.6, 16468, [AVar, BVar, CVar, 255]
' OR
' send as ASCII text strings separated by spaces with a comma at the end
Serout2 portc.6, 16468, [DEC AVar,32,DEC BVar,32,DEC CVar, 44]
```

BX-Basic

```
' send the numbers with a 255 character at the end
punctuationVar = 255
```

```
Call putQueue(outputVar, AVar, 1)
Call putQueue(outputVar, BVar, 1)
Call putQueue(outputVar, CVar, 1)
Call putQueue(outputVar, punctuationVar, 1)
' OR
' send as a text strings separated by spaces with a comma at the end
' make a message to send
OutputString =cstr(AVar)&chr(32)&cstr(BVar)&chr(32)&cstr(CVar)&chr(44)
Call putQueueStr(outputVar, outputString)
```

Call and Response

It is usually better to take a more controlled approach in which the microcontroller sends only one set of data at a time at the multimedia computer's request. Because there is only one set of readings at a time in the buffer, you can easily identify which sensor is which without the use of a delimiter simply by the order in which they arrived. The first one sent will be the first one received. The sequence would work something like this:

1. The microcontroller waits (usually with a blocking function) for bytes.

2. The multimedia computer sends bytes (sometimes an arbitrary byte just to prompt a reply).

3. The microcontroller sends bytes.

4. The multimedia computer receives bytes in order.

The whole process loops infinitely, as long as the two computers need to communicate. This method is termed *call-and-response*. The multimedia computer calls, and the microcontroller responds. This is where the blocking function of the microcontroller (discussed earlier in this chapter) really comes in handy. Sometimes you'll also hear it referred to as *handshaking*. This type of synchronization also ensures that the data is fresh. If your microcontroller is spewing readings faster than the multimedia computer can react to them, you may get a backlog of old readings in the buffer, or the old readings will get overwritten by new readings when the buffer gets full. It's an effective way of managing long strings of data moving from one device to another.

Sometimes this technique gets hung up when both sides are frozen, expecting the other to begin. If you have problems with this, it is a good idea to send a request at the start of your multimedia software and perhaps periodically thereafter, or possibly to have a timeout for the blocking function on your microcontroller's serial input function, as shown above. Here's an example in microcontroller code (the multimedia computer code will follow later):

Your Private Protocol

```
( PBASIC )   ' TX is connected to pin 6. RX is connected to pin 7
             ' switches are on pins 0, 1, and 2.
             SwitchAvar var byte
             SwitchBvar var byte
             SwitchCvar var byte
             ' declare a byte for incoming data:
```

```
RXData var byte

input 0
input 1
input 2

main:
    ' wait for serial input from the multimedia computer;
    ' if you get nothing in 10 ms, go to main:
    serin 7, 16468, 10, main, [RXData]

    ' read the switches:
    SwitchAvar = in0
    SwitchBvar = in1
    SwitchCvar = in2

    ' send the values out:
    serout 6, 16468, [SwitchAvar, SwitchBvar, SwitchCvar]
goto main
```

(MBasic)
```
' TX is connected to pin 6. RX is connected to pin 7
' switches are on pins 0, 1, and 2.
SwitchAvar var byte
SwitchBvar var byte
SwitchCvar var byte
' declare a byte for incoming data:
RXData var byte


input 0
input 1
input 2

main:
    ' wait for serial input from the multimedia computer;
    ' if you get nothing in 10 ms, go to main:
    serin 7, N9600, 10, main, [RXData]

    ' read the switches:
    SwitchAvar = in0
    SwitchBvar = in1
    SwitchCvar = in2

    ' send the values out:
    serout 6, N9600, [SwitchAvar, SwitchBvar, SwitchCvar]
goto main
```

PicBasic
Pro

```
' TX is connected to pin C6. RX is connected to pin C7
' switches are on pins B0, B1, and B2.
SwitchAvar var byte
SwitchBvar var byte
SwitchCvar var byte
' declare a byte for incoming data:
RXData var byte


input portb.0
input portb.1
input portb.2

main:
    ' wait for serial input from the multimedia computer;
    ' if you get nothing in 10 ms, go to main:
    serin2 portc.7, 16468, 10, main, [RXData]

    ' read the switches:
    SwitchAvar = portb.0
    SwitchBvar = portb.1
    SwitchCvar = portb.2

    ' send the values out:
    serout2 portc.6, 16468, [SwitchAvar, SwitchBvar, SwitchCvar]
goto main
```

BX-Basic

```
' TX is connected to pin 11. RX is connected to pin 12
' switches are on pins 5, 6, and 7.

dim SwitchAvar as byte
dim SwitchBvar as byte
dim SwitchCvar as byte
dim inByte as byte
dim gotaByte as boolean
dim inputBuffer(1 To 10) As Byte
dim outputBuffer(1 To 40) As Byte

sub main ()
    ' set up serial port:
    call defineCom3(12, 11,bx1000_1000)
    call openQueue(inputBuffer, 10)
    call openQueue(outputBuffer, 40)
    call openCom(3,9600,inputBuffer, outputBuffer)

    do
```

Your Private Protocol

```
                    ' read switches:
                    SwitchAvar = getPin(5)
                    SwitchBvar = getPin(6)
                    SwitchCvar = getPin(7)

                     ' read serial data in:
                    If statusQueue(inputBuffer) = true then
                        call getQueue(inputBuffer, inByte, 1)

                        call putQueue(OutputBuffer, SwitchAvar, 1)
                        call putQueue(OutputBuffer, SwitchBvar, 1)
                        call putQueue(OutputBuffer, SwitchCvar, 1)


                    end if
                loop
            end sub
```

Sending Bigger Numbers

The standard-sized package that you send is a byte. A byte can hold a range of values from 0 to 255. The problem we often encounter is that the range of our analog input doesn't fall perfectly within that range. You can send the number as text, which uses as many bytes as there are digits. You can scale your number down to fit into one byte. Or you can break the number down into multiple bytes, send them separately, and recombine them on the receiving end.

Send Your Numbers as Text

As we have discussed in the sections "Numbers or Letters: Using ASCII" and "Punctuation," sometimes it is useful to turn your numbers into a text string temporarily, for the purposes of transmission. This is less efficient because you have to use a byte for every digit and conversion functions on both ends of the transmission. However, it offers an advantage in that your numbers can be as big as you like. Check the code in the "Punctuation" section above.

Scaling Your Numbers

In Chapter 6 we discussed scaling functions to convert one range of numbers to another range of numbers. Serial communication gives you an opportunity to apply that idea in a simple way. If, for example, you're dealing with an analog sensor connected to your microprocessor's analog-to-digital converter, and you're getting the full range of the ADC, you know the number is 10 bits, or 0 to 1024. This can be scaled down to a byte-sized range simply by dividing by 4. In other cases, though, the answer is not as simple as that. For more complex cases, where your range is perhaps 30 to 600, use the ranging methods outlined in Chapter 6.

Whenever you scale down a number greater than 255 to fit in a byte-sized message, you're losing resolution. Sometimes this is desirable because it filters out irregularities, but at other times it makes your sensor response feel chunky.

Sending Big Numbers in Many Bytes

It is possible to send numbers greater than than 255 by sending two bytes. On the microcontroller end, this is simple. For example, to send out a word- or integer-sized variable, you have to break the variable into two bytes, then place them in the `serout`, `serout2`, or `putQueue()` functions. PBASIC, MBasic, and PicBasic Pro allow you to do this by using dot notation to refer to part of a variable, as shown below. In BX-Basic, you can send the integer as two bytes.

(PBASIC)   `WordVar var word`

(MBasic)

(PicBasic Pro)

Then send out as follows:

(PBASIC)   `Serout 6, 16468, [wordVar.lowbyte, wordVar.highbyte]`

(MBasic)   `Serout 6, N9600, [wordVar.lowbyte, wordVar.highbyte]`

(PicBasic Pro)   `Serout portc.6, 16468, [wordVar.lowbyte, wordVar.highbyte]`

(BX-Basic)   `Dim integerVar as integer`

Then send out as follows:

```
call putQueue(outputVar, integerVar, 2)
```

However, on the multimedia computer side, you will need to write code to recombine the two separate bytes into one variable, using this formula:

```
BigVar = firstbyte + (secondByte * 256)
```

Serial Communication on a Multimedia Computer

Many people reading this book already have some experience authoring on multimedia computers and are now champing at the bit to link them with the physical world. In this section, we will show you how to use serial communication to make a connection between a multimedia computer's authoring environment and a microcontroller. If you already know how to use one of the environments that we cover (or a similar one), you're in good shape. If you're new to programming on a multimedia computer, you should pick a language and then find other resources for programming beyond this book. It's not possible for us to recommend the single best multimedia authoring language because this is a personal choice. We use several for different purposes. Every programmer has a set of tools that they know best, and each tool has different strengths and weaknesses. We'll cover a couple of different languages here.

We find Macromedia's Director MX to be the best mix of power and ease of use, but a little pricey. Microsoft's Visual Basic is also very powerful and has a big following, but it's more typically used in business-oriented applications than in multimedia applications. Cycling '74's Max/MSP is the easiest to use, and it's great for MIDI, sound, and video control, but it's not as useful for developing onscreen human interfaces as the others. Java is free and widely used, but a bit too low-level for doing interesting things very quickly. Processing is a new environment that we like; it provides a simple environment for making graphic applications, and it can be extended by incorporating Java once you know what you're doing. It is also free (http://www.processing.org). Macromedia's Flash MX is limited mostly to Web graphics and not extensible for serial communication, but it is easy to use and very popular. We built a tool in Java so it can communicate with a microcontroller serially. Future versions of Flash MX may have extensions for serial communication. You can also communicate with Flash MX using a serial-to-Ethernet converter like the Cobox Micro mentioned in Chapter 12 and Flash's XMLSocket command.

Most programming environments cannot control the serial port out without being extended. The operating system procedures to drive the serial port are different on each hardware platform, and the tools for manipulating it are specific to the operating system. Cross-platform authoring environments like Flash and Director MX usually leave out these platform-specific details and rely on third-party developers to add extensions to the environment. Often the biggest obstacle to serial communication is tracking down the extensions that you need to access the serial port and placing them in the right folders.

After you have added any extensions to your programming environment, you'll need to learn the commands for using those extensions. The basic steps are as follows:

1. Access the commands in the extension file (referred to as *creating a serial object*).
2. Pick which serial port you want to use.
3. Set the serial configuration and the baud rate.
4. Send bytes.
5. Receive bytes.

A few general principles for all serial programming follow. We'll go over the details for each of our examples as we cover the code for each environment.

Setting the port to be used (for example, COM1, COM2) is sometimes done when creating the serial object and sometimes done afterwards with a separate command. Port names can sometimes be a little different from the usual COM1 or COM2, particularly if you are using a USB adapter or serial expansion card. In those cases, the port names might be more proprietary, like USA19IIS1.1. Your serial library will hopefully have a means for querying the machine for the names of all the ports available.

Commands for setting the configuration are usually straightforward, and some serial interfaces just default to the standard 9600-N-8-1.

Sending bytes is easy, usually a single command. Receiving bytes requires that you deal with the fact that this is asynchronous communication; in other words, you don't know exactly when bytes are arriving. Receiving bytes on the multimedia computer is easier than receiving on the microcontroller because multimedia computers have serial buffers. The operating system automatically stores incoming bytes into this serial buffer until your code has a chance to deal with them. There are two main techniques for finding out about bytes waiting in the serial buffer. The first technique is to continually poll the serial buffer using a command that tells you how many bytes are waiting there. The second way is to specify a function to be called when something arrives in the serial buffer. This is known as creating a *callback* or a *listener*.

Serial in Lingo

This section assumes you are familiar with Macromedia Director MX and its scripting language, Lingo.

Although there is no serial programming interface built into Director MX, the environment is easily extensible using an architecture called Xtras. The first step in adding an Xtra to Director MX is finding and buying it. We recommend the SerialXtra from http://www.physicalbits.com, which is far and away the best one. Much of what follows applies to any Lingo Xtra, so if you have used Xtras before it should be a snap.

The Xtra is a file that we recommend you place in the same folder as your Director MX movie (Macromedia recommends you place it in the Xtras folder of the application folder; we find it simpler to do it our way. If you ever have problems with an Xtra, try their way too). Xtras are platform-specific, so there will be one file for the Macintosh and a different file for Windows. To use this with Shockwave in a browser you currently have to manually copy the Xtra file into the shockwave/xtras folder.

The next step is to open the Xtra from within your movie file using the command

```
openxlib "serialXtra.osx"
```

You'll need to match the extension to your platform. On the Macintosh (OS X), the extension is .osx. In Windows, it's .x32.

This is usually done in your startMovie or prepareMovie handler. You can confirm that the movie has recognized the Xtra if you type **showxlib** in the message box, SerialXtra should now appear in the list of Xtras.

The next step is to make an object, as follows:

```
SerialObj = new( xtra "serialXtra")
```

The new command creates an object using the SerialXtra as the blueprint.

The command above creates a reference to the serial object that this command creates and stores that reference in the variable SerialObj. For those of you not familiar with object-oriented programming, this might be the first time you ever put anything other than text or numbers into variables. You should make this variable global because you will use it anywhere in your program you need to use any of the serial commands.

Once you've created the serial object, you need to open a serial port. To find the names of all serial ports available, you can use the put findports() command in the message window once you've created the object (make sure the movie is running when you do it). You'll get a list like this (this list is from a Macintosh running OSX):

```
[[#portName: "/dev/cu.IrDA-IrCOMMch-b", #MaxBaudRate: "N/A", #FullName:
"/dev/cu.IrDA-IrCOMMch-b", #InUse: "No"], [#portName: "/dev/cu.modem",
#MaxBaudRate: "N/A", #FullName: "/dev/cu.modem", #InUse: "No"], [#portName:
"/dev/cu.USA19HS191P1.1", #MaxBaudRate: "N/A", #FullName:
"/dev/cu.USA19HS191P1.1", #InUse: "No"]]
```

Copy the port name of the serial port you want to use, and add the following line to your startMovie or prepareMovie handler:

```
serialObj.openPort(portName)
```

For example, from the list above, the port for the Keyspan USA19HS USB-to-serial adaptor is /dev/cu.USA19HS191P1.1

```
serialObj.openPort("/dev/cu.USA19HS191P1.1")
```

NOTE
Don't be confused by the dot notation. What this command says is that you want to use the openPort() command, which can be found in the serial object that's contained in the variable SerialObj.

Next you set the serial protocol, using the setProtocol() command:

```
SerialObj.setProtocol(9600, "n", 8, 1)
```

The default is 9600, N-8-1, so you can skip this command if those are the settings you want.

That's everything that you need at the start of your program to use the serial port. All of it should go in the startMovie or prepareMovie handler. The only other housekeeping detail you need to know is that you should dispose of the serial object when your program ends. To do this, put the following code in your stopMovie handler:

```
SerialObj = 0
closeXlib
```

If you don't dispose of the serial object, Director MX won't be able to access the serial port the next time you run your movie. If your program halts due to an error, you may have to manually call stopmovie using the message box in order to kill the serial object releasing the port and the memory. If that doesn't work, you'll need to restart Director MX to fix this problem.

Sending data is easy. You just say

```
SerialObject.writeChar("A")
```

or

```
SerialObject.sendNumber(65)
```

and a byte gets sent out.

Receiving data is a little more complicated. The Xtra is always listening to the serial port and placing bytes into a serial buffer as they come in. The serial buffer gives you some breathing room so that you don't have to stop everything in order to catch the incoming information (as you do on a microcontroller), but you still have to check it frequently if you want your program to respond in a timely fashion to what the microcontroller's sending out. The main command for reading the serial buffer is the readNumber() command, which takes the first byte off the buffer and reads its value as a number from 0 to 255. You can also interpret the byte as an ASCII character by using readChar(). For example, if the microcontroller sent the value 65, readNumber() would return 65, and readChar() would return A. If you want the entire buffer as a string of characters, you can use readString().

Commands that you want to repeatedly happen in Director MX should be placed in an on ExitFrame handler. For example:

```
On ExitFrame
    MyVar = SerialObject.readNumber()
End
```

This handler would read bytes out of the serial buffer once each frame. If your microcontroller is continually sending one byte over and over (for example, sending the value of a switch), you'll notice a definite time lag between the time the switch changes and the time Director MX responds. This is because the microcontroller can fill the serial buffer faster than Director MX can read it. For this reason, it's usually better to use a call-and-response approach.

If you are expecting a number of bytes, you can use the charsAvailable() function to check that the number of bytes you expect has arrived. Don't use readNumber() or readChar() until you have the number of bytes that you expect in the serial buffer. Every time you use either of those commands, a byte is removed from the buffer, making the byte that arrived next first on the queue. By waiting until charsAvailable() returns the right number of bytes, you ensure that you get the entire string. The bytes are kept in order as they arrive in the serial buffer so that the first one you sent from the microcontroller will be the first one you get when you call readChar() or readNumber().

The code below will wait for three or more bytes in the serial buffer, then read them and place them in variables. If there's nothing in the buffer, it will send out a byte to ask for data. This code assumes you've set up the ports correctly and have opened the one you want, as described above.

```
global serialObject
On ExitFrame
    -- see if the port's been opened:
    If serialObject.isPortOpen() then
    If serialObject.charsavailable() = 0 then
        --send a byte to ask for data
        SerialObject.writeChar("A")
    End if

    If SerialObject.charsAvailable() >=3 then
        --first byte sent by microcontroller:
        MyVar = SerialObject.readNumber()
        --next byte sent by microcontroller:
        MyVar2 = SerialObject.readNumber()
        --third one sent by microcontroller:
        MyVar3 = SerialObject.readNumber()
    End if
End
```

In an entirely different approach, you can use readString() to read everything out of the serial buffer in one fell swoop and then parse through the string. We don't usually recommend this approach. It's messy. This would work well if you were sending readings from the microcontroller as ASCII text strings with punctuation. Here's how you would do this:

```
global serialObject, textSoFar
On ExitFrame
    TextSoFar = textSoFar & SerialObject.readString()
    --if you sent your readings separated by spaces with a comma at the end
    If textSoFar.word.count >= 3 then
    --the integer function converts from the ASCII string back into a number
```

Putting all together:

```
global serialObject, serialObjectName, serialObjectFilename
global myVar1, myVar2, myVar3

on startMovie
  clearglobals
  -- variables for setting up the xtra.
  serialObjectFilename = "SerialXtra"
  serialObjectName = "SerialXtra"
  -- make a new instance of the xtra. Fill in the extension for your OS below:
  openxlib the pathname & "serialXtra.osx"
  serialObject = new (xtra serialObjectName)
  -- check that it has been created correctly
  if objectP( serialObject ) then
    put serialObject
  else
    alert("Instance not valid")
  end if
  -- fill in the name of your serial port below:
  serialObject.openPort("/dev/tty.USA19HS191P1.1")
  -- set the data rate, start bits, etc:
  serialObject.setProtocol(9600, "n", 8, 1)
end

on stopMovie
  -- dispose of the xtra and close the xtra file
  serialObject.closePort()
  set serialObject to 0
end

on exitFrame
  doSerial
  go the frame
end

on doSerial
  -- see if the port's been opened:
  If serialObject.isPortOpen() then
    If serialObject.charsavailable() = 0 then
      --send a byte to ask for data
      SerialObject.writeChar("A")
    End if
    If SerialObject.charsAvailable() >=3 then
      --first byte sent by microcontroller:
      MyVar = SerialObject.readNumber()
      --next byte sent by microcontroller:
```

```
        MyVar2 = SerialObject.readChar()
        --third one sent by microcontroller:
        MyVar3 = SerialObject.readChar()
      End if
    End if
  end
```

If you put all of this text in your main movie script, and make sure the Xtra file is in the same directory as your movie, this will work with the call-and-response microcontroller examples above. You'll see the variables myVar, myVar2, and myVar3 change with your switches.

Finally, you can use a callback with the SerialXtra. A callback basically takes all the work you were doing in the exit frame and offloads it to the Xtra. This is particularly nice when it saves you from parsing through text to find a punctuation character that you may have used to signify the end of a transmission.

You should supply the name of the handler you want the Xtra to call in startMovie. This line would cause the Xtra to call your function RecievedChars after 10 characters have arrived.

```
        SerialObject.ReadUsingCallback("ReceivedChars", 10)
```

Of course, you are then obliged to have such a handler:

```
    On RecievedChars data
        Put theData.Buffer
        Put theData.String
        --send a byte to ask for data
        SerialObject.writeChar("A")
    End
```

The buffer is then delivered to you as a parameter variable in the form of a property list. TheData.Buffer will contain all serial data in the input buffer as raw values and theData.String will contain everything as a string. Note that the characters in the string will be the ASCII characters for the raw values, not ASCII-encoded values. In other words, if the microcontroller sends three bytes with raw values of 65, 66, and 67, theData.String will contain the string ABC, not 656667.

You can also supply the name of the handler you want the Xtra to call in startMovie after a specific character has arrived. This line would have the Xtra calling your function RecievedChars after a comma has arrived.

```
        SerialObject.ReadUsingCallbackOnToken( " RecievedChars ", chartoNum(","))
```

You are again obliged to have such a handler:

```
    on RecievedChars thedata
        put theData
        --send a byte to ask for data
        SerialObject.writeChar("A")
    end
```

Serial in Processing

Serial communication in Processing is simple. Before you can do it, however, you'll need to make sure to follow the installation instructions carefully before you start coding. As part of the installation (as of version 0091) installs serial port extensions for Java (remember, Processing is built on Java). We'll assume you were able to get Processing installed and able to recognize your serial ports for the purposes of this explanation.

Processing's serial commands are in an external library, so in order to use them. you have to import the library at the beginning of your program, using the `import` command, like so:

```
import processing.serial.*;
```

Then in your `setup()` handler, you can get a list of the available serial ports using the `Serial.list()` command, like so:

```
println(Serial.list());
```

This will print a list of all the available serial ports on your computer in the debugger pane. To open a serial port, use the `new()` command:

```
Serial port = new Serial(this, portname, baudrate);
```

The `Serial.available()` command from the serial library lets you know when there is new incoming serial data to read. If there's new data, `Serial.available()` returns true. If not, it returns false. When there's new data available, you can read each byte using the `Serial.read()` command. To constantly listen for serial data, check `Serial.available()` in your `main()` method, and when it's true, read a byte, like so:

```
Serial port = new Serial(this, portname, baudrate);
...
if (port.available() == true) {
  int newData = port.read();
}
```

To send serial out, use the `Serial.write()` command. `Serial.write()` can take just about any data type as its parameter: bytes, ints, strings, or arrays of any of the above.

It's that simple.

Okay, we lied. Handling multiple bytes through call and response is a little more complicated in Processing. There are many methods you could use, but the underlying idea is that you need to collect the bytes as they come in and put them in a variable that can handle multiple bytes. For this example, you put them all into an array When the array gets long enough, you parse each element and convert it to whatever data type you need in order to use it:

```
void serialEvent() {
  processByte(port.read());
}
```

```
void processByte(int inByte) {
  // Add the latest byte from the serial port to array:
  serialInArray[serialCount] = inByte;
  serialCount++;
  // If we have 3 bytes:
  if (serialCount > 2 ) {
    xpos = serialInArray[0];
    ypos = serialInArray[1];
    fgcolor = serialInArray[2];
    // Send a capital A to request new sensor readings:
    port.write(65);
    // Reset serialCount:
    serialCount = 0;
  }
}
```

This example expects three bytes from the microcontroller, all of which range from 0 to 255, coming from analog sensors and putting it all together to move a ball on the screen:

```
// import the Serial library:
import processing.serial.*;

int bgcolor;                // Background color
int fgcolor;                // Fill color
Serial port;               // The serial port
int[] serialInArray = new int[3];      // Where we'll put what we receive
int serialCount = 0;        // A count of how many bytes we receive
float xpos, ypos;            // Starting position of the ball
boolean firstContact = false;   // Whether we've heard from the
// microcontroller
void setup() {
  size(256, 256); // Stage size
  noStroke();      // No border on the next thing drawn

  // Set the starting position of the ball (middle of the stage)
  xpos = width/2;
  ypos = height/2;

  // Print a list of the serial ports, for debugging purposes:
  println(Serial.list());

  // I know that the first port in the serial list on my mac
  // is always my  Keyspan adaptor, so I open Serial.list()[0].
  // On Windows machines, this generally opens COM1.
  // Open whatever port is the one you're using.
  port = new Serial(this, Serial.list()[0], 9600);
  port.write(65);     // Send a capital A to start the microcontroller sending
```

```
    }

void draw() {
  background(bgcolor);
  fill(fgcolor);
  // Draw the shape
  ellipse(xpos, ypos, 20, 20);
  // Get any new serial data
  while (port.available() > 0) {
    serialEvent();
    // Note that we heard from the microntroller:
    firstContact = true;
  }
  // If there's no serial data, send again until we get some.
  // (in case you tend to start Processing before you start your
  // external device):
  if (firstContact == false) {
    delay(300);
    port.write(65);
  }
}

void serialEvent() {
  processByte(port.read());
}

void processByte(int inByte) {
  // Add the latest byte from the serial port to array:
  serialInArray[serialCount] = inByte;
  serialCount++;
  // If we have 3 bytes:
  if (serialCount > 2 ) {
    xpos = serialInArray[0];
    ypos = serialInArray[1];
    fgcolor = serialInArray[2];
    // Send a capital A to request new sensor readings:
    port.write(65);
    // Reset serialCount:
    serialCount = 0;
  }
}
```

Serial in Java

The classes that you will need to perform serial communication are not included with your standard installation of Java. Your first step is to find the classes that will work with your hardware platform. For Windows, this is easily done by visiting the Sun Java site: http://java.sun.com/products/javacomm/index.html. For the Mac and other platforms, you can buy classes from http://www.serialio.com/. For free versions for the Mac OS 9, try http://homepage.mac.com/pcbeard/javax.comm.MRJ/. For Mac OS X or Linux, try http://www.rxtx.com; this still requires part of the download from Sun. For other platforms, try http://republika.pl/mho/java.comm/. Theoretically, all of these will conform to Sun's communications API, so your code can be pretty close to the same.

The installation is the hardest part, so you should actually read the readme file that comes with whatever package you use. On a PC you need to copy three files: "comm.jar" in your <JDK>/jre/lib/ext/, "javax.comm.properties" in <JDK>/jre/lib/, and "win32com.dll" in <JDK>/jre/bin/. Using RXTX on OSX, you need to put "libSerial.jnilib" and "RXTXcomm.jar" into /Library/Java/Extensions/. If you have ever used external classes with Java before, you know that getting all the files in the right directories is at least half the battle, particularly if you have more than one version of Java on your machine. If you don't like to dwell on this stuff too much, just put the necessary files in the folders of every installation of Java.

To query the machine for available ports, the code looks like this:

```
Enumeration portList = CommPortIdentifier.getPortIdentifiers();
while (portList.hasMoreElements()) {
    CommPortIdentifier portId = (CommPortIdentifier) portList.nextElement();
    if (portId.getPortType() == CommPortIdentifier.PORT_SERIAL){
        System.out.println(portId.getName() + " " +portId.getCurrentOwner());
    }
}
```

The code for finding the correct port and creating a serial object looks like this:

```
CommPortIdentifier portId=CommPortIdentifier.getPortIdentifier("COM1");
SerialPort mySerialPort = (SerialPort) portId.open("myApplicationName",2000);
```

The line for setting the configuration looks like this:

```
mySerialPort.setSerialPortParams(9600,
SerialPort.DATABITS_8,
SerialPort.STOPBITS_1,
SerialPort.PARITY_NONE);
```

Reading and writing with the serial port is done with InputStreams and OutputStreams, just like any other I/O operation in Java. Using these streams will seem familiar to anyone who has used Java for Internet programming. The code for getting these streams looks like this:

```
InputStream in = mySerialPort.getInputStream();
OutputStream out = mySerialPort.getOutputStream();
```

Once again, sending is easy.

```
out.write(x); //x is a byte sized variable
out.write("Hello".getBytes()); //covert "Hello" to bytes and send
```

When it comes to receiving bytes in Java, there are a couple of ways to do it. The first way is to just say

```
int input = in.read();
```

You can wrap your InputStream in other types of streams like the BufferedReader, which would be very useful for sending text strings punctuated with an end of line character. You turn the strings back into integers with the parseInt method.

```
BufferedReader lineIn = new BufferedReader(new InputStreamReader(in));
String newLine = lineIn.readLine(); //wait for char13, char10 or char13 and 10;
StringTokenizer st = new StringTokenizer(newLine," ");
// or you can use String.split instead of StringTokenizer in Java 1.4
if (st.hasMoreTokens()) int light = Integer.parseInt(st.nextToken());
if (st.hasMoreTokens()) int head = Integer.parseInt(st.nextToken());
if (st.hasMoreTokens()) int pressure = Integer.parseInt(st.nextToken());
```

The problem with these read functions are that they are blocking functions. In other words, they wait at the read() or readLine() function, halting further execution of your Java code until something comes in the serial port. You have already seen this freezing with the microcontroller, and even used it to your advantage in synchronizing call-and-response operations. You can avoid this by putting the read() command into a separate thread. A simpler solution is to first check if there are any bytes available in the serial buffer.

```
if (inputStream.available() > 0) {
    int input = in.read();
}
```

The above methods require that you are in a repeat loop or thread that is continually polling the serial object to see if there is anything available. Alternatively, you can set up a callback and have the SerialPort object do this continual checking. You do this by adding an event listener:

```
mySerialPort.addEventListener(this);
```

You have to do two other things to get this to work. First, your class must implement the SerialPortEventListener class. To do this, add these two words to the end of your class declaration:

```
public class YourClass implements SerialPortEventListener {
```

Second, you have to include a SerialEvent() method in your class. This is the method that will be called anytime there is new stuff coming in the serial port.

```
public void serialEvent(SerialPortEvent event) {
    if (event.getEventType()== SerialPortEvent.DATA_AVAILABLE) {
        if (inputStream.available() > 3) {
            int input = in.read();
```

```
            }
            System.out.println ("stuff came in" );
        }
    }
```

Putting it all together, you get a class to read in three bytes and send one back with the horizontal mouse position.

```
import javax.comm.*;
//import gnu.io.*; //use this instead of javax.com if you are using RXTX
import java.io.*;
import java.awt.*;
import java.util.*;

public class SerialExample extends Frame implements SerialPortEventListener {
    static SerialExample myFrame;
    //we are making this into a frame so we can track the mouse
    SerialPort mySerialPort =null;
    InputStream in;
    OutputStream out;
    byte x = 50;

    static public void main(String[] args) {
        // Print out the list of serial ports,
        //in case you don't know the name"
        Enumeration portList = CommPortIdentifier.getPortIdentifiers();
        while (portList.hasMoreElements()) {
            CommPortIdentifier portId = (CommPortIdentifier)portList.nextElement();
            if (portId.getPortType() == CommPortIdentifier.PORT_SERIAL){
                System.out.println(portId.getName() + " " +portId.getCurrentOwner());
            }
        }


        // Change the port name below as needed on the Mac:
        myFrame= new SerialExample("COM1",9600);

        //the following is all just window management
        myFrame.setVisible(true);
        myFrame.setLocation(new java.awt.Point(0, 0));
        myFrame.setSize(new java.awt.Dimension(255, 450));
        myFrame.setLayout(null);
        myFrame.setTitle("Serial");
        //add a listener for closing the window, in that event call the
windowClosing method
        myFrame.addWindowListener(new java.awt.event.WindowAdapter() {public void
windowClosing(java.awt.event.WindowEvent e) {myFrame.thisWindowClosing(e);}});
```

```
        //add a listener for moving the mouse in the window, in that event call the
mouseMoved method
        myFrame.addMouseMotionListener(new java.awt.event.MouseMotionAdapter()
{public void mouseMoved(java.awt.event.MouseEvent e) {myFrame.mouseMoved(e);}});
    }

    public SerialExample (String whichPort, int whichSpeed) {
        //which port you want to use and the baud come in as parameters

        try {
            //find the port
            CommPortIdentifier portId = CommPortIdentifier.getPortIdentifier
(whichPort);
            //open the port
            mySerialPort = (SerialPort)portId.open("SerialExample" + whichPort, 2000);
            //configure the port
            try {
                    mySerialPort.setSerialPortParams(whichSpeed,
                    mySerialPort.DATABITS_8,
                    mySerialPort.STOPBITS_1,
                    mySerialPort.PARITY_NONE);
            } catch (UnsupportedCommOperationException e){System.out.println
("Probably an unsupported Speed");}
            //establish streams for reading and writing to the port
            try {
                in = mySerialPort.getInputStream();
                out = mySerialPort.getOutputStream();
            } catch (IOException e) { System.out.println("couldn't get streams");}
            try {
                mySerialPort.addEventListener(this);
                mySerialPort.notifyOnDataAvailable(true);
            } catch (TooManyListenersException e) {System.out.println
("couldn't add listener");}
            try {
                //send an initial character in case your microcontroller is waiting:
                out.write("A".getBytes());
            } catch (IOException e) {System.out.println("couldn't send byte");}
        }
        catch (Exception e) { System.out.println("Port in Use");}

    }

    public void serialEvent(SerialPortEvent event) {
        if (event.getEventType()== SerialPortEvent.DATA_AVAILABLE) {
            try {
                if (in.available() >= 3) {
                // we will wait for three sensor readings
                    int heat = in.read();
```

```
                    int light = in.read();
                    int pressure = in.read();
                    //do something with these numbers
                    System.out.println(heat + " " + light + " " + pressure);
                    out.write(x); //send the mouse position back
                } //end if for data available
            } catch (IOException e) {}
        } //it's a serial port event
    }

    void thisWindowClosing(java.awt.event.WindowEvent e) {
        myFrame.setVisible(false); // Close the window when the close box is clicked
        myFrame.dispose();
        System.exit(0);
    }
    public boolean mouseMoved(java.awt.event.MouseEvent evt){
        x = (byte) evt.getX();
        // Put the mouse coord into a variable called x
        return(true);
    }
}
```

Theoretically, these classes can work within the security sandbox of an applet, but it would have to be signed for other people to use it. Due to a bug in Sun's code, you need to add these lines when using a signed applet:

```
String drivername = "com.sun.comm.Win32Driver";
try {
    CommDriver driver = (CommDriver)Class.forName(drivername).newInstance();
    driver.initialize();
} catch (Exception e) {System.out.println (e.getMessage ()); }
```

You can test an applet on your own machine without signing it by editing your java.policy file. On a PC you may find multiple versions of this file for each installation of Java. In OSX you can find this in /Library/Java/Home/lib/security/. You might have to unlock the file before you are able to change it.

```
grant codeBase "http://localhost/*" { permission java.security.AllPermission;
};
grant codeBase "file:///C:/YOURFOLDERS../-" {
permission java.security.AllPermission;
};
```

An applet adds many places to go wrong, so we recommend getting things working first in a Java application.

Serial in Max/MSP

Max/MSP is a visual programming language from Cycling '74. Until recently, it was available only on the Macintosh. As of version 4.3, it's available for Windows XP, too. It was originally designed as a tool for creating elaborate MIDI-based control systems. Recently, with the addition of MSP, it's become an excellent tool for real-time sound synthesis and processing as well. While it's a good control interface for sound and MIDI applications, its graphics tools are not as simple to use as those in Director MX, Processing, or Flash, so it tends to be a tool for performer/programmers rather than a tool for building standalone applications to be given to an end user. Nevertheless, it's an excellent tool for performance, and with the recent addition of Jitter, a toolkit for real-time video processing, it's an excellent multimedia tool.

Programs, called *patches* in Max/MSP, are not written in text. They're assembled onscreen from a toolkit of functional objects. The outputs of one object are connected to the inputs of another to create a sometimes elaborate collection of objects and connecting strings. It may seem daunting at first, but for those who dislike coding in written form, it can be a real treat. For more details, see http://www.cycling74.com.

Serial communication in Max/MSP is handled by using a serial object. There are five possible arguments to be placed in the body of the object:

- ▶ Letter to represent the port. The two default ports (COM1 and COM2 on the PC, modem and printer on the Mac) are a and b. Any additional ports are ports c through z, in the order they are installed. To find the name of your ports, attach a message box containing the word print to the serial object's input, lock the patch, and click the message box. You should get a list of the ports and the letters they're assigned to in the Max window.
- ▶ Baud rate (the default is 4800)
- ▶ Data bits (the default is 8)
- ▶ Stop bits (the default is 1)
- ▶ Parity (the default is 0).

The serial object has one input. The input is for sending data or asking for data. Any number or character is automatically sent out as a byte or an array of bytes. A *bang* (Max/MSP's equivalent to "true") causes the object to read in one byte of data from the port.

The serial object has two outputs. The left port outputs data bytes, and the right port outputs status messages and error messages.

Figure 7.3 is a simple serial reader. The metro object, which is just a metronome, bangs on the serial object every 5 milliseconds, looking for new data. Banging on the button above the number object to the left of the serial object or scrolling that number object will send the value of the number object out serially. The sprintf object and the print object beneath the serial object take the incoming bytes, format them as ASCII, and print them to the Max debug window. To get help on any object, select the object and choose "Help" from the Help menu, and Max will show you a working example of how to use the object.

Figure 7.4 shows another example using the punctuation method described above. In this case, Max/MSP reads in bytes until it gets a byte of value 255 (using the select object), then

Figure 7.3
A simple serial Max
patch.

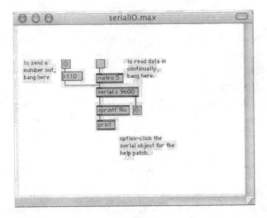

Figure 7.4
A punctuation Max
patch.

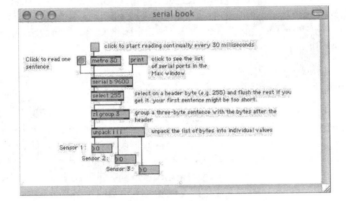

reads the next three bytes. When it gets them (the z1 object makes a list of the bytes, reading until it gets three bytes), it then parses the bytes, and puts each one into a separate number box. The metro object at the top sends a message every 30 milliseconds to read again.

Conclusion

The principles in this chapter are widely applicable throughout computing. Creating a set of agreements, a protocol, is a key skill for getting any two computers to talk to each other. Being able to follow and build on a communication protocol is a core skill at every level of our highly networked world. It may even help your love life.

Serial communication is the last core technical concept of this book. Everything in the advanced section is a variation on one of the ideas in the preceding chapters: interaction design, basic electronics, basic programming, digital input and output, analog input and output, and serial input and output. In fact, every physical computing project we've created has used a combination of these same principles. By now, you've undoubtedly built a few projects using the ideas we've covered, and you've got an understanding of how the ideas work in practice. If you haven't started building, what are you waiting for? Do it now. The best way to learn this material is to use it.

Part II
Advanced Methods

IN PART I we covered the general things that you need to know for almost any project. In this second part of the book, we'll introduce more advanced methods for accomplishing a number of more specific tasks. Most of these methods in Part II are just special cases of the basic ideas in Part I. We won't repeat the circuits and code from those chapters, but we will refer to them frequently. For example, we might talk about a sensor and say that it fits into a normal digital input circuit and uses the usual BASIC commands for digital input without supplying a schematic or sample code. If you encounter something that you're not comfortable with, go back to the earlier chapters (usually Chapter 6) and try the examples there again. You can't make an omelette until you've learned to scramble an egg. In the preceding chapters, you scrambled a few eggs. In the following chapters, you'll learn to make the physical computing equivalent of omelettes, frittatas, huevos rancheros, and maybe even eggs Florentine.

8

Physical Interaction Design, or Techniques for Polite Conversation

By now, you've got the basic electronic and programming techniques down and you are starting to combine them to pull off your particular idea. This is a good time to step away from the technology for a moment and consider how well your project works for your users. For the first part of this chapter, we'll discuss some ways to approach that problem and lay out some basic interaction design guidelines. In the second part of the chapter, we'll provide some techniques for putting these approaches into action.

The Conversation: Listening, Speaking, and Thinking[1]

In any well-designed physical computing application, the flow of activity between the person and the computer should follow the same comfortable flow of a good conversation. Designing the system so that this happens is what interaction design is all about. This means balancing the timing of your listening, thinking, and speaking to coordinate with the expectations and patterns of the user. When you do this work well, the interaction between the person and the computer flows naturally enough that the person doesn't have to think consciously about their performance, but only about the overall result.

Listening

In actual conversation, we don't often plan the taking of turns. Human beings are capable (to a limited degree) of talking and listening at the same time. When a listener wants to interrupt a speaker, she gives subtle physical cues, and the speaker knows to stop talking and listen. There are also natural pauses in a conversation for the listener to

---

[1] The ideas in this chapter rely heavily on Chris Crawford's explanation of computer interactivity in *The Art of Interactive Design: A Euphonious and Illuminating Guide to Building Successful Software* (No Starch Press, 2002).

digest information and prepare a response. We know intuitively that when we present information in conversation, we have to give our listeners time to digest the information. We know how long it takes to perceive a change or digest an idea consciously, and we factor that knowledge into our conversation. We give each other that time, and if we feel that the person we're speaking to should have responded, we prompt them to see if they're still understanding us: "Do you get it?" Listening for cues while speaking takes a level of sophistication that we seldom give ourselves credit for, because we're so well trained in doing it that we don't give it a second thought.

When you program a computer to interact with the world, however, you realize how much we take for granted in the course of everyday human interaction. A computer can't spontaneously react to a shout or a movement. If it's not listening when the event happens, it misses it. In fact, the very idea that a shout or a movement is an event that requires response is something that's got to be programmed in advance. It's an important notion because all interaction is made up of events or physical phenomena that must be sensed, interpreted, and responded to. In order to plan interaction between computers and humans (or anything else in the world) at a physical level, the first step is to teach it to listen. You have to articulate the possible events that the computer will respond to, define those events in terms the computer can sense, assign meanings to the events you've defined, and choose an appropriate response to each event. If an event's meaning changes based on the events that precede it, you've got to give the computer instructions about that, too.

There are two main quantities you need to consider when you detect actions with sensors: how intense the sensation was, and how long it took. When you're dealing with digital input sensors, you'll only have two possible values for how intense the sensation was: either you sensed something or you didn't. With analog sensors, you'll have a range from the most intense to the least. Since your sensors convert other forms of energy into electrical signals, you measure the intensity of the signal in volts. To measure how long the event took, you use seconds, microseconds, or milliseconds, depending on the event. To describe the event, then, you can use a graph of voltage and time. For example, an analog sensor might produce a graph like the one in Figure 8.1.

And a digital sensor might produce a graph like the one in Figure 8.2.

Figure 8.1
Analog sensor readings over time.

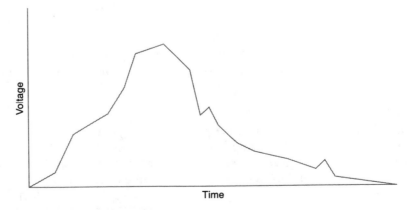

Figure 8.2
Digital sensor readings
over time.

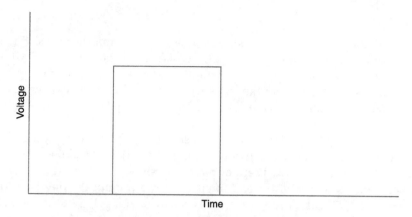

Keep these images in your head, as they'll come in handy when we begin to talk about things like threshold setting, edge detection, peak detection, and other sensor-reading methods.

In planning the range of possible microcontroller responses, the first thing you should do is to describe the events that you expect to occur over time. Plot out some of the dynamics that you expect the microcontroller to sense so that you can decide what techniques you'll need to use for your sensors to work optimally. Think through the actions to be sensed, and draw a rough graph of what they should look like. In some cases, this is simple enough that you can do it in your head, but in any complex system, it's often useful to have it on paper.

For example, Figure 8.3 is a rough graph of a person walking down a hallway, past several distance ranging sensors.

Figure 8.3
A person walking
down a hallway,
as seen by a
microcontroller.

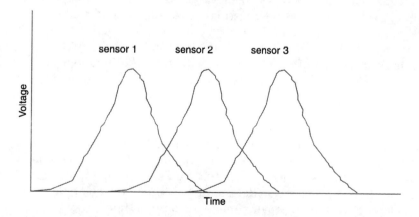

If you just wanted to know where the user is, you could look for the sensor with the highest reading and assume she's near that sensor; but on which side? Checking the readings of the sensors on either side would give you a better picture because the one she's nearer to might read higher than the one she's farther from. If you want her direction, you have to keep track of which sensors have already sensed her presence and which haven't. To get her speed, you could time the delay between sensing a peak on sensor one and sensor two. The possibilities can get very complex, and having a visual model of what you expect to sense can make it much easier to interpret what you actually sense.

Speaking

When we listen, whether we're listening to humans or non-humans, we bring with us similar expectations about how the pattern of a conversation will go. We know that pets, for example, react to our actions in about the same amount of time as people (and in some cases faster). We expect the same from our devices.[2] We expect that when we push a button, flip a switch, wave our hand, shout, or take whatever action is expected, the device will react with at least conversational immediacy. Let's take the Clapper, which can turn on or off a light when it hears a loud sound (such as the clapping of our hands), as an example. If the Clapper reacts too quickly and the lights come on when our hands first touch, we are startled. If the Clapper reacts too slowly, and the lights aren't on by the time we're consciously aware of the end of our clap, we prompt the device again, just as we do in conversation. Think of the number of times you've jiggled the toilet handle, flipped a light switch off and on in rapid succession, or jabbed repeatedly at a remote control power button, and you know what we're talking about.

When you design interactive devices, you have to factor this expectation in, and either meet it or give the person using it a new set of expectations that the device can meet. Your device should respond in ways a person expects or can learn to expect. Once you get to know the pace of response of your devices, you learn to factor that in when you interact with them. If you know the garage door opener takes a second to start moving, you don't jab it again right away. If the fluorescent lights take a few seconds to warm up, you give them time. We're especially tolerant with computers, because we figure they're computing, and we think computing takes time. The truth of the matter is often quite different.

Unlike humans, computers can do only one thing at a time. However, they can do things much faster than us, so it's possible for a computer to have completed several tasks—for example, reading a sensor, interpreting the result, using it to adjust the image onscreen or the position of a motor, and preparing to read again—all before the human that's interacting with it is aware that she's finished speaking. They're so fast, in fact, that multimedia designers often have a tendency to overburden them with complex tasks, making them seem slower than they really are. If you've ever had a computer react sluggishly as you attempt to drag a window across the screen, you've seen this in effect. Each time the computer reads the sensor (the mouse position sensors), it then has to complete several million tasks: figuring the new position of the window; examining what's already drawn there; calculating the effect of fancy things like drop shadows of the window on the images beneath it; redrawing the cursor, the window, and the screen beneath the window's edges; and making a cute dragging sound. One challenge an interaction designer faces is to determine how much the computer can do before the user expects a reaction and to provide that reaction in a timely way.

---

[2] In *The Media Equation: How People Treat Computers, Television, and New Media like Real People and Places* (Cambridge University Press, 1998), Byron Reeves and Clifford Nass make a very interesting case that people unconsciously treat computers like real people.

Expectations and Misunderstandings

Sometimes the problem of interaction is not one of precise timing but of clear indication of expectations.[3] Going back to our conversational model, if you enter into a long and detailed explanation of an idea that causes your listener to go silent for several minutes, you need to continue to pay attention to him in order to gauge his level of interest. You may need to cue him to respond at the end, perhaps through a silent pause and a questioning look. If he wants to interrupt you, you need to pay attention to him as you speak so that you can offer a response. If you want to finish your sentence, you might raise your finger to acknowledge his interruption so that he knows you heard him and will let him respond once you finish.

It's wise to incorporate similar small indicators for feedback into any system to acknowledge user input and to avoid misinterpretation. For example, turning an LED on when a button is pushed and off when the button is released takes negligible processing work, but gives the user a definite sign that the input was "heard" by the computer. The button may start or interrupt many other tasks besides lighting the LED, but lighting the LED lets the user know that those other tasks have been put in motion. Having been acknowledged immediately, the user is prepared to wait for the other tasks to finish as long as the wait is reasonable. If no indication is given, the user might push the button again, triggering unexpected consequences.

In many physical computing applications, the participant is more actively physically engaged than in multimedia computer applications, and her tolerance for delay is lower as a result. The patience that we're willing to give to computers doesn't generally extend to devices where the computer is not visible. Because of this, it's very important to keep system response time as low as possible, on a par with human reaction time or faster at all times.

At other times, you might need to prompt user input. For example, if the user's footsteps trigger a complex series of sound or video that brings her to a standstill, then perhaps a subtle visual cue could be used to prompt her to walk again when it's appropriate. This is particularly true when an output sequence has a subtle ending or does not have a definite ending point.

A narrative description of the participant's experience of your work can be very useful at this point. In describing what she will see, hear, feel, touch, speak to, step on, and so forth, in sequence, or using a branching diagram of possible sequences, you can identify points where her focus on a particular phenomenon is crucial. From there, you can plan ways to get the focus there or keep it there. For example, if the experience depends on the participant hearing and responding to a sequence of tones in a particular order and a particular rhythm, then audio cues to acknowledge her input could be counterproductive. On the other hand, a subtle—and quick—visual acknowledgement could enhance the precision of her responses.

---

[3] Donald Norman writes about people's mental models of systems and how those models affect the interaction with the systems in *The Design of Everyday Things* (Basic Books, 2002). His explanation goes into more depth on the idea presented here.

The Conversation

These kinds of cues are important because they're the cues on which a person builds her mental model of how a system works. If the system doesn't respond, she may think it's broken. For example, in a system we designed once, a series of buttons triggered playback of a series of video clips on a screen above the buttons. When a given clip was playing, the clients did not want another button press to interrupt the clip. In order to discourage viewers from hitting buttons at will, we put lights in the buttons, and dimmed them when a video clip was playing. When the clip was over, the buttons lit up again. This cue told viewers that the system was working properly, but that pressing a button when a video clip was playing was not a desired behavior. If they pressed a button during a video clip, the button would brighten very slightly while it was pressed, to ensure the viewer that the system was working, but then would fade again when the button was released, to limit distraction from the video. All the feedback in the world will not stop some users from feeling locked out by not being able to change the video. The designer must decide which is worse, interrupting the video or alienating that user.

Avoiding Modal Behavior

Software interaction designers are lucky people. They have the luxury of unlimited real estate on which to design. In software, you can always add another menu item, another pop-up list, or go to another screen when the number of steps to complete a task gets to be too much to fit on one screen. Virtual real estate is infinitely expandable. Physical interfaces lack this luxury because the device can only be so big, the room is only so many steps across, the camera's field of view can take in only so much, or the microcontroller can only read so many switches (at least until you get to Chapter 14, "Managing Multiple Inputs and Outputs"). Because you're combining a software control system with a physical interface, you can add features as long as you've got the program memory to fit it, but you won't have enough hardware sensors to trigger these new functions. You may be tempted to have the same sensors control multiple functions. This is a slippery slope, and utter confusion lies at the bottom.

For example, imagine you're building a musical instrument with a distance sensor as the main sensor. Normally, the sensor controls the pitch of the instrument. But if the user presses a green button, the distance sensor gets shifted from controlling the pitch of a sound to controlling the volume. What if the user wants to modulate the volume and the pitch at the same time? A red button changes the key signature the instrument plays in. But there are lots of key signatures, so she's got to press the button repeatedly to get to the next one. How does she know which key she was in last or which is next? What if she learns the whole sequence of key signatures, then presses the button repeatedly but overshoots the one that she wants. Can she go backwards?

Systems like this, where the behavior of the controls changes depending on the mode the system is in, work against the clarity of the physical interface. They give the user a layer of organization to remember that's not indicated in the controls themselves. One workaround to this is to change the ambient conditions depending on the mode. For example, you might cause the color of the instrument to change from blue to green when the sensor is shifted from pitch control to volume control. This solution still requires the user to memorize the colors of the modes. Another solution is to force the user to maintain contact with the mode-changing control in order to maintain the mode. The sustain pedal on a piano is an excellent example of this. It's not possible to forget that you're in sustain mode because your foot is strained in order to maintain the mode.

Unless the mode can be clearly indicated with no need for the user to remember what the change means, modes tend to be confusing. A better solution is to avoid modal systems whenever possible by mapping each control to a unique and consistent response.

Complex Responses

We have been proposing a kind of straightforward interaction scheme that may sound a little too dry and methodical if you're planning an ambient musical installation or a responsive sculpture that changes subtly over time. However, these are precisely the kinds of physical computing projects that need this kind of planning the most. Humans love patterns. We automatically look for patterns in everything from clouds to tea leaves to cracks in the sidewalk. In interactive systems, we look for patterns in the connections between the inputs and the outputs. The more abstract or subtle those connections are, the harder it will be for a viewer or participant to find a pattern. Sometimes the connections are too complex, or they're based on a set of conventions common only to you and other people with your training and experience. After the user gives up on finding the pattern, she might feel bored by a seemingly random sequence of events. She might even feel angry that you were implicitly inviting her to find a pattern where none apparently exists. This is also true in performance; the classic example of this is the "laptop music performance," in which several people sit onstage typing on laptops while the audience hears music, apparently generated by the performers. The audience may not appreciate the music as much if they cannot find patterns between the actions of the performers and the music coming out. Musical performance is often more satisfying when there's an apparent connection between the gestures of the performer and the sounds heard.

When you're planning interactive systems, no matter how abstract, keep in mind the tendency to look for patterns. You should give the viewer or participant a general sense of the connection between the inputs and outputs. To give your project a more complex feel, consider using multiple inputs. Let each input have a straightforward response, but design the system so that they combine in complex ways. Think about the ripples produced by throwing stones in a pond. The response to each stone is simple and predictable, yet the pattern generated by throwing in several is rich, layered, and unpredictable.

In addition to clear reactions, clear interfaces are also essential. If you choose to hide or disguise the sensors so that the person doesn't know how she is triggering this behavior, you might as well play a pre-recorded sequence because she won't understand how she is a part of the system. This doesn't mean, for example, that she needs to see a large red footprint labeled "stomp here" if you're sensing her footsteps. However, if her footsteps are what your system is responding to, then she should be able to see a connection between a single footstep and the system's response when the system is at a state of rest. You may want to design a system in which it takes a thousand footsteps in order to elicit a response, but she'll never get to the thousandth step if she's not clued in early on that "the game is afoot." In general, it's always best to err on the side of simple responses to simple actions, letting the combination of simple responses generate a complex pattern.

Random Numbers

We have been warning against interactions that appear to the user to produce random results. On the other hand, noise or random variation is everywhere in our lives. The movement of whiskers on your robotic cat or the flickering of stars on your ceiling would feel wrong without some random variation. The frustration of random responses is often exactly what you want in a game or simulation. For example, a roll of the dice or the roulette wheel, shuffled deck, or a phonebook flipped open to a random page are all events that rely on the randomness of the physical world to introduce surprise and excitement. While these random patterns are ubiquitous in life, the computer has a hard time generating random events. The beauty and utility of random numbers is not that they are random, but that they spring from patterns too complex to identify immediately. When these patterns come from mathematical algorithms divorced from physical reality, they're not always very convincing. Instead of generating randomness with algorithms, consider tapping into the noisy patterns that we see all around us in our physical environment for random numbers.

Every time you think you need a random number, ask yourself if there is a way to get that number from the noise in the physical system you are building. The standard trick on a multimedia computer is to use the milliseconds since the user last touched the keyboard, because unlike computers, people are unpredictable in their actions, touching the keyboard at erratic intervals. With the microcontroller, you have many more opportunities for sensing noise in the world. One simple example is to use the random static electricity generated by people, radio waves, and so on. Try this: stick a bare wire on an analog input of your microprocessor. Make the wire a long one, say, a foot or more. Strip off the insulation. Coil it if you want. Don't attach the other end to anything. Program the chip to read the wire as an analog input. As it's running, touch the wire. The changes appear to be random, and you should see a marked difference, but still a random pattern, when you touch it. This is because you're reading micro-voltage changes due to anything in the room that generates an electrical signal: you, a TV monitor, a cell phone, and so on. The bare wire is an antenna for your chip. Use its results as a random number. You could do the same thing with a pressure sensor or a tilt sensor in environments where pressure and tilt are changing.

These examples take advantage of complex processes in the physical world and use them as design elements. They allow you to include the unexpected but also to control it. A truly random system can often be very frustrating for the person using it, whereas a complex but ordered system is more engaging. It gives the person using it a structure on which to model her idea of how it works. Ultimately, she has a better chance of mastering such a system, and therefore finding it more satisfying to work with.

Your mindset as programmer will really benefit from including the possibilities and constraints of the physical world in your work. Without physical computing, everything that the user interacts with is abstracted. You have to simulate buttons and handles, movement, and orientation. With physical computing, you factor all of your user's physical understanding of the physical world into your interface. You get to take advantage of the fact that she knows how buttons and springs and doors and all kinds of other physical things work.

Thinking

Even though computers can do only one thing at a time, it only takes a few microseconds to execute each line of code. You can use this to your advantage by programming the computer to listen to its inputs for short periods, then control its output for short periods. If all of these periods are shorter than the human reaction time, it can appear to a human being as if the computer is doing many things, like speaking and listening at the same time.

Sensing and reacting in momentary fragments necessitates a good bit of work if the computer is going to sense events and respond at a human time scale. In order for the computer to be able to interpret events, it has to reconstruct events from the fragments it senses each time it listens to its sensors. To interpret a shout as a cue to play a song, for example, it must first have sensed silence, and be able to tell how much noise is different enough from silence to interpret as a shout. If two shouts constitute a cue to play music, it's got to hear both the shouts, and the silence in between, and be able to count.

In a similar fashion, a computer has to react in ways that a human can interpret. If its output happens in small bursts, it has to create longer responses from a sequence of small bursts. If it's meant to play a song all the way through when cued, and not respond to cues while playing, it's got to be able not only to start playing the music, but also to keep track of when it ends, as well as to offer an alternate response if it senses a "play" cue while the music is playing. Though this may seem like a lot of work, it's not too bad when you understand a few of the techniques below.

Techniques for Effective Interaction

Following are some examples that put the principles described above into action. These examples give you ways to make your microcontroller handle multiple tasks simultaneously and recognize the beginnings and ends of complex events based on what it senses.

Multitasking

Imagine you want to make an LED flash three times in response to the push of a button. You want the flashing to happen once per second. Here's the pseudocode for it:

```
read button
if button is pushed then
    loop 3 times:
        turn on LED
        pause 1 second
        turn off LED
        pause 1 second
    end loop
end if
```

If you were to write this routine using pause commands (or delay commands on the BX-24), there would be six seconds in between the time when the button is pushed and the next reading. If you want to make the LED react to a button push in the middle of the flashing sequence, you're out of luck. In the middle of the flashing loop, the microcontroller isn't reading the button at all.

You could find a flashing LED processor to flash the LED for you, attach that to your microcontroller, and turn it on and off in response to the sensor, but that would be more technology than the project needs. In this case, it would be better to write a more responsive program so that there's not a six-second pause between readings of the sensor.

You need a way to make sure that you're listening to the user at a rate faster than human response time, while still controlling the blinking LED at a rate you want. Ideally, you would have two different loops (or threads): one that runs very fast, like the main loop, to keep checking the sensor, and one a bit slower, to blink the LED if necessary. This way, if something changes with the sensor while the LED is blinking, you can provide an appropriate response. One way to do this is by using counters to count the number of times through the main loop. Let's assume the main loop will run in a thousand times a second (in most cases, it's faster than that, but this makes for easy math). You can use the counter to listen to the sensor every loop and change the LED every thousandth loop.

Here's an example:

```
Set counterForLEDs = 0
Set LEDFlashCounter = 0
Set flag = down
Loop:
    Check the switch
    If the switch is pressed then
        Put up a flag to tell the LEDs to flash
    end if

    If the flag is up then
        Subtract one from the counterForLEDs
        If the counterForLED has reached zero
            Reset counterForLEDs to 1000
            If we have not flashed three times
                Add one to the flash counter
                Flash
            Else
                You have finished flashing so
                Reset flash counter
                Reset counterForLEDs
                Reset the flag
            End if
        End if
    End if
End loop
```

You may be confused by the flag in the pseudocode above; so far, we haven't talked about making computers control flags. A *flag* is just a variable used to send a message from one loop to another. Think of it like a semaphore flag, or the flag on the mailbox that you put up to tell the mail carrier that there's outgoing mail inside. In the example above, it's possible that the user might stop pressing the switch before the LED stops flashing, so you can't rely on just the state of the switch to know whether the LED should flash. The flag gets set to 1 every time you're supposed to start flashing the LED and set to 0 when you've successfully flashed the LED. Using loop counters and flags like this, you can set one process in motion at its own pace (the flashing of the LEDs), while keeping the previous process in motion at another pace (checking the sensor).

Here's an example in code:

PBASIC

MBasic

```
counterVar VAR Word    ' we want to count to 1000, so we need a word
needFlashingFlagVar VAR  Bit
timesFlashedVar VAR  Byte
ledState VAR Bit


INPUT 7      ' the Switch is on this pin
LOW 8             ' the LED is on this pin
counterVar = 1 'set the countdown close to zero
Main:
    'check every loop for the button press
    IF IN7 = 1 THEN
        needFlashingFlagVar = 1 'set the flag
    ENDIF

    IF needFlashingFlagVar THEN
        counterVar = counterVar - 1 'count down to next change
        IF counterVar = 0   THEN 'if you have counted down to zero
            counterVar = 1000 'set the counter back up
            IF timesFlashedVar < 3 THEN ' if you have not done all the flashes
                IF ledState = 0 THEN 'flash the led
                    timesFlashedVar = timesFlashedVar + 1
                    HIGH 8
                    ledState = 1
                ELSE
                    LOW 8
                    ledState = 0
                ENDIF
            ELSE
                'if you have finished flashing the led set variables to initial state
                timesFlashedVar = 0
                needFlashingFlagVar = 0
                ledState = 0
                counterVar = 1
                LOW 8
```

```
                    ENDIF
                ENDIF
            ENDIF
        GOTO main
```

PicBasic
Pro

```
counterVar VAR Word    ' we want to count to 1000, so we need a word
needFlashingFlagVar VAR  Bit
timesFlashedVar VAR  Byte
ledState VAR Bit


Input portb.0         ' the switch is on this pin
Output portb.1        ' the LED is on this pin


Low portb.1
counterVar = 1 'set the countdown close to zero
Main:
    'check every loop for the button press
    IF portb.0  = 1 THEN
        needFlashingFlagVar = 1 'set the flag
    ENDIF


    IF needFlashingFlagVar THEN
        counterVar = counterVar - 1 'count down to next change
        IF counterVar = 0   THEN 'if you have counted down to zero
            counterVar = 1000 'set the counter back up
            IF timesFlashedVar < 3 THEN
                ' if you have not done all the flashes
                IF ledState = 0 THEN 'flash the led
                    timesFlashedVar = timesFlashedVar + 1
                    High portb.1
                    ledState = 1
                ELSE
                    Low portb.1
                    ledState = 0
                ENDIF
            ELSE
            'if you have finished flashing the led set variables to initial state
                timesFlashedVar = 0
                needFlashingFlagVar = 0
                ledState = 0
                counterVar = 1
                LOW portb.1
            ENDIF
        ENDIF
    ENDIF
GOTO main
```

```
BX-Basic    DIM counterVar as Integer     ' we want to count to 1000, so we need a word
            DIM needFlashingFlagVar as   Byte
            DIM timesFlashedVar as   Byte
            DIM ledState as Byte

            Sub Main()

                Call putPin(13,0)
                counterVar = 1 'set the countdown close to zero
                Do
                'check every loop for the button press
                IF getPin(12) = 1 THEN
                    needFlashingFlagVar = 1 'set the flag
                END IF


                IF (needFlashingFlagVar = 1) THEN
                    counterVar = counterVar - 1 'count down to next change
                    IF counterVar = 0   THEN 'if you have counted down to zero
                        counterVar = 1000 'set the counter back up
                        IF timesFlashedVar < 3 THEN
                        ' if you have not done all the flashes
                            IF ledState = 0 THEN 'flash the led
                                timesFlashedVar = timesFlashedVar + 1
                                call putPin(13,1)
                                ledState = 1
                            ELSE
                                call putPin(13,0)
                                ledState = 0
                            END IF
                        ELSE
                        'if you have finished flashing the led set variables to initial state
                            timesFlashedVar = 0
                            needFlashingFlagVar = 0
                            ledState = 0
                            counterVar = 1
                            call putPin(13,0)
                        END IF
                    END IF
                END IF
                loop
            End Sub
```

Keeping track of the timing of processes like this doesn't do much good, though, if the processes don't interact in some useful way. For example, what happens if the user presses the switch again while the LED flashing sequence is happening? Currently, nothing, which makes the program the same as if you just used pauses. If you want a second switch press to interrupt the flashing sequence and bring it to an end, you need a little more information. You'd first need to watch changes (see the "Edge Detection" section below) in the switch's state, so you only get one event for each press of the switch. When you detect a press you would toggle the current state of the flag and counters.

Notice that the output routine happens relatively infrequently (every 1,000th loop), while your input routine happens very frequently (every loop). Generally, you want to place a priority on listening frequently so that you can change your response quickly.

You have to factor in the time taken to run the rest of our program as well, so you might have to make your pause smaller or change your counting. Perhaps you'd change to activating the LED process every 500th loop or every 100th loop. There's usually not an easy way to calculate this in advance, so you end up starting with an arbitrary value that you think is close enough, then changing the program until you find a value that works.

Certain commands that you give a processor will take more time than others. For example, any command that sends bytes out serially will take as long as needed to send the bytes (9600 bits per second). Even the if-then statements in the example above slow the processor down somewhat. The surest way to find out how a given command affects your program is to try it in practice. Your interaction with the user and with your output will be helped by removing any unnecessary commands, so when you've learned what you need from a debug statement, for example, you should comment it out or remove it.

This timing loop is not the only way to balance timing between input and output. There are as many schemes for this as there are programmers, and everyone has their own method. The key factor to keep in mind is that any time the processor is constrained to one task, like a pause, or a print statement, or any other command that takes time, then the system is not listening to the user. Whenever this happens, you must have a way of letting the user know and when it's appropriate for them to respond again.

Some processors have a more advanced operating system, and can handle the precise timing of multiple tasks for you. For example, the BX-24 has limited multitasking capability. (For details, see the BX-24 documentation.) Not many small microprocessors have such a capability built in, so you often have to find your own ways of handling it, like we've done above. The BX-24's multitasking is based on the idea of *timer interrupts*. Interrupts are basically routines that are scheduled to run every time the processor's timer counts off a certain interval, no matter what. On other microcontrollers, interrupts are somewhat more complex to use and involve knowing some lower-level programming. Besides timer interrupts, there are also *hardware interrupts*, which are input pins that are designed to stop the flow of a program when they receive an input, no matter what's going on in the code. Interrupts are beyond the scope of these notes, but see the documentation of your microprocessor to see if it supports interrupts and how to use them.

Another approach to the multitasking problem is to have separate processors handle the separate tasks. This could involve things like using a separate processor to drive a motor in a moving sculpture, letting a MIDI sampler handle the playback of music in a sound installation, or letting a desktop computer control a complex visual display while a microcontroller reads the input sensors. You're processing the task of interaction in parallel: each part of the job is given to an individual processor. All the processors talk to each other only when needed, such as when an event occurs that another processor needs to handle. Their attention to each other is minimal relative to the attention they give to their tasks. Because each task is simple, each processor can do it quickly, so overall response time of the system is within the range of human expectations.

Dividing the task among several processing devices is a higher-level solution that saves you the trouble of having to coordinate tasks at the programming level on one processor. It comes at a cost, however. First, there's the cost of equipment. Then there's the cost of time in figuring out the connections between components. Then there's the cost of coordinating what has become a complex system of many components. You always have to balance these costs against the costs of building your own programming and electronics. Even when you do use several processors, you still have to manage when they're listening to their sensors or controlling their outputs, and when they're passing that information along to each other. If it's easier to use several devices, and the financial costs aren't too extravagant, then that's the way to go. For example, we often resort to using serially controlled servo motor controllers whenever we're building projects using multiple servos. The mini-SSC from Scott Edwards Electronics (http://www.seetron.com) is an excellent example. On the other hand, when the cost becomes prohibitive or the complexity of the system gets out of hand, then the best solution is to manage everything on one central processor.

Edge Detection

Let's take the simplest possible event you might want to sense. A person presses a button, and you want to know when she pressed and when she released. You already know how to read a digital input continually. Here's the pseudocode:

```
Loop:
    If input is high then
        Print "Input is high"
    Else
        Print "Input is low"
    End if
End loop
```

If you've written a program like this, you know that what you get is something like this:

```
Input is low Input is low Input is low Input is low Input is high Input is high
Input is high Input is high Input is high Input is high Input is high Input is
high Input is low Input is low Input is low Input is low Input is low Input is
low Input is low Input is low Input is lo Input is low
```

Say you want to count the number of times a button (digital sensor) is pressed and turn on an LED when it's been pressed three times. You might be tempted to do something like this:

```
Set ButtonCounter to 0

loop:
    If the button is pressed then
        Add one to the ButtonCounter
```

```
        End if

        If the buttonCounterVar > 3 then
            Light the LED
            'reset the buttonCounterVar to 0
        end if
    end loop
```

However, this loop gets run several thousand times a second on a microcontroller. If it takes a human being a tenth of a second to take her finger off the button once she's pressed it, then the loop will get run hundreds of times during what she perceives as one press of the button. That's not a reliable way to count button presses at all!

To get around this problem, you need to consider not only the state of the button, but also the state of the button during last time the loop was run. If the button is high and the last state of the button was low, then you know that the person just began pressing the button. If the button is low and the last state is high, then you know she just stopped pressing the button. This is sometimes called *edge detection* because you're finding the beginning and ending edges of the button press (refer to Figure 8.2). By counting the ending edges, you know how many times the button's been pressed. For those readers used to multimedia programming in Lingo, Flash, or other GUI environments, this is the equivalent to a mouseUp or mouseDown event.

The steps used in edge detection are simple:

1. Read an input.
2. Compare it to the last reading.
3. Take action based on the comparison.
4. Store the current reading as the last reading so you can take a new one.

Here's a program that uses edge detection and properly counts button presses:

PBASIC

```
ButtonStateVar var byte
LastButtonStateVar var byte
ButtonCountVar var byte
Input 7  ' the button is on pin 7

main:
    ButtonStateVar = in7
    ' if the button isn't the same as it was last time through
    ' the main loop, then you want to do something:

    if buttonStateVar <> lastButtonStateVar then
        if buttonStateVar = 1 then
            ' the button went from off to on
            ButtonCountVar = ButtonCountVar + 1
            debug "Button is pressed.", 10, 13
        else
```

```
                        ' the button went from on to off
                        debug "Button is not pressed", 10, 13
                        debug "Button hits: ", DEC buttonCountVar, 10, 13
                    endif

                    ' store the state of the button for next check:
                    lastButtonStateVar = buttonStateVar
                endif
        goto main
```

MBasic

```
ButtonStateVar var byte
LastButtonStateVar var byte
ButtonCountVar var byte
Input 7  ' the button is on pin 7

main:
    ButtonStateVar = in7
    ' if the button isn't the same as it was last time through
    ' the main loop, then you want to do something:

    if buttonStateVar <> lastButtonStateVar then
        if buttonStateVar = 1 then
            ' the button went from off to on
            ButtonCountVar = ButtonCountVar + 1
            debug ["Button is pressed.", 10, 13]
        else
            ' the button went from on to off
            debug ["Button is not pressed", 10, 13]
            debug ["Button hits: ", DEC buttonCountVar, 10, 13]
        endif

        ' store the state of the button for next check:
        lastButtonStateVar = buttonStateVar
    endif
goto main
```

PicBasic
Pro

```
ButtonStateVar var byte
LastButtonStateVar var byte
ButtonCountVar var byte
Input portb.7    ' the switch is on RB7
ButtonStateVar = 0

main:
    ButtonStateVar = portb.7
    ' if the button isn't the same as it was last time through
```

```
                    ' the main loop, then you want to do something:

               if buttonStateVar <> lastButtonStateVar then
                   if buttonStateVar = 1 then
                       ' the button went from off to on
                       ButtonCountVar = ButtonCountVar + 1
                       serout2 portc.6, 16468, ["Button is pressed.", 10, 13]
                   else
                       ' the button went from on to off
                       serout2 portc.6, 16468, ["Button is not pressed", 10, 13]
                       serout2 portc.6, 16468, ["Button hits: ", DEC buttonCountVar, 10, 13]
                   endif

         ' store the state of the button for next check:
                   lastButtonStateVar = buttonStateVar
               endif
         goto main
```

(BX-Basic)

```
         Dim ButtonStateVar as byte
         Dim LastButtonStateVar as byte
         Dim ButtonCountVar as byte
         ' the button is on pin 12


         Sub main()
             do
                   ButtonStateVar = getPin(12)
                   ' if the button isn't the same as it was last time through
                   ' the main loop, then you want to do something:

                   if buttonStateVar <> lastButtonStateVar then
                       if buttonStateVar = 1 then
                           ' the button went from off to on
                           ButtonCountVar = ButtonCountVar + 1
                           Debug.print "Button is pressed."
                       else
                           ' the button went from on to off
                           debug.print "Button is not pressed"
                           debug.print "Button hits: "; Cstr( buttonCountVar)
                       end if

                       ' store the state of the button for next check:
                       lastButtonStateVar = buttonStateVar
                   end if
             loop
         end sub
```

The basic four steps of edge detection come up constantly when designing any kind of interactive system. Edge detection routines enable the microcontroller to interpret changes in sensor readings as higher-level actions. You'll use these steps all the time, whether you're reading digital or analog sensors.

Analog Sensors: Thresholds, Edges, and Peaks

When you're working with analog sensors, the beginnings and endings of the events you might sense are slightly different than for digital sensors. We will talk about three kinds of changes that you might look for: thresholds, edges, and peaks.

Finding Thresholds in an Analog Signal

Sometimes you only care whether your sensor has passed a threshold. For example, if you're working with a photocell, and you want to sense a flashlight falling on the photocell but not the ambient light in the room, you might write a routine to filter out all readings below a certain threshold. Testing whether or not your reading is above or below a threshold essentially turns your analog sensor into a digital sensor.

You could detect a threshold with a routine like the following:

```
establish threshold from a reading of ambient conditions at start up
Loop:
Read sensor
If sensor reading is higher than threshold then
        React
End if
End loop
```

This code is simple but it all depends on having a good number for the threshold. If you are in a controlled setting, you may be able to use a fixed number for your threshold. But if your sensor were a photocell, for example, this threshold might work in the morning but not at night. You might need to calibrate the threshold to different ambient conditions. One quick way of doing this it to grab a sensor reading before you enter your main loop and use that for the threshold. You would just have to make sure that your microcontroller is powered up under normal ambient conditions to get a good threshold and restart the chip to recalibrate the threshold. Another approach is to continually read a *control* sensor that is situated in an area away from the area where you expect change. The reading from the control sensor gives you the current baseline of ambient conditions and is used to set the threshold for the sensor that is actually changing. For thresholds that automatically recalibrate over time, you will need to average your readings over time. See the section called "Smoothing, Sampling, and Averaging" for more on this.

Finding Edges in an Analog Signal

If you think about the threshold as an edge, the process of sensing when the sensor is activated is similar to the digital sensor example above. You take a reading, determine if it's above your threshold, and if the previous reading was below the threshold, the sensor has just been triggered. If the reading is below the threshold and the previous reading was above, then the sensor has just ceased to be triggered.

Techniques for Effective Interaction

This is a very simple routine. It's much like the digital input reading routine before you added edge detection. A slightly more refined routine might incorporate an analog version of edge detection, like so:

```
Loop:
      Read sensor
      If sensor reading is higher than threshold then
            If previous sensor reading was below threshold then
                  React
            End if
      End if
      Save the current sensor reading as the last reading
End loop
```

Since the logic of analog edge detection is the same as it is for digital edge detection, we'll leave it to you to write your own actual code for this.

You might find that find your readings are fluctuating slightly above and then below your threshold, giving you many apparent edges when you are really being still. For example, in the photocell graph in Figure 8.4, you can see lots of ripples in the edge of the curve. These could appear as multiple threshold crossings when in reality there's only one crossing that you care about. You can use some of the techniques in the section called "Smoothing, Sampling and Averaging" to reduce this problem.

Finding Peaks in an Analog Signal

Analog threshold detection is great for testing when an analog sensor crosses a threshold when it's rising or falling. Sometimes, however, you want to know when it's reached a peak and is headed back down again. For example, imagine the sensor in the graph on the right in Figure 8.4 is the sensor for a key on a piano keyboard. To know how loud the note is to be played, you would want to know the peak, which tells you how hard the key was hit. In this case, a slight variation on the edge detection routine would do the trick. Instead of an edge, you have a peak, where the sensor reaches its maximum value. In order to find the peak, you look for the sensor's reading to cross the threshold going up, then wait until it reaches a maximum and take that maximum as the peak.

In order to determine a peak, you have to set a threshold for when you start and stop looking for the peak. Figure 8.4 shows readings from two different sensors. The figure on the top shows what happens when you cover a photocell with your hand quickly. The figure on the bottom shows several taps on a force-sensitive resistor (FSR). You can see that the taps on the FSR happen much quicker than the covering of the photocell. There's a clear peak on each tap on the FSR. The readings start at zero (which is the threshold where you start and end looking for the peak) and end at zero. In the photocell graph on the left there is a peak, but the beginning and ending point is not as clear, so you need to set a threshold to determine which readings you care about and which you don't. With the photocell, you might only care when the light crosses the threshold, because the change is so gradual. On the other hand, because the change in the FSR readings is sudden, you might need to look for the peak.

Figure 8.4
Analog sensor readings. On the top, a photocell being covered and uncovered quickly. On the bottom, several taps on a force-sensitive resistor.

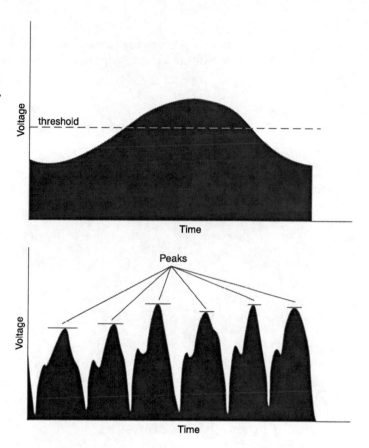

In pseudocode, finding a peak looks like this:

```
Loop:
    Read sensor
    If sensorValue >= threshold then
        If sensorValue >= lastSensorValue then
            PeakValue = sensorValue
        End if
    Else
        If peakValue >= threshold then
            this is the final peak value; take action
        end if
        Set the peak value to 0 so we can start it rising next loop
    End if
End loop
```

You might have to set your threshold fairly high in order to eliminate false peaks like the ones you see at the beginning of each reading in the graph on the bottom in Figure 8.4.

Peak finding is useful when your sensor changes very fast, like the key on the keyboard mentioned above, but it's not as useful for sensors that change slowly, like a volume knob. Before you implement a peak-finding routine, decide whether your sensor lends itself to finding peaks first.

Here's the actual code:

PBASIC

```
PeakValue VAR Word
SensorValue VAR Word
LastSensorValue VAR Word
Threshold VAR Word
Noise var word

Threshold = 50      ' set your own value based on your sensors
PeakValue = 0     ' initialize peakValue
Noise = 5

Main:
    ' read sensor on pin 0:
    HIGH 0
    PAUSE 1
    RCTIME 0, 1, sensorValue

    ' check to see that it's above the threshold:
    IF sensorValue >= threshold + noise THEN
        ' if it's greater than the last reading,
        ' then make it our current peak:
        IF sensorValue >= lastSensorValue + noise THEN
            PeakValue = sensorValue
        ENDIF
    ELSE
        IF peakValue >= threshold THEN
            ' this is the final peak value; take action
            DEBUG "peak reading", DEC peakValue, 10, 13
        ENDIF

        ' reset peakValue, since we've finished with this peak:
        peakValue = 0
    ENDIF

    ' store the current sensor value for the next loop:
    lastSensorValue = sensorValue
GOTO main
```

MBasic

```
PeakValue var word
SensorValue var word
```

```
LastSensorValue var word
Threshold var word
noise var word


Threshold = 50     ' set your own value based on your sensors
Noise = 7
PeakValue = 0      ' initialize peakValue
Main:
    ' read sensor on pin 0:
    ADin 0, sensorValue

    ' check to see that it's above the threshold:
    If sensorValue >= threshold + Noise then
        ' if it's greater than the last reading,
        ' then make it our current peak:
        If sensorValue >= lastSensorValue + noise then
            PeakValue = sensorValue
        endif
    Else
        If peakValue >= threshold then
            ' this is the final peak value; take action
            debug ["peak reading", DEC peakValue, 10, 13]
        endif

        ' reset peakValue, since we've finished with this peak:
        peakValue = 0
    Endif

    ' store the current sensor value for the next loop:
    lastSensorValue = sensorValue
Goto main
```

```
PicBasic        ' Define ADCIN parameters
 Pro            DEFINE    ADC_BITS       10        ' Set number of bits in result
                DEFINE    ADC_CLOCK      3         ' Set clock source (3=rc)
                DEFINE    ADC_SAMPLEUS   20        ' Set sampling time in uS


                PeakValue var word
                SensorValue var word
                LastSensorValue var word
                Threshold var word
                Noise var word


                Threshold = 50     ' set your own value based on your sensors
                PeakValue = 0      ' initialize peakValue
```

```
                noise = 5

                ' Set PORTA to all input
                TRISA = %11111111
                ' Set up ADCON1
                ADCON1 = %10000010

        Main:
                ' read sensor on pin RA0:
                ADCin 0, sensorValue

                ' check to see that it's above the threshold:
                If sensorValue >= threshold + noise then
                    ' if it's greater than the last reading,
                    ' then make it our current peak:
                    If sensorValue >= lastSensorValue + Noise then
                        PeakValue = sensorValue
                    endif
                Else
                    If peakValue >= threshold then
                        ' this is the final peak value; take action
                        serout2 portc.6, 16468, [ "peak reading", DEC peakValue, 13,10]
                    endif

                    ' reset peakValue, since we've finished with this peak:
                    peakValue = 0
                Endif

                ' store the current sensor value for the next loop:
                lastSensorValue = sensorValue
        Goto main
```

```
BX-Basic    Dim PeakValue as integer
            dim noise as integer
            Dim SensorValue as integer
            Dim LastSensorValue as integer
            Dim Threshold as integer

            Sub Main()
            Threshold = 300        ' set your own value based on your sensors
            noise = 7
            PeakValue = 0      ' initialize peakValue

                do
                    ' read sensor on pin 13:
```

```
sensorValue = getADC(13)
'debug.print cstr(sensorValue)
' check to see that it's above the threshold:
If sensorValue >= threshold + Noise then

    ' if it's greater than the last reading,
    ' then make it our current peak:
    If sensorValue >= lastSensorValue + noise then
        PeakValue = sensorValue
    End if
Else
    If peakValue >= threshold then
        ' this is the final peak value; take action
        debug.print "peak reading: "; cStr(peakValue)
    end if

    ' reset peakValue, since we've finished with this peak:
    peakValue = 0
End if

' store the current sensor value for the next loop:
lastSensorValue = sensorValue
        loop
    end sub
```

Debouncing

If you were using a homemade switch, or any switch with loose contacts, you may have noticed when you ran the edge detection routine that every once in a while, the button count advanced by more than one when you pressed the button. What happened?

If you've ever been shocked by static electricity jumping from your hand to a metal doorknob on a cold, dry day, you know that it's possible for electricity to jump through air when two conductors are close to each other and when the charge is great enough. At the lowest physical level, a switch is just two mechanical contacts that can be brought into contact with each other or separated. When the contacts are brought close together, but not touching, the same phenomenon can occur. For the last few fractions of a second before the contacts make a solid connection, they bounce off each other and grind together. It's possible for them to make and break electrical contact several times in a few milliseconds, and current tries to leap the gap, sometimes succeeding and sometimes failing. Because the microcontroller is reading the switch several thousand times a second or more in our applications, it's not uncommon for it to detect these false contacts before the switch is properly closed. The microcontroller might read the press of a button something like in Figure 8.5.

During the time between the arrows, the switch is being closed. This may be less than a millisecond long, but the microcontroller can still take several readings during that time.

Figure 8.5
Readings from a
switch on a time scale
of milliseconds or
microseconds.

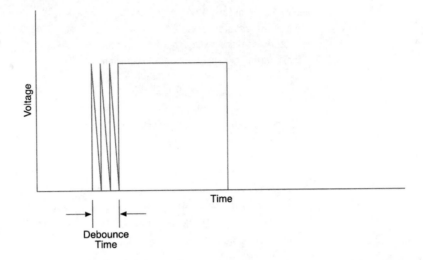

This can mean that sometimes, even when you're using an edge detection routine like
the one above, you might still get false readings. To prevent this, you can use a debounce
routine. *Debouncing* a switch is the process of checking its reading two or more times
over a very short interval (less than human reaction time) to ensure an accurate reading.
It works like this:

```
If the switch is on
    Wait a fraction of a second
    If the switch is still on then
        Take action
    End if
End if
```

Here's a simple debounce routine:

PBASIC

MBasic

```
SwitchOnVar var byte
Input 7

Main:
    If in7 = 1 then
        Pause 10 ' 10 milliseconds; change the time to suit your needs
        If in7 = 1 then
            SwitchOnVar = 1
        Else
            SwitchOnVar = 0
        Endif
    Endif
Goto main
```

PicBasic Pro

```
SwitchOnVar var byte
Input portb.7


Main:
    If portb.7 = 1 then
        Pause 10 ' 10 milliseconds; change the time to suit your needs
        If portb.7 = 1 then
            SwitchOnVar = 1
        Else
            SwitchOnVar = 0
        Endif
    Endif
Goto main
```

BX-Basic

```
Dim SwitchOnVar as byte


Sub Main()
    do
        If getPin(12) = 1 then
            Call delay(0.01)' 10 ms; change the time to suit your needs
            If getPin(12) = 1 then
                SwitchOnVar = 1
            Else
                SwitchOnVar = 0
            End if
        End if
    Loop
End sub
```

Debounce routines can be used with analog sensors as well, though it's more common to check an analog reading to see if it's higher or lower than a given threshold or within an acceptable range than to check if it's identical to its past reading. Unlike digital sensors, which can have only two states (on or off), analog sensors can have multiple states. Sometimes the difference between one state and another may be imperceptible to humans, but readable by microprocessors.

Smoothing, Sampling, and Averaging

Much of what you do in programming physical computing projects is to figure out how to deal with the world's natural randomness and make it look smooth. A photoresistor read through an analog-to-digital converter, for example, will never give you a steady value. It always fluctuates with tiny changes in lighting that your eye automatically filters out. Because the microcontroller will read these changes that you don't see,[4] the changes get reflected in

---

[4] For more on this, see Donald Hoffman's *Visual Intelligence: How We Create What We See* (W.W.Norton & Co., 1998) or Tor Nørretranders' *The User Illusion* (Viking, 1999).

Techniques for Effective Interaction

the output. Your sensors and their supporting circuitry will also introduce noise that is not actually in the environment. In practice, you often need to smooth out your readings.

Whenever you start to work with a new sensor, you should get in the habit of testing the sensor with a simple piece of code that just reads it and returns the values continually so that you can watch its behavior over time. The simple digital and analog input programs from Chapter 6 do this job nicely.

A quick way to smooth out your numbers is simply to divide each reading by the amount of fluctuation you typically see. For instance, if your numbers fluctuate within a range of five points when the sensor is at rest, just divide by 5 and the numbers will appear to be still as well. This will give you a smaller range of numbers, however, so your smoothness comes at the expense of resolution. By reducing the resolution to the minimum needed to begin with, you can reduce the jitter you get from noisy readings before it's a problem. For example, if your instrument only plays 12 notes, try dividing your analog range down to 1–12 right away. The process of scaling down your numbers was covered in Chapter 6.

Taking a number of recent readings into account is another approach that can help smooth your results. To do this, you keep an array of recent readings and have a variable to keep track of the last reading that you put into the array. Averaging the recent readings will keep your resolution high and will appear to smooth things out as long as the readings are fluctuating within a limited range.

```
make an array for recent readings
loop
     read sensor
     find the next place in the array
     if you are at the end of the array go the beginning
     insert the current reading to the array, replacing the oldest one
     total all the readings together in a repeat loop
     divide the total of all recent readings by the number of recent readings

end loop
```

If the fluctuations are caused by random noise, the best way to eliminate those freak readings is to take the median (the middle of a sorted set) rather than the average of recent readings. In this way, freakish readings are discarded without affecting normal readings as much. To do this, you have to sort the array of past readings and pick the middle item.

```
make an array for recent readings
loop
     read sensor
     find the next place in the array
     if you are at the end of the array go the beginning
     insert the current reading to the array, replacing the oldest one
     sort all the readings into a separate array by value
     take the middle reading of the sorted array

end loop
```

Any scheme that takes recent readings into account will make your system slower to respond because past readings are still weighing down the average as your sensor heads in a new direction.

Here's the actual code for both averaging and median filtering. Note that this code uses two big arrays, which take up a lot of memory, particularly for the Basic Stamp.

```pbasic
lastPositionInArray CON 2 ' keep a history of the past 3 readings
temp VAR Word
average VAR Word
median VAR Word
positionInPastArray VAR Byte
past VAR Word(lastPositionInArray)
sortedPast VAR Word(lastPositionInArray) 'we all have one

' variables for subroutines:
i VAR Byte
total VAR Word
j VAR Byte
position VAR Byte


positionInPastArray = lastPositionInArray

PAUSE 500 ' start program with a half-second delay

main:
    'get the reading:
    HIGH 8
    PAUSE 1
    RCTIME 8,1,temp



    'add the reading to an array of past readings,
    ' and reposition the oldest:
    positionInPastArray = positionInPastArray + 1
    IF positionInPastArray > lastPositionInArray THEN
        positionInPastArray = 0
    ENDIF
    past(positionInPastArray) = temp

    ' subroutine averageArray averages the array (see below):
    GOSUB averageArray

    ' subroutine medianArray() gets the middle of the array:
```

```
        GOSUB medianArray

        ' print the results:
        DEBUG " Average = ", DEC average, " Median = ", DEC median,  13
    GOTO main

averageArray:
        'average the values in the array:
        total = 0
        FOR i = 0 TO lastPositionInArray
            total = total + past(i)
        NEXT
        temp = (lastPositionInArray + 1)
        average = total /temp
    RETURN


medianArray:
        'simplest sorting routine; this could be faster
        FOR i = 0 TO lastPositionInArray
            position = 255   'same as -1 for a byte
            FOR j = 0 TO lastPositionInArray
                IF past(i) >= past(j) THEN
                    position = position + 1
                ENDIF
            NEXT
            sortedPast(position) = past(i)
        NEXT

        ' get the middle element:
        median = sortedPast( (lastPositionInArray / 2))

        ' just for debugging purposes, print the sorted array:
        FOR i = 0 TO lastPositionInArray
            temp = sortedPast(i)
            DEBUG DEC temp, 32 ' 32 = ASCII space
        NEXT

    RETURN
```

```
MBasic    lastPositionInArray CON 4 ' keep a history of the past 5 readings
          temp VAR Word
          average VAR Word
          median VAR Word
          positionInPastArray VAR Byte
          past VAR Word(lastPositionInArray)
```

```
sortedPast VAR Word(lastPositionInArray) 'we all have one

' variables for subroutines:
i VAR Byte
total VAR Word
j VAR Byte
position VAR Byte


positionInPastArray = lastPositionInArray

PAUSE 500 ' start program with a half-second delay

main:
    'get the reading:
    ADIN 0, temp

    'add the reading to an array of past readings,
    ' and reposition the oldest:
    positionInPastArray = positionInPastArray + 1
    IF positionInPastArray > lastPositionInArray THEN
        positionInPastArray = 0
    ENDIF
    past(positionInPastArray) = temp

    ' subroutine averageArray averages the array (see below):
    GOSUB averageArray

    ' subroutine medianArray() gets the middle of the array:
    GOSUB medianArray

    ' print the results:
    DEBUG [" Average = ", DEC average, " Median = ", DEC median,   13]
GOTO main
averageArray:
    'average the values in the array:
    total = 0
    FOR i = 0 TO lastPositionInArray
        total = total + past(i)
    NEXT
    temp = (lastPositionInArray + 1)
    average = total /temp
RETURN

medianArray:
    'simplest sorting routine; this could be faster
```

```
            FOR i = 0 TO lastPositionInArray
                position = 255   'same as -1 for a byte
                FOR j = 0 TO lastPositionInArray
                    IF past(i) >= past(j) THEN
                        position = position + 1
                    ENDIF
                NEXT
                sortedPast(position) = past(i)
            NEXT

            ' get the middle element:
            median = sortedPast( (lastPositionInArray / 2))

            ' just for debugging purposes, print the sorted array:
            FOR i = 0 TO lastPositionInArray
                temp = sortedPast(i)
                DEBUG [DEC temp, 32 ]' 32 = ASCII space
            NEXT

        RETURN
```

PicBasic
Pro

```
' Define ADCIN parameters
DEFINE ADC_BITS 10 ' Set number of bits in result
DEFINE ADC_CLOCK 3    ' Set clock source (3=rc)
DEFINE ADC_SAMPLEUS 50     ' Set sampling time in uS

TRISA = %11111111 ' Set PORTA to all input
ADCON1 = %10000010 ' Set PORTA analog and right justify result
Pause 500 ' Wait .5 second

lastPositionInArray CON 9 ' keep a history of the past ten readings
temp VAR Word
average VAR Word
median VAR Word
positionInPastArray VAR Byte

' variables for subroutines:
i VAR Byte
j VAR Byte
total VAR Word
position VAR Byte
past VAR Word(lastPositionInArray)
sortedPast VAR Word(lastPositionInArray) 'we all have one
```

```
positionInPastArray = lastPositionInArray

PAUSE 500 ' start program with a half-second delay

main:
    'get the reading:
    ADCIN 0, temp


    ' add the reading to an array of past readings,
    ' and reposition the oldest:
    positionInPastArray = positionInPastArray + 1
    IF positionInPastArray > lastPositionInArray THEN
        positionInPastArray = 0
    ENDIF
    past(positionInPastArray) = temp
    ' subroutine medianArray() gets the middle of the array:
    GOSUB medianArray
    ' subroutine averageArray averages the array (see below):
    GOSUB averageArray


    ' print the results:
    serout2 portc.6, 16468, [" Average = ", DEC average, " Median = ",
        DEC median, 10, 13]
    serout2 portc.6, 16468, [" Median = ", DEC median, 10, 13]
GOTO main

averageArray:
    ' average the values in the array:
    total = 0
    FOR i = 0 TO lastPositionInArray
        total = total + past(i)
    NEXT
    Temp = (lastPositionInArray + 1)
    average = total /temp
RETURN

medianArray:
    'simplest sorting routine; this could be faster
    FOR i = 0 TO lastPositionInArray
        position = 255 'same as -1
        FOR j = 0 TO lastPositionInArray
            IF past(i) >= past(j) THEN
                position = position + 1
            ENDIF
        NEXT
```

```
            sortedPast(position) = past(i)
    NEXT


    ' get the middle element:
    median = sortedPast(lastPositionInArray / 2)


    ' just for debugging purposes, print the sorted array:
    FOR i = 0 TO lastPositionInArray
    temp = sortedPast(i)
    serout2 portc.6, 16468, [DEC temp, 32] ' 32 = ASCII space
    NEXT


    serout2 portc.6, 16468, [10, 13]
RETURN
```

BX-Basic

```
const lastPositionInArray as byte = 4 ' keep a history of the past 5 readings
dim past (0 to lastPositionInArray) as integer
dim sortedPast (0 to lastPositionInArray) as integer 'we all have one
dim average as integer
dim median as integer
dim positionInPastArray as byte


Sub Main()
    Debug.Print "start"
    positionInPastArray = lastPositionInArray
    call delay(0.5) ' start program with a half-second delay


    do


        ' add the reading to an array of past readings,
        ' and reposition the oldest:
        positionInPastArray = positionInPastArray + 1
        if positionInPastArray > lastPositionInArray then
            positionInPastArray = 0
        end if
        'replace the oldest reading with a new reading
        past(positionInPastArray) = getADC(13)


        ' subroutine averageArray() averages the array (see below):
        call averageArray()


        ' subroutine medianArray() sorts the array
        ' and takes the middle of the array:
        call medianArray()


        ' print the results:
```

```
            debug.print " Average = " ; cstr(average);
            debug.print " Median = " ; cstr(median)


      loop
End Sub

Sub averageArray()
    ' average the values in the array:
    dim i as byte
    dim total as integer
    total = 0
    for i = 0 to lastPositionInArray
        total = total + past(i)
    next
    average = total\cInt(lastPositionInArray+1)
end sub

sub medianArray()
    dim i as byte
    dim j as byte
    dim position as byte
    dim arrayElement as integer

'simplest sorting routine fine for short array; could be faster
    for i = 0 to lastPositionInArray
        position = 0
        for j = 0 to lastPositionInArray
            if past(i) > past(j) then
                position = position + 1
            end if
        next
        sortedPast(position) = past(i)
    next

    ' get the middle element:
    median = sortedPast((lastPositionInArray\2))

' just for debugging purposes, print the sorted array:
    for i = 0 to lastPositionInArray
        arrayElement = sortedPast(i)
        debug.print cstr(arrayElement); ",";
    next
end sub
```

Conclusion

The techniques above will help you in realizing a well-designed interaction scheme. Multitasking will give your system the ability to sense and respond at a human rhythm; edge detection, threshold setting, and peak finding will allow you to define discrete events, and debouncing and smoothing will allow you to smooth out noise and the fluctuations that are insignificant to human senses so that the system can sense change on a broader time scale. These techniques won't solve all of your interaction problems, but they'll give you a basis for defining the interaction in terms that humans can understand. When applying these techniques, keep in mind the principles of interaction discussed in the first section of this chapter.

One of the first rules of performance is that actors need to be given something to do, not told what to feel. From the action, they will find their own way to the emotion or the logic of the story. There's a similar principle at work to physical interaction design: participants need to be given something to do in an experience. If there's meaning to be had in the work, they'll interpret it themselves based on the action. If they aren't given logical sequences of action to follow or to discover, they won't engage with the work. Actions must be clearly indicated or suggested, and there must be a progression from one action to the next, whether it's action taken by the participant, by the system, or by both.

When planning your project, picture not only what it is you're making, but also the person who will be experiencing it. Picture her actions as an integrated part of the whole system, and balance the rhythm of the experience so that all participants are an active part of the whole, not just passive observers who occasionally trigger another prerecorded or computationally generated sequence. Don't tell them what to think; show them what to do.

Finally, it's important to watch how people use your project. When a user can't operate it, you'll be tempted to instruct him, and might even get impatient and argue with him. Don't do this. His interpretation of what's going on is based on his observations. If he doesn't understand part of the system, it's an indication that what you built for him to observe doesn't provide enough for his mental model of the system's workings to match yours. The best thing you can do at this point is to drop your theories about what works and watch the user carefully with an open mind. Consider conforming the interaction to his expectations, or consider what would make his model of the system match yours.

9
Sensing Movement

Some of the most popular interactions in physical computing tap into the sometimes unnoticed but unavoidable tendency people have to express themselves through bodily movement. People move in order to position themselves best for a given activity, to get a better look at something they're interested in, to respond to music or some other stimulus, or just because they're uncomfortable and need to shift their weight. Body movement is exploited in some of the most common everyday applications, from the auto-flush mechanisms on public toilets to the light switches in our offices that turn on automatically when they detect movement. Position and motion sensors make it relatively simple to take advantage of body position and movement for a wide range of projects, from making ghosts in haunted houses leap out when a person passes a door threshold to changing the lighting and projections in a dance club based on the combined movement of bodies on a dance floor.

What all these interactions have in common is the ability of the computer to sense the position of objects in space. Given that the toilets at the airport know when you are standing in front of them,[1] you would think that this is an easy task. In fact, this can be a very difficult problem, depending on how much information you need and how much you can control the environment. In this chapter, we'll discuss a number of techniques for detecting position, motion, and orientation. We'll also discuss ways to constrain the environment to make the most effective use of the sensors described.

Assessing the Problem

In order to sense bodies in motion, you have to begin by determining how much you need to know about their motions. There are a few basic factors of motion to consider:

▶ *Position*. Do you need to know where something is within a space?

▶ *Orientation*. Do you need to know if they're rotating about an axis? Which way they're facing?

▶ *Velocity*. Do you need to know how fast they're moving, and in which direction they're moving?

---

[1] Bill Buxton, former chief scientist at Alias Research, is famous for exhorting computers manufacturers to make computers at least as smart as the toilets at O'Hare airport.

> *Absolute or Relative*. Do you need to know an object's absolute position in a space, or just the change from its previous position?

> *Identity*. Do you need to discern between multiple objects?

When talking about position and orientation, you have to consider the *degrees of freedom* the body has in which to move. The fewer degrees of freedom you are interested in, the easier the job. There are three degrees of freedom for position: left to right (X axis), up and down (Y axis), and front to back (Z axis). On top of these, there are three more degrees of freedom for orientation or rotation: rotation around the X axis (*tilt* or *pitch*), rotation around the Y axis (*pan* or *yaw*), or rotation around the Z axis (*roll*).

Range of sensitivity is one of the most important criteria when choosing a sensor. Many of the sensors discussed below are ranging sensors, meaning that they sense distance of a body from the sensor or movement in front of the sensor. The range of most sensors is constrained on the maximum end and on the minimum end. Most sensors will have an effective range of under 9 feet. Video tracking is an exception to this because you can adjust the range by adjusting the zoom on the lens. In addition, distance-ranging sensors will not operate uniformly at all distances, so you have to work with the zone in which they're most sensitive. Figure 9.1 illustrates the typical cone-shaped zone of sensitivity that most ranging sensors have.

Figure 9.1
Many of the sensors in this chapter have a cone-shaped field of sensitivity.

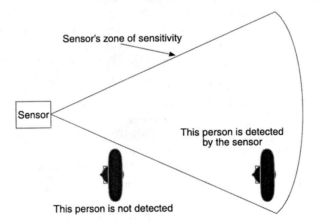

The best course of action in dealing with the various challenges of position tracking is not to apply more sophisticated technology. Better results usually come from constraining the environment to make your job easier. For example, ask yourself how many people should be able to experience your project at one time. Consider constraining the space or the entrances and exits so only one person at a time can fit through rather than dealing with identifying multiple targets. There will be times when this is inappropriate or limits the project too much, but if it doesn't make any difference, or if it improves your project to work with a constrained space, do so. Like a good magician, you should make your necessary constraints look like a perfectly natural part of your system.

How Ranging Sensors Work

Most sensors that read the distance from a target send out some form of energy (light, magnetism, or sound) as a reference signal. They measure the amount of energy that reflected off the target and compare it with the energy that went out. Then they convert the difference into an electrical voltage or digital signal that you can read on a microcontroller. For example, a very cheap low-tech solution for making your computer as smart as the toilets at the airport would be to place a photocell and a flashlight on your computer monitor facing the user (see Figure 9.2). As a person gets closer to the computer, more of the light from the flashlight will bounce off of her body back to the photocell. The photocell would then give you a reading of whether a person was sitting in front of the computer and roughly how close she was sitting.

Figure 9.2
Many distance sensors work by sending a beam of energy (light, sound, and so on) out and bouncing it off the target.

Source

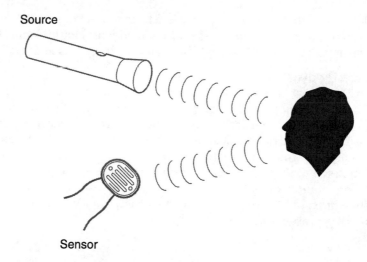

Sensor

This principle is common to many different sensors and across many scales. On a small scale, there are the finger sensors in virtual-reality gloves. In some of these gloves, light is sent down an optical fiber that rides along each finger.[2] The fiber is scratched at each knuckle so that a little light escapes when the fiber is bent. Bending a finger causes less light to reach the end of the fiber. A photocell at the end captures the light and reads the change as an analog value. On a large scale, airplane radar systems operate by sending out a radio signal and measuring the time it takes for the signal to bounce back from a target.

This simple theory might inspire you to start making lots of homegrown sensors like the flashlight example above. Keep in mind that ambient conditions in the field might wreak havoc on a project that you've only tested in the lab. In the virtual-reality glove example above, both the light source and the sensor could be completely encased and never affected by ambient conditions. In real life situations, people with different wardrobes, hairstyles, and skin pigmentation will reflect light differently. Because there is no lens over the photocell, light coming from other sources and from every direction will affect the

---

[2] Unless you have a manufactured version of this, we recommend using flex sensors instead for most glove projects. Flex sensor finger sensors are much easier to build.

photocell. Changing ambient lighting conditions can interfere with your expectations of how much light should bounce back. Finally, your user may not enjoy having a flashlight shining in her face. We do not want to discourage your homegrown sensors, especially for very contained environments. However, it's generally worth the money to buy a commercial sensor module when it is available. These modules typically use lenses or filters to narrow the field of sensitivity. They use infrared light, ultrasonic sound, or other energy sources that are not perceptible by humans. In addition, they often send out energy that is modulated at a distinctive frequency to make it easier to distinguish it from other sources in the environment.

Detecting Presence

Sometimes all you want to know is whether someone is present or not. This only requires a simple digital input sensor. For example, if your haunted house multimedia extravaganza is started when a person enters a doorway, all you need is a digital sensor to tell when he enters.

One common use for distance sensors is to track a person moving in front of an object in order to trigger the object to action when the person gets close enough. This can be very effective, but keep in mind that being present and paying attention are not the same thing, as any parent or teacher can confirm. Imagine that you want to sense when a person is looking at your painting so that you can make the painting respond in some way. You could put a ranging sensor in front of the painting and look for a person to get close enough, but this sensor alone won't tell you whether she's got her back to the painting or not. Sensing attention is a more complex problem. The sensors we'll cover in this section are good for sensing presence only, but the sensors in the next section, "Determining Position," can be useful for detecting presence as well.

Foot Switches

Foot switches are the most straightforward means of detecting a person's presence, especially within a small area. The most common type is made of long strips of metal tape separated at intervals by foam tape. When someone steps on these sensors, the foam tape compresses and the metal strips touch each other like the contacts of any other switch. The biggest problem with these sensors is that they need to be robust enough to withstand the weight of people constantly stepping on them. For this reason, it's probably better to use a commercial version, even though they seem very simple to make. There are some good ones available at http://www.tapeswitch.com. For a higher-end analog version, see the TapTiles made for Infusion Systems' I-Cube (http:// www.infusionsystems.com). Floor pads tend to be ugly and should be concealed beneath some sort of carpet.

Photoelectric Switches

In a photoelectric switch, a light beam hits a target sensor. When the beam is broken by a body passing between the sensor and the light source, the switch is activated. These are the "electric eye" switches that have been used for decades in such things as automatic door openers. They're great for detecting passage through some threshold, such as a body through a doorway or a hand through a hole in a box. You always see these in movies about jewel theft, sending red beams of light across the room around the treasure. In reality, you seldom see the beam, and the jewel thief is never as attractive as the ones in the movies. Some photoelectric switches have an emitter on one side and a detector on the other. Others have the emitter and detector on one side and just a mirror on the other side. You can make your own with a cheap laser pointer on one side and a photocell or phototransistor on the other. Keep in mind that these sensors are digital, not analog. They won't tell you how far the body is from the light, just that the body crossed the beam of the light.

You can also buy photoelectric switches from any burglar alarm supply store (see Figure 9.3). These burglar alarm sensors can be effective across very wide areas and don't necessarily even need a microcontroller. They usually have two terminals, which get connected when the beam breaks. You can connect these as a switch into a digital input circuit or use it directly to turn on a relay or another low-amperage device. Quite often, they will delay their reset for some period of time after being tripped. There's usually a potentiometer in the device for lowering the delay. You may not be able to lower it to zero, though, depending on the sensor you buy. Highly Electric (http://www.highly.com) carries photoelectric switches if you're looking online for a source.

Figure 9.3
A photoelectric switch and its target, and an infrared sensor. These two sensors work on similar principles, but the photoelectric switch is digital (only detects if someone crosses the beam), and the ranging sensor is analog (measures the distance between the person and the sensor).

Motion Detectors

Motion detectors are those ubiquitous beige or black boxes with an LED that blinks when someone walks anywhere in the room (see Figure 9.4). These sensors respond to changes in the infrared light in the space. They only react to change, so will not tell you if someone is in the room and standing still, only if they are moving. The ones used for burglar alarms usually come with terminals that will connect as a switch into a digital input circuit. They offer a distinct advantage over photoelectric switches in that they are extremely easy to install, usually have a much wider field of sensitivity that can be adjusted by changing the lenses that usually come with them. Like photoelectric switches, these sensors will delay their reset for some period of time after being tripped. There's usually a potentiometer in the device for reducing the delay, but again, you may not be able to reduce it to zero, depending on your sensor. You can also hack into the motion sensors used for outdoor lights, which are cheaper and usually available in any hardware store. Though these

Figure 9.4
A motion detector.

sensors are usually designed to switch 120 volts AC, they usually operate well on as low as 5 to 12 volts DC, so they'll work with your microcontroller.

Magnetic Switches

Magnetic switches consist of a very thin pair of contacts in a protective housing. When exposed to a magnet they're drawn together, closing the switch. Sometimes you'll see the switches themselves (without the magnets) sold as *reed switches*. The magnetic switch is a favorite for sensing the position of moving objects because the magnet doesn't require any wires (see Figure 9.5). Suppose you want an object to be able to move unencumbered by wires, but you want to know when it is placed on a pedestal. You might simply put a magnet in the bottom of the object and the magnetic switch on the top of the pedestal.

Figure 9.5
A creepy doll head
with a magnetic switch
inside the neck. The
magnet is in the head.

Hall-effect sensors are similar to magnetic switches in that they detect a changing magnetic field. The simplest Hall-effect sensors are digital ones that change their output from low to high when the magnetic field around them changes. Analog Hall-effect sensors output a variable voltage as the strength of the magnetic field around them changes. Hall-effect sensors are very easy to use. Typically they have three leads: power, ground, and output. To use them, you give them voltage and ground, then connect the output to your microcontroller, reading it as digital or analog depending on the nature of the sensor. The range on a Hall-effect sensor is very short, a couple of inches at most, so they're really of most use for measuring very small changes between magnetic objects. Jameco and Digi-Key (http://www.jameco.com and http://www.digikey.com) both carry Hall-effect sensors.

Determining Position

The sensors we've covered so far allow you to tell whether a person is in a particular space or whether or not they've moved in the space, but they don't tell you where the person is or where she's moving. Following are a few sensors for determining that. Most of these will enable you to determine the person's or object's speed and velocity as well, if you keep track of the change in position.

It is common to equate digital sensors with detecting presence and analog proximity sensors with detecting distance. This is not always true. Given enough digital data points, you can create an analog feel from digital sensors. For example, if you put enough digital floor switches in a room, you would know roughly where in the room the person is standing by which floor switch they are standing on. Conversely, analog sensors can be used in a "binary" way by sensing if a particular threshold has been passed (see Chapter 8 for details on thresholds). You can change this threshold in software, giving you further flexibility for changing conditions.

IR Sensors

You really can't beat the Sharp GP2D family of IR sensors (carried by http://www.acroname.com, http://www.digikey.com, and other retailers) for determining short distance. They are cheap, relatively accurate, and easy to use. These sensors send out an infrared beam and read the reflection of the beam off a target (refer to Figure 9.2). Different models work at different ranges. The longest range sensor in the family, the GP2Y0A02YK, can sense from eight to 56 inches. The shortest range one, the GP2D120, can sense a range from about 1.5 to 12 inches. There are analog sensors in this family and digital sensors. The digital sensors trigger when a person or object moves within a given threshold distance of the sensor. The analog sensors output a variable voltage from 0 to 5 volts, which varies with the distance. We find the analog ones more useful because they can always be converted to digital use by measuring for a threshold. The standard analog input circuit (refer to Chapter 6) will work for these if your microcontroller has A/D conversion built in. Figure 9.6 shows the schematic and the wiring. If your microcontroller has no A/D converters, you can use a variation on the R-C circuit used with the rctime command, as shown in Figure 9.7.

Figure 9.6
The Sharp GP2D12 infrared sensor connected to a microcontroller with built-in analog-to-digital conversion.

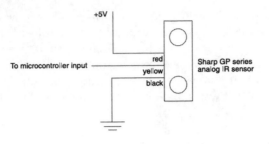

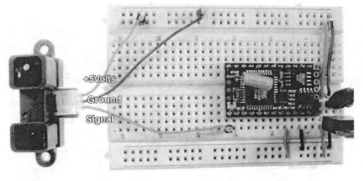

Figure 9.7
The RCTime circuit with a Sharp GP2D12 IR sensor.

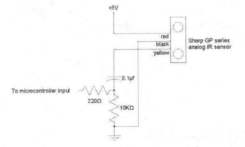

Ultrasonic Sensors

For longer ranges, ultrasonic ranging modules work well. Just like sonar devices, they send out a ping of ultrasonic sound, and then time how long it takes to bounce back. The longer it takes for the ping to return, the further away your target is. There are several different models. The SensComp/Polaroid sonar-ranging modules can read a range from six inches to 35 feet. They have an initiation pin and an echo pin. To use them, you set the initiation pin high, then use the rctime command on the echo pin to measure how long it takes to return a signal. These modules are useful but expensive, and they draw a significant current (up to two amps) when they send the ping.

The Devantech SRF family of ultrasonic sensors are a cheaper alternative to the Polaroids. The cheapest one, the SRF04, works in the same way as the SensComp/Polaroid model: you set an initialization pin high, then wait for a return on an echo pin. To determine the distance, you divide the time taken by the speed of sound in your microcontroller's software. More expensive models like the SRF08 allow you to just get the distance by communicating with the sensor using a protocol called I2C (for more on this protocol, see Chapter 12, "More Communication between Devices").

If you're using the Devantech SRF04 or the SenseComp/Polaroid module, you will need to do a little more programming. You can send out the ping with a simple pulsout command on the INIT pin of the module. You can time how long it takes the sound to bounce off the target and return using either a pulsin command or an rctime command. You will need a constant for the speed of sound to convert the microseconds returned by these commands into inches (73.746 microseconds per inch) or centimeters (29.033 microseconds per centimeter). Figure 9.8 shows the schematic and the wiring.

Figure 9.8
The Devantech SRF04
ultrasonic sensor.

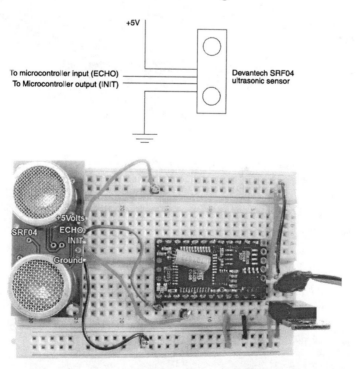

Here's the pseudocode for reading a Devantech SRF04 sensor:

```
Loop
    Pulse the init pin
    Time how long it takes to get a pulse back
    Divide the time by the speed of sound
    Pause to let the sensor reset
End loop
```

Because the minimum times on the pulsout and pulsin commands are not the same on the different microcontrollers we're using, you'll notice that the constant for the speed of sound changes from one microcontroller to the next. Here's the actual code:

PBASIC

```
distance var word
conversionFactor con 137    '54 for centimeters
initPin con 11          'pin number for init pin
echoPin con 8           'pin number for echo pin

debug "start"
pause 500 ' start program with a half-second delay
main:
    pulsout initPin,10 ' 10us init pulse
    pulsIn echoPin,1, distance
    distance = distance/conversionFactor
    debug "Distance: = ", DEC distance, "inches",13
    pause 100
goto main
```

MBasic

```
distance var word
conversionFactor con 137    '54 for centimeters
initPin con   11        'pin number for init pin
echoPin con   8         'pin number for echo pin

'unfortunately, using debug on the atom interferes with the timing of the pulses
'you need to program the atom rather than using debug mode,
'and see the results in a terminal window.
Serout 6, N9600, ["start"]
pause 500 ' start program with a half-second delay
main:

    pulsout initPin,10      ' 10us init pulse
    pulsIn echoPin,0,distance
    distance = distance/conversionFactor
    Serout 6, N9600, ["Distance: = ", DEC distance, "inches",13]
    pause 100
goto main
```

PicBasic Pro
```
DEFINE OSC 4' the constants in this code work for a 4 MHz clock,
' but need to be adjusted for other speeds.
' at 20MHz, for example, divide them by 5
distance var wordconversionFactor con 14     '6 for centimeters
initPin var portb.0          'pin number for init pin
echoPin var portb.1   'pin number for echo pin

serout2 portc.6, 16468, ["start"]
pause 500 ' start program with a half-second delay
main:
     pulsout initPin,1 ' 10us init pulse
     pulsIn echoPin,1, distance
     distance = distance/conversionFactor
     serout2 portc.6, 16468, ["Distance: = ", DEC distance, " inches"]
     pause 100
goto main
```

BX-Basic
```
dim distance as integer
const conversionFactor as integer = 137 '54 for centimeters
const initPin as byte = 16 'pin number for init pin
const echoPin as byte = 13 'pin number for echo pin

sub Main()
     debug.print "start"
     call delay(0.5) ' start program with a half-second delay
     do
          pulseout initPin,10,1 ' 10us init pulse
          distance = pulseIn(echoPin,1)
          distance = distance\conversionFactor
          debug.print "Distance = " ; cstr(distance); "inches"
          call delay(0.1)
     loop
end sub
```

Other Position Sensors

The infrared and ultrasonic modules are by far the easiest distance-ranging sensors and will probably take care of most of your distance measuring needs. For very close-range interactions, (less than the 1.5 inches that the Sharp GP2D120 is capable of measuring), consider analog Hall effect sensors. For very large-scale position sensing you can use GPS, which can pinpoint your position within a few meters almost anywhere on earth. GPS doesn't work indoors or in areas without a clear view of the sky, however. GPS is well covered in Chapter 12.

If you have very precise positioning requirements on the scale of the human body, consider magnetic motion trackers (http://www.polhemus.com or http://www.ascension-tech.com).

These give you extremely fast and accurate readings for all six degrees of freedom via RS-232 serial communication. The object that you're tracking has to be tethered to a small magnetic sensor. The range for the most accurate readings (less than 0.1") is about one yard radius, with a bigger range for less accurate readings. Large amounts of iron in the room will reduce the accuracy. These sensors are expensive. They cost thousands of dollars, but you can't beat their accuracy with any homegrown solution. They're great for applications where a person will stand still in one place and move parts of her body around or move objects around her body. Virtual reality designers love them. If you need precise positioning for these kinds of applications, then get one of these sensors; the investment will save you hundreds of hours trying to get precise six-degree tracking on your own.

In the $10,000 range, you can find a variety of sensors in the entertainment industry for motion capture for special effects and animation. Every year at the Association for Computing Machines' SIGGRAPH conference you will see new schemes for doing this. Often these systems require installation into a special purpose room. For example, Vicon (http://www.vicon.com) makes a system for motion capture that uses an array of cameras spread around the perimeter of an empty room. Retroreflective tape or balls (like the paint used in highway lines that reflects light very well) are attached to the body or object that you want to track. The cameras are designed to read only infrared light, which is reflected by the retroreflective tape. The data from all the cameras is combined to generate a three-dimensional track of the tape spots in space. To track a person, the spots are attached to all of the person's joints and whatever other body parts you want to track. Though motion capture systems are very accurate, they are also very expensive and require considerable computer expertise and horsepower to set up and maintain.

Determining Rotation

So far, we've introduced sensors that enable you to tell whether an object or person is present, and where they are in a space. In this section we'll talk about how to determine how the person or object is oriented with respect to other objects.

Potentiometers

The simplest rotation sensor is the ordinary potentiometer. For example, if you want your user to turn a wheel to adjust the rotation of an image or the pitch of a sound, you could attach a potentiometer to the pivot point of the wheel. The circuitry and programming for a potentiometer are very simple and are covered in the "Analog Input" section of Chapter 6. There are two challenges to using an ordinary potentiometer for sensing a full 360 degrees of rotation. First, most pots do not turn 360 degrees infinitely. Second, you have to find a way to attach them to the wheel that the user is supposed to rotate.

Most potentiometers don't turn a full 360 degrees. You can find multi-turn potentiometers, but eventually they have also a limit in both directions. You can pop the back off of a pot and eliminate the physical barrier to full rotation by cutting part of the metal casing off. However, a potentiometer's resistive band has a gap in it, positioned where the metal stops and keeps you from turning it further. You will get very erratic readings as the potentiometer's wiper moves over this gap. You might be able to live with this if the resolution that you need from the sensor is less than the error that the gap introduces. You can also buy dual potentiometers, or continuous rotation potentiometers, which contain two wipers, and rotate endlessly through 360 degrees. By reading the signal from both wipers, you get a continuously changing reading and can avoid the error caused by the gap. You do this by discarding the reading from whichever wiper is passing over the gap at any given moment.

Attaching a potentiometer to a larger wheel is usually a highly idiosyncratic problem, but there are a few guidelines that are helpful to remember. Generally, pots are too lightweight mechanically to take the force that an axle for a large wheel must take. Use a strong axle for the wheel, and then attach the pot to one of the axle's stationary supports. Next, couple the pot to the wheel itself to measure the rotation. Make sure there is a little give in the coupling so that the eccentricities of the wheel's movement don't produce wear on the pot. Figure 9.9 shows three different options for coupling a potentiometer to a wheel.

Figure 9.9
Three different methods for coupling a potentiometer to a wheel.

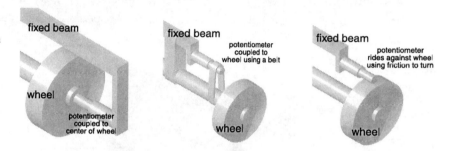

Accelerometers

Accelerometers measure the change in speed of movement, or acceleration. They typically have two (or sometimes three) axes of measurement. Accelerometers are commonly used in cars to measure acceleration and deceleration. If a car decelerates too fast, the accelerometer senses it and triggers the air bags to inflate. When the two axes are perfectly perpendicular to the earth, an accelerometer only measures changes from an outside force. For example, an accelerometer mounted on a toy car would measure the car's acceleration due to a push from you. When you tilt an accelerometer, however, it measures acceleration due to gravity. As a result, accelerometers will give you a relatively good measurement of the tilt of a body or object. Because they use gravity as a reference, they only need to be attached to the object you are sensing, thus avoiding all the mechanical hassles described above that come with attaching potentiometers to moving parts. Accelerometers will typically give you close to 90 degrees of sensitivity when it comes to measuring tilt in this way. Unless you're using a three-axis accelerometer, or two two-axis accelerometers mounted at 90 degrees relative to each other, you'll only get two directions of movement.

Analog Devices (http://www.analog.com) makes a number of good accelerometers, among them the ADXL202E. All of Analog's accelerometers are tiny chips, which are very difficult to solder by hand for the inexperienced solderer. However, they make a demonstration board, the ADXL202EB, that's very easy to integrate with a breadboard. The ADXL202E

SLIP RINGS

There is a problem that frequently accompanies sensing rotation. If you have electronics on a turning part that's wired to a non-turning part, the wires will get tangled and eventually limit the rotation. The simplest way to solve this problem is to make the rotating part's electronics self-contained, or to use wireless technologies. This means the rotating part will probably need batteries at least and much more supporting electronics at most. To avoid this, you can use slip rings as conductors for the wires on the rotating parts. *Slip rings* contain bands of metal conductors, typically on the shaft, to which the rotating electronics are attached. Springy conductors attached to the non-rotating part press against these bands to conduct without being attached. Slip rings introduce some electrical noise because the conductors are grinding against each other, so they're usually machined very precisely to reduce this. They're usually fairly expensive as a result. A quarter-inch stereo phono jack can work as a cheap and dirty slip ring for three conductors. Figure 9.10 shows a phono jack used as a slip ring and a professional slip ring.

Figure 9.10
A phono jack used as a slip ring (left) and a professional slip ring (right).

has two output pins, one for the X axis and one for the Y axis. Both pins output a digital pulse whose width varies with the acceleration on that axis. You can measure the pulse width using the rctime command or the pulsin command. Analog also makes a second demonstration board, the ADXL202-EB-232, that gives you the X and Y accelerations via RS232 serial communication. This board costs over $200, though, so we don't recommend it. Figure 9.11 shows how to connect the ADXL202EB to a microcontroller.

To read the ADXL202E from a microcontroller, you simply listen for pulses coming in on the X pin and the Y pin. For most human-scale applications, just reading the varying numbers will give you a good enough resolution to do what you need to do. If you actually need to calculate the acceleration in meters per second squared, consult the data sheet available for download from Analog Devices (http://www.analog.com). The example below returns the raw numbers only.

Figure 9.11
An ADXL202EB
accelerometer module
connected to a
microcontroller.

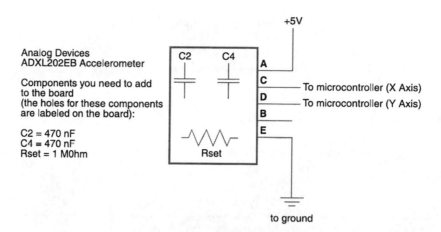

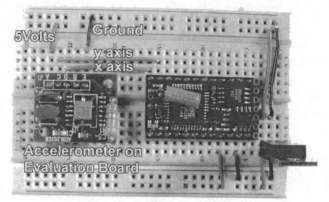

PBASIC

```
xTilt var word
yTilt var word
XPin con 6 'pin number for init pin
yPin con 7 'pin number for echo pin

debug "start"
pause 500 ' start program with a half-second delay

main:
    pulsIn XPin,1, xTilt
    pulsIn YPin,1, yTilt
    debug "xTilt = ", DEC xTilt, " yTilt = ", DEC yTilt
    pause 100
goto main
```

MBasic

```
xTilt var word
yTilt var word
XPin con 6 'pin number for init pin
```

```
yPin con 7 'pin number for echo pin

debug ["start"]
pause 500 ' start program with a half-second delay

main:
    pulsIn XPin,1, xTilt
    pulsIn YPin,1, yTilt
    debug ["xTilt = ", DEC xTilt, " yTilt = ", DEC yTilt]
    pause 100
goto main
```

PicBasic
Pro

```
DEFINE OSC 4
xTilt var word
yTilt var word
XPin var PORTB.0 'pin number for init pin
yPin var PORTB.1 'pin number for echo pin

serout2 portc.6, 16468, ["start"]
pause 500 ' start program with a half-second delay

main:
    pulsIn XPin,1, xTilt
    pulsIn YPin,1, yTilt
    serout2 portc.6, 16468, ["xTilt = ", DEC xTilt, " yTilt = ", DEC yTilt]
    pause 100
goto main
```

BX-Basic

```
dim xTilt as integer
dim yTilt as integer
const XPin as byte = 11 'pin number for init pin
const YPin as byte = 12 'pin number for echo pin
sub Main()
    debug.print "start"
call delay(0.5) ' start program with a half-second delay
    do
        xTilt = pulseIn(XPin,1)
        yTilt = pulseIn(YPin,1)
        debug.print "xTilt = " ; cstr(xTilt); " yTilt = ";cstr(yTilt)
        call delay(0.1)
    loop
end sub
```

Compass

Accelerometers cannot read rotation around the vertical axis, or *pan* angle. For this you can use an electronic compass. Electronic compasses work just like conventional compasses, using the earth's magnetic field to determine rotation. Readings from a compass are not perfectly accurate (±5 degrees) and they don't react very quickly, but for rough readings, they're relatively easy to use. Reasonably priced models like the Devantech CMPS03 (available from http://www.acroname.com and others) send their reading back to your microcontroller using synchronous serial communication (see Chapter 12 for details on this method of communication).

Encoders

Encoders combine a rotating wheel and a light sensor to sense rotation. The heart of a common encoder is a wheel with slits cut in it. A phototransistor and an LED are mounted on either side of the wheel, aimed at it. The LED's light will pass through the slits and be received by the phototransistor, but it will be blocked by the spokes between the slits. Your microcontroller can then count pulses from the phototransistor to find out how many slits have passed and, therefore, how far the wheel has turned. This is a relative reading as opposed to the absolute reading that a pot gives you. If your microcontroller misses a pulse, your relative position shifts, and you have inaccurate information about the wheel's position. Generally, encoders are more effective for measuring speed than position. Encoders are common in older computer mice. Two encoders are positioned on two sides of a ball, which rotates both encoders at once. One encoder is used for reading movement along the mouse's long axis, and one measures movement laterally. If you've ever picked up your mouse to continue dragging across the screen, you've seen how encoders are relative and not absolute. The mouse's position on the pad isn't measured, but its speed across the pad is. This is why the cursor doesn't move much when you lift the mouse but does move when you drag the mouse across the pad. Figure 9.12 shows an encoder in a typical mouse.

Figure 9.12
A rotary encoder in a mouse.

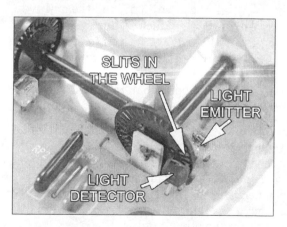

There is another type of encoder, called an *absolute encoder*, that does the work of counting the pulses for you and delivers an absolute position. Absolute encoders sound great, but they typically have less resolution than potentiometers. Both types of encoders can continuously move 360 degrees around a circle.

Speed of Rotation

Quite often, you need to know speed of rotation rather than distance of rotation. A tachometer is a typical device for measuring rotational speed. To build a tachometer, you only need one digital sensor on the side of the wheel. Magnetic switches work well for this because they require no physical connection to the wheel. You put the magnet on the wheel and the magnetic switch in a fixed position beside the wheel. With each rotation, the magnet turns on the switch. Count the on-off transitions per minute, and you've got the revolutions per minute (RPMs). Edge detection and debouncing (refer to Chapter 8) will be important for fast moving wheels. You will see this set up on most bicycle tachometers. To measure rotation speeds of less than a full rotation, you'll need to add more magnets at a regular spacing, or you'll need a potentiometer or an encoder.

Gyroscopes

Gyroscopes are sensors that measure angular acceleration. They're similar to accelerometers, except that they measure how fast the angle of rotation is changing, rather than measuring acceleration in a straight line. They can be very useful for measuring rotation around an axis and for measuring speed of rotation.

Video Tracking

Photocells have a very seductive quality when you first play with them as an analog input into your microcontroller. It seems magical to get a beautiful range of numbers just by waving your hand without any wires attached. When you use photocells in an actual installation, however, they start to give you a lot of headaches. You can look at video cameras as a dense array of thousands of photocells, but without many of the weaknesses of individual photocells. Video cameras have a lens to scale the range of light you are interested in, an iris to adjust for lighting conditions, and the ability to separate the incoming light by color. Welcome to the even more seductive world of machine vision. Multimedia computers have become fast enough for you to manipulate video on a pixel-by-pixel level rather than frame-by-frame. If you want to know where a person is in a room, you could put a camera on the ceiling and then use software to look for the X and Y position of any pixels that are a different color than the floor. When you want details of a person's motion in a large space, this is often the best solution.

As you get into video tracking, you will have new appreciation of your body's ability to see and process what it's seeing. One of the things that makes computer vision so difficult is that cameras and computers do not automatically adjust for changing conditions the way our eyes and brains do. For example, if you see a fire engine at noon, and then again in the evening, your eye compensates for the lighting differences. The fire engine appears to be the same color, even though the light reflected from it is very different at those two times of the day. The computer, on the other hand, will just see the fire engine as different colors at the different times of day. Making matters worse, when you're using analog video standards (NTSC, PAL, and so on) that are very noisy, blips in the signal will make the color of individual pixels appear to change even if the color is not changing. Even if you could solve color-correction problems with better equipment, you are still left with the most difficult problem: object recognition. Our brains effortlessly pick out objects in a scene. For example, we can recognize a head, a hand, or a snake, regardless of the angle at which it's viewed. When you sit down to write software to do the same kind of recognition, it's hard to even know where to start.

Computer vision experts spend many years tackling these problems. Even if you're not eager to get a Ph.D. in this subject in order to realize your project, you can solve 80 percent of the problems fairly easily and then constrain your environment to account for the rest. For example, it might be very difficult to find a person against some changing and arbitrary background (the stuff of computer science dissertations) but very easy to find them against a uniformly colored background (the stuff of art school projects). It is very difficult to recognize a person's face, but trivial to find a particular red hat. If you want to make your life easy, have the person wear a red hat and ensure that there is a uniform non-red background. This may seem too constrained, but it gives you the general idea.

Whenever you're planning a project using video tracking, the first factor to consider

COLOR SPACES

Your illumination changes more than the colors of the objects change. When you're analyzing an image from camera software, it's better to use colorspaces that separate out brightness from color. A *colorspace* is a way of describing and analyzing the light and color in an image. For example, you can describe an image by its hue (what color it is), saturation (how deep the color is), and brightness (how bright the light is). Unfortunately, most camera digitizers convert camera images into an RGB colorspace, meaning that every pixel is described by its red value, green value, and blue value. You can convert RGB values to HSB, or you can use *normalized RGB*. To normalize RGB values, use these formulas:

$$nR = r/(r+b+g)$$
$$nG = g/(r+g+b)$$
$$nB = b/(r+g+b)$$

Normalizing your RGB values might improve your results with the Processing and Java code listed below.

is the lighting. Strong, even light throughout the space to be tracked will make the image on camera much clearer with higher contrast and will simplify the task of picking out change from the background. Your camera will often automatically try to boost the lighting artificially and introduce noise in low-light conditions. Despite your best efforts, most video signals will be noisy. Blurring the video in software (not in the lens) will lessen the effects of noise and bad lighting, but it will lower your resolution and drastically slow down your processing.

Using infrared light is a great trick for video tracking. Although your eye cannot see infrared light, video cameras can. Try clicking your television's remote control in front of a video camera to prove it. If you place an infrared filter[3] in front of a camera in a room with fluorescent lights, you will only see the remote control surrounded by darkness.

---

[3] Infrared filters should be called *visible light filters* because that is what they really filter. You can buy them from most photographic suppliers, or you make one very inexpensively by using a piece of ordinary photographic film that has been processed without being exposed. Sometimes just the trailer on an old negative that you have lying around the house (the black strip that you normally throw out) will work.

Fluorescent lights do not give off infrared light, but incandescent lights do, as does the sun. If you can discreetly attach an infrared source to your target, it can easily be singled out of an otherwise black field for rock-solid tracking. For example, a wand or a badge with an IR LED in it, or an incandescent source like a flashlight covered by an infrared filter, will do the job nicely. Retroreflective tape (the kind you see on biker's helmets and ankle straps) is highly visible under infrared light. You can buy it in strips from 3M (http://www.3M.com). It can improve visibility if you have no way of putting a powered IR source on the person or object you want to track. When it's difficult or impossible to attach an IR source to the target, you can wash the entire scene with IR illuminators and look for moving shadows.

Overriding automatic exposure and focus is usually desirable so you have greater control over the changes in light. It is hard to find inexpensive manual video cameras these days. Most of them have auto-irises to correct the light levels automatically, so check this before choosing a camera. Look for cameras with manual override, if possible. Quite often the best camera position is on the ceiling because you will be able to track two dimensions of horizontal movement, and people don't move vertically very much. A zoom lens that goes to a very wide angle is the most useful for this type of installation because the area covered at human head level is less than that covered on the floor. For example, if the camera is 10 feet high and has a 45-degree viewing angle, it will cover 8 foot 4 inches on the floor, but only 3 foot 8 inches at head height. See Figure 9.13 for the details.

Figure 9.13
When using a camera on the ceiling to track horizontal movement, try to hang the camera as high as possible and use a very wide-angle lens.

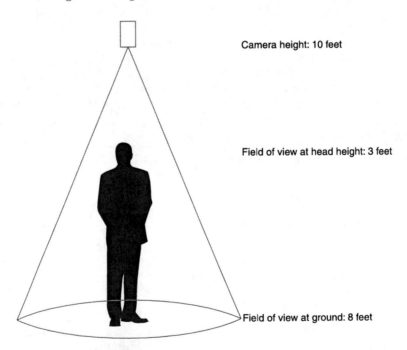

Camera height: 10 feet

Field of view at head height: 3 feet

Field of view at ground: 8 feet

You need a fast processor to look at each pixel as fast as they come into a video camera (up to 12 million pixels per second). None of the microcontrollers that we have covered in this book is fast enough to do this. We will show you how to connect to another microcontroller that is fast enough (the SX chip in the CMUcam, available from http://www.acroname.com), but for the greatest functionality and flexibility in camera types, connect a video camera to a multimedia computer. More and more software environments have extensions to access video pixel by pixel. Below are examples for video tracking in Director MX, Max/MSP, Processing, Java, and the CMUcam. We've just scratched the surface in each environment, giving you enough of an example to get a hold of something within the video pixels. The rest is up to you.

The first two examples in Director and Max/MSP are considerably easier than the second two in Processing and Java. This is because in Director and Max/MSP you are giving over most of the pixel-by-pixel work to extensions written by somebody else in C. In the latter two examples in Processing and Java, your code has to do all the work of processing each pixel individually. As usual, in return for this additional work you will get more control.

Configuring your computer with the various layers of drivers so that your software can make contact with the video pixels will often be more difficult than writing your code. More and more machines come ready for this kind of video input, so you might just get lucky, but don't be surprised if it does not work right away. There are too many different video input devices (USB webcams, firewire webcams, DV camcorders, NTSC video cameras) for your software to be able to accommodate each one individually. Instead, it will rely on a standard for video such as QuickTime, Video for Windows, or DirectShow to bring those disparate inputs into a common format. QuickTime is standard for the technologies listed in this book, so make sure it is installed (it's a free download from http://www.apple.com/quicktime/) on your machine. Next you have to be sure that your video hardware is ready to talk to QuickTime. To do this, you'll need a driver called a VDIG. Video hardware for the Mac will usually come with such a driver. Most video hardware for a PC usually only comes with WDM (DirectShow) or the older Video For Windows drivers. For a PC, you would then need a WDM to VDIG software adapter (downloadable from http://www.vdig.com or http://www.abstractplane.com.au). You should test your computer's configuration before you touch any of your own code using one of two utility programs: AmCap (for testing WDM drivers on the PC) and HackTV (for testing VDIG drivers or adapters on both the Mac and PC). These applications are freely available on the Web and often come with your video equipment.

Video Tracking in Director MX

The fastest way to get the most functionality is with an Xtra for Macromedia Director called TTC-Pro (which can be purchased and downloaded from http://www.smoothware.com). Although Director is not really fast enough to look through video pixel-by-pixel at normal video resolutions, it can ask this Xtra (written in C) to do it. For example, you can have the Xtra return to you the X and Y coordinates of the pixel that's closest to a particular RGB value. This is what the code listed below does. The Xtra can do much more than that. For example, you can make a motion tracker by asking it repeatedly for the X and Y coordinates of all the areas that changed from the previous frame. You can make a change tracker by asking for the X and Y coordinates of the areas that have changed from a reference frame that you had previously captured using the Xtra. At lower resolutions, you can even ask for all the pixels to be passed to Director for you to analyze in Lingo. Don't be put off by the complicated example movie that comes with TTC-Pro. The majority of your changes will be variations on a single line within the `exitframe` script. Download the demo of this Xtra and paste this code into a movie, put a quickdraw castmember into sprite 1, and you'll see video in a window with a sprite following the reddest point in the video. If you click on another color, the program will try to follow that color. The original and less expensive TrackThemColors Xtra from Smoothware would accomplish this task, but we recommend using the Pro version because it has a lot more functionality and works on more platforms.

```
global TrackObj, targetRed, targetGreen, targetBlue, videoWidth,videoHeight
on startmovie
    set videoWidth = 320
    set videoHeight = 240
    -- Tries to open any version of the TTC Xtra that is in the same folder
    OpenXlib "TTC-Pro Xtra (Carbon)"
    OpenXlib "TTC-Pro Xtra (Classic)"
    OpenXlib "TTC-Pro Xtra (windows)"
    OpenXlib "TTC-ProDemo Xtra (Carbon)"
    OpenXlib "TTC-ProDemo Xtra (Classic)"
    OpenXlib "TTC-ProDemo Xtra (windows)"

    --make a new object
    TrackObj = new(xtra "TTCPro")
    --initialize the object for the size that you want:
    put InitVideo(TrackObj,1,rect(0,0,VideoWidth,VideoHeight),1)
    targetRed = 255 --make the initial target red
    targetGreen = 0
    tagetBlue = 0
end

on exitframe
    --grab a frame to be tracked and displayed
    TrackObj.GrabOneFrame()

    --show the video, this may become optional later:
    TrackObj.ShowVideo([rect(0,0,videoWidth, videoHeight),rect(0,0,videoWidth,
videoHeight)])


    --ask the object for closest pixel to that color in the whole frame:
    location = TrackObj.TrackColors(1,[[targetRed,targetGreen,targetBlue,rect(0,0,videoW
idth, videoHeight)]])

--This is the line that you would most likely change for other functionality --

    -- it returns a list, but the first item is the best position
    sprite(1).loc = location[1][1]
    go the frame
```

```
end

on mouseDown
    --if they click within the video use that pixel to set a new target
    if inside(point(mouseH(),mouseV()), rect(0,0,videoWidth,videoHeight)) then
    -- ask the object for the color of the pixel that you clicked on
    pickedPixel = TrackObj.GetColors([point(mouseh(),mousev())])
    -- the object returns a list , [red, green, blue]
    targetRed = pickedPixel[1]
    targetGreen = pickedPixel[2]
    targetBlue = pickedPixel[3]
    put "New Target: " , targetRed, targetGreen, targetBlue
    end if
end

on keydown
    if the key = "s" then
        --when you press "s" you will get the standard dialog box for video settings
        trackObj.videoSettings()
    end if
end

on stopmovie
    --working with xtras, it is important to clean up the objects you make manually
    TrackObj.CleanUp()
    set TrackObj = 0
    closeXlib
end
```

Video Tracking in Max/MSP

For Max/MSP users, there are a couple of options. Jitter is an extensive addition to Max/MSP for video input and output. Jitter has some tracking capabilities, using the `jit.findbounds` object. There is an extension of jitter that has some more powerful machine vision capabilities as well. It's called `cv.jit`, and it's downloadable from http://www.iamas.ac.jp/~jovan02/cv/index.html.

Figure 9.14
A sample Max/MSP patch using the jit.findbounds object.

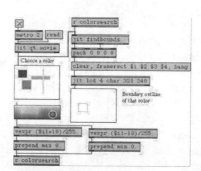

Jitter allows you to feed the findbounds object minima and maxima for the color that you are tracking. Findbounds will give you back the rectangular bounds (*rects* for short) of objects in the video that fall within those constraints. In the example in Figure 9.14, a QuickTime movie is played, and you are able to pick a color to track. Rects that contain colors within 10 values of the chosen color will be returned by findbounds.

Two other video input solutions for Max/MSP have been around for a while: the Very Nervous System (available from http://www.interlog.com/~drokeby/softVNS.html) and Cyclops (available from http://www.ericsinger.com). They let you set up hotspots in the video and return a value when the pixels in the hotspot differ by a threshold that you set. This gives you the functionality of hitting a virtual button when you gesture within the hotspot. The other examples in this book take an alternate approach; they allow you to follow a gesture anywhere in the screen by tracking a blob of pixels. Figure 9.15 shows the example help patch from Cyclops.

Figure 9.15
A sample Max/MSP patch using the Cyclops object.

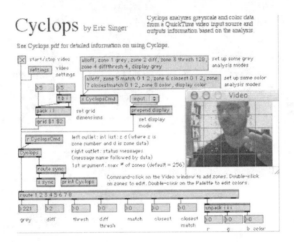

When you open the Cyclops patch or add the Cyclops object to a patch, a video window pops up and you are able to set sensitivities (zones) for any of the grid squares. When you place one of these numbered zones in the grid, the pixels from that square of the grid are treated as a single pixel. There are a few different things a zone can be sensitive to: color, grayscale, and change. In the patch in Figure 9.15, you can see that the final routing object is giving the results of each zone into a box.

Video Tracking in Processing

As we mentioned in Chapter 7, "Communicating between Computers," Processing is a simple programming environment for making graphic applications, and it can be extended by incorporating Java, once you know what you're doing. It gives you a lot of the power of Java while eliminating a great deal of the complexity. To see this in action, compare the following Processing example to the abbreviated Java example below. In addition to the configuration that we talked about in the "Video Tracking" section above, you will need some additional Java classes to connect QuickTime to Java. The QuickTime for Java classes are an optional part of the QuickTime install, but Processing will take care of that for you when you install it. This example uses Processing's video library, so you have to import it at the beginning of the code, like you did with the serial library.

When the code example below is working properly, you should see video in a window with a red dot following the reddest thing in the picture. If you click on another color the program will try to follow that color. You can see that the main loop contains a repeat loop that looks through all the rows of pixels, and then another repeat loop nested within that to scan all the columns within a row.

```
//Import the video library:
import processing.video.*;

Capture myCamera;      // our copy of the video library
float worldRecord = 1000.0; //intialize the worldrecord
int xFound = width/2;     // initialize the location of the tracking ball
int yFound = height/2;
boolean goodTrack = false; // whether or not we have something in the image
                   // that's close enough to our tracked color
color targetColor = color(255,0,0); // the target color: red

void setup()
{
  // set window size:
  size(320, 240);

  // List all available capture devices
  println(Capture.list());

  // capture from the second device in the list
  // change this to match whatever camera you're using.
  // in this case, the camera we used came second
  // in the list (Capture.list[1]):
  myCamera = new Capture(this, Capture.list()[1], width, height, 30);
}

// this gets called whenever there's a new frame of video available:

void captureEvent(Capture myCamera)
{
  // read the myCamera and update the pixel array:
  myCamera.read();
  // we don't have a pixel that matches our color yet:
  goodTrack = false;

  // scan all the pixels looking for a match:
  for(int row=0; row<height; row++) {
    for(int column=0; column<width; column++) { //for each column
      //get the color of this pixel
      //find pixel in linear array using formula: pos = row*rowWidth+column:
      color pixelColor = myCamera.pixels[row*width+column];
```

```
        // calculate the difference between this pixel's color
        // and our desired color:
        float diff = abs(red(targetColor) - red(pixelColor)) +
abs(green(targetColor) - green(pixelColor)) +
abs(blue(targetColor) - blue(pixelColor))/3;

        if (diff<= worldRecord){ // if this is closest to our target color
          worldRecord = diff;
          yFound = row; //mark the spot for drawing it later
          xFound = column;
          goodTrack = true;
        }
      }
    }
  }

  void draw()
  {
      // draw the camera image on the screen:
    image(myCamera, 0, 0);
      // if we got a good color match, draw a dot there:
    if (goodTrack) {
      fill(targetColor);
      ellipse(xFound, yFound, 10, 10);
    }
  }
  // if the user clicks on a spot, change
  // the tracked color to the color of
  // the spot clicked:
  void mousePressed() {
      targetColor = myCamera.pixels[mouseY*width+mouseX];
      fill(targetColor);
      ellipse(mouseX, mouseY, 10, 10);
  }
```

Video Tracking in Java

Java lags behind C for speed of execution, so you may not think that it's perfect for
processor-intensive tasks like video tracking. However, faster machines and just-in-time
compilers allow you to get good video frame rates along with the portability, extensibility,
networking capabilities, relative ease of use, and wide knowledge base of Java. In addition
to the configuration that we talked about in the introduction to this section, you will need
some additional Java classes to connect QuickTime to Java. The QuickTime for Java classes
are an optional part of the QuickTime install so you may have to update or even go back
to the installer to do a custom install with QuickTime for Java checked. In order to remove
some of the complexities of the QuickTime for Java classes, we are also using a package
called vpb.jar (downloadable from http://stage.itp.tsoa.nyu.edu/~dano/vbp/). If you want to

use the code below, you will have to put another file, vpb.jar, into your classpath. The same folder as your class should be part of your classpath. To be sure, you can put it in /jre/lib/ext/ (PC) and /Library/Java/Extensions/ (Macintosh OSX).

When the code example below is working properly, you should see video in a window with a red dot following the reddest thing in the picture. If you click on another color, the program will try to follow that color. The main action of this code happens in the LookAtFrame method, where there is a repeat loop that looks through all the rows of pixels; another repeat loop is nested within that to scan all the columns within a row. This quick and dirty program might do the trick for some applications. If you want to go further once you get the pixels, we recommend the books *Digital Image Processing: A Practical Introduction Using Java* by Nick Efford (Addison-Wesley, 2000) and *Machine Vision Algorithms in Java: Techniques and Implementation* by Paul F. Whelan and Derek Molloy (Springer Verlag, 2000).

```java
import java.awt.*;
import java.util.*;
import java.awt.event.*;
import java.awt.image.*;


public class PickNTrack extends Frame {
    static int kWidth ; //The overall size of your video
    static int kHeight ;
    static long elapsedTime; //For evaluating performace
    static long now;
    static int x = 0; //these are the x and y position of the dot you are drawing
    static int y = 0;
    static int redGoal = 210; //these describe the color you are chasing
    static int greenGoal = 20; //255, 255, 255 would be white
    static int blueGoal = 20;
    static PixelSource ps; //this object from vbp.jar gives you access to video pixels
    static ImageWrangler iw; //this object from vbp.jar converts from arrays to images
    static PickNTrack myWindow;
    static Image myImage; // An image for displaying the video frame
    static boolean scanning = true;

    PickNTrack() { //this is like startmovie
        kWidth =320;
        kHeight =240;
    }
    public static void main(String args[]) { //always the first method called
        myWindow = new PickNTrack();
        myWindow.setSize(kWidth,kHeight);
        myWindow.show();
        myWindow.toFront();
        myWindow.setLayout (null);

        //These are the two objects that you are using out of vpb.jar
```

```
        ps = new PixelSource(kWidth,kHeight);
        iw = new ImageWrangler(ps.vidWidth,kHeight,ps.getMasks());


        //add a listener for shutting the window, give it a method to call
(thisWindowClosing)
        myWindow.addWindowListener(new java.awt.event.WindowAdapter() {
            public void windowClosing(java.awt.event.WindowEvent e) {
                myWindow.thisWindowClosing(e);
            }
        });
        //add a listener for clicking the mouse in the window, give it a method to call
(MouseClicked)
        myWindow.addMouseListener(new java.awt.event.MouseAdapter() {
            public void mouseClicked(java.awt.event.MouseEvent e) {
                myWindow.MouseClicked(e);
            }
        });
        //add a listener for pressing a key, give it a method to call (KeyPressed)
        myWindow.addKeyListener(new java.awt.event.KeyAdapter() {
            public void keyPressed(java.awt.event.KeyEvent e) {
                myWindow.KeyPressed(e);
            }
        });


        /////////This is the main loop///////
        while (scanning) //you may want to farm this out to a thread
            {
             LookAtAFrame(); //we look through all the pixels
             myWindow.repaint(); // we paint the winner
            }


    }
    static void LookAtAFrame() { //this is where the action is, where we go pixel by
pixel through the video
        int[] rgb;
        int worldRecord = 60000; //some huge number
        ps.grabFrame(); //grab a frame
        for (int row = 0; row < kHeight; row++) {
//REPEAT FOR EACH ROW OF PIXELS
            for (int column = 0; column < kWidth; column++){
//REPEAT FOR EACH PIXEL IN THE ROW
                rgb = ps.getPixel(column,row);
                int diff = Math.abs(rgb[0] - redGoal) +Math.abs(rgb[2]-blueGoal) +
Math.abs(rgb[1 ] - greenGoal);
                    if (diff < worldRecord) {
                        //if the difference is smallest for this pixel
                        x = column; //remember this position
                        y = row;
```

```
                            worldRecord = diff ;
                            //reset the record
                        }
                }//END FOR EACH PIXEL IN A ROW
            }//END FOR EACH ROW OF PIXELS
            try {Thread.sleep(1);} catch(InterruptedException e) {}
            myImage = iw.imageFromArray(ps.getPixelArray()); //make a picture
            elapsedTime = System.currentTimeMillis()-now; //for checking performance
            now = System.currentTimeMillis();
        }     // end of lookat frame

    public void update(Graphics g){ //avoid flicker, don't clear the screen
        paint(g);
    }
    public void paint(Graphics g) { //this is where we paint
        if (myImage != null){
            g.drawImage(myImage,0,0,this);//the background video
            g.setColor(Color.black);//black
            g.fillOval( x-5,y-5,10,10);//the dot for tracking
            g.setColor(new Color(redGoal, greenGoal, blueGoal));//black
            g.fillOval( x-4,y-4,8,8);//the dot for tracking
        }
    }
    public boolean MouseClicked(java.awt.event.MouseEvent evt){
        //this repicks the color you are chasing
        int[] rgb;
        int x = evt.getX();
        int y = evt.getY();
        rgb = ps.getPixel(x,y);
        redGoal = rgb[0];
        greenGoal =rgb[1];
        blueGoal = rgb[2];
        System.out.println ("clicked x" + x + " y" + y + " R" + redGoal + " G" +
greenGoal + " B" + blueGoal);
        return(true);
    }
    public boolean KeyPressed(java.awt.event.KeyEvent e){ //pop up dialog
        String whichKey =e.getKeyText(e.getKeyCode());
        if (whichKey.equals("S")) { //press "s" to get video settings
            ps.videoSettings();
        }else if (whichKey.equals("T")) { //press "t" to see performance
            System.out.println ("Time: " + elapsedTime + " ms/frame ");
        }
        return(true);
    }
    void thisWindowClosing(java.awt.event.WindowEvent e) {
        scanning = false;
        System.out.println ("quit");
```

```
                    dispose();
                    ps.killSession();
                    System.exit(5);
            }
        }
```

CMUcam

If you cannot have a multimedia computer involved in your project at all, for example, if you want to attach a camera to the back of your head so you can detect car headlights, or if you're building a musical baton that generates musical tones from video patterns, one option is to use the CMUcam (available through http://www-2.cs.cmu.edu/~cmucam/). The CMUcam uses an SX microcontroller to look through the pixels. The SX works at 100 million instructions per second (MIPS). That is fast enough to look at each pixel of incoming video, while a PIC microcontroller with a 20 Megahertz crystal, which operates at 5 MIPS, is not. You can talk to the CMUcam from your microcontroller via a TTL or an RS-232 serial connection. Figure 9.16 shows the CMUcam.

Figure 9.16
The CMUcam.

We highly recommend that, before you start connecting the CMUcam directly to your microcontroller, you get to know the CMUcam's serial commands first, using a terminal program on your multimedia computer or using the Java application that comes with the CMUcam. Set the baud rate in HyperTerminal or Zterm to 115200, then send a line of text: TC 130 255 0 10 0 30 followed by a carriage return to the CMUcam. It will look for blobs with red values between 130 and 255, green values between 0 and 10, and blue values between 0 and 30 and return the coordinates of all the blobs that meet those criteria.

The calls you make to the CMUcam are similar to the calls you make to the TrackThemColors Xtra in Director or the Cyclops extension of Max/MSP. One important difference is that there's not enough memory on the CMUcam to store a reference frame necessary for background removal or motion detection. Though the CMUcam may seem like an attractive option because it eliminates the need for a multimedia computer, we recommend (as usual) that you start at the highest level possible. Before you spend the money on a CMUcam or any other low-level solution, ask yourself if it's necessary to do it the low-level way. Even if your project eventually needs to be free from a multimedia computer, we recommend that you learn the basics of video tracking there and prototype your concept using the easiest environment possible.

Identity

Tracking objects in a space becomes more complicated when you're trying to track more than one. Not only do you need to know *where* each object is, but also *which* one is where. Many of the sensors covered here will not support multiple targets. For example, our beloved IR and ultrasonic sensors will bounce off the closest target, not noticing any targets behind it. The main technique for establishing identity of multiple targets is to give each target a distinct signature.

Three of the most common commercial identification technologies can interface relatively easily with a microcontroller or a multimedia computer: barcode scanners, RFID tags, and magnetic swipe card readers. *Radio Frequency Identification (RFID) tags* are stickers or small tokens that carry a unique ID number. When radio waves are bounced off an RFID tag, the tag reflects the radio wave back, but the reflection carries the ID number with it. *Passive RFID tags* get their energy from the radio wave itself and require no battery or other form of power. Passive RFID tags only work over short distances. If you've ever bought a book or a CD and have seen the sticker with a spiral metal pattern on it, you've seen a passive RFID tag. *Active RFID tags* have their own power source and can work over longer distances. These are much more expensive than passive tags. They're used in commuter tollbooth passes like EZ-Pass. The receivers for RFID range in cost from $100 and up. SkyeTek (http://www.skyetek.com) sells a small receiver for about $100 that interfaces via RS-232 serial to a microcontroller and can be embedded into many projects. Passive RFID tags cost less than a dollar apiece, generally. *Barcode scanners* use a laser to scan the pattern of light and dark bands on a UPC symbol and convert it into a string of text. They're ubiquitous in retail stores these days. You can find barcode scanners with RS-232 serial ports relatively easily. Symbol Technologies (http://www.symbol.com) is the biggest manufacturer of barcode scanners and has a wide range available. Used barcode scanners are easy to find on eBay as well. They usually come with software for printing out the barcode stickers. Magnetic swipe card readers use a magnetic tape recorder head to read the magnetic tape on a credit card or ID card and convert it to a string of text. They're also easy to find on eBay and many of the electronics retailers mentioned in this book. Interfacing them to a microcontroller is a little trickier; it generally involves synchronous serial communication (see Chapter 12 for more on that).

While commercial ID systems aren't terribly difficult to use, they don't work well at longer ranges (greater than a meter). In addition, the expense and overhead of learning the protocols may be more than you need. There are many more homegrown solutions for identifying objects as well. Generally, any property that you can sense can be assigned in varying degrees to use as a signature to distinguish each object that you want to track.

Following are three approaches to one problem, the tracking of game pieces on a board (for example, chess, checkers, and so on).

▶ *Color.* You could give an individual game piece a unique color, and place a camera above the board. Then you're able to track all the game pieces using any of the video tracking techniques covered in this chapter. This relies on very controlled lighting and on the players' hands not obscuring the game board too much. You can also get the TCS230 color sensor (available from http://www.parallaxinc.com) that senses differences in color. It's basically a low-resolution camera that outputs the color differences only, with no information about the shape of what it sees.

▶ *Flashing sequence.* You could give each piece its own microcontroller (consider the cheaper PICs here) and have each one emit a different serial string, which pulses an infrared LED. Use an infrared phototransistor attached to a serial input pin to read the serial data. The receiving microcontroller will know each different game piece by its serial signature. In order to do this, you need to be able to make an infrared LED visible on the top of each game piece. You should also make sure that each piece isn't constantly sending its signal, so that there's less chance that they'll overlap. One method to control this overlap is to have the receiver work much like an orchestra conductor, constantly sending data to each piece and waiting for a reply before it prompts the next piece for an update.

▶ *Resistance.* You could make the board a tracking device. Put two electrical contacts in each square of the board; one connects to an analog input pin, and the other to 5 volts. Put a different value resistor in each game piece, and position the ends of the resistor so that it makes a connection between the contacts of a game square whenever it's put down. When you read all the inputs on the game board, you'll be able to sense which piece is where because each will return a different analog value.

Another common technique for establishing identity is to rely on continuity. To do this, you assign a unique ID to each object when your sensors first find it. You then assume that objects don't move drastically and that an object from each subsequent sensor reading will be the same one as the closest object in the previous reading.

Conclusion

Your fingers are already well represented as input on the keyboard and mouse into the computer. This chapter discussed ways of giving your software a larger view of the world and the things in it. Position and movement are two of the most fundamental factors you need to know in order to distinguish objects and people in space, and there are many good sensors available to do this. Many of them seem very easy to use, especially under workshop conditions, but are prone to misbehave in the field. Test your work with users early and often, and work in the actual environments that you're designing for as much as possible. Keep in mind that problems in sensing movement in space are often solved by fixing the ambient conditions rather than by fixing the technology. Now that you have a few techniques for sensing movement, you can move on to creating movement.

10
Making Movement

By now, you've learned a good bit about how to make the computer listen well to human expression, and you've also learned a few techniques for responding, through light and sound coming out of either the microcontroller or the multimedia computer. The next step is actually animating physical media. This can give you a more unexpected, compelling, even magical response than you get from run-of-the mill-multimedia. For example, even the simplest of animatronic characters in a haunted house (a skeleton arm tapping the visitor on the shoulder, perhaps) can evoke a louder scream from visitors than the most realistic, blood-curdling recorded screams or the largest projection of a ghost. This chapter introduces techniques for creating motion. We'll discuss various types of motors and discuss their characteristics in general, and then we'll talk about some special electrical needs of motors. Following that, we'll discuss the various motor types in detail and describe how to control them from a microcontroller. Finally, we'll discuss some basic mechanical principles, so that you can convert motors' movements into movements that work with your particular system.

Types of Motion, Types of Motors

There are two basic types of motion covered in this chapter: *linear motion*, or motion in a straight line, and *rotary motion*, or motion in a circle. Most of the devices we'll talk about create rotary motion, so the first challenge you'll often face once you get them working will be to convert that rotary motion into linear motion.

The most basic motor you'll use is the *DC motor*. DC motors have two electrical connections. They spin continually when given enough electrical current at the proper voltage. When the current is reversed, they spin in the opposite direction. If the voltage is lowered, they spin slower. If it's raised, they spin faster.

Most DC motors run at fairly high speeds but don't have a lot of pulling force, or *torque*. In order to give them more torque and lower their speed, a series of gears can be added. The next most basic motor, the *gearhead motor*, is just a DC motor with a gearbox on the top. Gearhead motors don't move very fast, but they are much stronger than regular DC motors without a gearhead. The gearbox reduces the speed of the motor, exchanging speed for increased turning strength, or *torque*.

You've already encountered one type of gearhead motor in this book, the *RC servo motor*. A servo motor is a special type of motor that gives feedback about its position (generally using a potentiometer). The RC servo motor is particularly beloved among physical computing enthusiasts because it combines the advantages of a gearhead with a self-contained feedback system that allows you to pulse it in order to move it to a particular position within a 180-degree range. RC servos can't move a full 360 degrees like other motors, but they can be positioned precisely within their range of movement.

The *stepper motor* combines both precise positioning and a full 360-degree range of motion. Stepper motors move in discrete steps around a circle. For example, a 200-step motor moves 360 degrees in 200 steps (1.8 degrees per step). They can be rotated continuously in either direction by continuing to step them forward or backward. They have reasonably good torque, as well. However, they are more complex to connect than other motors.

Figure 10.1
Motor types (clockwise from top left): DC motor, gearhead motor, RC servo, stepper motor.

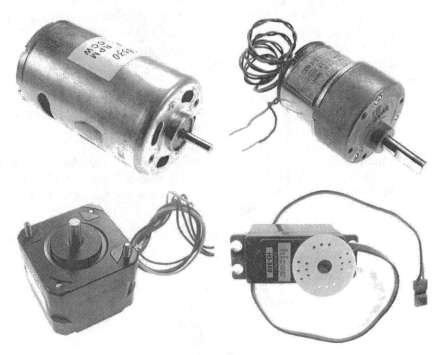

All of the motors in Figure 10.1 create rotary motion and have to be attached to one of the mechanical devices described in the second part of this chapter to create other motions. In order to create linear motion directly, we'll introduce the *solenoid*, a device with a moving rod that pulls in or pushes out when it's given current. You will also come across other actuators that are not motors. In particular, nickel-titanium (*nitinol*) wire has some initial appeal because it contracts like a muscle (it's also known as *muscle wire*) when you apply power. For most applications it is slow to respond, offers minimal movement for the effort needed to get it working, and is finicky about power. You can find products using muscle wire and a related device called *air muscle* at SI Images (http://www/imagesco.com), but we think you will usually get better results using motor and solenoids.

Characteristics of Motors

There are a few characteristics common to all motors that you should keep in mind when looking for a motor for your project.

The *rated voltage* of a motor is the voltage at which it operates at peak efficiency. Most DC motors can be operated somewhat above or below their range, but it's best to plan to operate them at their rated voltage. Dropping below the motor's rated voltage reduces the motor's torque, and operating too high above the rated voltage can burn the motor out. If you're varying the motor's voltage in order to vary its speed, plan on the motor's top speed being at the rated voltage, and its slowest speed at no less than 50 percent of the rated voltage.

Motors draw *current* depending on the load they're pulling. Usually more load means more current. Every motor has a *stall current*, which is the current it draws when it's stopped by an opposing force (like the weight it's pulling). The stall current is much greater than the *running current*, or current that it draws when it has no load. Your power supply for a motor should be able to handle the stall current with extra amperage to spare. For example, if a motor's stall current is two amps, you should use power that can supply at least three amps, to be safe. Likewise, any components that regulate the motor's current should be able to handle three amps. Motors draw almost the stall current for a brief period of time when they start up, to overcome inertia.

Often you'll see a motor rated in ohms. This gives you the *resistance* of the motor. Using Ohm's Law (current = voltage/resistance), you can calculate the motor's running current if you know the rated voltage and the resistance.

Motor *speed* is given in revolutions per minute (RPM) or revolutions per second (RPS). Very occasionally, you'll see motor speeds in Hertz (Hz), which is the same as revolutions per second. Speed is more important when selecting DC and gearhead motors because they're used for continuous motion. For RC servos and stepper motors, speed is usually less important than accurate positioning. However, when quick positioning is a priority, the speed of a stepper may be given as well. For example, hard disk motors are rated by their speed and their positional accuracy because being able to read data off a disk quickly is important when you're reading data for real-time playback, like playing music files or movies.

Position resolution is only a factor for RC servos and stepper motors. It's usually given in degrees or in steps per revolution. Greater resolution means you can create a smoother motion from the steps or achieve greater accuracy when you're positioning whatever it is that the motor is moving.

Torque is the measure of a motor's pulling force. A motor's torque is a measure of how much force it can generate at a given distance from its center of rotation. For example, if a motor can lift a one-pound load that's suspended one foot from the center of its shaft, the motor's torque is one pound-foot. Motor manufacturers haven't standardized this measurement, so sometimes you will see it as lb.-ft., oz.-in., g-cm (gram-centimeter), and any other weight-to-length variation you can think of.

Figure 10.2
Torque of a motor. This
motor can deliver 1
pound-foot of torque.

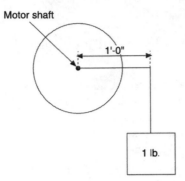

Special Electrical Needs of Motors

Motors work on the electrical principle of *inductance*. When you put electric current
through a wire, it generates a magnetic field around the wire. By placing a charged coil of
wire in an existing magnetic field (say, between two magnets), the coil will be attracted
to one magnet and repelled by the other. Which magnet it's attracted to and which it's
repelled by will depend on the direction of the current flow. A higher current will generate
a greater magnetic field, and therefore a greater attraction or repulsion.

Inductive Loads and Back Voltage

At the heart of a DC motor is a coil with a current running through it mounted on a
spinning shaft. The coil is positioned between two magnets. As the coil is alternately
attracted to one magnet and repelled by the other, it spins, and you get circular motion.
All *inductive loads* (like motors, electromagnets, and solenoids) work on this same
principle: you induce a magnetic field by putting current through a wire, and then use
that magnetic field to attract or repulse a magnetic body.

However, the principle works in reverse as well. When you move a coil of wire in an
existing magnetic field, the field induces a current in the wire. So if you've got a motor
spinning near a magnet, and you turn it off, the magnetic field will induce a current in the
wire for a brief amount of time. This current moves in the reverse direction of the current
flow you generated to run the motor. It's called *blowback*, or *back voltage*, and it can
cause damage to your electronics. You can stop it by putting a diode in parallel with the
electronics that you want to protect, facing in the opposite direction of the normal current
flow. A diode used in this way is called a *snubber diode*. It should be able to carry the full
stall current of the motor. You should protect the rest of your circuit with a snubber diode
any time you're using an inductive load. Otherwise your microcontroller will continually
reset itself, and you'll probably damage the microcontroller, the transistor that's controlling
the motor, and other components in the circuit. The schematic in Figure 10.3 shows a
snubber diode protecting a transistor that's controlling a motor. You can also put the
snubber diode in parallel with the motor, facing in the opposite direction of the current
flow. Whether or not you're using a transistor to control your motor, it's a good idea to use a
snubber diode in this way.

Figure 10.3
A snubber diode used to protect a transistor that's controlling a motor.

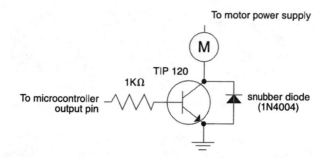

SHOPPING FOR A POWER SUPPLY

Most motors require more electrical power than the ones we've recommended so far, so you need to find a power supply that matches the electrical characteristics of your motor. Power supplies can be expensive, but you can use surplus supplies for many motor applications. You can often repurpose power supplies from other applications.

There are a few terms you should be familiar with before looking for a power supply. Many supplies are *regulated*, meaning that the voltage will not drop as the current increases. This is vital for electronic circuits and useful for motor applications as well. You'll also see power supplies listed as *switching* supplies or *linear* supplies. Switching supplies are generally more efficient than linear supplies, and generally more expensive. If you can afford a switching supply, get it.

Computer power supplies can be particularly useful, as they often have the amperage you need and are available inexpensively or free (if you've got access to a discarded machine). Most computer supplies will tell you their ratings on the side and the amperages they can supply at various voltages. The most common voltages available are 5 volts and 12 volts, though many will also supply −5 volts and −12 volts at low currents as well. Most of the supplies we've seen have black wires for ground, red for +5, and yellow for +12 volts. To be sure, measure the voltage with a meter if you don't have the data sheet on the supply.

The ideal power supply for electronic and motor applications is the variable bench top supply. These allow you to vary the voltage and current while you test your application. After you see what you need, you can then buy a dedicated power supply. They're not cheap, but they're very handy when you do a lot of motor and electronics work. Marlin P. Jones & Associates carry a nice 0-20V, 0-10A model, stock no. 7036 PS (http://www.mpja.com). Once you've found the voltage and amperage needed by using a bench top supply, you can get a fixed power supply to replace it for your project.

Please be careful when using and handling these power supplies. They can be dangerous. In particular, be careful of the large capacitors in them, which can hold a significant charge even after the power supply is turned off.

When possible, it's wise to separate your motor's power supply from your microcontroller's power supply.

Smoothing Current Drops Using Decoupling Capacitors

Because motors draw so much current when they start up, they affect the current going to the circuit that controls them. Often, when a motor attached to a microcontroller starts up, it will draw so much current that the voltage in the circuit drops and the microcontroller resets itself. We recommend that you put a debug statement at the very start of your program, outside the main loop, to expose this problem when it happens. To prevent the problem, you should use capacitors to *decouple* your microcontroller's voltage regulator, and for the microcontroller itself (see the "Decoupling Capacitors: Stabilizing Your Voltage Regulator" sidebar in Chapter 6 for more on decoupling capacitors). These will smooth out the dips in the current. In fact, it's good practice to put a decoupling capacitor between the power and ground of every IC in your circuit whenever you're using an inductive load in your project (it doesn't hurt to do it whether you've got an inductive load or not). Figure 10.4 shows a properly decoupled voltage regulator. Even when your motor power supply is separated from your microcontroller's supply, they will have a common ground, and the motor will affect the microcontroller. So always decouple your microcontroller when using motors. It's also helpful to use separate voltage regulators for the motor and the microcontroller when possible.

Figure 10.4
Use decoupling capacitors liberally when you're working with inductive loads.

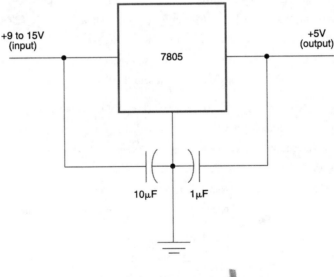

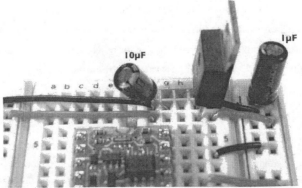

Controlling Motors

Motors require more current than a microcontroller's output pins can supply, so they must be controlled using a combination of transistors or relays, depending on the application. The different types of motors we've mentioned require different control techniques.

The easiest way to control most motors is to get a motor control module that interfaces to your microcontroller. For example, there is a module called the MotorMind B from SolutionsCubed that controls DC motors based on serial commands sent to it from a microcontroller. Solarbotics makes a cheaper module called the L293D Secret Motor Driver that's controllable directly from the microcontroller, using two output pins to set the direction and one to set the speed via pulse width modulation. The Mini-SSC II from Scott Edwards Electronics controls up to eight servomotors with serial commands from a microcontroller. There is also the Little Step-U module from Parallax that can be used for controlling stepper motors in a similar fashion. With these modules you will be finished controlling your motor and you'll be ready to move on to other problems much faster than if you build your own circuitry as described later in this chapter. In some cases they will even provide extra functionality, like ramping up and ramping down the speed of the motor, which will also save you a lot of programming time. In keeping with the high-level approach of this book, we recommend them. The main disadvantage is cost. They are not particularly expensive, but if you are controlling many motors, the cost would add up. Also, if the motor you need to control needs more voltage or current than these modules can provide, you would have to build your own circuitry. We will not cover how to use these modules because they all come with good instructions. Instead, this section of the chapter is about controlling motors at a lower level than these devices. Even if you do use a high-level controller, reading what follows may help you to understand what's going on.

Figure 10.5
A variety of motor controllers: the MotorMind B from SolutionsCubed (a DC motor controller), the Mini-SSC from Scott Edwards Electronics (a servo motor controller), and the Little Step-U from TLA Microsystems (a stepper motor controller).

Controlling DC Motors and Gearhead Motors

DC motors and most gearhead motors are functionally the same in that they have two electrical connections. There are two easily controllable parameters of a DC motor, direction and speed. To control the direction, you reverse the current so that positive becomes negative, and vice versa. This is also called *reversing the polarity* of the motor. To control the speed, you vary the input voltage using pulse width modulation (PWM), as described in Chapter 6.

DC Motor Control Circuit

To control a DC motor from a microcontroller, you use a switching arrangement called an *H-bridge* (see Figure 10.6).

Figure 10.6
Switches arranged in
an H-bridge.

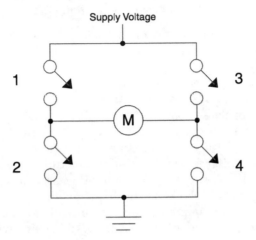

When switches 1 and 4 are closed and 2 and 3 are open, voltage flows from the left lead of the motor to the right. When 2 and 3 are closed and 1 and 4 are open, polarity is reversed and voltage flows from the right lead of the motor to the left.

An H-bridge can be built from transistors so that a microcontroller can switch the motor. Although you can make your own H-bridges, it's usually easier to use an H-bridge controller manufactured specifically for the job. A pre-manufactured H-bridge chip will include diodes to protect the transistors from back voltage, sometimes a current sensing pin to sense the current the motor is drawing, and much more. There are many motor drivers available from various electronics suppliers. Look around to find one that suits your needs and price range.

Any H-bridge chip will have certain elements:

- Pins for logic input (control from the microcontroller)
- Pins for supply voltage (supply for the motor)
- Pins for logic voltage (for the transistors inside the H-bridge that read the signals from the microcontroller)
- Pins for supply output (to feed the motor)
- Pins for ground

The logic voltage pins usually take the same voltage and current as your microcontroller. The supply voltage takes whatever voltage and current you need to run your motor. The logic inputs connect to the pins on your microcontroller that you use to output control signals to the H-bridge, and the supply output pins go to your motor. The configuration of these pins might vary slightly depending on the manufacturer of the H-bridge. They might also use slightly different names, but the concepts are the same.

The following example uses an H-bridge integrated circuit, the SN754410, made by Texas Instruments and other manufacturers. These are fairly common chips; Acroname, Digi-key, and other retailers carry them. This particular chip has two H-bridges and can therefore control two motors. It can drive up to one amp of current at between 4.5 and 36 volts. The L293 is another motor driver with the same pin connections. It can be used interchangeably with the SN754410 if you can't find that chip. If your motor needs more voltage or amperage, look around for a different H-bridge. The principles will be similar to this example.

Figure 10.7
A microcontroller connected to a SN754410 dual H-bridge chip.

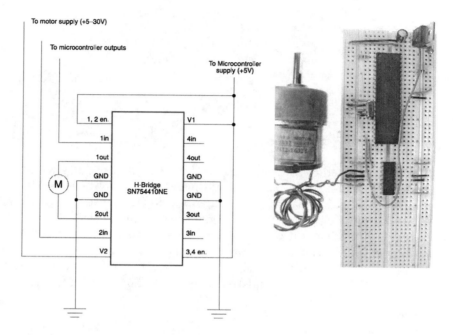

The pins of this H-bridge that you're using are as follows (taking a pin high means attaching it to 5 Volts):

> *1,2 enable.* Allows inputs 1 and 2 to control outputs 1 and 2, respectively, when this pin is at 5V.

> *3,4 enable.* Does the same as 1,2 enable for outputs 3 and 4.

> *V1.* Voltage supply for logic.

> *V2.* Voltage supply for motors.

> *1in.* Input from controller.

> *1out.* Current flows from V2 to this pin when 1in is high.

> *heat sink/GND.* All four of these pins are ground.

> *2in.* Input from controller.

> *2out.* Current flows from V2 to this pin when 2in is high.

Since you're not using the 3rd and 4th ins/outs, don't bother to take the 3,4 enable pin high.

DC Motor Control Programming

DC motor direction control using an H-bridge is very simple. The following pseudocode illustrates what needs to happen. In this example, if the switch is off, the motor turns one direction, and if the switch is on, the motor turns the other direction. Because this example is so basic, we'll leave it to you to translate into code for your particular microcontroller:

```
loop
     if the switch is off
          make pin 1 high
          make pin 2 low
     else
          make pin 2 high
          make pin 1 low
     end if
end loop
```

To control the speed of a motor using an H-bridge, you use pulse width modulation. There are two ways you can do this. You could pulsewidth modulate (PWM) whichever motor pin should be high instead of just giving it 5 volts. However, there is a simpler approach. You can pulse the enable pin on the H-bridge. This pin is basically an "on-off" switch for the H-bridge, so pulsing it will pulse whichever output pin is active. This has the added advantage of letting you control speed with a different output pin and a different routine than the one that controls direction. To do this, you need to add another connection between the H-bridge and the microcontroller, as shown in Figure 10.8.

Figure 10.8
Connect the enable pin of the H-bridge to your microcontroller to control speed.

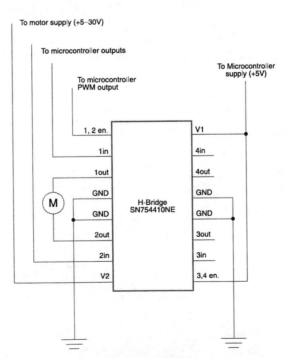

Controlling RC Servos

As we discussed in Chapter 6, RC servo motors are very easy to control. They can be precisely positioned along a 180-degree arc. For instance, you could place a webcam on an RC servo and pan to particular places of interest in your room. You control an RC servo by sending a pulse on the control line every 20 milliseconds. Depending on the pulsewidth (duration of the pulse), the motor moves to a position within the 180-degree range. A 1-millisecond pulse moves the motor to 0 degrees, a 2-millisecond pulse moves it to 180 degrees. Any pulse between 1 and 2 milliseconds moves the motor to a position proportionally between 0 and 180 degrees.

HARDWARE PWM

Keeping a constant PWM signal going while juggling other tasks is tricky because when you're not pulsing the pin, the motor's not moving. On all of the processors except the Basic Stamp, there is another solution to this problem. *Hardware pulse width modulation (HPWM)* is a method for sending a constant PWM signal on a given pin while other tasks are being executed. For more on hardware PWM, consult the manuals and examples for your particular processor and programming environment.

There are several servo motor controllers on the market that interface easily to a microcontroller. If you're planning a project that needs more than one servo, it's wise to invest in a controller so you don't have to spend programming time getting the timing right. The Mini-SSC2 from Scott Edwards Electronics (http://www.seetron.com) will control up to eight servos using serial commands. There are dozens of others on the market that control varying numbers of servos.

If you're controlling only one or two servos, they're very easy to control directly from your microcontroller. The two examples in Chapter 6 give you all the code you need to make that happen.

Controlling Stepper Motors

Stepper motors are different than regular DC motors in that they don't turn continuously but move in a series of very precise steps. They are different from the RC servo in that they can turn continuously in a full circle and they don't give you any feedback about their absolute position. They're useful any time you want to move a precise distance around a circle, or when you want to translate that distance to a precise linear distance. For example, you could attach one to the knobs of an Etch A Sketch toy to draw pictures with more detail than human patience and muscle control allows. Or you might put a sonar ranging device on a stepper motor at the center of a room so you can rotate the sensor around the room, taking distance measurements at regular intervals to learn the contours of the room.

Stepper motors have several coils of wire inside, not just one. The center shaft has a series of magnets mounted on it, and the coils surrounding the shaft are alternately given current or not, creating magnetic fields which repulse or attract the magnets on the shaft, causing the motor to rotate. Figure 10.9 shows the inside of a stepper motor.

Figure 10.9
The inside of a stepper motor. In this motor, many of the coils around the edge are wired together so that there are only four coil circuits.

This design allows for very precise control of the motor: by proper pulsing, it can be turned in accurate steps of set degree increments (for example, 1.8-degree increments, half-degree increments, and so on). They are used in printers, disk drives, and other devices where precise positioning of the motor is necessary. In fact, old printers and scanners are an excellent source for good steppers for physical computing projects. If you see a printer in the garbage, don't pass it up. There are at least two steppers in there that you can use.

Steppers usually move much slower than DC motors, since there is an upper limit to how fast you can step them. However, unlike DC motors, steppers often provide more torque at lower speeds. They can be very useful for moving a precise distance or a specific number of rotations. Furthermore, stepper motors have very high torque when stopped, since the magnetic field of the motor coils holds the motor in place like a brake.

Steppers can slip if they're moving a heavy load, so it's wise to devise a system to continually check their position against an absolute position, if needed. The methods for sensing rotation in Chapter 9 will come in handy here. The simplest method is to use the homemade tachometer described in that chapter. Place a magnet on the disc that the stepper is turning and a Hall-effect sensor or a reed switch on the fixed base on which the motor is mounted. Each time the motor passes the switch, you know one rotation has passed, and you can start counting steps from zero again.

To control a stepper, you need to energize the coils in the right sequence to make the motor move forward. To do this, you need to understand the how the wires are connected. There are two basic types of stepper motors, unipolar steppers and bipolar steppers. There are, of course, a number of stepper motor controller modules available, such as Parallax's Little Step-U module, and if you've got the cash, these will save you time. But if you don't, here's how to do it on your own.

Unipolar Stepper Motors

The *unipolar stepper* motor has five or six wires and four coils (actually two coils divided by center connections on each coil). The center connections of the coils are tied together and used as the power connection. They are called unipolar steppers because power always comes in on this one pole. Figure 10.10 shows the typical wiring for a unipolar stepper.

If you're lucky, your stepper will come with instructions as to which wire is which, and you can wire it up simply. They don't often come with clear wiring instructions (especially

Figure 10.10
Wiring for the coils
of a six-wire unipolar
stepper (for a five-wire
unipolar stepper, wires
5 and 6 are connected).

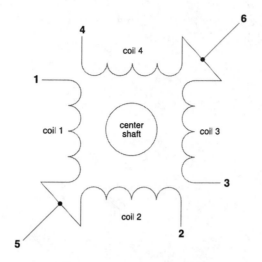

if you ripped them out of something you found in the garbage), so you might have to determine which wire goes to which coil by yourself. To do this, take an ohmmeter to the wires and measure the resistance from one wire to another. The outer wires for each coil will have a resistance that is double the resistance between the inner wire and either of the two outer wires. For example, if the resistance between wires 1 and 5 is x ohms, then that between 1 and 2 is $2x$ ohms. Remember, two wires that are not connected (for example, 1 and 3, 4, or 6) have infinite resistance, which should read as an error on your meter. When you put voltage across two wires of a coil (for example, 1 to 2, or 3 to 4), you should find that the motor is very difficult to turn (don't force it, that's bad for the motor).

Like other motors, the stepper requires more power than a microcontroller can give it, so you'll need a separate power supply for it. Ideally, you'll know the voltage from the manufacturer, but if not, get a variable DC power supply, apply the minimum voltage (hopefully 5 volts or so), apply voltage across two wires of a coil (for example, 1 to 2 or 3 to 4), and slowly raise the voltage until the motor is difficult to turn. It is possible to damage a motor this way, so don't go too far. Typical voltages for a stepper might be 5 volts, 9 volts, 12 volts, or 24 volts. Higher than 24 volts is less common for small steppers, and, frankly, above that level it''s best not to guess.

To control the stepper, apply voltage to each of the coils in a specific sequence. The sequence would go like those shown in Table 10.1.

Table 10.1
Unipolar Stepper Motor Stepping Sequence

STEP	COIL 1	COIL 2	COIL 3	COIL 4
1	high	low	high	low
2	low	high	high	low
3	low	high	low	high
4	high	low	low	high

Note: wires 5 and 6 are wired to the supply voltage.

You drive the stepper by connecting the four coils to a transistor and the two common wires to the supply voltage, as shown in Figure 10.11.

Figure 10.11
A transistor control for a four-wire unipolar stepper motor.

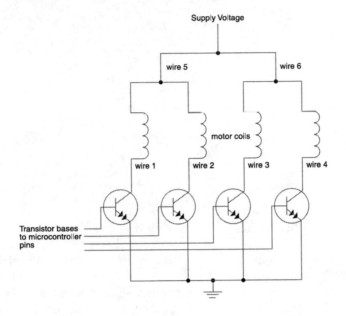

In Figure 10.11, the transistors are TIP120 Darlington transistors. A convenient way to do this is with a Darlington transistor array, such as the ULN2004. Most of the major online electronics retailers will carry Darlington arrays, and they're cheap. Figure 10.12 shows the schematic for wiring a unipolar stepper to a Darlington transistor array.

Figure 10.12
A unipolar stepper motor control with a Darlington transistor array. Many steppers use this color scheme for the four coils:

coil 1: orange

coil 2: yellow

coil 3: black

coil 4: brown

Power: red

This may or may not work for your stepper.

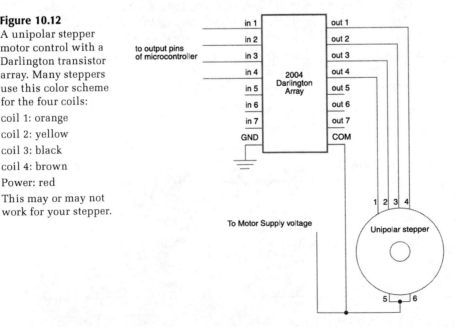

If you have trouble getting a unipolar stepper to work with the stepping sequence in Table 10.1, try stepping one coil at a time, like Table 10.2.

Table 10.2
Alternate Unipolar Stepper Motor Stepping Sequence

STEP	COIL 1	COIL 2	COIL 3	COIL 4
1	high	low	low	low
2	low	high	low	low
3	low	low	high	low
4	low	low	low	high

Note: wires 5 and 6 are wired to the supply voltage.

Once you have the motor stepping in one direction, stepping in the other direction is simply a matter of doing the steps in reverse order. Knowing the position is a matter of knowing how many degrees per step, and counting the steps and multiplying by that many degrees. So for example, if you have a 1.8-degree stepper and it's turned 200 steps, then it's turned 1.8 × 200 degrees, or 360 degrees, or one full revolution.

Bipolar Stepper Motors

The *bipolar stepper motor* usually has four wires coming out of it. Unlike unipolar steppers, bipolar steppers have no common center connection. In practice, there's not a lot of difference between unipolar steppers and bipolar steppers, for your purposes. However, it's worthwhile to know about both because you never know what kind you'll end up using, particularly if you're salvaging them from trashed appliances. They have two independent sets of coils instead. You can distinguish them from unipolar steppers by measuring the resistance between the wires. You should find two pairs of wires with equal resistance. If you've got the leads of your meter connected to two wires that are not connected (that is, not attached to the same coil), you should see infinite resistance (or no continuity).

NOTE
A six-wire unipolar stepper motor is really a bipolar stepper motor with center connections on each coil. When we connect the two center taps together, we're turning it into a unipolar motor. With four-wire bipolar steppers, it's not possible to do this.

To control a bipolar stepper motor, you give the coils current using the same steps as for a unipolar stepper motor. However, instead of using four coils, you use both poles of the two coils and reverse the polarity of the current. This may seem confusing at first, but let's look at the stepper motor stepping sequence again, and see what it means when we apply it to a bipolar stepper. Figure 10.13 shows the way that current flows in a bipolar stepper motor's coils when we apply current using the steps below.

Table 10.3
Bipolar Stepper Motor Stepping Sequence

STEP	WIRE 1	WIRE 2	WIRE 3	WIRE 4
1	high	low	high	low
2	low	high	high	low
3	low	high	low	high
4	high	low	low	high

Note: wires 2 and 5 are wired to the supply voltage.

Figure 10.13
A bipolar stepper motor
stepping sequence.

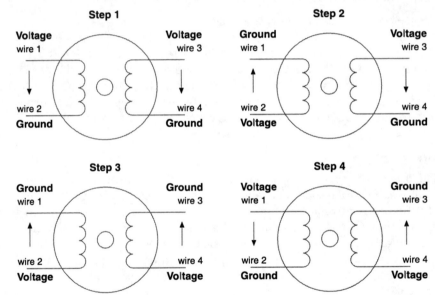

The easiest way to reverse the polarity in the coils is to use a pair of H-bridges. The SN754410 dual H-bridge that you used in the DC motor example above has two H-bridges in the chip, so it will work nicely for this purpose. Figure 10.14 shows the connections you need to make.

Stepper Motor Control Programming

Because both unipolar and bipolar stepper motors are controlled by the same stepping sequence, we can use the same microcontroller code to control either one. In the code examples below, connect either the darlington transistor array (for unipolar steppers) or the dual H-bridge (for bipolar steppers) to the pins of your microcontroller as described in each example. There is a switch attached to the microcontroller as well. When the switch is high, the motor turns one direction. When it's low, it turns the other direction.

Figure 10.14
A bipolar stepper
motor controlled by
a SN754410 dual H-
bridge.

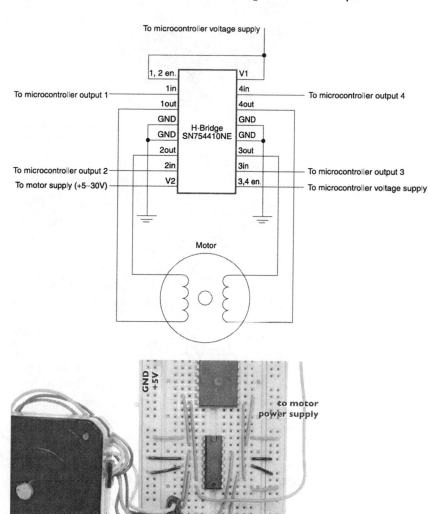

Here's the pseudocode for this example:

```
If switch is high then
    Turn motor one direction:
        Set coils to step 1 of sequence
        Set coils to step 2 of sequence
        Set coils to step 3 of sequence
        Set coils to step 4 of sequence
Else
    Turn motor the other direction:
```

```
                    Set coils to step 4 of sequence
                    Set coils to step 3 of sequence
                    Set coils to step 2 of sequence
                    Set coils to step 1 of sequence

        End if
```

PBASIC

MBasic

```
' switch is on pin 8
' stepper motor connections are on pins 0 to 3, as follows:
' connection 1: pin 0
' connection 2: pin 1
' connection 3: pin 2
' connection 4: pin 3
' we will set all of pins 0 to 7 at once, rather than setting each pin individually.

' set variables:
steps        var word         ' keeps track of which step we're on
stepArray    var byte(4) ' an array to hold the stepping sequence


' set the pins 0 to 3 to output:
DIRL = %00001111

' set all the pins 0 to 7 high:
OUTL= %11111111
' set in 8 (the switch) to input:
input 8
' set the values in the step array:
stepArray[0] = %00001010
stepArray[1] = %00000110
stepArray[2] = %00000101
stepArray[3] = %00001001

' pause half a second at startup:
Pause 500

main:
    ' if the switch is high, add one to steps; otherwise, subtract one:
    if IN8 = 1 then
        steps = steps + 1
    else
        steps = steps - 1
    endif
    ' the modulo operator (//) gives the remainder of the division of the
    ' two quantities in the operation. So x // 4 can never be more than 3,
    ' since anything divided by 4 has a maximum remainder of 3.
    ' below, we use modulo to convert the number in steps to a number
```

```
          ' between 0 and 3. Then we set all the pins from 0 to 7 by setting
          ' OUTL equal to one of the 4 elements of the step array:
          OUTL = stepArray[steps // 4]

          ' pause sets the speed between steps:
          pause 3
      GoTo main
```

PicBasic Pro

```
' switch is on portb.4
' stepper motor connections are on portD, pins 0 to 3, as follows:
' connection 1: portd.0
' connection 2: portd.1
' connection 3: portd.2
' connection 4: portd.3
' we will set all of portD at once, rather than setting each pin individually.

' set variables:
steps        var word         ' keeps track of which step we're on
stepArray    var byte(4) ' an array to hold the stepping sequence


' set the four lower pins of portD to output:
TRISD = %11110000

' set all the pins of portD high:
PORTD = %11111111
' set portb.4 (the switch) to input:
input portb.4
' set the values in the step array:
stepArray[0] = %00001010
stepArray[1] = %00000110
stepArray[2] = %00000101
stepArray[3] = %00001001

' pause half a second at startup:
Pause 500

main:
    ' if the switch is high, add one to steps; otherwise, subtract one:
    if portb.4 = 1 then
        steps = steps + 1
    else
        steps = steps - 1
    endif
    ' the modulo operator (//) gives the remainder of the division of the
    ' two quantities in the operation. So x // 4 can never be more than 3,
```

```
                    ' since anything divided by 4 has a maximum remainder of 3.
                    ' below, we use modulo to convert the number in steps to a number
                    ' between 0 and 3. Then we set all the pins of portD by setting
                    ' portD equal to one of the 4 elements of the step array:
                    portD = stepArray[steps // 4]

                    ' pause sets the speed between steps:
                    pause 3
            GoTo main
```

BX-Basic

```
    ' switch is on pin 13
    ' stepper motor connections are on pins 9 to 12, as follows:
    ' connection 1: pin 9
    ' connection 2: pin 10
    ' connection 3: pin 11
    ' connection 4: pin 12
    ' we will set all of pins 5 to 12 at once,
    ' rather than setting each pin individually.


    dim motorStep(1 to 4) as byte
    dim thisStep as integer

    Sub main()
        call delay(0.5) ' start program with a half-second delay

        ' save values for the 4 possible states of the stepper motor leads
        ' in a 4-byte array. the stepMotor routine will step through
        ' these four states to move the motor. This is a way to set the
        ' value on four pins at once. The eight pins 5 through 12 are
        ' represented in memory as a byte called register.portc. We will set
        ' register.portc to each of the values of the array in order to set
        ' pins 9,10,11, and 12 at once with each step.

        motorStep(0) = bx0000_1010
        motorStep(1) = bx0000_0110
        motorStep(2) = bx0000_0101
        motorStep(3) = bx0000_1001

        ' set the last 4 pins of port C to output:
        register.ddrc = bx0000_1111

        ' set all the pins of port C low:
        register.portc = bx0000_0000

        do
```

```
            if getPin(13) = 1 then
                thisStep = thisStep + 1
            else
                thisStep = thisStep - 1
            end if

            call stepMotor(thisStep)
        loop
    End Sub


    sub stepMotor(byref whatStep as integer)
        ' the modulo operator (//) gives the remainder of the division of the
        ' two quantities in the operation. So x // 4 can never be more than 3,
        ' since anything divided by 4 has a maximum remainder of 3.
        ' below, we use modulo to convert the number in steps to a number
        ' between 0 and 3. Then we set all the pins form 5 to 12 by setting
        ' register.portc equal to one of the 4 elements of the step array:

        ' sets the value of the eight pins of register.portc to whatStep:
        register.portc = motorStep(whatStep mod 4)

        call delay (0.01) ' vary this delay as needed to make your stepper step.
    end sub
```

If you're having trouble getting your stepping sequence to work correctly, try setting the pause or delay between steps to a full second. Then watch the motor step by step as it moves in its sequence. It should move consistently in the same direction each time. If it doesn't, perhaps taking three steps forward and one back, you probably have the wires connected incorrectly. Try changing the arrangement of the connections between the H-bridge or transistor array and the motor until you get it right.

Controlling Solenoids

All the motors we've discussed so far create rotary motion, and therefore need some sort of mechanical system to convert their motion to linear motion. In contrast to the motors we've discussed, *solenoids* create linear motion. A solenoid is basically a coil of wire with an iron shaft in the center (see Figure 10.15). When the coil is given current, it creates a magnetic field, and the shaft is pulled or pushed as a result. When the current is turned off, the magnetic field disappears and the shaft moves back, either because gravity pulls it back down or because it's attached to a spring mechanism that pushes or pulls it back into place. Solenoids operate much like electromagnetic relays, which we described in Chapter 6. Solenoids cannot be positioned variably. They have only two positions, on or off. The shaft can be at full extension or compression, or not. There is no way to position the shaft halfway. In that sense, they are digital output devices.

Figure 10.15
A solenoid.

Since they are made up of charged coils that induce a field, solenoids share many of the same characteristics as motors. They have a characteristic operating voltage and amperage, the coil has a fixed resistance, and they can exert a certain fixed amount of force. They have a few additional characteristics that you need to know in order to use them as well.

Solenoids can be push-type or pull-type. In a *push-type solenoid*, the shaft is pushed out of the barrel when the coil is given current. In a *pull-type solenoid*, the rod is pulled into the barrel when current is applied. Both types require some mechanism for returning the shaft to its rest position. If the system to which the solenoid is attached doesn't pull or push it back into place, this is usually done using a spring.

A solenoid's *draw* refers to how far the shaft travels. Most solenoids do not have a very long draw. An inch is a long draw. Solenoids are useful for applications where you need a short linear movement, like automatic door locks, valve closing and opening, and so forth. In cases where a long linear motion is needed, motors are the better tools.

Solenoids have a given *duty cycle*, which is a measurement of the on time divided by the on time plus the off time. For example, if a solenoid is on for 1 second and off for 3 seconds, its duty cycle is 1/1+3, or 1/4, or 25 percent

Solenoids also have a given *maximum on time*, after which they need to be turned off for the rest of the duty cycle. A solenoid operated consistently for more than its maximum on time, or for a greater duty cycle than it's rated for, will usually overheat and stop working. For example, if a solenoid has a 20 percent duty cycle and a maximum on time of a tenth of a second, then it can't be turned on for more than 0.1 seconds every half second. Solenoids with short maximum on times or duty cycles are usually referred to as *momentary solenoids*, and those that can stay on continually are called *continuous solenoids*.

Though there are some reversible solenoids, they are rare (reversible solenoids use a magnetic shaft). Most solenoids cannot be reversed, so changing the polarity on a push-type solenoid will not make it a pull-type solenoid. Make sure to get the one you need.

Most electronic and mechanical retailers and surplus suppliers carry a variety of solenoids, as they're very common in electronic appliances. All Electronics is our favorite source for solenoids, but many of the other retailers listed in this book will carry them, too.

Controlling a solenoid is very easy. All you need is a relay or transistor that can switch the voltage and current that the solenoid requires, and a diode to block the back voltage generated by the solenoid (remember, it is an inductive load). You can use the circuit shown in Figure 10.16.

Figure 10.16
A solenoid control circuit.

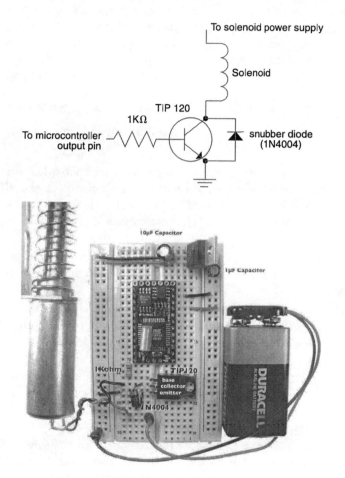

Programming for a solenoid is the same as programming for a digital output. All you need to do is to take the output pin that the solenoid's connected to high to turn it on, and take it low to turn it off. Make sure that your program can't keep the solenoid on for longer than the maximum on time or duty cycle, however.

Basic Mechanics: Converting Motor Motion to Usable Motion

With any motorized system, the first problem you face after you get the motor working is how to convert the motor's motion into something you can use. There are a number of methods common to mechanical systems of all sorts that are useful to know about when you want to control motion of any sort. While this section is by no means comprehensive, it will help get you started on understanding a few basics of how to move things, as well as introduce some of the terminology you'll need when you start looking for parts.

The most important thing to keep in mind when planning any mechanical system is this: all machines are used to do work of some kind. This may seem obvious, but work, in this case, is defined as a force applied over a certain distance (work = force × distance). Machines are designed to allow you to vary the ratio of force to distance in order to get more work for less force. They are mechanical transducers: they convert one form of mechanical energy into another. Some systems are more efficient than others, but no machine converts 100 percent of the input force into output force. They all lose some energy along the way, to friction, heat, and so forth. Deciding what system will do the work best for the least amount of effort is your prime task in dealing with mechanical systems.

When you build or adapt a mechanical system to do your bidding, you always have to consider a few factors:

▶ *Can it be done with a servo motor?* You might consider working backward from the easiest motor to use with a microcontroller, the RC servo motor. Even if you have to add a small mechanical linkage to make your project work with one of these, it will probably save you work compared to powering, wiring, and controlling anything else.

▶ *Does it do the work you need it to do?* If the mechanical system you're designing won't convert the force that your motor can deliver into the force that you need, it's no good.

▶ *Will it work with the motor you have to work with?* Is there a simple way to connect the system to your motor? If not, don't waste tons of time trying to adapt one to the other. Figure out which one is easier to replace, and replace it.

▶ *Will it fit the space you've got to work with?* If you've got to fit everything in a one-foot cube, and you've got a gear system that takes twice that space, it's no good. Find a better way. Alternately, ask yourself if you can hide the mechanism somewhere behind the one-foot cube.

▶ *Is it more cost- and time-effective to modify an existing mechanism to do what you want rather than to make your own from scratch?* Like electronics, mechanics can be very seductive. Making your own gear train or system of linkages can be very satisfying. But if doing so takes all the time you've got for your project, such that you never get to consider the other issues brought up in this book, then you shouldn't build your own. Many toys, appliances, and other everyday devices have mechanisms built into them that can be cannibalized for physical computing systems. Take a look inside that old VCR, CD player, Baby Poops-A-Lot, or cymbal-playing monkey that you broke years ago. You're likely to find some useful mechanisms.

Simple Machines

There are a handful of simple machines that occur in almost every mechanical system. Combinations of these machines are the building blocks of devices that create motion. Understanding how these simple machines convert mechanical energy will make it easier for you to design ways of creating motion in your work.

The Lever

The *lever* is about the simplest of machines, one you're used to dealing with every day, from can openers to car jacks and millions of other everyday devices. A lever is used to change the direction and distance of a force. Every lever has a *fulcrum point* about which the lever pivots. The two arms of a lever are not equal. A lever lets you move a heavy weight with a small force, by taking advantage of this inequality. Imagine that you have a lever whose long arm is twice the length of the short arm. If you place the load you need to move on the shorter side of the lever, and apply half the force needed to move that load to the longer side of the lever, you move the load. You have to apply the force for twice the distance in order to do the same amount of work, however. You can see this in action in Figure 10.17. A one-kilogram weight is moved half a meter by putting a half-kilogram weight on the long arm of the lever and letting it push down one meter.

Figure 10.17
The lever.

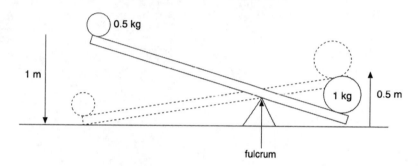

The ratio of the long arm to the short arm gives you the *mechanical advantage* of the lever, which is the ratio of work put into the system to work coming out of the system. If the long arm is twice as long as the short arm, the ratio is 2:1, and the mechanical advantage is 2. So you could move the weight with half the force needed if you're willing to apply your force twice as far. This comes in handy when you've got a motor that can apply only a limited amount of torque, but you've got a lot of space to work with.

The Pulley

A *pulley* is a series of moving wheels and ropes, chains, or wires used to reverse the direction of an applied force or to gain mechanical advantage. A single pulley just allows you to change the direction of the force, which is very useful when you want to add a counterweight to a moving load, but multiple pulleys in a system add mechanical advantage. However, if the single pulley is moving, it doubles the force because it makes you pull twice as far. Look at the pulleys in Figure 10.18. In the system on the left, the pulley is fixed and there is no mechanical advantage. Only the direction of the force is changed. In the system on the right, the mechanical advantage is 2, because you have to pull the rope up two meters to move the weight one meter. What you lose in distance, you gain in force, because it takes only half the force that gravity applies to the weight to pull it up.

The more moving pulleys you add, the greater the mechanical advantage you get. At the same time, you increase the distance you have to pull in order to move the weight. Adding fixed pulleys, on the other hand, only allows you to change the direction of the force. Figure 10.19 illustrates this with a few pulley arrangements and their mechanical advantages.

Figure 10.18
Single-pulley systems:
fixed pulley (left) and
moving pulley (right).

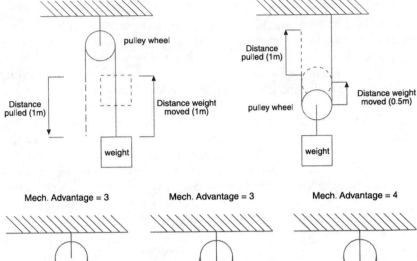

Figure 10.19
Multiple-pulley
systems.

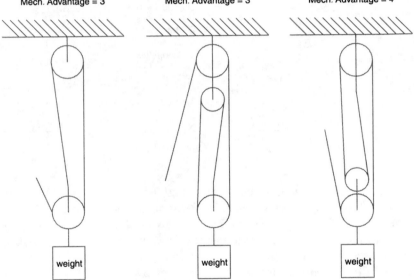

The Gear

Gears are used to convert rotational motion, both by changing direction and by trading speed for torque. The mechanical advantage of a gear train is called the *gear ratio*, which is determined by measuring the ratio of the radii of the gears. In the gear train in Figure 10.20, the smaller gear is half the size of the larger, so the gear ratio is 2:1. The larger gear will move half the speed of the smaller but will provide twice the torque.

The gears in Figure 10.21 move in opposite directions. So if the smaller gear were attached to a motor, the larger gear would move at half the speed of the motor and provide twice the torque in the opposite direction of rotation.

Certain gears can be used to change the axis of motion as well. *Bevel gears* have their teeth mounted at an angle to the axis of the gear so that the mating gear does not have to be mounted at the same angle. *Helical gears* have their teeth cut at an angle to the face of the gear. This increases the power of the gear train because more of the face of each gear tooth is exposed to the other gear.

Figure 10.20
A simple gear train.

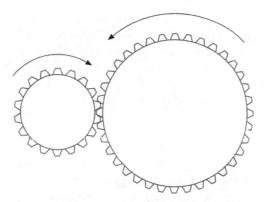

Screws can be used not only as fasteners, but also as gears. Screws convert rotational motion into linear motion. A screw mounted to a motor with a moving head fastened to it is at the core of most handheld CD players, for example, to move the laser beam from the edge of the disk to the outside. Screws are also used in vises, clamps, and many other common tools.

Worm gear mechanisms combine a regular, or helical, gear and a screw. They generally have very high gear ratios and shift the axis of motion by 90 degrees. Figure 10.21 shows a typical worm gear.

Figure 10.21
A worm gear.

Rack-and-pinion gears are also used to convert rotary motion to linear motion. In a rack-and-pinion, teeth are mounted along a linear track (rack) that moves by being run against a normal gear (pinion). Rack-and-pinion systems are common steering mechanisms in cars; the rack is attached to the axle mount, and the pinion is attached to the steering wheel. Figure 10.22 shows a rack-and-pinion.

Figure 10.22
A rack-and-pinion.

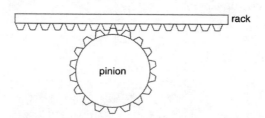

Although there are many sources for individual gears and gear trains, it's often easiest to look for gear trains in existing toy and hobby sets. Kits like K'NEX, LEGO, Erector, and others have very useful gears, gear trains, axles, shaft collars, and other parts for making customized motor systems. Even if you're not interested in the look of these parts, consider them for the infrastructure of your project, if they can be clothed in materials that match the look you want. Using existing parts like this will save you hours of construction time.

The Cam

The *cam* is a wheel mounted eccentrically (off-center) on a shaft. It seems very simple, but serves a number of purposes. The simplest use of a cam is as a vibrator. By spinning the motor, the weight of the cam causes the motor's axis to shift. If the motor is attached to some solid surface, say, a pager or cell phone body, the surface vibrates. In fact, pager motors are very common (available from most of the retailers mentioned), very small, and very useful for creating vibration in all kinds of projects. You can also create your own vibrating motors just by gluing a nut eccentrically on a small DC motor.

Cams can also be used to create oscillating or periodic motion from rotary motion. By placing a shaft against the edge of a cam, the shaft will move up and down as the cam rotates eccentrically on the motor. Cams can also produce periodic motion.

For example, the cam in Figure 10.23 would produce motion with three sudden jumps per revolution, moving the lever nearby to hit the switch on the other side of the lever.

Figure 10.23
A cam used to create
periodic action.

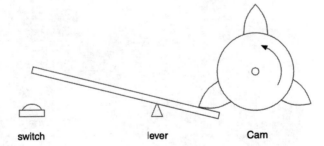

switch   lever   Cam

Another useful form of cam is the *camshaft*, in which a rotating shaft has bends in it to produce several cams all on the same shaft. Camshafts are used in car engines to move the valves in opposition to each other. A typical camshaft would look like the one in Figure 10.24.

Camshafts are also used in mechanical automata, where one crank may turn several dancing figurines at a time. Any time you want to move several objects from one motor in a periodic motion, a camshaft will do the job.

Figure 10.24
A camshaft.

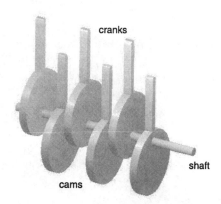

The Ratchet

The *ratchet* is related to the gear in that it's a wheel with teeth, but it's used for a different purpose. Ratchets allow the wheel to move in one direction, but not the other. The teeth of a ratchet are cut with one vertical edge and one diagonal edge. An external lever hook called a *pawl* can slide up the diagonal side of each tooth, or catch against the vertical side of the tooth. In Figure 10.25, a pull-type solenoid pulls in when given power, moving the ratchet clockwise a few degrees. Ratchets can be useful in systems where you can apply force in one direction, but not the other, and need to continually apply force for longer than the distance of your motor. Ratchets are often used in combination with levers to create winches.

Figure 10.25
A ratchet.

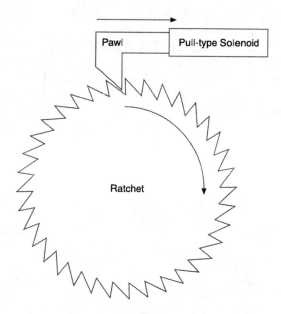

Joints

There are endless ways to join structural elements together to create movement, and each unique system of connections will give you a different type of motion. There are three types of joints that are most common, however: rotating joints, sliding joints, and bending joints. Each type of joint will have its own advantages and limitations, its own weak points, and points of greatest friction.

Bending joints, like a *hinge*, will give you limited motion in one axis. A hinge will be able to move at most 180 degrees, most likely less, depending on where your two structural pieces are hinged together. Figure 10.26 shows the effect of hinge placement on the range of motion between the two joined pieces.

Figure 10.26
Hinges.

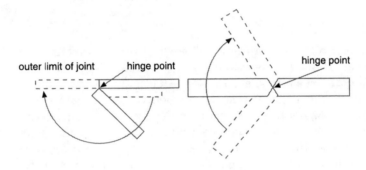

Rotating joints are joints where circular structural elements rotate around a common axis. In a rotating joint, there is friction between the rotating shaft and the collar, or *bushing*, in which it's rotating. Figure 10.26 shows a typical shaft and bushing. This can be managed by using some form of oil or grease lubricant, a high-density plastic bushing that has very little friction, an oil-impregnated bushing, or by using a bearing of some sort. The job of a bushing is to keep the rotation of a joint in one axis, so you want to make sure the shaft and the bushing fit together snugly, with just enough room to turn. Too tight, and it won't turn. Too loose, and the shaft will shift off the ideal axis of rotation and bind up. *Bearings* consist of a metal chassis containing balls or cylinders that are free to roll within the chassis so that they provide friction relief by turning. Bearings are often used to lessen the friction in a rotating joint.

When dealing with any rotational motion, it's important to know where the system will bear the load, or weight. An *axial load* is a load parallel to the shaft, and a *radial load* is a load perpendicular to the shaft. Both stress the joint in different ways. An axial load will tend to grind the shaft against the end of the bushing, and a radial load will pull or push the rotation off-axis and place extra stress on one side. Every load has both axial and radial components. A well-balanced load is one that limits both as much as possible. Almost any application where you're converting the rotational motion to linear motion, for example using the motor as a winch, will place a radial load on the shaft. Wheels place a radial load on the shaft of an axle. Axial loads will place pressure on the socket where the shaft sits in the bushing and will cause the joint to wobble unless they're perfectly balanced. Turntables place an axial load on the shaft that turns them and a radial load when they're off-balance.

Basic Mechanics

Figure 10.27
A rotating joint (shaft
and bushing).

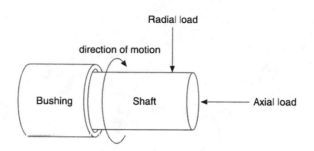

Rotating joints are perhaps the most common joints due to the flexibility they offer; for example, many bending joints, such as hinges, are made of a rotating joint with two radial loads. In addition, to get more than one axis of motion, a spherical rotating joint called a *ball-and-socket joint* (like your hip joint) is necessary. In a ball-and-socket joint, a rod with a spherical end (ball) is fitted into a cup (socket) at the end of a second rod. Lubricant is placed between the ball and socket to reduce friction.

Sliding joints are joints where one surface slides against another. Like rotating joints, you have to take care to reduce friction but also ensure a snug fit, as well as avoid binding because of a misfit. Ideally, the sliding section of a sliding joint should be at least twice as long as the width of the slot. This will minimize the chance of the piece binding up. Sliding joints can generally be lubricated with the same materials as rotating joints. Figure 10.28 shows a typical sliding joint.

Figure 10.28
A sliding joint.

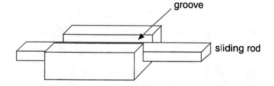

Linkages

Stiff and flexible support members can be linked using various joints to create a variety of movement and support systems. Linkages can also convert one type of motion to another, similar to cams.

The *four-bar linkage* is a common tool for creating complex motion from simple rotational motion. It consists of four stiff bars connected by joints about which they can rotate. One bar is kept stationary, and is called the *ground*. The bar being moved is the *coupler*, and it's opposite the ground. The two joining bars can be of varying lengths, depending on the application. If a joining bar can rotate a full 360 degrees, it's called a *crank*, and if it's constrained by the rest of the system from rotating all the way around, it's called a *rocker*. Systems with joining bars of unequal length change the speed of motion similar to gears, but they also change the path of motion. The system in Figure 10.29 creates a very complex pattern of movement from the end of the coupler as the crank turns all the way around, not unlike the shape of a windshield wiper blade (the pattern of movement is shown on the right). Furthermore, if you turn the whole mechanism on its side clockwise, use the crank as a ground instead, and attach the end of the former ground to the edge of a wheel, you get a back-and-forth motion that's not too far off from the movement of a walking leg.

Figure 10.29
A four-bar linkage, showing the movement pattern of the tip of the coupler.

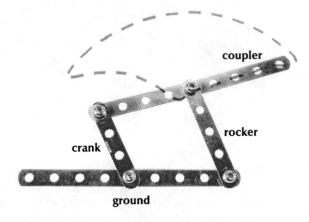

SHAFT COUPLERS

No matter what you need to attach your motor to, you'll need some extra hardware in order to attach it. The part you're looking for is usually called a *shaft coupler*, or a *collar*. It's basically a metal sleeve that fits over the shaft of the motor. It attaches securely to the motor shaft and the part you're attaching to the motor. You can find couplers with different-sized holes on either end to be able to join shafts of differing diameters. The most basic shaft couplers rely on friction to do the job. These can slip, however, so some shafts and couplers are designed with a notch taken out of them, so that the coupler can fit the shaft in only one way. (See the gearhead motor in Figure 10.1 for an example of a notched shaft.) *Set screws* are often used with couplers to assist in making a solid connection as well. A set screw is a screw mounted perpendicular to the shaft that screws through the coupler to bind against the shaft, securing the coupler. There are many varieties of couplers, but most will be a variation on what's described here. When you're looking for a motor to match a gear, pulley, or wheel, or vice versa, make sure you know the necessary shaft diameter and what kind of coupling is possible. Figure 10.30 shows a variety of shaft coupling methods.

Figure 10.30
Collars and couplers.

Scissor linkages combine several stiff supports in an X fashion, with rotating joints at the corners. A scissor can retract and extend a great distance with reasonable support. Figure 10.31 shows a typical scissor linkage.

Figure 10.31
A scissor linkage.

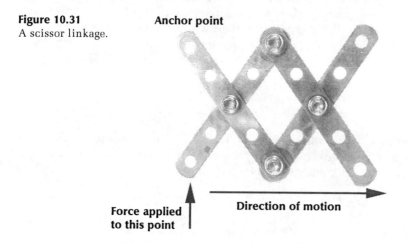

The Piston (Rod and Crank)

A *piston* is a combination of a wheel and a series of linkages. It's a simple way to convert rotary motion to back-and-forth linear motion. A crank is attached to the side of the wheel by a rotating link, with its other end attached to a rod or block (piston head). The rod or block is constrained to move in a line, so when the wheel turns, the rod or block moves forward and backward (see Figure 10.32). Pistons are used in most engines, but can also be adapted for applications like animatronics, hydraulics, pneumatics, and more.

Figure 10.32
A piston.

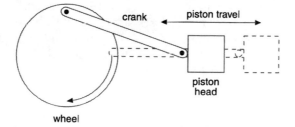

Construction

Whenever you create motion, you need a solid structure on which to mount your moving parts. We haven't talked about construction materials in this book because we feel it's a topic that merits its own book. However, there are a number of materials that we use for quick and easy construction of prototypes that are worth mentioning here.

If we had to single out one supplier for construction and mechanical parts, it would be McMaster-Carr. They carry a very wide variety of hardware and construction materials, and their catalog and Website is very detailed and helpful. If you can't find what you're looking for locally, check out http://www.mcmaster.com.

Foamcore

Foamcore is a wonderful construction material for quick projects, because it's lightweight and very easy to cut and form. Though it tends to buckle when you put too much weight on it or apply too much force, it's very easy to strengthen with ribs and struts made from foamcore placed on end, or from wood. It holds together well with white glue or wood glue, and is very fast to build with. Many fabricators, designers and architects use it for initial models because it's so easy. Your local art store will carry it in varying colors and thicknesses.

Tupperware

Tupperware and other household plastic containers make useful housings for electronic parts. They're relatively easy to make holes in and can be sealed up with hot glue. While it's certainly not a professional-grade housing, we see it used in physical computing projects all the time.

Wood

If you've got the saws necessary to work with wood, it's great for large physical structures, of course. However, carpentry is its own discipline, and can take as much or more time as the electrical and programming work laid out in this book. It's electrically non-conductive, which is handy when working with circuits, but sawdust can carry static electricity, so make sure you dust off any wood structures before you introduce your electronics.

Plexiglas

Plexiglas (acrylic) makes good housings, and can also make good, lightweight structures. You can cut thin Plexiglas sheets by simply scoring it with a matte knife along a straight edge and snapping it apart. Many industrial plastics retailers will have laser cutters for cutting custom forms out of Plexiglas and will cut it for you for a fee. Some of them will simply have you bring in a graphics file from CorelDraw or Adobe Illustrator as a template. Drilling good holes in Plexiglas can be done with regular bits, but to make clean holes that don't have chipped edges requires a special drill bit. A special adhesive called Weld-On works well for joining Plexiglas, but it's very toxic. You can get it at most plastic retailers.

Adhesives

Hot glue is great way to adhere two things together. It may not last forever, but it will adhere two things long enough to see if they are worth attaching more permanently. It fills gaps and is also an excellent insulator. Self-tapping drywall screws allow you to work very quickly with wood. Gaffer's tape (not to be confused with duct tape) is a cloth tape that is easily hand-torn to different length and widths. You can write on it, it neatly covers seams, and it can be applied and taken off very easily. It's also got a strong adhesive, and holds well to many materials. Cable ties should already be in your kit for neatening and providing strain relief to your electronics. They also come in handy for strapping anything to anything with considerable force. Hose clamps are also very useful, especially when you have a lot of wires or a few heavy wires to contain.

Erector, Meccano, K'nex

Many toy kits make great structural material for projects. If you don't want your project to look like it was made from toys, build a skin or housing to cover it. The advantage these offer is the freedom to build stable structures to hold motors, gears, and other moving parts securely without having to fabricate your own struts and supports.

There are countless other construction materials, of course; these are just a few that we find convenient and quick to work with. If you've never done any construction of this sort, we recommend browsing the handyman section of your bookstore for more information or seeing if your local university, high school, or community organization offers any basic construction classes.

Black Cloth

Black cloth (canvas, velour, and duvetyn curtains and the like) is not structural, but it hides a multitude of sins. It makes a great backing and discreetly hides your ungainly contraptions and electronics. It draws the eye to brighter and more lively things in front of it, and tells people to pay no attention to that computer behind the curtain. This frees you up to concentrate on getting the interaction right by getting your project in front of real people and worrying about neatening up the implementation later. We get a lot of our fabrics from Rose Brand (http://www.rosebrand.com), who will also custom-tailor stage curtains, but any local fabric store will do as well.

Conclusion

Motion can be one of the most exciting and expressive tools in the physical computing toolbox. By now, most people are desensitized to motion onscreen, whether it's a monitor or a movie screen. We respond to it, but only as filtered through our conscious mind. When you see an object that has its own physical mass move, however, it triggers a more visceral reaction. We've seen the simple movement of a motor electrify students hundreds of times. However, creating motion is one of the most time-intensive physical computing tasks and can create more confusion than sense if it's not carefully considered as part of the whole system. Just as a screen filled with animated icons for no reason can seem overly busy, a space filled with moving things can overwhelm anyone in it. Used sparingly and thoughtfully, it can get your users' attention like no other form of output. The first time you make something move with a microcontroller is the second most exciting moment after you light your first LED. When you've had some luck with this chapter, reward yourself with another celebratory hokeypokey.

11

Touch Me

This chapter is about the point of physical contact between your body and your software. There are great opportunities for input and output through the huge sensitive membrane that is your skin and through the muscles under it. Two modes of sensation used in concert (for example, touch and hearing, or touch and sight) have much greater effect than either one alone, particularly when you're trying to build the illusion of immersive virtual reality. The study and implementation of techniques and psychological effects of this type of physical interface is called *haptics*. Some areas of your body come quickly to mind when imagining tactile interface, like the hands and feet, because we manipulate things with them, or the face and head because we're very sensitive to touch there. On the input side, there are some very easy-to-use items like force sensitive resistors, thermistors, and capacitance sensors. We will even touch on some techniques for sensing changes across your skin to read your unconscious reactions. On the output side, there are some easy devices that allow you to generate sensations of vibration and temperature. There are many other areas of the body worth considering as points of contact. Output that reaches your larger muscles falls into an area called *force feedback*, which is mostly by the use of larger motor and mechanical systems, covered in Chapter 10.

Force-Sensitive Resistors

The force-sensitive resistor (FSR) is one of the best sensors in the physical computing tool kit. FSRs convert mechanical force into electrical resistance. Like any other variable resistor, they generally have two leads and fit very easily into the analog input circuit shown in Chapter 6. They come in a variety of forms, as shown in Figure 11.1, but all are generally small and flat. They require a firm yet slightly pliable backing to work properly, so even if you are embedding them in something amorphous like a pillow, be sure to mount them on a flat surface first. The leads can be quite flimsy, and their movement will add error to the sensor's reading. To prevent this, mount everything, including your connection to the FSR, on a stiff backing and encase the contact end with heat shrink or hot glue (don't encase the whole sensor in hot glue, or it won't work!).

Figure 11.1
Force-sensitive
resistors come in
various shapes and
sizes.

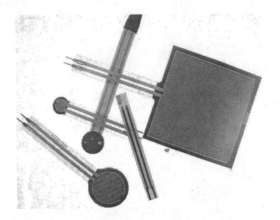

FSRs are typically designed to sense small amounts of force, such as the force of your finger pressing a button or keypad. The force of your body weight will quickly bring these sensors to their peak reading. This is useful if you only want to use them as a digital input to tell if a person is stepping on them or not. Digi-Key carries a range of good FSRs made by CUI Incorporated. You can find them on Digi-Key's site listed as force sensors. Look for part number 102-1212-ND thorough 102-1227-ND. Tekscan's FlexiForce sensors are also popular. Parallax (http://www.parallax.com), Images SI (http://www.imagesco.com), and others carry them. Interlink Electronics sells a design kit (part number 50-76247 at http://www.interlinkelec.com) with a variety of FSR forms, including long strips and small circle pads. They sell these sensors individually as well, at about $3.00 per sensor, but only in lots of about $60.00 or more. If you need a large number of FSRs, it's a good deal. You can also get FSR pads that sense position, like the Infusion Systems' SlideLong and SlideWide (http://www.infusionsystems.com).

Homegrown FSRs

FSRs have a conductive form of rubber inside that lessens its resistance to current flow the more it is compressed. You can build your own FSRs using materials like conductive foam or conductive rubber (Zoflex) that behave this same way. You probably have some conductive foam because chips like your microcontroller are generally shipped in a small piece of it. You can also buy larger pieces of it (Radio Shack part number 276-2400, or Jameco part number 13864). You simply sandwich the conductive foam between two conductors and read the resistance between the conductors. Any copper foil or copper mesh that solder will stick to will work for the conductors. Metal screen door mesh works well. Building your own FSR allows you to vary the sensitivity by adding more material between the sensors. Creating your own sensor might also be necessary if you need to fit it into an unusual space like a small nose on a doll. Conductive foam will tend to lose some of its sensitivity over time, and you will have to recalibrate. You can buy Zoflex conductive rubber (http://www.irmicrolink.com) in sheets, or your can form it yourself. It works similarly to conductive foam.

Force sensors are inherently subject to wear and tear, and getting consistent values out of them is difficult. Unless you are a skilled fabricator, you're better off buying the professionally produced FSRs.

Flex Sensors

Flex sensors, shown in Figure 11.2, look and work much like FSRs, but they vary resistance based on how much you bend them instead of how much you press on them. They come in the form of a flat plastic strip that can be bent up to 180 degrees, increasing resistance from about 10 kilohms to 40 kilohms. They have two leads and connect easily into an analog input circuit. The obvious application is for sensing things that bend like fingers and hinges. They show up in a number of different virtual reality control gloves. They are so easy to work with you can consider them for sensing other types of rotary or linear movement. For example, a flex sensor could be used to sense how far out a small drawer has been pulled or how far a door has been opened. You can find flex sensors at Infusion Systems, Jameco, and Images SI.

Figure 11.2
Flex sensors.

Pressure Sensors

One common mistake people make when they're looking for force sensors is to search for pressure sensors. Pressure sensors measure pressure exerted by a gas or fluid. They're most commonly used in hydraulic or pneumatic applications, where you need to know the pressure of a gas or a liquid as it moves through a tube or a valve. Sometimes they're used in meteorological applications too, for example, to take measurements of atmospheric pressure (barometers). These sensors often have a small tube attached in order to couple with a valve. They can also be used as breath sensors, such as Infusion Systems' Air sensor. Digi-Key and Jameco also carry a number of pressure sensors that produce a varying voltage or resistance in response to changing pressure. Look for one that operates at the voltage or resistance levels that your microcontroller can sense.

Sensing Touch Using Capacitance Sensors

For sensing the very lightest touch, you should look into capacitance sensors. Your body is something of a capacitor, always storing a small electric charge. The shock you get when you touch a grounded object after walking across a carpet is the discharging of your body's stored charge. Some capacitance sensors can detect your body's charge from distances of up to a meter and are used to measure analog distance. This is the technique used by the

Theremin musical instrument (http://www.thereminworld.com). Most capacitance distance sensors require quite a lot of additional circuitry, so they aren't as precise or reliable as the infrared or ultrasonic sensors mentioned in Chapter 9. Capacitance sensors are most useful as touch sensors or near-touch sensors. You can create buttons that work with only the slightest touch of a finger. Capacitance sensors can be adjusted to detect your finger just before it actually touches (within a few millimeters), which can give an object a magical feeling. Because they have no moving parts and can be hidden below thin conductive or non-conductive surfaces like cloth or cardboard, they offer many options for making your buttons not look like buttons. Capacitance sensors are not limited to sensing your finger or your body. These sensors can detect any object that carries a static charge.

Quantum Technologies' Qtouch sensor ICs put all the circuitry for capacitive sensing into a chip for you. Digi-Key sells many models, for example the QT113H, part number 427-1012-ND. The QT113H, shown in Figure 11.3, produces a digital output at 5 volts when a person touches the sensor. A microcontroller can read this as a simple digital input.

Figure 11.3
The QT113H capacitive sensor schematic (top) and circuit (bottom). Note that the shield foil from the cable is connected to ground.

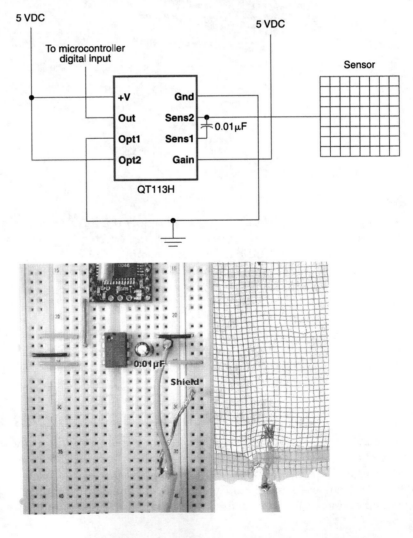

You have to connect a sensor, which does not come with the chip. We've found copper mesh or copper foil works nicely as the sensor. The connection between the sensor chip and the sensor itself also reacts to changes in capacitance, so you'll find that even touching the wire between the two will trigger a reaction. This can be a problem if you only want a very localized area to be sensitive, or if the sensor wire has to run near other current-carrying wires. To get around this, use a shielded conductor between the chip and the sensor. A *shielded conductor* is a wire or a group of wires wrapped in a foil or mesh wrapping. Many video and speaker cables and computer cables are shielded. If you strip back the outer insulation jacket of these cables, you'll find the foil or mesh wrapping surrounding the inner wires. Don't remove it. Connect it to the ground of your circuit to make the conductors insensitive to capacitive changes.

The important pins on this chip are power and ground, the sense pins, and the output. You can use either of the sense pins for your sensor, then put a capacitor in between them, as shown in the schematic in Figure 11.3. The option pins on the Qtouch ICs allow you to set various options like the sensitivity, the reset time (how long the sensor takes to go low again if no change is detected), and more. Read the data sheet for all the options.

Quantum makes a whole family of these chips (http://www.qprox.com) with various options, including having multiple switches per chip. They also make a few analog capacitance sensors, like the QT300, which give you a changing value when they detect movement within a centimeter or so of the sensor.

Off-the-Shelf Touch Interfaces

Touch screens are the easiest way to connect touch with computer graphics. There are many suppliers that integrate touch screens into ordinary monitors at increasingly affordable prices. In addition to the usual video connection these will have a serial or USB connection for the touch information. After you install the drivers, your software can get the touch location by simply reading the mouse coordinates. You can also buy screens that can be attached to conventional monitors. Elo TouchSystems (http://www.elotouch.com) makes a number of both integrated touch screen monitors and add-on touch screens. You can usually find these in surplus at very reasonable prices. All Electronics (http://www.allcorp.com) frequently has a number of different models in stock. You may even consider using these as sensitive touch panels without attaching them to a monitor.

The disadvantage of touch screens is that they generally will only read contact at one point at a time. This means that if you put all five fingertips on the screen, you won't get five discrete locations. Instead, the screen will report several different locations in succession in an inconsistent order. If you want a multitouch touchpad, your options are more limited. Tactex Systems made a wonderful multitouch sensor board, the MTCExpress, but it has been discontinued. Used models show up on eBay frequently and are coveted by musicians.

Sensing Vibrations Using Piezoelectric Sensors

Piezoelectric sensors are often used to detect strain or very slight force changes. These sensors produce a varying voltage when they are bent. They respond very quickly, and to slight changes. Microphones are made of piezoelectric film. In fact, if you connected a piezo to the microphone amplifier circuit in Chapter 13, "Controlling Sound and Light," it would work well as a knock detector. With a fast processor like a PIC, you could use two piezos on a table and time the arrival of their signals to determine the position of a knock on the table. Piezos are used for all kinds of sensors beyond microphones, from sensing strain on bridges to the hitting of a drum to the pitter-patter of children's footsteps in flashing sneakers.

The voltage range that a piezo sensor can produce can be up to a few thousand volts, and it can generate changes as small as a few microvolts. Because of this, piezos can be difficult to read across their entire sensitivity range. One common way to read miniscule changes from a piezo is to use an *operational amplifier*, or *op amp*. Op amps take a very small voltage signal and amplify it to a range that's readable. They can be used for many other functions as well, like reading the difference between two voltages, the sum of two voltages, and more. They've got a reputation among physical computing hobbyists for being difficult to use, but they don't have to be.[1] Figure 11.4 shows one very simple-to-use op amp used to measure the changes from a piezo.

Figure 11.4
A piezo sensor and an LM358 op amp to amplify the voltage changes.

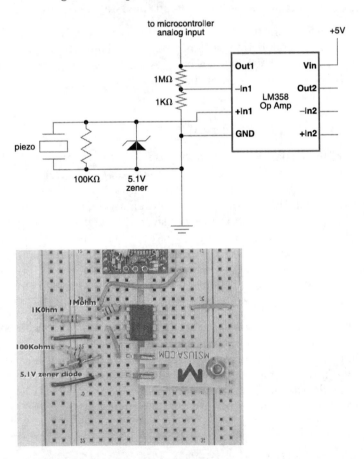

[1] There's much more to be said about op amps. For a more lengthy and technical introduction, see *Practical Electronics for Inventors* by Paul Scherz (McGraw-Hill/TAB Electronics, 2000). If you're really itching to dive into the subject in depth, see *The IC Op Amp Cookbook* by Walter C. Jung (Prentice Hall PTR, 1986).

This op amp, the LM358, is called a *single-supply* op amp because it only needs a positive voltage and ground. Many op amps are *dual-supply*, meaning that they need a positive voltage, ground, and a negative voltage. The output from this circuit will vary between 0 and 5 volts, depending on your piezo and what it's physically mounted to. You can read it with an analog-to-digital converter. If you're using the BS-2, you'll find that the RCTime circuit doesn't catch all the changes from this circuit because the piezo changes voltages very fast. The more extreme the piezo is bent, the more voltage it will produce.

The sensor in the circuit in Figure 11.4 is a piezo film sensor with vibrating mass from Measurement Specialties (http://www.msiusa.com/sensors). It's available from many other suppliers, including Digi-Key as part number MSP-1007-ND. You can use almost any piezo element, though. A piezo speaker cut out of a child's toy used with the same circuit is sensitive enough to respond to a very delicate touch, even to blowing.

You can change the amplification factor of the op amp by changing the two resistors attached to the negative input pin. In this circuit, they're 1 kilohm and 1 megohm, giving an amplification of 1000:1.

The unusual diode attached to the piezo is called a *zener diode*. You'll see it again in Chapter 13, when you build a telephone line interface. A zener diode allows electrical energy to pass up to a certain voltage and cuts the rest off. In this circuit, the zener diode is rated for 5.1 volts, and it's used to send to ground any voltage that the piezo produces above 5 volts.

Creating Vibrations

The most common method of creating vibration is to put a weight off center on the shaft of a motor and spin the motor. You can easily build this by crimping a fishing weight on to any DC motor, or you can hack open a massaging vibrator. You can also find surplus supplies of tiny vibrating motors used in cell phones and pagers. Jameco Digi-Key, All Electronics, and others carry these. They work great in any application where they're positioned near the body. We've seen them put in hat bands, money belts, and many other clothing items as a way to give the wearer an alert without calling attention visually or aurally. Solarbotics (http://www.solarbotics.com) sells them without the weights, so you can use them as regular motors as well, though they're not very powerful. Controlling them is no different than any other DC motor (see Chapter 10). Most of them run on about 1.5 volts, so make sure you're using a supply that doesn't provide more voltage than they can handle.

Taking Your Temperature

A byproduct of human touch is heat. You can determine if someone is touching an object by detecting an increase in heat using a thermistor. Thermistors convert heat into electrical resistance. They are easy to find, cheap, and they plug easily into the standard analog input circuit. Changes in ambient heat conditions can throw off your readings, so it is important to also have a control thermistor to measure current ambient conditions for comparison. Heat does not dissipate as quickly as light, so your readings may seem a little slow in changing. For this same reason you can tell a little bit about how long something has been touched by how warm it has become. We mention thermistors here because heat is associated with human touch, but they are more widely useful. For instance, you could use them to sense whether someone is blowing or breathing on an object. The temperature change from the breeze created by breath is detectable. They can also be used in safety applications because fire and things that lead to fires (like overheating electronics) are hot.

If you are just looking for relative changes in temperature, stick with a simple and cheap thermistor. If you're looking for precise readings, there are temperature sensors like the Dallas DS1820, available from http://www.maxim-ic.com, which measure temperature to within half a degree Fahrenheit. The DS1820 interfaces to a microcontroller using synchronous serial communication like that mentioned in Chapter 12, "More Communication between Devices." These are not as simple to use as thermistors, but they are more precise when precision is needed.

Cooling Things Off and Heating Them Up

For creating hot or cold surfaces, you can use a Peltier junction, shown in Figure 11.5. A *Peltier junction* is a solid-state heat pump. You apply current and it makes one side hot and the other side cool. They are available from many surplus electronic suppliers, like All Electronics (http://www.allcorp.com), the Electronic Goldmine (http://www.goldmine-elec.com), and others. Peltier junctions consume a large amount of current, so you have to control them using a transistor or relay. The darlington transistor circuit for motor control in Chapter 6 will control many smaller Peltier junctions as well. Generally these are used for cooling a very small area, though there are some compact refrigerators made that use them for cooling.

Figure 11.5
A Peltier junction.

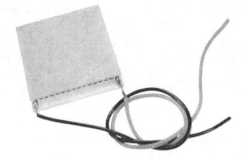

Although Peltier junctions also create heat, they are usually only used for cooling because heat is more easily produced with a simple resistive coil. To localize the heating for tactile applications, you might look at compact heating elements. Minco (http://www.minco.com) makes a variety of them. Surplus models from Minco and others show up frequently on the Electronic Goldmine (http://www.goldmine-elec.com/), Marlon P. Jones Associates (http://www.mpja.com), and others. Like Peltier junctions, these take a lot of current and need to be controlled using a transistor or relay.

Getting Under Your Skin

There is a whole range of techniques for getting at your body's unconscious responses by attaching electrodes to your skin. Reading involuntary responses like your heart rate, skin reactions, and brain wave activity can be intriguing because these reactions are hard to control, but for the same reason they make for unsatisfying interactions. Biometric sensors have gotten cheaper and more reliable, but so far they haven't gotten especially easy to use. Most are still fairly customized, and there are few off-the-shelf solutions that interface directly with a microcontroller.

Galvanic skin response is one measurable quantity generated involuntarily by the body. It's well known as the basis for the polygraph, or lie detector. The theory behind it is basically that you sweat more when stressed, and that telling a lie is stressful. You place two conductors near each other on your skin. When you tell a lie, your increased sweat between the conductors will lessen the resistance between them. Your body becomes a variable resistor. To read the changing values, however, you'll need an op amp, as the voltage changes will be miniscule.

Your brain and your muscles (including your heart) generate small electrical signals that can be picked up by electrodes strapped to your body. Aside from the dangers implicit in strapping electronics to your body, the challenge here is the circuitry for amplifying and filtering the signal coming from those electrodes for use with your microcontroller. First, you need an op amp to amplify the signals above a microvoltage level. Next, you need to filter the individual frequencies out. Brain waves, for example, alternate at varying frequencies between 0 and 60 Hz, so to read the individual frequencies you'd need to filter them out using a fast Fourier transformation (FFT; see Chapter 13 for more on FFT). This is too computationally intense for a microcontroller but possible on a multimedia computer. There are a few manufacturers of hobbyist brainwave (electroencephalograph, or EEG) sensors and muscle movement (EMG) sensors, but they are not cheap. Infusion Systems makes an electromyograph, or EMG sensor, the Curl, for use with their controller box. IBVA Technologies (http://www.ibva.com) makes an EEG and EMG sensor that interfaces with a Macintosh or PC for about $1000. Brain Actuated Technologies (http://www.brainfingers.com) makes a similar system for about $2000.

Heart rate measurements are relatively easy to sense using light. Many commercial pulse meters use a superbright LED or a laser on one side of a finger and a photodiode on the other side. As blood pulses through the finger, it changes the amount of light reaching the photodiode. The photodiode's signal is sent to an op amp, and the resulting peaks in light level give an indication of the person's pulse. If you don't want to build an op amp circuit, you can hack into many consumer pulse meters because most of them have an LED that blinks in time with the pulse. Remove the LED (this might require some careful soldering) and connect the contacts to your microcontroller as a digital input. The pulses used to turn on the LED will give you an indication of the user's pulse. You can read the pulses using the `Count` command (`CountTransitions()` on the BX-24) or the `Pulsin` command.

Force Feedback

Most of the output we have discussed so far in this chapter has a light touch. More impressive haptic feedback, the kind that can resist the force of your muscles, usually requires more power and more mechanical expertise. At the extremes of this are the mechanical systems used in simulators for training astronauts and for amusement park rides. Chapter 10 should give you some ideas for the mechanics needed. Force feedback requires a more sophisticated system of feedback between the sensors and the actuators. For instance, to realistically simulate a mechanical hand pressing against your hand, you need to know how hard your hand is pressing, how hard the mechanized hand is pressing, how far to try moving the mechanized hand, and where the hand actually is. Our trusty RC servo motor comes in handy here with some build-in feedback. As long as you continue to pulse one of these motors to go to a given position, it will continue to fight to get there even if a stronger force is not allowing it to do so. You should also investigate more sophisticated DC motor control drivers that include current sensing from the motor, so you can detect when extra force is being applied and respond accordingly. The 3959 H-bridge from Allegro Micro (http://www.allegromicro.com) is such a driver. One of the more impressive force feedback devices on the consumer market today is the Phantom from Sensable Technologies (http://www.sensable.com). This six-degrees-of-freedom modeling tool is a stylus attached to a moving arm that allows you to shape 3D virtual objects as if you were modeling clay. As you press into the 3D surface, the stylus responds with resistance, becoming harder to move the deeper you press into the object. It's still too expensive for the home user, but it points the way to usable force feedback in everyday life.

Conclusion

The physical computing adage that input is easier than output is particularly true in the realm of touch. Some of the best and easiest sensors available to us are geared towards touch, but they're usually aimed at your hands. There is no reason this has to be the case, however, and most sensors designed for hands can be readily adapted to respond to other body parts. On the output side, you face all the usual difficulties of power and mechanics compounded by a complicated and vulnerable target, the human body. Of course, time is on our side, as work in areas like automation for the physically challenged, biometrics for security, and teledildonics are continually spinning off interesting toys in our direction.

12
More Communication between Devices

In Chapter 7, "Communicating between Computers," we introduced techniques for communicating between your microcontroller and a multimedia computer using serial communication. We talked about how to create your own protocol for transferring data between two devices. This chapter picks up where that one left off. When you identify a part of your project that you cannot or do not want to do with your microcontroller, it's possible that you can find an off-the-shelf device with a serial port that can accomplish the job. Some examples that show up quite often in physical computing projects are video switchers, video mixers, cameras with automated pan/tilt mounts, modems, 3D sensors, and medical equipment like simple pulse meters. Devices like these can make your work much easier. To use them, you'll need to learn their protocols. We'll discuss how to learn the protocol of most anything with a serial port, and we will give a specific example, using a Global Positioning System (GPS) receiver. We'll also introduce MIDI, the Musical Instrument Digital Interface protocol. Understanding MIDI gives you access to a wide array of devices, including sound synthesizers, audio mixers, lighting controllers, and various input devices.

Sometimes a standalone serial device is more than you need. Perhaps your project requires something simpler, like a sound volume controller that you can command from your microcontroller, or a way to read more inputs than your chip has. Many special-purpose IC chips and modules use another form of serial communication called *synchronous serial communication*. We'll cover the principles of this form of serial communication and show an example so that you understand where to start when you encounter ICs and modules that have a synchronous serial interface.

We could hardly have a chapter about communication between computers without some discussion of networking and of the Internet. There are many ways to connect microcontrollers to the Internet. We'll introduce one device to do the job. We'll also briefly introduce modems for communication over phone lines, whether connected to the Internet or not.

Microcontrollers are small and cheap, which opens up all sorts of possibilities for mobile computing. In this chapter, we discuss briefly how radio frequency (RF) and infrared communication work and touch on some higher-level options for making your devices communicate wirelessly.

Synchronous and Asynchronous Communication

Serial communication can be broken up into two broad categories: synchronous and asynchronous. *Synchronous serial communication* uses two wires, one for the data and one called the *clock* that controls the rate at which the data is sent. One device acts as the master and sends a timing pulse on the clock wire every time it is ready to send or receive a bit of data. The term *shifting* is used for synchronous serial communication, because with each clock pulse you shift over the next bit of data. The microcontrollers in this book all have commands called `shiftin` and `shiftout` for sending and receiving synchronous serial communication. There are many styles of synchronous serial communication. Looking at the data sheets for various devices, you'll see I2C, SPI, and Microwire, among others. Though there are some differences between the styles, they all shift bits between devices on the clock pulse.

In *asynchronous serial communication* both devices have their own separate clock to keep track of time. The sender sends pulses representing the data being transmitted at an agreed-upon data rate, and the receiver listens for pulses at that same rate. The timing of the pulses is called the *data rate* or the *baud rate*. One side effect of asynchronous communication is that you never know when the pulses will be coming in, so you have to listen at all times. This is where it helps to have a serial buffer, as we mentioned in Chapter 7. You're already familiar with asynchronous serial communication from that chapter. You'll also use it for MIDI, Internet communication, and most communication between computers of all kinds.

Asynchronous Serial Protocols

Communication between two devices requires that both sides agree about how the messages will be sent. This is called a *protocol*. For example, you have to establish a set of agreements about the physical connection, about the number of wires used, each wire's purpose, and about the type of connectors. You also need a set of agreements for electrical characteristics of the pulses (what voltages will be used), another for the timing of the pulses, another for the grouping and formatting of pulses, and finally, an agreement as to the meaning of the pulses. Communications protocols are commonly organized in this way, as layers of agreements. This allows you to use the layers of an existing protocol where convenient, and depart from it when you need to. In this book we try to use the lower layers of existing protocols as-is, so that we can focus on the upper layers, where the bits sent are assigned meaning.

Most of the protocols that we've already mentioned differ mainly at a physical and electrical level. We have already discussed RS-232 and TTL serial protocols that differ only in the voltage levels of their pulses. They are great when you're only communicating between two devices and for short distances. Because RS-232 is only for one-to-one communication, it's called a *point-to-point* protocol. Other protocols vary at the network level, in how the devices that use them can be arranged. For example, RS-232's cousin, RS-485, is a *multidrop* protocol because the same serial signal can be split between many devices so that several receivers and transmitters can share the same serial line. RS-485 is the basis for a number of other standards, including DMX-512, a popular protocol for lighting and entertainment control systems. Ethernet, the most popular network communications protocol, and MIDI are also multidrop serial protocols. Multidrop protocols will have different electrical requirements from RS-232, but you can buy boxes or ICs to convert from one to another. When you're shopping around for a device to meet your needs on a given project, look for ones that work with protocols you already know, particularly at a physical and electrical level. A little extra search time can save you lots of development time.

Learning a Protocol

Even if you use all the layers of an existing protocol, the content and probably the syntax of your messages will be specific to your project. Each message is like a sentence that needs to be broken apart and interpreted. In Chapter 7, you had some experience creating your own protocol for formatting data because you wrote the software on both ends of the wire. When you're working with an existing device, you don't always have that luxury, and you have to conform to the device's protocol.

It is better to find a device that uses an industry-wide *open* standard[1] than a *proprietary* standard used only by one manufacturer. Sometimes these protocols are maintained by professional organizations (see the GPS example below) and other times the standard of the dominant company is copied by others (for example, the Hayes protocol, established by the Hayes Corporation and adopted by many other manufacturers of modems and other devices). With an open protocol, you can talk to many different models and brands of devices without changing your code. If you have to use a proprietary protocol, hopefully you have the manual for the device you are talking to. It is possible to reverse engineer a protocol by just banging on the keyboard in a terminal program and analyzing what comes back, but it takes a lot of time. If you don't have the manual or the manual does not mention serial control, you can find a lot of old manuals on the Web. You can also usually find the proud reports there of others who have slogged through some of the more mysterious protocols before you.

The first thing you want to learn is how the messages are delimited. Sometimes messages are delimited by length. For example each message might be three bytes long. Other protocols will use a special character to mark the end of each message. The most common end-of-message delimiter is the ASCII carriage return character (ASCII value 13). Sometimes this is preceded by the ASCII linefeed character (ASCII value 10). The null character (ASCII 0) is also frequently used to delimit a message's end, particularly with Internet socket connections. These delimiters are essential, not only for receiving information from a device but also for sending. Quite often you will send the right commands and nothing happens because you forgot to append the end-of-message delimiter. Sometimes there will be delimiters to separate, different parameters within a single message. Space characters (ASCII 32), commas (ASCII 44), or tabs (ASCII 9) are most commonly used for this. If every parameter is of a fixed length, like a byte, there is no need for characters to separate them.

It is also quite common to have a header at the beginning of the message. The header might contain the address of the device you're speaking to, if several devices share the same serial line, or it might contain a byte with the length of the message to follow.

The next thing you will want to learn is whether the bytes are being sent as ASCII text or as raw binary values (refer to Chapter 7 for the difference). Some devices will have both an ASCII mode and binary (raw value) mode, so you will have to decide which to use. ASCII-encoded values can be read by people, so they're easier to debug when you see them onscreen. To make use of the bytes on the receiving side, you might eventually have to convert your bytes to a raw value, though. Most programming environments have built-in functions for doing this.

If you know that only the computers need to see the actual values (for example, if you're sending the values from an analog sensor to move an object onscreen, or you're sending channel values to a video mixer), then using raw values makes a lot of sense. Raw values greater than 255 can't be sent in a single byte and have to be converted on the receiving end (refer to Chapter 7). Negative numbers are often tricky when sent as raw values because the receiver might not interpret the byte in the same way. For example, one device may assign the eight bits of a byte the values 0 to 255, and another might assign it the values -127 to 128.

Finally, you'll want to find out if there is anything like the "call and response" communication scheme that we suggested in Chapter 7. Some sensor devices will wait for you to send a request and will then send a reply. This is sometimes called a *polled* mode. Some devices can also work in *continuous* mode, where they are constantly spewing everything they know as fast as they can. If you have a choice, polled mode is usually easier for working out the protocol.

Before you get started trying to write software to talk to your device, always use a terminal program like Telnet (for the Internet), HyperTerminal (serial on PC), or Zterm (serial on Mac) to manually send messages back and forth. This will allow you to get the hang of the protocol before you introduce the rest of your software. These terminal programs will interpret everything as ASCII text. They are of more limited use for raw binary values, but it can be useful just to see garbage characters going back and forth to prove that the physical connection is working. When you finally write your own software, start with a simple program that sends messages from a text box and looks at returning messages in the output window. You'll need that functionality anyway, and it's useful to have this program as a debugging tool in your bag.

RS-232 Boxes

Many commercial or industrial devices use RS-232, and the basic configuration of most of them is hard-wired to 9600 baud, 8 data bits, 1 Stop Bit, No Parity. If the device allows you to change this configuration, it's often done with hardware switches like jumpers or DIP switches.

If you are connecting to another RS-232 device, chances are good that it has a DB9 connector like the ones you're familiar with from Chapter 7. You may need to buy an adaptor if it is the wrong gender or connector type. It's also possible that the connections are non-standard, or reversed, even if your device has a DB9 connector. This may lead to the TX pin of one device being connected to the TX pin of the other, which will not make for very good conversation. If you are sending from your microcontroller, you can simply switch the wires on your breadboard. If you are connected to a multimedia computer, you need to add a *null modem adaptor*, which crosses the TX and RX lines, to your cable.

Global Positioning System Data

Now that you know the general issues of connecting to RS-232 devices, let's look at a specific example. The Global Positioning System, or GPS for short, is a system for determining your latitude, longitude, and altitude. It's commonly used in navigation, geological surveying, and other commercial applications where it's important to know your location on the surface of the earth. In recent years, consumer-grade GPS receivers have gotten cheaper, and it's become popular with hikers, climbers, and other outdoor hobbyists. Almost every receiver on the market these days has an RS-232 serial port.

To find your position, a GPS receiver listens for radio signals from an array of satellites above the earth owned and operated by the US military. By determining how long the signal took to reach the receiver, and by reading the relative signal strengths of the signals it receives, the receiver can triangulate how far it is to the satellites. Since they're in geostationary orbit (meaning that their locations are always the same relative to the planet), it's possible for the receiver to work out its position on the earth once it knows how far it is from at least three satellites. If it's got signals from at least six satellites, it can work out its altitude above sea level as well. GPS doesn't work well indoors or in areas with a lot of tree cover or tall buildings, but it does a pretty good job outdoors under open sky. Some manufacturers claim accuracy of 15 meters or less, though your accuracy may vary depending on your surroundings, the quality of your receiver, and the signals it receives.

Finding a GPS Receiver

If you're shopping for a GPS receiver, you've got several options. There are GPS modules available for plugging into a breadboard or circuit board, such as the TF10 from http://www.sparkfun.com, or the R217-TR-GPM from http://www.acroname.com. Both of these need an external antenna. You can also buy a handheld GPS receiver that's got a screen, a keypad interface, and a serial port. Lower-end models are in the same price range as the modules mentioned above and are often cheaper. We recommend the handheld units because their user interface makes debugging much easier. The receiver we used for our examples, a Garmin 12XL, also has a simulator mode. In simulator mode, it will output GPS data as if you're walking in a given direction, even if it isn't receiving any signals from satellites. This is invaluable when programming and debugging, unless you have the luxury of doing your programming outdoors under open sky. Many units available now have a simulator mode. Look for it when shopping.

Learning the GPS Protocol

GPS devices make a nice example for this book because they all use the open protocol, NMEA (http://www.nmea.org). As we mentioned, an open protocol means that your same code will work for many different brands. In fact, some receivers will speak their own

WHAT'S A CHECKSUM? WHAT'S PARITY?

A checksum is a method for checking if the data sent in a message got transmitted correctly. To checksum a string, you add up all the bits that make the string and place the sum in a single byte or two bytes at the end of the message before you send it. Upon receiving a message, you go through the same process of adding up the bits. If they don't add up to the sum at the end, then you know something went wrong in transmission and the message is not valid. This is very similar to using a *parity* check. Parity is a system for checking the validity of each byte you send. You use the 8th bit of the byte to mark whether the first seven bits add up to an even number or odd number. Parity is very seldom used anymore because it sacrifices a bit of every byte and will not work if there is an even number of errors. Here's a very simple example of using checksum:

Say you were sending a string that contained three bytes. Each byte contained a value ranging from 0 to 255. If your string's decimal values are as follows:

235, 127, 65

Then the binary values are

11101101, 01111111, 01000001

There are 15 bits whose value is 1 in the message. So our checksum is 15. If you were expected to send a checksum byte as the fourth byte of our string, you'd send

235, 127, 65, 15

This is a very simple checksum. Some checksums require you to do more work. The NMEA checksum, for example, requires you to do an XOR (exclusive or) on all the bytes in the string. XOR is a *logical* or *bitwise* operation, explained in more detail in Chapter 14, "Managing Multiple Inputs and Outputs." For more information on this, check out any book or Web site explaining logical or bitwise operations. The Basic Stamp manual has examples explaining these operations, as does Charles Petzold's book *Code: The Hidden Language of Computer Hardware and Software* (Microsoft Press, 2000).

---

proprietary protocol as well. Be sure to set the receiver's preferences to the NMEA protocol before you begin. For our purposes, we'll be looking at the NMEA 0183 protocol, version 2.0. For more information on the NMEA protocol, search the Web for the NMEA FAQ. It's kept in a number of locations by volunteers and is updated regularly.

The NMEA 0183 protocol is set to the same configuration we used in Chapter 7, 4800 or 9600 bps, 8 data bits, No Parity, 1 stop bit, inverted logic. The protocol is ASCII-based and works in continuous mode, so you can connect it to a terminal program like HyperTerminal or Zterm, set the configuration, and watch the text fly.

The text that actually comes back to you contains several different types of sentences. Some give speed and heading, some give course correction data, some give information about the satellites, and so forth. The simplest ones just give you latitude, longitude, altitude, the time of the reading, and whether the data is valid. Each sentence starts with a "$" character, then two letters to identify the device that's sending, then three letters to identify the type of sentence. After that, each data item is separated by a comma. At the end of the sentence, there is a "*" character, followed by two bytes for *checksum* error-checking (see the sidebar called, "What's a Checksum? What's Parity?"). The checksum is optional, and not all devices use it. Every sentence ends with a carriage return and linefeed (ASCII characters 10 and 13, like we've been using in our debug messages).

If you connect your GPS receiver to a terminal program like HyperTerminal or Zterm, you'll see something like this:

```
$GPRMC,185310,V,4032.2945,N,07359.7921,W,0.0,0.0,180204,13.3,W,S*24
$GPRMB,V,,,,,,,,,,,,A,S*0E
$GPGGA,185310,4032.2945,N,07359.7921,W,8,10,2.0,89.9,M,-34.1,M,,*4D
$GPGSA,A,3,01,04,07,09,10,13,17,20,24,28,,,3.6,2.0,3.0*36
$GPGSV,3,3,10,24,44,258,46,28,18,166,41*74
$GPGLL,4032.2945,N,07359.7921,W,185310,V,S*54
$GPBOD,,T,,M,,*47
$GPBWC,185310,,,,,,T,,M,,N,,S*67
$GPVTG,0.0,T,13.3,M,0.0,N,0.0,K*7F
$GPXTE,V,V,,,N,S*43
```

These are the various NMEA sentences that the receiver is transmitting. They're explained in depth in the NMEA FAQ. The simplest sentence that gives you position is the GLL sentence ($GPGLL). This gives your position in latitude and longitude and the time of the reading. As you can see, each parameter is separated from the others in the string by a comma. This makes reading the sentence on a microcontroller easy; you read the incoming bytes, and every time you see a comma (ASCII value 44), treat what follows it as a new parameter. The GLL sentence parameters are as follows:

- ▶ Latitude, in degrees and minutes
- ▶ Latitude direction
- ▶ Longitude, in degrees and minutes
- ▶ Longitude direction
- ▶ Time the position was determined, in hours, minutes, and seconds Greenwich Mean Time
- ▶ Whether the data is valid
- ▶ Checksum

To break down the GLL sentence in the example, you can see that the latitude is 40 degrees, 32.2945 minutes North; the longitude is 73 degrees, 59.7921 minutes West; the position was determined at 18:53:10 GMT[2] the data was Valid (V). The * and the two characters following it are the checksum. If we wanted to interpret this on a microcontroller, the pseudocode would look like this:

```
Loop:
        Listen for $ at the beginning of a sentence
        Skip the next two bytes
        If the next three bytes are "GLL", then
        Loop until we get a carriage return or linefeed
                Add the incoming byte to a sentence array
                End loop
                Interpret the sentence
        End if
End loop


Interpret the sentence:
        Set an item counter to 0. (We know we have 7 items to read)
        Loop until we run out of bytes to read
        Read bytes from the sentence array until we get a comma
                Convert the bytes from ASCII into a numerical value
                Place the numerical value into the right item variable:
                        Item 1 = latitude
                        Item 2 = lat. direction
                        Item 3 = longitude
                        Item 4 = long. Direction
                        Item 5 = time
                        Item 6 = whether data is valid
                        Item 7 = checksum
                Increment the item counter, so we know which item this is
        End loop
End interpret
```

This program can run to several pages, so we'll leave writing the actual code to you. Numerous examples can be found online for the various microcontrollers used in this book.

MIDI

MIDI, or Musical Instrument Digital Interface, is a protocol developed for communication between digital synthesizers and other digital music devices. If you're a musician,

---

[2] If you're a GPS aficionado, you've probably already worked out by now that the reading was taken on a sunny afternoon in Washington Square Park in Manhattan, just about lunch time (12:53:10 EST). The NMEA data wouldn't tell you that it was sunny, however.

you probably own a MIDI device, perhaps a keyboard controller or synthesizer, or a combination of both. Using your microcontroller to communicate with a synthesizer or sampler using MIDI, you open up lots of possibilities for creating interfaces for new musical instruments. In the other direction you can tap into the highly evolved and well-known interfaces of existing musical instruments to control video or motorized systems. If you're not a musician, but you're looking for a way to generate higher-quality sound than your microcontroller can produce, you'll find that MIDI synthesizers and samplers are an easy way to do this. There are also MIDI-controlled controller lighting dimmers, sound and video mixers, and many other devices unrelated to music that use the MIDI protocol.

MIDI does not define the nature or timbre of a synthesized sound, it just describes the action of playing preexisting sounds. MIDI is to a digital audio file as a word processing document is to a fax. The former describes the music generally, and the latter is an exact copy of the music that's less easily changed. You may not be able to guarantee the exact same fonts when you send a word processing document to a friend, but when it arrives, you can change the composition of the document much easier than you can change a fax. Because it describes musical performance in a general way, MIDI has also been expanded to other performance-related applications, such as control of lighting systems, synchronization of playback for film and soundtrack editing, and more.

MIDI Physical and Electrical Connections

If you look at the back of MIDI equipment you will see the characteristic 5-pin female connector that you see in Figure 12.1. The ends of MIDI cables are all 5-pin male plugs, and they come in lots of nice colors. MIDI is a multidrop protocol, meaning that several devices can be connected together and all share the same wires. Each device only responds to the messages that are addressed to it. Commercial MIDI devices have jacks for MIDI out, MIDI in, and MIDI thru. Anything that comes in the MIDI in jack is received by the device and sent out the MIDI thru jack as well. If the device also generates MIDI messages, they go out the MIDI out jack. This is one of the benefits of MIDI over a point-to-point protocol like RS-232. MIDI devices can be networked so that several devices can all share messages.

Your multimedia computer and your microcontroller have no MIDI connector. In order to send MIDI into or out of a multimedia computer, you'll need a MIDI interface. Most modern MIDI interfaces connect to the multimedia computer via USB; Mark of the Unicorn's FastLane USB (http://www.motu.com) or Midiman's MIDISport 2x2 are good inexpensive examples.

You can build a MIDI interfaces for your microcontroller yourself. The wiring schematic for MIDI output from a microcontroller is shown in Figure 12.1. The input circuit is shown in Figure 12.2. We've left out the physical details on the MIDI in circuit because in many applications, you'll only need the MIDI out circuit. If you're building something that just generates MIDI data played on a synthesizer, for example, you don't need the MIDI in circuit.

MIDI operates at 5 volts DC. The MIDI specification calls for all MIDI devices to be *opto-isolated*. This means that you've got a chip in the circuit called an *opto-isolator* that separates the input circuit from the rest of the synthesizer. This prevents one manufacturer's controller from damaging another manufacturer's synthesizer if the voltage

Figure 12.1
The MIDI output
circuit.

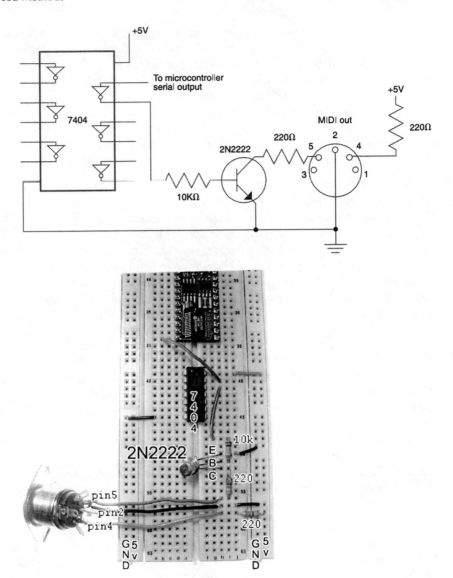

Figure 12.2
The MIDI input circuit.

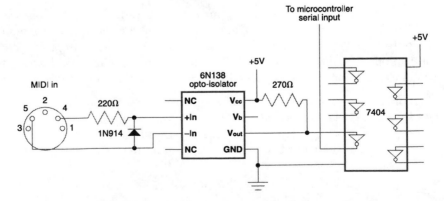

levels aren't quite the same. Unless you're making a commercial product, the opto-isolator isn't strictly necessary, but it's not hard to use, so we're including it here to keep in line with the MIDI spec.

As a protocol for performance, MIDI must be fast. Even the smallest delay between the time you press a key on a keyboard and the time you hear the note would be intolerable to a musician. Unlike RS-232 where we had our choice configuration and data rates, the MIDI protocol specifies a configuration of 31,250 bits per second (see the following sidebar).

Although MIDI is a simple protocol to grasp, there are many facets to it. It's very powerful for that reason. We're going to give you a glimpse of what MIDI can do, but for more detail, you'll need to look elsewhere.[3]

MIDI devices can be grouped in two groups, controllers (devices that send MIDI messages) and receivers (devices that receive MIDI messages and do something as a result). Many MIDI synthesizers are both controllers (the keyboard part) and receivers (the synthesizer part). It's not unusual to find the two separated, however. One keyboard's keys might be used to control its own built-in synthesizer and several other synthesizer or sampler modules. It might also control a MIDI lighting dimmer, motor controller, or other devices. It's very easy to build a MIDI controller using a microcontroller and a few sensors.

There are several small synthesizer modules on the market that offer a wide range of synthesized instruments. Any half-rack or third-rack sized unit will be smaller than a laptop and easy to hide in any device larger than a handheld device. Used modules are easy to find on eBay or in your local music store. If you're using a multimedia computer, there are many software synthesizers available online that can be addressed via MIDI messages.

Sending MIDI Messages

Once you've got the physical and electrical connections done, you can deal with the content of MIDI messages. This is where the MIDI protocol goes further than the RS-232 or TTL protocols because it also specifies the syntax and the meaning of the content. It is this further specification of the syntax of the message that allows you to plug your microcontroller into any MIDI synthesizer without rewriting any code.

Any MIDI command consists of at least two bytes, a *status byte* and a *data byte*. Status bytes are equivalent to commands in programming languages, and data bytes are the parameters that follow those commands. All MIDI status bytes are values greater than 127, and all MIDI data bytes are values from 0 to 127. This allows you to tell a status byte from a data byte right away. The most common MIDI messages have three bytes, a status byte followed by two data bytes. There are some exceptions, like pitch bend, which uses two data bytes to represent one value (much like word or integer variables on your microcontroller) for better resolution. In a typical MIDI message, four pieces of information are sent: the action (for example, note on, note off, pitch bend, and so on), the channel that it is addressed to, the pitch (musical pitch) that you want to affect, and the amount of change (for example, how loud you want the sound to play, or how much you want to bend

---

[3] There are lots of good sources of information on MIDI on the Web and elsewhere. Paul Lehrman and Tim Tully's book *MIDI For The Professional* (Music Sales Corp, 1993) is an invaluable reference for MIDI information.

Sending Serial Messages at MIDI Data Rates

The common serial libraries of some multimedia machines, especially Windows machines, don't have 31,250 as a data rate option. To get around this, you'll have to use software that's tailored for MIDI communication. Sometimes you can come close to the number and it will work. For example, the BX-24's MIDI examples actually operate at 30,270 bps. The BX-24 can't send data at this rate using COM3, and the PIC can't send data at this rate using a 4-MHz crystal, so you'll need to make some adjustments if you're using one of these microcontrollers.

In order to send MIDI from the BX-24, you have to use COM1, the serial port that's permanently assigned to pins 1 and 2. Pin 1 is the serial out (TX) pin, and pin 2 is the serial in (RX) pin. Previously, you've only used these pins to download new programs to the chip and to send debug messages. COM1 always sends inverted data (meaning that a logic 1 is 0 volts, and a logic 0 is 5 volts), so you won't need the hex inverter from the circuit above. Just run a connection from pin 1 to the 10 kilohm resistor, and you're done. Using COM1 for MIDI means your debug messages won't work, and you'll get garbage characters in the monitor window whenever MIDI messages are sent. This is because the monitor window is set for a different data rate, and the MIDI byte values don't map to readable ASCII values. The code example below will send MIDI from COM1.

To send and receive MIDI from the PIC using PicBasic Pro, you'll get the best results from a different set of serial commands: HSERIN and HSEROUT. These commands control the Universal Asynchronous Receiver-Transmitter (UART) that's built into some PICs, including the 18F452. The UART is permanently connected to pins RC6 (output, or TX) and RC7 (input, or RX) on the 18F452, so you have to use those pins. The code example below gives you the correct syntax for MIDI out, and the circuitry in Figures 12.1 and 12.2 (with the hex inverter) gives you the correct circuitry for both MIDI out and MIDI in.

In addition, you'll need to use a faster crystal. We typically use a 20-Mhz clock for MIDI. You can buy 20-MHz crystals, but you'll find that they don't always work well on a breadboard. To get around this, you can use a 20-MHz powered oscillator, which is a crystal with its own power source. These produce a better clock signal than an unpowered crystal. Figure 12.3 shows the schematic and wiring for a PIC using a powered oscillator.

When you program your PIC for 20 MHz, make sure that you put the following code at the top of your program:

```
DEFINE OSC 20 ' this is case sensitive
```

And when you download the code using EPICWIN, make sure you've set the oscillator preferences for high speed by clicking the Configuration menu, Oscillator, HS. If you don't do this, the program won't start running.

Figure 12.3
A PIC 18F452 using a
powered oscillator.

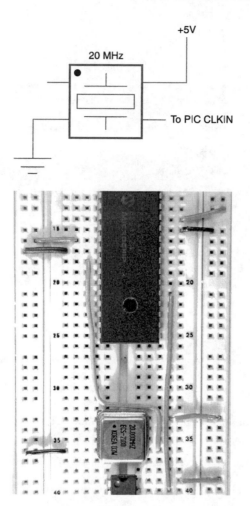

the pitch). For example, the first message below would cause middle C to be played at a
medium loudness on the first channel (probably a piano). These values are in hexadecimal
notation to make it easier to read the command. For example, 0x90 means "note on channel
0," and 0x80 means "note off, channel 0." You don't have to write the MIDI values in
hexadecimal if you find it cumbersome, since MIDI values are sent as raw binary values,
not ASCII-encoded values.

```
0x90 0x45 0x45    or in decimal form    144 60 60
```

This message would play a middle C on the second MIDI channel, medium volume.

```
0x91 0x45 0x45    or in decimal form    145 60 60
```

Notice that we got four pieces of information into three bytes. To keep the messages short
(and thus fast), the command and the channel are both jammed into one status byte. The
first half of a status byte gives the command, and the second gives the channel.

Table 12.1 shows the most common MIDI messages.

Table 12.1
Typical MIDI messages

Value (decimal)	Value (Hex)	Command	Data Bytes
128-143	80-8F	Note Off	2 (note, velocity)
144-159	90-9F	Note On	2 (note, velocity)
160-175	A0-AF	Key Pressure	2 (note, key pressure)
176-191	B0-BF	Control Change	2 (controller no., value)
192-207	C0-CF	Program Change	1 (program no.)
208-223	D0-DF	Channel Pressure	1 (pressure)
224-239	E0-EF	Pitch Bend	2 (least significant byte, most significant byte)

HEXADECIMAL VALUES

Often hexadecimal notation is used to show the values of the bytes sent in a serial protocol. You'll recognize it because it's usually preceded by the prefix "0x" or followed by the suffix "H." Even though a text representation of hexadecimal notation is used, you usually send the data as raw values. For an explanation of binary, decimal, and hexadecimal notation, refer to Chapter 7.

Hexadecimal is useful for seeing the two different sides of a byte separately. For example, in the MIDI protocol both the action and the channel are stuffed in a single status byte. In decimal notation, MIDI messages appear to be arbitrary. For example, note on messages are 144 for channel 0, 145 for channel 1, and so on, up to 159 for channel 15. In hexadecimal notation, MIDI messages are easier to read and remember because the first hexadecimal digit shows you the top of the byte (action), and the second digit shows you the bottom of the byte (channel). For example, all note on messages start with 9 and end with the channel number. 90 is channel 0, 91 is channel 2, and so on, through 9F for channel 15. This works because MIDI allows for 16 channels, hexadecimal has 16 different digits, and four bits (half a byte) have 16 possible combinations.

Fortunately, you don't have to convert from hexadecimal to decimal notation in your microcontroller code. You can use either notation in your code for all of the microcontrollers we're using. In pBasic, MBasic, and PicBasic Pro, numbers in hexadecimal notation are preceded by the character $. In BX-Basic, hexadecimal numbers are preceded by the characters &H. For example, 255 in decimal notation is $FF (in pBasic, MBasic, and PicBasic Pro) or &HFF (in BX-Basic) in hexadecimal notation.

As we mentioned, MIDI devices can be chained together into a network. MIDI allows for 16 data channels, so up to 16 devices can all listen for messages on the same line. The channel information allows you to address a message to a specific device or to a specific instrument within that device. Many synthesizer manufacturers adhere to an extension of the MIDI specification, called the *general MIDI* format which specifies which musical instrument will be on which channel. You would want to adhere to this if you are playing orchestrations of several instruments across different synthesizers. Otherwise, feel free to assign any channel to a device.

Note on tells the synthesizer to start playing a note at a specified pitch and velocity; *note off* tells it to stop playing a note at a specific pitch and velocity. Whenever you send a note on, you have to send a note off when you want it to stop. You could also send a note on with a velocity of 0, which has the same effect as a note off (it stops the sound). There is no command to play a note for a given duration. These two are the most common MIDI messages, and likely the only ones you'll use from a microcontroller most of the time.

Key pressure is the pressure on a key that's being pressed; it would affect things like the vibrato on a note that's already playing. *Channel pressure* is similar to key pressure, but it applies to all notes on a given channel.

Pitch bend changes the pitch of a note that's already playing; it's got a two-byte resolution, so the range of pitch bend is from 0 to 16,383 (128 × 128; remember, MIDI data bytes have a range of 0 to 127, not 0 to 255). Pitch bend is usually generated by a wheel or joystick, with the original pitch at the center of the wheel. A pitch bend value of 0 represents maximum bend down, and 16,383 represents maximum bend up.

Control changes are changes that can happen to a note in progress; controllers can do things like change the volume (volume affects all notes playing; velocity affects only one note), add sustain to a note, and so on. Controllers might also select a different bank of sounds to change the sound that's playing. Control changes are often used for non-musical MIDI devices. For example, the Topaz MIDI-controlled lighting dimmer uses control change messages to dim six channels of lighting.

One useful controller message to know about is 0x7B, which sends an "all notes off" message on a designated channel. It's useful for when you've got notes that you can't stop playing and can't figure out why. The first time you make a MIDI controller, it's not uncommon to get stuck notes. Perhaps you sent a note on message for one pitch and never sent a corresponding note off message because the sensor that determines the pitch changed. Even commercial MIDI devices sometimes get "stuck notes." To stop all notes on channel 1, you'd send 0xB0 0x7B. No second data byte is necessary.

Once you've got your microcontroller wired for MIDI output as shown in Figure 12.1, sending MIDI out is easy. The example below is a variation on the tone generator program from Chapter 6 using a MIDI synthesizer as output. To run this, you'll need a synthesizer to connect your microcontroller to. The program takes a value from an analog sensor, and uses it to generate the pitch of a note played once every quarter of a second. Here's the pseudocode:

MIDI

```
loop:
    read sensor
    convert sensor value to a note
    play MIDI note
    pause a quarter second
    stop MIDI note
end loop
```

Here's the actual code:

PBASIC

```
' the sensor is on pin 8
' the MIDI out is on pin 7
' declare an array of 12 word variables:
pitch var byte(12)

' declare other variables:
note var byte
RCTimeVar var word

' the 12 elements of the array called pitch are 12 notes of a scale.
pitch(0) = 60' middle C
pitch(1) = 61 ' C#
pitch(2) = 62 ' D
pitch(3) = 63 ' D#
pitch(4) = 64 ' E
pitch(5) = 65 ' F
pitch(6) = 66 ' F#
pitch(7) = 67 ' G
pitch(8) = 68 ' G#
pitch(9) = 69 ' A
pitch(10) = 70      ' A#
pitch(11) = 71      ' B


main:
    ' read the sensor. My flex sensor gave a range from 0 to 750:
    HIGH 8
    PAUSE 1
RCTime 8, 1, RCTimeVar
    ' convert to a range from 0 to 11
    note = RCTimeVar / 65
    ' note on, at the desired pitch, middle loudness:
    Serout 7, 12, [$90, pitch(note), $40]
    Pause 250
```

```
        ' note off:
          Serout 7, 12, [$80, pitch(note), $00]
    goto main
```

NOTE

On the Basic Atom Pro24, the MIDI code would be identical to the PBASIC code except for the data rate, which should be 0x401B ($401B in MBasic notation). To date, we've found MIDI out from the Basic Atom Pro24 to be erratic enough to send us to other platforms, but we welcome you to try it if you've already got a Basic Atom.

PicBasic Pro

```
' the sensor is on pin RA0.  The MIDI out is on pin RC6
' Make sure to select Configuration, Oscillator, HS
' in EPICWIN when programming:
DEFINE OSC 20
DEFINE ADC_BITS 10          ' Set number of bits in result
DEFINE ADC_CLOCK 3          ' Set clock source (3=rc)
DEFINE ADC_SAMPLEUS 15      ' Set sampling time in uS

' set up serial UART registers:
define HSER_RCSTA 90h ' enable the receive register
define HSER_TXSTA 20h ' enable the transmit register
define HSER_BAUD 31250 ' set the baud rate

TRISA = %11111111       ' Set PORTA to all input
' Set up ADCON1
ADCON1 = %10000010

' declare an array of 12 word variables:
pitch var byte(12)

' declare other variables:
note var byte
ADCVar var word

' the 12 elements of the array called pitch are the 12 notes of a scale:
pitch(0) = 60 ' middle C
pitch(1) = 61 ' C#
pitch(2) = 62 ' D
pitch(3) = 63 ' D#
pitch(4) = 64 ' E
pitch(5) = 65 ' F
pitch(6) = 66 ' F#
```

MIDI

```
pitch(7) = 67 ' G
pitch(8) = 68 ' G#
pitch(9) = 69 ' A
pitch(10) = 70    ' A#
pitch(11) = 71    ' B

main:
        'My potentiometer gave a range from 0 to 1023:
        ADCin 0, ADCVar
        ' convert to a range from 0 to 11:
        Note = ADCVar / 100
        ' play note:
        hserout [$90, pitch(note),$40]
        pause 250
        ' noteoff:
        hserout [$80, pitch(note), $00]
goto main
```

BX-Basic

```
' Don't forget, if you're using the BX-24, you don't need
' the hex inverter in your circuit.

' set up serial buffers
dim inputBuffer(1 To 13) As Byte '4-byte output buffer.
dim outputBuffer(1 To 10) As Byte '1-byte output buffer.

' declare an array of 12 byte variables:
dim pitch (0 to 11) as byte

' declare other variables:
dim note as byte
dim ADCVar as integer
dim midiCmd as byte
dim velocity as byte

Sub Main()
    ' the 12 elements of the array called pitch are the 12 notes of a scale:
    pitch(0) = 60 ' middle C
    pitch(1) = 61 ' C#
    pitch(2) = 62 ' D
    pitch(3) = 63 ' D#
    pitch(4) = 64 ' E
    pitch(5) = 65 ' F
    pitch(6) = 66 ' F#
```

```
                pitch(7) = 67 ' G
                pitch(8) = 68 ' G#
                pitch(9) = 69 ' A
                pitch(10) = 70      ' A#
                pitch(11) = 71      ' B

        ' open serial queues:
        Call OpenQueue(inputBuffer, 13)
        Call OpenQueue(outputBuffer, 10)

            ' open serial port on COM1:
            call openCom(1, 9600, inputBuffer, outputBuffer)

            ' set baud rate to 30,270:
            register.ubrr = 14

        do
                ' my distance ranger gave a range from 0 to 1024:
                call getADC(13, ADCVar)
                ' convert to a range from 0 to 11:
                note = cByte(ADCVar \ 98)

                ' sent a note on message, channel 1, velocity 64:
                midiCmd = &H90
                velocity = &H40
                call putQueue(OutputBuffer, midiCmd, 1)
                call putQueue(OutputBuffer, pitch[note], 1)
                call putQueue(OutputBuffer, velocity, 1)
                call delay(0.25)

                ' noteoff:
                midiCmd = &H80
                velocity = 0
                call putQueue(OutputBuffer, midiCmd, 1)
                call putQueue(OutputBuffer, pitch[note], 1)
                call putQueue(OutputBuffer, velocity, 1)
            loop
        End Sub
```

MIDI is also very useful if you're using Max/MSP on a multimedia computer. However, if you own Max/MSP, you already knew that. Max/MSP allows you to use MIDI messages to play back existing sounds, to generate sound waves from scratch, or to control video or other multimedia events. Many Max programmers prefer to use the MIDI protocol for even the most basic sensor projects because it simplifies sending data into Max.

MIDI is a venerable open protocol. The protocol has been widely adopted, and you will find great consistency between MIDI devices. It is flexible enough to be stretched to serve purposes that have nothing to do with musical instruments. What we've shown and discussed here is only the tip of the iceberg of what you can do with MIDI, so if this much gets you excited, then you have much more to explore.

Connecting to the Internet

Maybe you want people to be able to throw virtual balls from a Web page to dunk a real person into a real tank of water. Or maybe you want people all over the world to be able to jam together over the Internet with the great new electronic musical instrument you've made. Maybe you want to take advantage of an existing network (wireless even) to get your data from your microcontroller in the lobby of your building to the computer in your office. Or maybe you just have a lot of skills with Internet programming in Flash's ActionScript, for example, or another language with no serial port access, and would prefer to use an Internet connection to get data from the microcontroller to your computer. If you want your microcontroller to connect to the Internet, you will need to use an intermediary device (at least for now).

You could use your multimedia machine as an intermediary to the Internet. To do this, you would use serial communication to pass all the information between your software on the multimedia machine and the microcontroller, as you already saw in Chapter 7. The software on your multimedia could then relay everything back and forth to the Internet. This would require that you know how to make Internet connections in whatever multimedia program you are using. If your software will be running in a Web page, there will be security restrictions to work around for connecting to the serial port or for making some forms of Internet connections. Your multimedia computer may seem like an awfully big box for such a simple job as handing bytes from one protocol to another. But if you already own the multimedia computer and know how to use it, remember that quick and dirty often wins the race in the world of prototyping.

Communication between devices on the Internet happens as a result of a number of protocols all layered on top of one another. At the bottom are protocols that define the physical and electrical connections, similar to the connections we've described in other serial protocols. This is referred to as the *physical* layer of the network communication model[4]. Next are the protocols that define how computers connected to a local area network identify each other. If you're connecting to a LAN at home or in the office, you're probably using *Ethernet* for this, through a cable modem or a DSL connection. If you're connecting through a modem, you're using *Point-to-Point Protocol* (PPP). These protocols are in the *datalink* layer. Once the computers are talking to each other locally, they need an address that tells computers elsewhere on the Internet how to find them. This is handled by the *Internet Protocol* (IP). This is the *network* layer. Next, applications need to know whether to establish a connection to another machine for an extended time, in order to exchange lots of data, or whether to just squirt packets of data at each other as fast as

---

[4] This multi-layer scheme is based on a network model called the OSI (open systems interconnection) model that's the basis of Internet networking protocols. We've cheated a bit to simplify it for our purposes.

possible. The former is done using *Transmission Control Protocol* (TCP), and the latter using the *Universal Datagram Protocol* (UDP). This is called the *transport* layer. Finally, there's a layer of protocols that defines the format of information for each particular application. For example, you might be transferring files using the *File Transfer Protocol* (FTP), browsing HTML documents on the Web using the *Hypertext Transfer Protocol* (HTTP), or reading mail using the *Simple Mail Transfer Protocol* (SMTP). All of these rely on TCP. TCP includes automatic error checking, so it's slower than UDP, but more reliable. You might also be watching a streaming video or listening to an audio stream, using Real Media or Windows Media or QuickTime. These use protocols like *Realtime Streaming Protocol* (RTSP), which relies on UDP. The blips you sometimes see in a stream of video are the result of lost bytes in the transmission. That's the tradeoff you make to get the speed of transmission that UDP allows. This final layer actually combines a few layers, but we'll refer to it as the *application* layer for simplicity's sake. Figure 12.4 gives you a basic idea of how all these protocols are related.

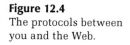

Figure 12.4
The protocols between you and the Web.

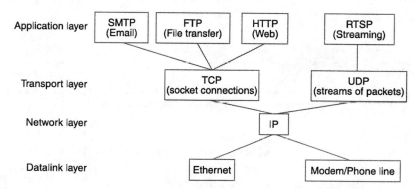

There are many devices that are designed to fill the gap between the Internet and your microcontroller. The exact type of Internet connection you need to make will guide your decisions about what to use. For infrequent transmissions that are always initiated by one side, HTTP connections will work. These connections are short exchanges between computers, just long enough for your computer to download the files in a Web page. If you have done some programming for the Web, then you are probably familiar with the GET and POST methods of an HTTP connection. The SitePlayer module from NetMedia (http://www.siteplayer.com) acts as a Web server that attaches to your microcontroller. It can take GET requests from the Internet and return information from your microcontroller. HTTP connections work for applications like Web pages in which all the activity originates from one side of the connection and only comes along every few minutes or even every few days. This would work well if you wanted to be able to occasionally jiggle one of your cat's toys remotely from a Web page at the office.

For applications where timing is a little more critical, like chat, instant messaging or gaming, you may want to use a persistent TCP socket connection.[5] HTTP connections are made through TCP sockets, but the socket is closed after each HTTP request. If you're

---

[5] Because persistent sockets are better for time-critical communication, they are sometimes called *synchronous connections*. From a serial communication standpoint, these are still asynchronous connections. Synchronous in this case mostly refers to an application where people are expected to be at either end of the connection at the same time.

running a chat or trying to play ball with your cat over the Net, opening and closing a socket each time is a bit of a chore. By keeping the socket open, you avoid this. In addition, TCP sockets are kept open in both directions, allowing either side to send a message without waiting for a new request. The end result is that generic TCP/IP sockets make for much faster, more responsive interaction than HTTP connections.

Network Connection Using the CoBox Micro

The details of Internet protocols are beyond the scope of this book, but we will go into some detail on one device for making a generic TCP socket connection. The CoBox Micro from Lantronix is a serial-to-Ethernet converter (http://www.lantronix.com). The CoBox connects to the Internet via an Ethernet connection, using TCP/IP. You can make TCP socket connections to and from it to other computers. Once a socket connection is made, all data exchanged between it and the other computer will be transferred to its serial port. This allows you to connect your microcontroller to the Net using the serial methods you're already familiar with.

NOTE

The following explanation assumes you're familiar with some of the basics of the Internet, like assigning an IP address and so forth. If you're totally confused, we'd recommend picking up a basic book on Internet protocols and configurations first.

The CoBox Micro can be used with Lantronix's embedded integration kit (EIK), which costs extra, or it can be used on its own. The connector on the CoBox Micro has twelve pins, which have the functions listed in Table 12.2.

You'll only need the TX, RX, ground, and reset connections in the example below. Figure 12.5 shows how the pin connections relate to the physical module.

Figure 12.5
CoBox Micro Pin connections.

Table 12.2
CoBox Micro Pin Connections

Pin 1	+5VDC
Pin 2	Ground
Pin 3	Rx channel 1
Pin 4	Tx channel 1
Pin 5	CTS channel 1
Pin 6	DCD channel 1
Pin 7	RTS port 1
Pin 8	DTR channel 1
Pin 9	Reserved
Pin 10	Reset (active low)
Pin 11	Reserved
Pin 12	Reserved

If you're using a breadboard, as we've shown in all the other projects in this book, the easiest way to connect the CoBox Micro to the board is to use an IDC-type connector and a multiconductor ribbon cable, as shown in Figure 12.6. The parts you'll need to build this cable are listed in Table 12.3. You can get them from many online retailers, but for the sake of convenience, Table 12.3 lists the Jameco part numbers.

Table 12.3
CoBox Micro Connector Cable Parts

PART NUMBER	DESCRIPTION	NOTES
42657	IDC connector, DIP plug, 14 pin*	Used to connect the ribbon cable to the breadboard
153947	IDC connector, 14-pin socket*	Used to connect CoBox Micro to ribbon cable
105671	28AWG 16-conductor ribbon cable, flat, rainbow colored	Used to connect everything together
73251	IDC crimp tool	Tool used to crimp the connectors onto the cable. You can do this by hand with a pair of pliers, but it's messy and you're likely to break a connector.
49040	7404 Hex Inverter	Used to supply adequate signal levels

*You're likely to break a connector your first time, so get a couple of spares.

Though the CoBox Micro uses TTL serial, we found it useful to use a hex inverter to provide good signal levels between the CoBox Micro and the microcontroller. In addition, you'll need the hex inverter when you connect the CoBox Micro to a multimedia computer's serial port for initial setup and debugging, so it's convenient to have the circuit already laid out. Figure 12.6 shows the schematic and the connections.

Figure 12.6
CoBox Micro connections. The top right shows the connections underneath the ribbon connector. The photo on the bottom right shows the connections to a serial cable.

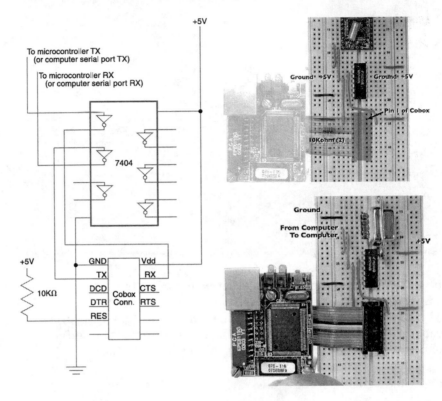

The first thing you need to do once you've powered up the CoBox Micro is to configure its serial port and Internet connection. To do this, connect its serial port to a multimedia computer through a hex inverter, as shown in Figure 12.6, and open a terminal program at 9600 bps, 8 data bits, No Parity, 1 stop bit (9600, 8-N-1).

Once you've opened the serial connection, hold down the X key on the computer, and press the Reset button on the CoBox Micro. You'll get a message like the following. Press the Enter key, and you'll get the setup menu that follows:

```
*** Lantronix Universal Device Server ***
Serial Number 6602000 MAC address 00:20:4A:66:07:D3
Software version 04.5 (011025)
Press Enter to go into Setup Mode


*** basic parameters
Hardware: Ethernet Autodetect
```

```
IP addr 192.168.000.010, gateway 192.168.000.001,netmask 255.255.255.000

***************** Security *****************
SNMP is enabled
SNMP Community Name:
Telnet Setup is enabled
TFTP Download is enabled
Port 77FEh is enabled
Web Server is enabled
Enhanced Password is disabled

***************** Channel 1 *****************
Baudrate 9600, I/F Mode 4C, Flow 00
Port 10001
Remote IP Adr: 192.168.001.023, Port 10002
Connect Mode : D4 Disconn Mode: 80
Flush Mode : 77

***************** Expert *****************
TCP Keepalive : 0s

Change Setup : 0 Server configuration
 1 Channel 1 configuration
 5 Expert settings
 6 Security
 7 Factory defaults
 8 Exit without save
 9 Save and exit Your choice ?
```

First, choose option 0 to set up the Internet protocols. Configure them as follows:

▶ *IP address*: as given to you by your network administrator

▶ *Gateway address*: as given to you by your network administrator

▶ *Netmask* (number of bits for host part): 8 (equates to 255.255.255.0)

Next, choose option 1 to configure the serial port. Use the following settings:

▶ *Baudrate:* 9600

▶ *I/F Mode:* 4C (sets the various baud mode bits; see manual for details)

▶ *Flow:* 00

▶ *Port number:* 10001 (or whatever other port number you choose)

▶ *Connect mode:* D4

▶ *Remote IPaddress:* Address of whatever machine you want it to connect to automatically on startup (check your multimedia computer's network IP address and use that)

Connecting to the Internet

▶ *Remote portnumber:* 10002 (you can use other numbers, but the example below uses 10002)

▶ *Disconnect mode:* 80

▶ *Flush mode:* 77

▶ *Disconnect time:* 00:00

▶ *SendChar1:* 00

▶ *SendChar2:* 00

If you set the connect mode to D5 instead of D4, the CoBox Micro will automatically connect to the remote address above. Though this can be useful, it's not used in the example below. See the CoBox Micro User Guide for more details on the configuration settings.

Once you've set the serial port configuration, choose option 9 to save and reset the CoBox Micro.

Just as with serial communication, network communication involves a conversation between two computer devices. In this case, you need to write code on the microcontroller to control the CoBox Micro, and you need to write code on the multimedia computer to connect to the CoBox Micro. Before you do that, however, you should test your serial-to-Ethernet connection using a terminal program. If you left things set up as in the image on the bottom right in Figure 12.6, then you've already got the CoBox Micro connected to your multimedia

GIVING YOUR COBOX AN INTERNET ADDRESS

There are two parts of an address used for TCP sockets. The *IP address* specifies which physical machine you want to talk to and the *port*, which specifies the software process within that machine. The port is a single number that you can make up. To avoid stepping on the port reserved for other pieces of software (for example, 23 for Telnet, 25 for mail, 80 for HTTP) you might start with a number above 8000. This is why we're using 10001 and 10002 in our examples. IP numbers are a little trickier because they generally need to be unique to the device within the network. The idea of every microcontroller having its own IP address will exhaust remaining unused numbers quickly, so the next versions of the Internet Protocol (IPv6) allow for many more addresses. In the meantime, if your network's system administrator has an experimental streak, ask them for a dedicated IP address for your CoBox. You will also have to ask them for your gateway address. Otherwise you might have to operate on your own private network. If you're configuring the CoBox on a home router, then you are your own network administrator. The gateway address will be the router's address, and you'll pick an address within the same range for the CoBox Micro's IP address. For example, if your router's address is 192.168.1.1 (the default for many home routers), then you can pick any address in the range 192.168.1.x for the CoBox Micro. Many home routers have an administration screen that lets you see all the addresses currently assigned. Pick an address that's not used by any of the computers on your network.

computer's serial port. Open Zterm or HyperTerminal as you did before, but don't hold down the X key this time. To connect through the Internet, you'll use a program called Telnet. Telnet is the terminal program that Zterm and HyperTerminal are both based on. It dates back to mainframe computers, and it only runs from the command line. To run it in Windows, click on the Start menu, choose Run, and type **telnet** followed by the IP address of your CoBox Micro and the port number that you assigned to the serial port. For example,

```
telnet 192.168.1.3 10001
```

On a Macintosh running OSX, look in the Applications folder for the Utilities folder. In there, you'll find an application called Terminal. Launch it and type the same command. You won't get a lot of feedback. In Windows, you'll get a blank window if you succeed and nothing if you don't. The Macintosh Terminal program is a bit more friendly, and will tell you when it's trying to connect and whether it succeeded or not. Once you've got a connection, type **Hello World!** in the telnet window and then hit the Return key. You should see the text show up in your HyperTerminal or Zterm window. If so, go to the HyperTerminal or Zterm window and type, **Hello yourself, you big fat hairy CoBox!** followed by the return key. You should see the text show up in the Telnet window. Keep typing from one to the other as long as it amuses you. This is cause for a small hokeypokey. When you're ready to move on, the example below shows you how to connect to a multimedia program.

In this example, the microcontroller will wait for bytes to come in from the CoBox Micro. The CoBox Micro sends an ASCII "C" when a new connection is made. When a connection is broken, it sends an ASCII "D." When there's no connection, it sends an ASCII "N" about once every second. When it's connected, it passes through whatever bytes come from the remote computer. We'll make the remote computer initiate a connection, then send various messages to prompt the microcontroller to take action. The digits 1 through 8 (ASCII values 49 through 56) will make the microcontroller light up one of 8 LEDs. The digit 9 (ASCII value 57) will make the microcontroller send back the value of an analog sensor.

The pseudocode on the microcontroller is as follows:

```
Loop:
Read an analog sensor
     Listen for a byte from the Cobox Micro
     If the byte is "C', then another computer has connected to the Cobox from the
net
     If the byte is a "D" or an "N", then the Cobox is disconnected from the other
computer
     If the byte is "1" through 8", then light an LED
     If the byte is "9", then
         send the analog sensor value back
     end if
End loop
```

Here's the actual code:

```pbasic
' Serial out is on pin 6
' serial in is on pin 7
' an analog sensor is on pin 0
' pins 8 through 15 have LEDs on them.

' variables and constants for the serial port:
dataByte var byte
tx   con 6
rx   con 7
inv9600 con 16468 ' baudmode for serin2 and serout2: 9600 8-N-1 inverted

' general-purpose counter:
i var byte

'variables for analog sensor:
RCvar var word        ' Create variable to store result
DIRH = %11111111      ' set pins 8 through 15 as all outputs

Pause 1000 ' Wait a second at startup

main:
    ' read the ADC value:
    high 0
    pause 1
    RCtime 0, 1, RCvar

    ' check for incoming serial data:
    serin rx, inv9600, [dataByte]
    gosub checkByte
goto main

checkByte:
    if (dataByte > 48) then
        ' convert the ascii value of 1-9 to a numeric value
        ' (e.g. ascii "0" = 48)
        dataByte = dataByte - 48

        ' if the number is between 1 and 8, light an LED:
        if (dataByte  > 0) & (dataByte <= 8) then
            ' the dcd command takes a number and
            ' converts it to the position of a bit in a byte:
            outH = dcd (databyte - 1)
```

```
                    endif

                    ' if we get "9", send the ADC message.
                    if dataByte = 9 then
                        serout tx, inv9600, ["ADC: ", DEC Rcvar, 10, 13]
                    endif
                endif
        return
```

MBasic

```
' Serial out is on pin 6
' serial in is on pin 7
' an analog sensor is on pin 0
' pins 8 through 15 have LEDs on them.

' variables and constants for the serial port:
dataByte var byte
tx   con 6
rx   con 7

' general-purpose counter:
i var byte

'variables for analog sensor:
ADCVar var word         ' Create variable to store result
DIRH = %11111111        ' set pins 8 through 15 as all outputs

Pause 1000 ' Wait a second at startup

main:
    ' read the ADC value:
    Adin 0, ADCVar
    ' check for incoming serial data:
    serin rx, N9600, [dataByte]
    gosub checkByte
goto main

checkByte:
    if (dataByte > 48) then
        ' convert the ascii value of 1-9 to a numeric value
        ' (e.g. ascii "0" = 48)
        dataByte = dataByte - 48

        ' if the number is between 1 and 8, light an LED:
        if (dataByte  > 0) & (dataByte <= 8) then
```

```
                        ' the dcd command takes a number and
                        ' converts it to the position of a bit in a byte:
                        outH = dcd (databyte )
                    endif

                    ' if we get "9", send the ADC message.
                    if dataByte = 9 then
                        serout tx, N9600, ["ADC: ", DEC ADCVar, 10, 13]
                    endif
                endif
            return
```

PicBasic Pro

```
' Serial out is on pin RC6
' serial in is on pin RC7
' an analog sensor is on pin RA0
' pins RB0 through RB7 have LEDs on them.

' Define ADCIN parameters
DEFINE ADC_BITS 10 ' Set number of bits in result
DEFINE ADC_CLOCK 3    ' Set clock source (3=rc)
DEFINE ADC_SAMPLEUS 50    ' Set sampling time in uS

' variables and constants for the serial port:
dataByte var byte
tx   var portc.6
rx   var portc.7
inv9600 con 16468 ' baudmode for serin2 and serout2: 9600 8-N-1 inverted

' general-purpose counter:
i var byte

'variables for ADC:
ADCvar var word        ' Create variable to store result
TRISA = %11111111 ' Set PORTA to all input
ADCON1 = %10000010 ' Set PORTA analog and right justify result
TRISB = %00000000     ' set all the pins of PORTB to output

Pause 1000 ' Wait a second at startup

main:
    'read the ADC value:
    adcin 0, ADCvar
    ' check for incoming serial data:
    serin2 rx, inv9600, [dataByte]
    gosub checkByte
```

```
        goto main

    checkByte:
        if dataByte > 48 then
            ' convert the ascii value of 1-9 to a numeric value
            ' (e.g. ascii "0" = 48)
            dataByte = dataByte - 48

            ' if the number is between 1 and 8, light an LED:
            if dataByte > 0 && dataByte <= 8 then
                ' the dcd command takea a number and
                ' converts it to the position of a bit in a byte:
                portb = dcd (databyte - 1)
            endif

            ' if we get "9", send the ADC message.
            if dataByte = 9 then
                serout2 tx, inv9600, ["ADC: ", DEC ADCVar, 10, 13]
            endif
        endif
    return
```

BX-Basic

```
' Serial out is on pin 11
' Serial in is on pin 12
' LEDs are on pins 13 through 19    ' (only 7 of them on BX24, not 8)
' ADC is on pin 20     ' takes up the 8th LED pin
' set up input and output buffers in memory:
dim outputBuffer(1 To 50) as byte
dim inputBuffer(1 To 20) as byte

' variables for dealing with incoming serial data:
dim gotaByte as   boolean
dim dataByte as   byte
dim dataValue     as   byte

' strings for sending out through the CoBox:
dim sendString    as String
dim connectString as String

' variables for dealing with the ADC:
dim adcval        as integer
dim byteval       as byte

' constants for the serial port and the ADC:
const   serOutPin     as   byte = 11
```

```
            const     serInPin as   byte = 12

        Sub main()
            call delay(1.0) ' start program with a half-second delay

            ' set up serial port:
            call defineCom3(serInPin, serOutPin, bx1000_1000)

            ' open the input and output buffers:
            call openQueue(outputBuffer, 50)
            call openQueue(inputBuffer, 20)
            call openCom(3, 9600, inputBuffer, outputBuffer)

                ' main loop:
                do
                    ' read the value of the ADC on pin 20, convert to a byte:
                    adcval = getADC(20)
                    byteval = cByte(adcVal \ 4)

                    ' check for incoming serial data:
                    call serialCheck()
                loop
        End Sub

        sub serialCheck()
            ' Find out if anything is in the queue.
            gotaByte = statusQueue(inputBuffer)

            ' If there is data in the input buffer,
            ' get the first byte of it:
            if (gotaByte = true) then
            ' there's data available: read it here
            call getQueue(inputBuffer, dataByte, 1)

            ' do stuff in response to serial data here
            call checkByte()
            end If
        end sub

        sub checkByte()
            dim i as byte ' local variable for for-next counter

            ' convert the ascii value of 0-9 to a numeric value
            ' (e.g. ascii "0" = 48)
            dataValue = dataByte - 48

            ' iterate over the pins, turn on the one asked for,
```

```
        ' and turn the others off:
        for i = 13 to 19
            if dataValue + 12 = i then
                call putPin(i,1)
            else
                call putPin(i,0)
            end if
        next

        ' if we get "9", send the ADC message.
        if dataValue = 9 then
            call sendADCVal()
        end if

    end sub

    sub sendADCval()
        ' format a message with the ADC value at the end:
        sendString = "ADC" & cstr(byteVal) & chr(10) & chr(13)
        call putQueueStr(outputBuffer, sendString)
    end sub
```

On the multimedia computer, you'll initiate the Net connection to the CoBox Micro at the start of the program. Then you'll listen for keystrokes on the keyboard for the keys 1 through 9, and send the value to the microcontroller through the CoBox Micro. When you get a reply, you'll display it onscreen. Below are examples for Director MX, using the Multiuser Xtra and Processing. Java code has been omitted for brevity's sake, but if you're comfortable with Java you will see that the Processing code is almost identical. In fact, this example uses existing Java network classes rather than using Processing's network libraries. You can also find many objects for making Internet connections in Max/MSP but we don't have room here to begin covering all the differences.

Network Connection in Lingo

This example uses the Multiuser Xtra for Director. Macromedia advocates use of the Flash Communication Xtra for net communication nowadays, but it's less flexible for peer-to-peer connections like this. You can find the Multiuser Xtra in the goodies directory on your Director installer CD. Put it into your Xtras folder before you launch Director.

In this example, there are three text fields, called server, status, infield, and outfield, respectively. The server and outfield fields are editable fields. All the rest are not. There are two buttons, a start/stop socket button and a send message button. Name the cast member containing the code "Main Movie Script." All the buttons and fields are in one frame of the movie, which looks like that in Figure 12.7.

Figure 12.7
Interface for socket
connection movie for
Director.

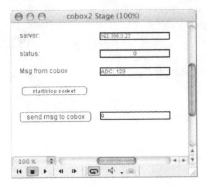

The movie will attempt to connect to the IP address in the server field when it starts. Change this address to the address of your CoBox Micro before starting the movie. While the movie is running, type the digits 1 through 9 into the Out field, then click the Send button and see what happens on your CoBox Micro.

The following code goes in the main movie script:

```
--Basic socket connection for CoBox Micro embedded processor connections
--using MultiUser Xtra (note: this does not use
-- the MultiUser Server itself, just the xtra)

global socketObj -- variable to hold our instance of the xtra

on startmovie
    startSocket
end

on startSocket
    -- get the IP address from the field "server":
    coboxAddress = member("server").text

    -- open the multiuserXtra:
    socketObj = new(xtra "Multiuser")

    -- give the xtra the name of the handler for incoming messages,
    --and the script that it's in:
    socketObj.setNetMessageHandler(#MessageFromXtra, script "main movie script")

    -- open a socket connection:
    err = socketObj.connectToNetServer("Blank","Blank",coboxAddress,10001,"Blank",1)

    -- return any messages from the xtra:
    member("status").text = string(err)
```

```
        end

on stopSocket
     SocketObj = 0
end

on MessageFromXtra
     -- when we get any incoming messages from the socket, this handler runs:

     netMsg = socketObj.getNetMessage()
     errCode = netMsg.errorCode

     if (errCode = 0) then
     senderID = netMsg.senderID
     subject = netMsg.subject
     messageList = netMsg.content

     --handle the message
     -- if the message isn't empty:

     if not voidp(messageList) then

          member("infield").text =  messagelist
          end if
     else
          --do error processing here, if there's any to be done
     end if

end

on exitFrame
     go the frame
end

on sendSomething someString
     -- sends a string out to the socket:
     themsg = someString
     socketObj.SendNetMessage( "Blank", "Blank", themsg)
end
```

The following code goes in the sprite script for the send button:

```
on mouseUp me
     -- sends the contents of the field "outfield" out the socket:
     sendSomething member("outfield").text
end
```

The following code goes in the sprite script for the connect button:

```
global socketObj
on mouseUp me
    if objectP(socketObj) then
    stopsocket
    else
    startsocket
    end if
end
```

Network Connection in Processing

This Processing example is similar to the Director example above. At the start of the program, it attempts to connect to the CoBox Micro. If it gets a connection, it sends every keystroke to the CoBox Micro and displays the keystroke's ASCII value onscreen. If it gets anything from the CoBox Micro, it displays it onscreen. It also displays the state of the connection at the beginning of the program.

```
/*
socket_to_Cobox
Connects Cobox Micro and sends keystroke ASCII values once connected.
Also displays any messages received from Cobox Micro.
*/

// variables for the socket connection:
Socket coboxSocket = null;
BufferedReader netInput = null; // used to read text from the Cobox
String netString = ""; // converts netInput to a string
String coboxAddress = "192.168.1.23"; // fill in your Cobox's IP address
PrintWriter remote = null; // used to send text to the Cobox
int remotePort = 10001; // fill in your Cobox's receiving port
boolean isConnected = false; // whether we have a good connection or not

//variables for the keyboard and display:
String inputString = "Hello"; // input from the keyboard
String displayString = "";
BFont metaBold; // our display font

void setup()
{
    // The font "Meta-Bold.vlw.gz" must be in the
    // current sketch's data directory in order to load:
    size(400, 300);
    background(0,0,64);
    metaBold = loadFont("Meta-Bold.vlw.gz");
```

```
            textFont(metaBold, 18);
            text(inputString, 20, 50);
            displayString = "Trying to connect to " + coboxAddress;
            text(displayString, 20, 100);
}


void loop ()
{
    // open a connection to the Cobox. try once a second until connected:
    while (isConnected == false) {
        isConnected = connectToCobox();
        try { Thread.sleep(1000); } catch (InterruptedException interrupted) { }
    }
    try {
        // update the screen:
        background(0,0,64);

        // update what we get from the keyboard:
        text(inputString, 20, 50);

        // if we're connected, update what we get from the net:
        if (isConnected == true) {
            if (netInput.ready() == true) {
                netString = netInput.readLine();
            }
        }

        // if the netString is longer than two bytes, then display it:
        if (netString.length() > 2 ) {
            displayString = netString;
        }
        text(displayString, 20, 100);
    } catch (IOException e) { println(e);}
}


boolean connectToCobox()
{
    // flag to return whether we're connected or not.
    // if the connection try below fails, it'll return false:
    boolean gotConnected = false;
    try {
        // open a socket to a Cobox Micro:
        coboxSocket = new Socket(coboxAddress, remotePort);
        // once we have a connection, let the user know:
        netString = "Connection accepted";
        // set up a bufferedReader to get stuff from the Cobox:
```

```
                netInput = new BufferedReader(new InputStreamReader(coboxSocket.
        getInputStream()));

                // set up a printWriter to send stuff to the Cobox:
                remote = new PrintWriter(coboxSocket.getOutputStream());
                remote.flush();

                //update the state of the connection:
                gotConnected = true;
            } catch(IOException e) {netString = "Status: " + e;}
            return gotConnected;
        }

    void keyPressed()
    {
        int keyValue = Integer.parseInt("" + key);
        // update the message onscreen:
        inputString = "ASCII value entered: " + key;

        // if we're connected to a Cobox,
        // then send the key string to it:
        if (isConnected == true) {
            remote.write(keyValue);
            remote.flush();
        }
    }
```

Connecting over Telephone Lines Using Modems

Modems make data communications over phone lines possible. A modem has a serial port that you connect to your microcontroller, allowing you to connect it to another computer via a second modem on the other end of the phone connection. The modem then handles all the work converting your digital data into audio tones and back. It *modulates* and *demodulates* the data over voice lines. It also generates the tones necessary for dialing, and connects and disconnects the line for you. You can get modem modules that fit on a board like the Cermetek modem from Parallax (also available from its manufacturer, at http://www.cermetek.com), but any modem you find will probably do the job. Microcontrollers usually don't send large quantities of data, so even slower modems that have been discarded will work just fine. Modems will generate touch tones, but will not decode them, and most modems will not allow you to use the same line for voice communications and data communications simultaneously. If you need to do either of these, you'll need to build your own phone line interface as described in Chapter 13, "Controlling Sound and Light."

You connect to a modem just as you would any other serial device. The microcontroller's serial receive pin connects to the modem's transmit pin and vice versa. Modem communications are divided into two modes: data mode and command mode. In data mode, the bytes you send to the modem are sent straight through to the modem on the other end of the phone line. In command mode, the bytes you send to the modem are commands to configure the modem, tell it to dial or hang up, and so forth. The commands used to control a modem are the Hayes AT protocol. All the commands are in ASCII, meaning that to make a connection, for example, you'd send the address as a string of ASCII alphanumeric characters rather than the raw values. They all begin with the letters AT (ASCII 65 and 84) and end with a carriage return (ASCII 13).

To dial a number you would send the string ATDT followed by the ASCII-encoded phone number, like this:

```
ATDT12125551212, CR
```

To hang up:

```
ATH0, CR
```

To put the modem in auto answer mode on first ring:

```
ATS0=1, CR
```

When the modem hears a ring, it will automatically connect the line and send you a "?" character. To switch from data mode to command mode, you send the string +++. Once you've established a basic connection, there's not much need to drop into the command set, and your communications between computers are regular serial exchanges.

See Table 12.4 for some of the most common AT commands.

Special-Function ICs and Modules

So far in this chapter, we've discussed devices that have a built-in microcontroller and can function independently when they're not connected to another device. There's a simpler class of devices, IC chips and modules, that don't function independently. Some of these are simple ICs, and some are modules, mounted on separate printed circuit boards because they need some extra supporting circuitry. There are countless modules and ICs on the market that can meet many of your physical computing needs. They may give you a simple interface to a particular sensor or actuator, or allow you to manage multiple inputs or outputs from one chip. Some handle timing functions, amplify signals, generate signals, and more.

Regardless of what a particular module or IC does, you need to know a few things about it to decide if it's right for you. Most of the information you need will be contained in the device's datasheet. A *datasheet* gives all the specifications of the chip, including a description of how it works and how to use it. You can get this, usually in PDF form, from the manufacturer or retailer before you buy. Use them to make more informed purchasing decisions. Typing the part number into a search engine usually yields the datasheet pretty quickly.

Table 12.4
Common AT Commands

COMMAND	FUNCTION
+++	Escape sequence switches from data mode to command mode.
,	Sometimes you need a pause, for example, when you need to wait for a prompt after dialing. The comma adds a two-second pause. For example, the string ATDT9,12125551212<CR> dials the number 9, waits two seconds, then dials the rest of the number. If you need to dial 9 to get an outside line at work, this is how you do it.
A/	Repeats the previous command. This command won't work if preceded by the AT command or followed by <CR>.
ATA	Puts the modem in answer mode; in other words, it picks up the phone.
ATDL	Redials the last-dialed number.
ATDP	Pulse dial (for phone lines with no touch tone service; not used much anymore).
ATDT	Tone dial.
ATDW	Resume dialing after dial tone is detected.
ATD,	Pause before dialing.
ATH0	Hang up.
ATH1	Open the connection but don't dial (what you do when you pick up the receiver).
ATI0	Return modem model and speed. Useful if you pulled the modem out of the trash.
ATI6	Return data connection info.
ATI7	Return manufacturer and model info. Useful if you pulled the modem out of the trash.
ATL0	Mute speaker.
ATL1	Set speaker volume low.
ATL2	Medium volume.
ATL3	High volume.
ATM0	Disable speaker.
ATM1	Enable speaker until a connection is established.
ATM2	Enable speaker all the time.
ATM3	Enable speaker after dialing but disable after a connection is established.
ATSn	Set special-function registers. For example, S0 sets the number of rings for auto-answer.
ATZ	Restore default modem settings.

Datasheets contain a wealth of information, more than you usually need. Some of it is written in very technical terms and can be intimidating to the non-engineer. Don't let it scare you off. You usually do not have to understand everything on the datasheet to get the device to work. Start with the general description. Even the most cryptic general descriptions give you clues as to what a device does if you read them two or three times. Latch on to terms you know and work backwards.

If you're lucky you will also find *application notes*, which explain, usually in friendlier prose, how to use the chip or module for a particular purpose. Even if you're not using it for the same purpose, you can learn a lot about how it works from other application notes. Finally, look on the Web and in newsgroups and mailing lists to see if anyone else who's used the device has posted any useful tips.

Pay attention to the physical form, or the *package*. If you're using a breadboard, you want ICs in a SIP or DIP package with pins that are spaced 0.1 inches apart. You'll see many other acronyms describing the package, like SOIC, PLCC, TQFP, and BGA. Avoid these and other packages that don't have pins arranged in a way that you can use.

The most useful part of a datasheet is usually the *pin diagram*. This is a map of the chip or module, telling you what each pin does. Somewhere nearby you'll find a description of the pin functions as well. Look for the things you know you'll need, like power and ground. Other pins are used for input and output or to control the device's optional functions.

You'll also find a section of the datasheet called "Electrical Characteristics." This will tell you the operating voltage and current of the device. Most of the time it's given as a range, showing the minimum, maximum, and typical operating values. Any device will need power to operate. Most of the time they can share 5-volt power that your microcontroller is using. You can still use a chip that requires a different power supply, for example, 3.3 volts, but you will have to supply power through a separate regulator. The two devices will most likely have to share a ground, though. The datasheet will often have other electrical specifications. For example, a motor controller will specify the maximum voltage and amperage of the motors that it can control. Make sure these match the requirements of the other components in your system.

Next, look for a form of output that you're familiar with and that your microcontroller can speak or listen to. Some devices have simple digital output that goes high or low when something happens (for example, the capacitance sensors in Chapter 11), or an analog output, that produces a changing voltage (for example, the GP2Dxx IR sensors in Chapter 9). Some may have a pulsewidth output that produces a changing pulsewidth as the sensor changes (for example, the ADXL202E accelerometers in Chapter 9). You can read this using the pulsin or count commands. Still others will have a frequency output that you read with something like the count command (for example, the photodiode array in Chapter 13). Your device may have a parallel interface, delivering the data on several pins as a binary value that you could read as a group (see Chapter 14, "Managing Multiple Inputs and Outputs"). Many ICs and modules use synchronous serial communication, which we will cover in detail in the next section of this chapter.

There may be other pins on your device besides the inputs and outputs that let you set its characteristics. Connecting these is like setting the preferences in software. Much of the time you can set the options once and forget them. Some pins are *active high*, meaning that they need to be connected to a positive voltage to activate the pin's function, and others are *active low*, meaning that they go to ground to activate the function. Active low pins have a bar over the top of the symbol in the pin diagram. Sometimes option pins should be connected through a resistor to voltage or ground. These are called *pullup* resistors if they go to power, and *pulldown* resistors if they go to ground. Typically, something in the 4.7-kilohm to 10-kilohm range will do the job if a value isn't specified. You might also need to add a few components, like a capacitor or a crystal, between pins. If you're lucky, the datasheet will also include some example schematics, showing how the device is to be wired. You may find that you can wire the device in a circuit that's simpler than the examples. Some pins may not require a connection at all.

Synchronous Serial Protocols

So far in this chapter, we've discussed devices that have a microcontroller built in and can function independently when they're not connected to another device. There's a simpler class of devices, usually small modules or IC chips that don't function independently but that still communicate serially. These devices use *synchronous serial communication*. You'll hear of a lot of different synchronous serial protocols: I2C, SPI, Microwire, and so forth. All of them are variations on the same principles.

Synchronous serial devices use an extra wire for sending pulses to control the rate of data transfer. Synchronous serial requires at least three connections: a serial data connection, a clock connection, and a ground. Often, there are connections for both sending and receiving, just as with asynchronous serial communication, for a total of four connections. One side of the communication is called the *master* because it supplies the timing pulses on the clock connection. The connections for synchronous serial are usually labeled MISO, for Master In, Slave Out (meaning that the data is going from the slave to the master) and MOSI, for Master Out, Slave In (going from the master to the slave). Sometimes you'll see the terms SDI (serial data in) and SDO (serial data out). The clock will sometimes be labeled SCK, SCLK, or CLK.

In addition to the data lines, there's usually a *chip select* connection. Several synchronous serial devices can be connected to one bus, meaning that you can run the data lines in parallel from one master controller to several slaves. You have seen multidrop connections like this before. In MIDI, it was dealt with by specifying a channel in the first byte sent. On the Internet, it was dealt with by giving each device a unique IP address. In order to direct the flow of data in synchronous serial, each slave gets its own chip select connection to the master. This way, the master can set a given slave's chip select pin to tell it to listen and to tell all the other chips to ignore the data. The schematic on the right in Figure 12.8 shows a typical arrangement for many synchronous serial devices attached to one master. Generally, the chip select is taken low (given 0 volts) to select a given chip and taken high (given 5 volts) to tell the chip to ignore data. This is called an *active low* pin, and it's indicated by a bar over the top of the pin in the schematic.

The master device sends clock pulses to keep the data exchange moving. There are two important parts to each clock pulse: when the clock goes from low to high (0 volts to 5 volts) and when it goes from high to low (5 volts to 0 volts). The former is called the *rising*

Figure 12.8
Synchronous serial
communication.
Communication to one
chip (left) and several
chips (right). Note how
each slave on the right
has its own chip select
pin, but they all share
data lines.

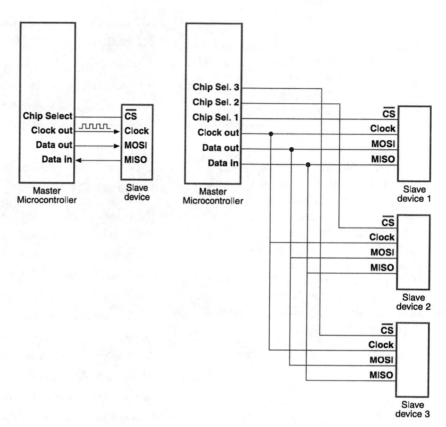

edge of the clock, and the latter is called the *falling edge*. Data is actually exchanged on these edges. Usually, the data coming from the master is expected on the rising edge, and the data coming from the slave is expected on the falling edge. This means that you can read data in both directions on one clock pulse. You'd do it like this:

```
Loop 8 times
      Put a bit of information on the data out connection
      Take the clock connection high
      Take the clock connection low
      Read a bit of information on the data in connection
End loop
```

When you're not reading and writing at the same time, you don't have to do all four steps. You'd only do the first three to send data and the last three to read it.

You could do all of this yourself, using the inputs and outputs of your microcontroller, one bit of data at a time, However, the programming environments we're using all have a number of commands to do some of the work for you. The most useful commands for synchronous serial communication are shiftin, which reads data from a synchronous serial device, and shiftout, which writes data to a synchronous serial device. These commands have a slightly different syntax from controller to controller, but they all do the same thing.

They pulse a clock pin while reading data from an input pin (shiftin) or writing it to an output pin (shiftout). These commands move bits into a variable or out from a variable one at a time, like a bucket brigade. Every synchronous serial device will have its own command set, detailed in its datasheet.

This example dims six LEDs by using a six-channel digital potentiometer that's controlled using synchronous serial communication. You already know how useful potentiometers are as physical input sensors. They can also be useful as output control devices. For example, you can use a potentiometer to control the volume of an audio signal or the brightness of an LED. However, a microcontroller can't turn a physical pot very easily.

The AD5206 digital pot from Analog Devices (http://www.analog.com) has six potentiometers on one chip. Each pot has three pins, just like a normal pot: a wiper (labeled W in Figure 12.9), a connection to ground (labeled B), and a connection to voltage (labeled A). The fact that there are so many pots on this chip might make some of the schematics and circuits in this example look a little scarier than they really are. Don't worry, though, because you're using the same components on each pot. When you connect A to 5 volts, B to ground, and W to the anode of an LED through a 220-ohm resistor, you get a circuit that can dim the LED. Each of the digital pots on the AD5206 has 256 steps; in other words, each pot goes from 0 to 255. So if a pot is set

FLIPPING BITS BEFORE SHIFTING OUT

For the BX-24, you have to do a little more work to shift bits out. The bits of each byte are shifted starting with the most significant bit. This means that to shift the three-bit values for the pot address from the BX-24, you have to put those bits in the first three bits of a byte to be shifted. It works like this:

Suppose you want to send the value 5 to change the level on the last channel. In binary notation, 5 = 00000111. To do this, you're shifting out three bits. The three bits have to be the first (most significant) three bits of the byte you want to send, though, so you want the byte you plan to send to look like this: 11100000. To make this happen, you need to move the value up five bits. If you multiply by 32 (which is 2^5), you move the bits where you want them. This kind of shifting is sometimes necessary when you need to move a value to a different position in a byte. For example, any time you want to shift out fewer than eight bits on the BX-24, you need to move those bits to the top (most significant bits) of the byte. Multiplying the value by any power of 2 will move it that many positions in the byte. To shift four bits out, multiply by 2^4. To shift 2 bits out, multiply by 2^6. In general, to move x bits to the top of a byte, multiply by 2^{8-x}.

to 127, for example (half the total), the voltage at the wiper is 2.5 volts. Each step is 5/255, or about 0.02 volts. That gives you fine-tuned control over the LEDs attached to it.

To set a pot to a specific resistance, you send the AD5206 commands via the serial connection. The commands are 11 bits long. The first three bits contain the address of the pot that you want to change, represented in binary notation. For example, pot 1 is address 0, so the first three bits would be 000. Pot 2 is address 1, or 001. Pot 3 is address 2, or 010, pot 4 is 011, and so forth. The final eight bits of the command message are the desired value for the pot.

Figure 12.9
An AD5206 digital
potentiometer wired to
dim six LEDs.

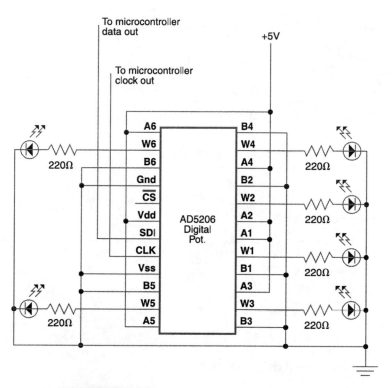

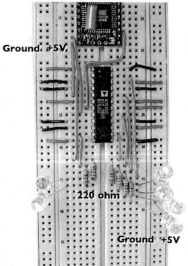

It's not uncommon for synchronous serial devices to have odd-length command strings like this. When you're working with a new device, check its datasheet for the details. Fortunately, it's relatively simple to deal with this using the shiftout commands. For all our platforms except the BX-24, you simply give the command two bytes to shift, and tell it how many of the bits to send.

Here's the pseudocode for what happens in this example:

```
Loop
    Loop through pots 0 to 5
        Fade the pot from 0 to 255
    End loop

    Loop through pots 5 to 0
        Face the pot from 255 to 0
    End loop
End loop
```

And here's the actual code:

```
' AD5206 is attached to pins 6, 7, and 9, as follows:
' Data in to AD5206: pin 9
' Shift clock: pin 6
' Chip Select: pin 7
SDO con 9
SCLK con 6
CS con 7
channel var byte
brightness var byte(6)
level var byte
dataOut var word

main:
    ' fade the LEDs up, one by one:
    for channel = 0 to 5
        for level = 0 to 255
            gosub fadeChannel
            pause 3
        next
    next

    ' fade the LEDs down, one by one:
    for channel = 5 to 0
        for level = 255 to 0
            gosub fadeChannel
            pause 5
        next
    next
goto main

fadeChannel:
```

```
        brightness(channel) = level
        ' take chip select low to activate AD5206:
        low CS
        ' put channel number in first byte to shift out:
        dataout.highbyte = channel
        ' put brightness in second byte to shift out:
        dataOut.lowbyte = brightness(channel)
        ' shift out 11 bits from dataout:
        shiftout SDO, SCLK, MSBFIRST, [dataOut\11]
        high CS
    return
```

```
' AD5206 is attached to pins 6, 7, and 10, as follows:
' Data in to AD5206: pin 10
' Shift clock: pin 6
' Chip Select: pin 7
SDO CON 10
SCLK CON 6
CS CON 7
channel VAR Byte
level VAR Byte
dataOut VAR Word

main:
' fade the LEDs up, one by one:
    FOR channel = 0 TO 5
        FOR level = 0 TO 255
            GOSUB fadeChannel
            PAUSE 3
        NEXT
    NEXT

    ' fade the LEDs down, one by one:
    FOR channel = 5 TO 0 step -1
        FOR level = 255 TO 0 step -1
            GOSUB fadeChannel
            PAUSE 5
        NEXT
    NEXT
GOTO main

fadeChannel:
    ' take chip select low to activate AD5206:
    LOW CS
    ' shift out 11 bits from dataout:
```

Synchronous Serial Protocols

```
              SHIFTOUT SDO, SCLK, MSBFIRST, [channel\3]
              SHIFTOUT SDO, SCLK, MSBFIRST, [level\8]
              HIGH CS
         RETURN
```

PicBasic
Pro

```
' AD5206 is attached to as follows:
' Data in to AD5206: RC5
' Shift clock: RC3
' Chip Select: RD0

' include the file that defines parameters for the shiftout command:
include "modedefs.bas"

SDO var portc.5
SCLK var portc.3
CS var portd.0
channel var byte
brightness var byte(6)
level var byte
dataOut var word

main:
    ' fade the LEDs up, one by one:
    for channel = 0 to 5
        for level = 0 to 255
            gosub fadeChannel
            pause 3
        next
    next
    ' fade the LEDs down, one by one:
    for channel = 5 to 0 step -1
        for level = 255 to 0 step -1
            gosub fadeChannel
            pause 5
        next
    next
goto main

fadeChannel:
    brightness(channel) = level
    ' take chip select low to activate AD5206:
    low CS
    ' put channel number in first byte to shift out:
    dataout.highbyte = channel
    ' put brightness in second byte to shift out:
```

```
            dataOut.lowbyte = brightness(channel)
            ' shift out 11 bits from dataout:
            shiftout SDO, SCLK, MSBFIRST, [dataOut\11]
            high CS
    return
```

(BX-Basic)
```
' AD5206 is attached to as follows:
' Data in to AD5206: pin 15
' Shift clock: pin 11
' Chip Select: pin 12

const SDO as byte = 15
const SCLK as byte = 11
const CS as byte = 12
dim brightness(0 to 5) as byte

sub main()
    dim channel as byte
    dim level as byte
    dim thisChannel as byte

    do
        ' fade LEDs up, one by one:
        ' (nb. There is a bug in BX basic, which causes for-next
        ' loops to behave erratically when counting to 0.
        ' because of this, we're counting from 1 to 6
        ' and subtracting when we call fadeChannel)

        for channel = 1 to 6
            for level = 1 to 254
                call fadeChannel(channel - 1, level)
                call delay(0.003)
            next
        next

        ' fade LEDs down, one by one:
        for channel = 6 to 1 step -1
            for level = 254 to 1 step -1
                call fadeChannel(channel - 1, level)
                call delay(0.005)
            next
        next
    loop
```

```
     end sub

     sub fadeChannel(byval thisChannel as byte, byVal thisLevel as byte)
         ' local variable, so we can shift out value in the byte:
         dim outChannel as byte
         brightness(thisChannel ) = thisLevel

         ' make sure the clock is low to begin with:
         call putPin(SCLK, 0)

         ' take the chip select low to activate the chip:
         call putPin(CS, 0)

         ' shift the channel number to the top three bits of the byte:
         outChannel = thisChannel * 32

         ' shift out the channel:
         call shiftout(SDO, SCLK, 3, outChannel )
         ' take the clock low for the next shift:
         call putPin(SCLK, 0)
         ' shift out the brightness:
         call shiftout(SDO, SCLK, 8, brightness(thisChannel ))
         call putPin(CS, 1)
     end sub
```

Wireless Serial Communication

Because physical computing applications tend to involve a lot of movement, wireless communication is a very attractive option. The easiest wireless communication typically takes output from an existing serial protocol, like TTL serial or RS-232, and sends it over a wireless connection. Theoretically, this means that only the physical connection is changing (the cables disappear), but the code still uses the old serial commands you know. There are two main methods of wireless serial communication: infrared (like your television remote) and radio, or RF (like your garage door). Infrared transmitters send bits using pulses of infrared light and require a line of sight between the transmitter and receiver. RF transmitters send bits on pulses of radio energy. RF doesn't require a line of sight but can be blocked by large metal objects. In order to differentiate the signal from other ambient radio or light waves, the data is sent on a *carrier wave*. If a receiver detects the energy coming in at the frequency of the carrier wave, then it knows it should be reading data, and if it doesn't detect it, then no one's sending. The actual information is encoded by slightly varying the frequency of the carrier wave (called *frequency modulation*, or *FM*) or its signal strength (amplitude; called *amplitude modulation*, or *AM*) to indicate a logic 0 or 1.

Infrared Serial Communication

Infrared serial communication is seen most frequently in remote controls and short message beaming from PDAs, cell phones, and other handheld devices. As a solution for microcontrollers, it is a little more work to get solid results, but it is less expensive and less prone to interference from nearby wireless sources. Because IR communication requires a line of sight between the transmitter and the receiver, it's great for applications where a person has to point at an object to activate it, or where a controller can see an overview of all the objects it's controlling. For IR communication, you send bits by pulsing an infrared LED that's aimed at a phototransistor. The phototransistor is covered by an IR filter so that visible light is blocked out. One of the most creative and delightful IR projects that we've seen involved a group of dancing toasters that were "choreographed" with instructions from an IR transmitter placed on the ceiling overhead.[6]

Many commercial infrared transmitter/receiver pairs use a 40 kHz carrier frequency and simply send serial data over it. If you have more money than time, you might consider something like the IR Buddy from Parallax (http://www.parallax.com) or the considerably less expensive TX-IRHS from Rentron (http://www.rentron.com) for more reliable results. Many consumer devices like palm pilots, pocket PCs, and even some multimedia computers come with an IR port for transferring data that uses a protocol called *IrDA*. You can buy a FlexiPanel module (http://www.hoptroff.com) to interface your microcontroller with this protocol.

If you're set on building your own IR transmitters and receivers, the simplest way to do this with a pair of serial devices (for example, a microcontroller and a multimedia computer) is to get a GP1U52X IR demodulator to receive the signal and a 555 timer chip to send it. Both of these should be available from Jameco, Digi-Key, or other retailers. The send circuit is shown in Figure 12.10, and the receive circuit is shown in Figure 12.11. To use this circuit, send any asynchronous serial data that you want into the send pin on the 555 circuit and listen for it at the same data rate on the receive pin of the receiver. It's best to do this at low data rates, 1200 bps or below if possible, since faster rates will give you more errors. Sunlight produces loads of infrared light, so you'll have little luck using IR serial communication outdoors or near sunny windows.

RF Serial Communication

Radio frequency serial communication, unlike IR serial, is omnidirectional and can go greater distances—even through walls, to a limited extent. This makes it great for applications like sensing movement of an acrobat's limbs or broadcasting data to a million tiny robots for world domination. You might have to work around problems of noise or interference from other transmitters, but these are generally reliable and easy to use.

Building your own transmitters and receivers from scratch requires more knowledge about RF engineering than we can pack in this book. Fortunately, there are a number of relatively inexpensive RF serial transmitters and receivers on the market. Just about any good robotics Website will sell some. We like the Glolab (http://www.glolab.com)

---

[6] Rania Ho's dancing toasters can be seen at http://www.dancingtoasters.com.

Figure 12.10
An infrared serial
communication
transmit circuit.

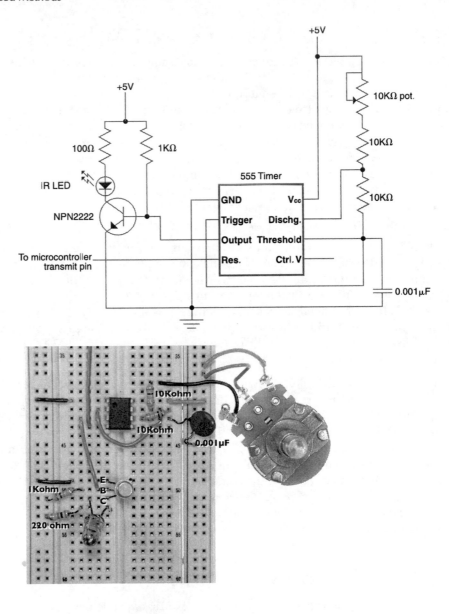

TM1V and RM1V transmitter and receiver pair because they're inexpensive and simple. They can transmit reasonably well over a range of one to two hundred feet. Glolab sells antennas for these, but you can also make your own antenna out of a piece of wire cut to the right length. Their antenna will be more reliable, but we've used homemade antennas on several occasions with relatively good results. You can also find good, inexpensive transmitter-receiver pairs from Abacom (http://www.abacom-tech.com), Rentron (http://www.rentron.com), and many other online retailers.

Using RF transmitters and receivers with a microcontroller is very similar to using infrared: you send serial data into the transmitter and listen for it on the output of the

Figure 12.11
An infrared serial communication receive circuit. We've removed the cover on this one to make the connections clearer, but you should keep your cover on to block out stray IR light sources.

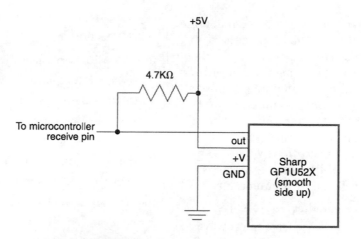

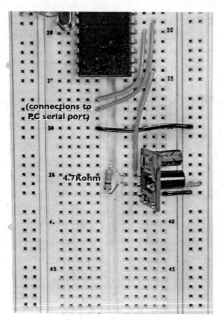

receiver. These RF modules won't operate at rates higher than 4800 bps and perform better when the rate is lower (2400 bps works well).

The most complex task in using RF communication is managing the data flow. When you're using a transmitter-receiver pair like these, you can't send data in both directions. This means that the sender never knows if the receiver got the message or not, and the receiver has no way of asking the sender to resend. One solution to this is to have the sender send regularly but infrequently, repeating its message even if the message hasn't changed. That way, the receiver never gets too much information (the problem you saw in the serial examples in Chapter 7 before we introduced the call-and-response method). Because the sender is repeating the message even when it hasn't changed, the receiver has a chance to catch any missed messages. A second, more expensive solution to the problem is to use transceivers. *Transceivers* are modules with a receiver and a transmitter built in. They can communicate in both directions. This allows you to implement a call-and-response method of communication in which the receiver confirms receipt of every message. In conditions where there's a lot of RF noise, it becomes necessary to do this to get reliable communication.

There are many sources of stray radio interference. Everything from microwave ovens to computers to metal filing cabinets can cause interference. Checksums are very useful for filtering out noise in RF communication (see the sidebar above, called "What's a Checksum? What's Parity?"). Sometimes one or more bytes in a long transmission can get garbled, so if the receiver checks the data against a checksum before using it, bad data can be thrown out. Engineering careers have been made on error correction for RF transmission, and there is plenty of material available in print and online should you wish to explore it further. There is also a scheme for encoding timing data with each byte, called *Manchester encoding*, that's commonly used with RF transmission. In this scheme, each byte is split in two so that a clock pulse can be sent in the middle. You can write your own Manchester encoding scheme, or you can use a Manchester encoding IC like the Glolab GL-104, which will encode your signal before sending it to the RF transmitter and decode it from the RF receiver. Manchester encoding and decoding can significantly improve the reliability of your RF transmission. Many higher-end RF transmitters, receivers, and transceivers have Manchester encoders built into the module.

Even in environments without noise, you have to worry about interference from other transmitters working at the same frequency. Everything may work perfectly when you're testing it, but if there's another prototype device with the same wireless module as yours in the vicinity, you'll get interference. You might consider adding a unique header byte to all your transmissions so you know which ones to act on.

Good, reliable RF communication is one area where it's worth spending a little extra money so you don't have to think about the details. There are a number of high-end RF modules available that will handle error correction for you and let you concentrate on your application. For example, Linx Technologies (http://www.linxtechnologies.com) make a number of more expensive transceivers that handle error correction and allow you to transmit both directions. Some of their transmitters can also go over 33 kbps, which is useful if you want to send MIDI via RF.

WIRELESS MIDI

Because MIDI is so commonly used in performance, it's common to want to send MIDI data wirelessly so that you can have a dancer's movement trigger music, for example, or a musician's improvisation control video. This is impossible to do at the lower serial rates that most RF modules support. While it's theoretically possible using the Linx modules mentioned, there are difficulties with these as well. A simple solution to this problem is to send the sensor data wirelessly from the performer's body to a base microcontroller over a low-speed wireless link, then have the base unit generate MIDI over a normal MIDI link.

Bluetooth

Bluetooth is a high-speed RF data protocol intended for connection between various mobile devices, like PDAs, cell phones, and handheld games. It operates at high speeds so that it can carry rich data like digitized audio and even limited digitized video. It's a relatively new protocol with a lot of promise. It's a useful serial data protocol because once two devices make contact over a Bluetooth connection, all the error correction is taken care of for you by the Bluetooth radios. They handle noise and crosstalk from other transmitters for you.

Bluetooth is a short-range protocol (the specification says 10 meters, and we've gotten about 30 feet in practice), so it's not as good for long-range wireless as some of the slower serial modules. But it is more error-free than other RF methods. It's also limited in that it's designed primarily for one-to-one connections. It takes about three seconds for Bluetooth devices to establish a connection, and once two devices are connected they ignore all other Bluetooth devices nearby until the connection is broken. It is less useful for broadcast-to-multiple devices, like the dancing toasters mentioned earlier.

In order to use Bluetooth for physical computing applications, you'll need a Bluetooth serial module such as the EmbeddedBlue module available from Parallax (http://www.parallax.com) or the Promi-SD 102 module, made by Initium and distributed by Lemos (http://www.lemosint.com) and others (see Figure 12.12). Both of these modules take TTL serial data in and out from a microcontroller and send it via RF to a receiver. The Promi-SD modules are nice because they use a standard DB-9 connector; for the Parallax units, you need to use one of Parallax's development boards or make your own cable with IDE connectors like the ones in the CoBox Micro example above. More modules are coming on the market every day, so shop around if you don't like the looks of these.

Figure 12.12
Bluetooth modules.
The EmbeddedBlue
module from Parallax
(left), and the Promi-
SD 102 from Initium
(right).

If you're communicating from one microcontroller to another, you'll need two Bluetooth modules. Otherwise you'll also need a multimedia computer with a Bluetooth receiver. Many laptops are shipping with Bluetooth radios built in now, but if you don't have one, there are a few decent Bluetooth adaptors you can buy. D-Link (http://www.dlink.com) sells a USB-to-Bluetooth adaptor, the DBT-120, that's simple and reliable.

Because Bluetooth can carry many other protocols, you'll need to tell your computer that you want to make a serial connection. On a Windows machine, software for your Bluetooth adaptor will associate a COM port with the Bluetooth radio, so connecting via Bluetooth is like connecting to any other serial port. The same is true on a Macintosh. If you've got a Mac with built-in Bluetooth, you'll need to run the Bluetooth Serial Utility program to establish a new serial port. If you're using a third-party adaptor, you'll use the adaptor's software to define the new serial port.

A Bluetooth radio has a unique address that other devices can use to identify it. To begin communication, the radio scans the area around it for other devices. When it discovers other devices, it can request a connection and begin communication. A Bluetooth device can also hide from other devices by setting itself to "undiscoverable" mode. This simply means it won't respond to a scan from other devices.

Bluetooth serial commands as defined in the Bluetooth specification are based on the Hayes AT command set that we discussed earlier in the section on modems. Manufacturers use different sets of commands for addressing their own modules, though, so you will need to read the manual for the particular one you buy. However, there are some functions common to all of them. You can

▶ Get the device's address

▶ Tell the device to scan for other devices (this returns a list of addresses)

▶ Connect to a given address

▶ Disconnect from a given address

▶ Enter or leave command mode

and more.

Like modems, all Bluetooth serial devices have two modes: command mode and data mode. In command mode, you can issue commands like the ones above. In data mode, all the bytes you send the device will get sent out just like normal serial data. Even when you're connected, you can toggle back and forth from command mode to data mode to issue other commands.

Because Bluetooth is showing up in a wide range of products, from phones to printers to handheld games, and because it can send fast, reliable serial data, it's got a lot of potential for physical computing. Simple, everyday devices like mobile phones can become controllers for dramatic interactive sculptures and more.

Wireless Ethernet

Wireless Ethernet has gone from being virtually unknown to being a necessity to many people almost overnight. If you work with computers at all, you trip over the terms "Wi-Fi" or "802.11" all the time. All of these are the same thing. The Ethernet protocol that we mentioned earlier is defined by the Institute of Electrical and Electronics Engineers (IEEE) and given the cryptic label IEEE 802.3. When a reliable method for transmitting Ethernet data over RF was created, it was called 802.11 as an offshoot of the original Ethernet protocol. There are various flavors of wireless Ethernet: 802.11a, 802.11b, and 802.11g are all on the market now, and there are probably more to come. The different flavors operate on different frequencies or different data rates, or both. Many wireless Ethernet transceivers can handle all three flavors. Not all of them can, so you have to be sure all the devices that you're networking can speak the same version of the protocol.

Connecting microcontrollers using wireless Ethernet is an attractive option, but for now it's an expensive one. The first thing you'll need is access to a wireless Ethernet network. These are sprouting up everywhere in public, and many home routers are wireless these days as well.

There aren't any modules to connect using wireless Ethernet on the market that are as simple as the CoBox Micro, though Lantronix recently released the WiPort. It's a wireless Ethernet module with similar command and configuration parameters as the CoBox Micro. It's still a new product, and its connectors are not designed to work with a breadboard, but adaptors will undoubtedly spring up by the time you read this.

If you've already got a wired module like the CoBox Micro or the Siteplayer, one option is to use it with a wireless Ethernet bridge like the D-Link DWL-810 or the Linksys WET-11. These devices have a connection for a regular wired Ethernet connection and a wireless Ethernet card. They retransmit the wired Ethernet signal to an existing wireless Ethernet network. You need both a bridge and an access point if you want to connect to an existing network.

Iosoft (http://www.iosoft.co.uk) sells the ER-22, a board that has a PIC 18F452 and a wireless Ethernet card on it. They also sell the software for the PIC to control the Ethernet card. However, it's all in C, so you'll need to know C and buy a PIC C compiler. Iosoft's code is written in CCS C, available from Custom Computer Services (http://www.ccsinfo.com). Buying the ER-22, its software, and the CCS C compiler will cost you over $400, so it's not the most cost-effective solution.

We mentioned earlier that the simplest approach to networking your microcontroller is to connect it serially to a multimedia computer. The same is true if you want to connect your microcontroller to the Internet wirelessly. If you connect serially to a laptop or a single-board computer, you gain the network connectivity of the larger computer and much more. A single-board computer contains the guts of a typical PC and not much else. Think of a laptop without the screen, keyboard, or hard drive, and you've got the idea. They typically cost in the $150 to $300 range. Most of them can run a simplified version of Windows, Linux, or some variation on Unix (sorry, there are no Macintosh single-board computers that we know of). They have serial ports and wired Ethernet ports, and some come with a CompactFlash or PCMCIA adaptor so you can add a wireless Ethernet card. Because they can use operating systems like Windows and Linux, you don't have to write your own software to talk to the card. You get to concentrate on writing the software to make the connection at a higher level, as you would on a multimedia PC or a server.

Wireless Ethernet Security

If you administer your wireless network yourself, you'll find that adding physical computing projects to that network is no more complex than adding another computer. If you rely on a network administrator, though, you're going to have to work with that person to get your device on the network. Wireless Ethernet is a headache for network administrators because anyone with a Wi-Fi card can connect to it. As a result, administrators tend to be more restrictive about what a device can do on the network, especially in a company setting. They don't want someone on the street corner connecting to the company intranet and running a server or getting into the company databases. Make sure you speak to your network administrator before you jump into the Wi-Fi pond with

RF Serial Communication

your project. If you find that it's more trouble than you can afford, consider connecting to the Internet with a wired connection and then connecting to that wired connection using the other RF methods we've outlined.

Conclusion

It's far easier to use existing hardware than to build your own. When you have the option to do so, it will make it possible to realize your goal much faster, and it will almost always involve needing to master some form of device-to-device communication. There are almost as many communications protocols as there are devices to receive them. While it's impossible to know them all, a little general knowledge will help you figure out most any communications protocol. Start at the physical and electrical level to see that you can connect to the device you're looking at. Then make sure you've got the data rate and other connection details correct. Finally, take a look at the syntax of the protocol and the order in which messages are exchanged. Remember that connecting to a terminal program is generally the easiest first step. With wireless communication, make sure you can exchange data over a wire first, then change the hardware. With the principles laid out in Chapter 7 and in this chapter, you should have a good start on decoding nearly any protocol.

13
Controlling Sound and Light

In physical computing, we would like to one day stretch the concept of multimedia to include physical media like wood, metal, and cloth and physical interaction such as movement, heat, and touch. That said, we are not interested in giving up any of the audiovisual capabilities traditionally associated with multimedia. The microcontrollers you've been using throughout this book lack the speed and data storage necessary to play back rich audio and visual display. However, as you saw in Chapter 7, it's easy to connect a microcontroller to a multimedia computer to add (old school) multimedia capabilities. Microcontrollers do have some limited capabilities for playing recorded sound and for creating screen graphics that can be good enough for creating functional interface feedback, if not emotionally stirring storytelling. The real strength of microcontrollers in the multimedia realm, though, lies in their ability to control light and sound at a more elemental level. For example, a microcontroller can register a thud better than it can determine the pitch of a sound. Similarly, a microcontroller may not be able to play video, but it can control a light source or sense a change in lighting more easily than a multimedia computer. In this chapter, we'll talk about ways of controlling light and sound from a microcontroller. We'll also talk a little about doing this on a multimedia computer, but we'll leave most of the techniques for video and sound production to other books. At the end of the chapter, we'll briefly discuss the single-board computer, a middle ground between the microcontroller and the multimedia computer, which is rapidly becoming a usable platform even for physical computing beginners.

Sound

Sound helps us break away from the typical rigid desktop interface because it offers more flexibility in terms of direction and it's less physically encumbering. On the input side, you can analyze an incoming sound signal in different ways for different purposes. To start with, you might want to know how loud a sound is. You could use a microphone to sense a person stomping his feet on the floor or to find the regular pattern of drum beat on the track of a CD. You might also want to know the pitch of a sound. For example, you might want to make a musical instrument that accompanies a singer respond to her pitch, or a lighting dimmer that changes the level of the lighting based on the pitch of your whistle. Because even the simplest sounds are made up of many pitches, however, detecting the pitch of a sound involves filtering out the various pitches and analyzing the relative amplitude of each one. This is harder than detecting the amplitude and takes more processing power. We will show you how to look for both volume and frequency on microcontroller and multimedia machines. You'll have more success finding pitch on a multimedia machine, but measuring pitch and volume are possible to a limited extent even on a microcontroller.

On the output side, we'll show you some techniques for generating sounds on the fly and for playing back prerecorded sounds. Generally, the quality of prerecorded sounds is better than the on the fly sounds, but the possibilities they offer for interaction are more limited. You have already used the freqout command in Chapter 6. If you varied the duration of the freqout command, you saw that you could allow for a quicker response from the microcontroller but it never sounded that good. On the other hand, using prerecorded audio, you'll get high-fidelity audio at the expense of quick response time. We'll also talk about MIDI and text-to-speech synthesizers, which offer a middle road: they generate sounds on the fly using small snippets of high-quality prerecorded sound, or they synthesize more complex sounds on the fly using more processing power than a microcontroller has.

Musicians are the pioneers of physical computing. They have solved lots of problems of getting physical gesture into electronic form. Typically their solutions are high-level and expensive; but if you just want to move past the technology to the expression, take a walk through a well-stocked music store or online music vendor, and you'll get lots of ideas. Many devices designed as musical controllers can be adapted to other purposes, thanks to MIDI and audio standardization.

We'll also show you how to connect your microcontroller to the telephone network in this chapter for audio communication, as opposed to the data communication afforded by modems in Chapter 12. This will open up possibilities for telecommunications between both humans and computers.

Sound Input

Regardless of what you're going to do with sound, the first step is to convert the sound energy into electrical energy. The microphone is the most basic of all audio transducers. In fact, it's one of the first transducers most people think of when they first learn what a transducer is. Unfortunately microphones aren't as easy to use for analog input as the variable resistors that we discussed in Chapter 6. Working with microphones presents a few challenges. Microphones convert air pressure changes to changing electrical voltages. Audio electrical signals are AC signals. This means that they're typically centered at 0 volts and vary in both the positive and negative direction. They're divided into two categories: microphone-level signals and line-level signals. *Microphone-level* signals range across a few microvolts or millivolts. *Line-level* signals vary from –1 volt to 1 volt. Line-level signals are produced by CD players, MP3 players, turntables, and other amplified devices. In order to bring a microphone signal to line level, you need an amplifier.

Any voltage from an audio input goes up and down in an AC wave. Figure 13.1 shows a graph of the voltage of a sound wave over time. When the sound energy is converted to electrical energy, the volume is represented by the height of the wave above or below the horizontal axis. This height is referred to as the *amplitude* of the sound. For our purposes, amplitude is the same as volume or loudness.

Figure 13.1
A typical graph of a
sound wave.

Audio signals change very fast. For example, the line-level signal of a recording of a tuning fork tuned at middle A, which has a dominant frequency of 440 Hertz (Hz) will vary from −1 volt to 1 volt and back again 440 times a second. In order to detect the frequency of a sound wave, you need a fast processor. If you don't measure it often enough you may miss the peak and get the wrong impression about the general amplitude of the signal. This is when an oscilloscope comes in handy.[1] The more often you measure, or *sample*, the sound level and frequency, the more accurate your representation of the sound will be. You could solve this problem by adding circuitry to filter changes so that you can only see the general amplitude changes. This is called following the *envelope* of the sound. Figure 13.2 shows what the envelope of a sound might look like, electrically. This is what you do when you're detecting the amplitude of a sound and don't care about the pitch. Detecting volume is not very difficult on today's fast computers, even on a microcontroller.

Figure 13.2
A sound's frequency
and its envelope.

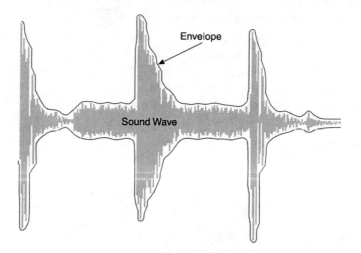

The pitch of a sound is also called the *frequency*. Finding the frequency requires that you again look at the fast-moving sound signal at the highest resolution, as you would to find loudness, but to also watch the signal over time to see how frequently it changes. For simple sounds, this will not be difficult for you to do.

---

[1] An *oscilloscope* is an electrical measuring tool, like a multimeter, that can measure voltage changes at very high rates. It's used to watch electrical signals, like audio waves or data signals, and make a graph in real time. They're generally more expensive than a hobbyist budget can afford, but if you have access to one, get to know it. You'll find it makes working with audio signals much easier.

Complex sounds like speech are made up of several frequencies all at once. Sometimes they have a dominant frequency, such as when a trumpet is played at a particular pitch, and sometimes they don't, as when a person is speaking. Even pitched sounds have *overtones*, which are frequencies produced as a side effect of the sound. To get an accurate measurement of the dominant frequency, you have to detect not just a single pitch, but several others as well. You separate out the various pitches and find the loudest. This is harder than detecting the loudness alone, and takes more processing power. There is a mathematical technique called *Fast Fourier Transformation* (FFT) that allows you to sort a sound into its component frequencies. It requires more computing expertise than this book expects of you, and more processing power than your microcontroller has. However, some of the multimedia environments we've covered include FFT tools, and we'll discuss how to use them below.

Sound Input to a Multimedia Computer

The simplest way to get microphone input to a computer is to use a multimedia computer's microphone or audio inputs. You don't need to add any additional circuitry; the multimedia computer can sample the sound wave very often, and there are many software tools available for analyzing the samples.

Max/MSP is particularly strong in this area. For volume, you just use the MSP `adc~` object and connect it to a `float~` box, which will show you the incoming instantaneous amplitudes. The best tool for doing a fuller analysis is Miller Puckette's `fiddle~` object, at http://www-crca.uscd.edu/~tapel/software.html. `Fiddle~` will work with both Max/MSP and PD, which is a shareware Max-like environment for Windows.

The Director MX Xtra `GetSoundLevel` (http://www.physicalbits.com) is also easy to work with for getting sound amplitude. It gives you the general sound input level, or two separate left and right levels if you use a stereo microphone. If you spread two microphones out, this could give you rough position information of a object emitting a constant sound. There are also Xtras for sensing pitch, using FFT. One that we like is the asFFT Xtra, available from ASCI (http://www.as-ci.net/asFFTXtra/).

Java can get sound input in several ways, but the most powerful way is to use the JSyn classes (http://www.softsynth.com/jsyn/). JSyn includes tools for both analysis and synthesis of sound using Java. Amit Pitaru has extended Processing using JSyn in a tool kit called Sonia (http://www.pitaru.com/sonia/). Live sound input and analysis is one of the many things you can do with Sonia.

Sound Input on a Microcontroller

In order to detect sound levels on a microcontroller, you will have to amplify the signal coming from your microphone. You can buy a kit like the Velleman K1803 (available from Jameco) or you can use a simple amplified speaker with output (like the Radio Shack 277-1008), or you can build your own amplifier with a few components. Regardless of which method you use, you will need to adjust the voltage levels to match your microcontroller. Figure 13.3 shows two circuits for audio input to a microcontroller. The circuit on the top is a line-level voltage converter. Use this if you're using the Radio Shack amplifier or from the Velleman kit. These amplifiers produce a *line-level* audio signal. If you're more adventurous, you can make your own amplifier using the circuit on the bottom.

Figure 13.3
Line-level converting
circuit and microphone
amplifier circuit for
audio input. In the
line-level circuit, a
female phono mini-
jack is shown for
convenient connection
to a store-bought
amplifier. The jacket
has been removed to
show the connections.

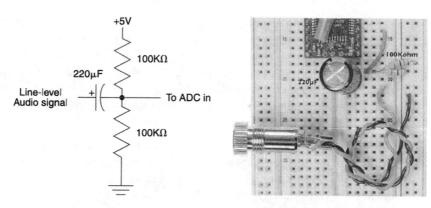

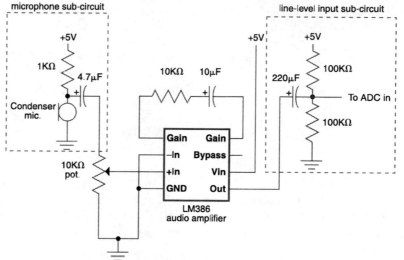

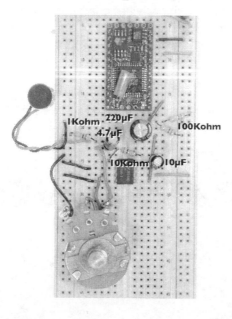

In the top circuit in Figure 13.3, the resistors are of equal resistance, so the voltage between them is exactly half the total voltage across them, or 2.5 volts. An incoming audio signal is line-level, so it varies from –1 volt to 1 volt. Added to the 2.5 volts, you get an input to the microcontroller that's between 1.5 volts and 3.5 volts. This should give you a wide range of values on any of the microcontrollers that use an ADC for analog input. The capacitor between the audio signal and the resistors acts as a low-pass filter so that you get the amplitude of the envelope of the sound, not the individual frequency changes.

If you're connecting to this circuit using a phono mini-jack, the tip of the connector is generally the signal, and the sleeve (the part nearest where you hold it) is the ground. If it's a stereo jack with three conductors, the center conductor (the ring) is the left channel, and the tip is the right channel.

Here's a code snippet to read the amplitude of the incoming sound. This will work in MBasic and PicBasic Pro with word variables and BX-Basic with integer variables:

```
' read an ADC value into the variable ADCVar, then do the following:
if adcVar >= 512 then
    AmplitudeVar = adcVar - 512
else
    AmplitudeVar = 512 - adcVar
 ' BX-BASIC: use "end if" instead of "endif":
endif
```

If you're using the BS-2, you won't be able to read this signal with the RCTime input, because RCTime is much slower than an ADC. Consider using an external ADC, like the MCP3208 from Microchip. This chip will give you eight channels of ADC, and it communicates with a microcontroller using synchronous serial communication, as discussed in Chapter 12.

Microcontrollers are fast enough to sample the wave frequently enough to get a reliable idea about its frequency, if the sound is a single-frequency wave. The count command in pBasic, MBasic, and PicBasic Pro (countTransitions on the BX-24) can give you an idea of the frequency. It counts the number of transitions on a pin. count can sample frequencies up to 25 kHz on a PIC using a 4 MHz oscillator, and up to 125 kHz using a 20 MHz oscillator, so you could measure within the range of human hearing. It won't work with complex sounds like speech or multitonal musical sounds like chords, but for simple pitches, it will work well.

NOTE

countTransitions on the BX-24 will count both the rise and the fall of each half of a sound wave, so the number it returns will be twice the actual frequency.

Here's a snippet of code to read the frequency of the incoming sound:

PBASIC
MBasic
PicBasic Pro

```
freqVar var word
' sample for one second (1000 ms) to get the frequency:
COUNT inputPin, 1000, freqVar
```

BX-Basic

```
dim freqVar as long
' sample for one second to get the transitions:
freqVar = countTransitions(inputPin, 1.0)
' divide by 2 to get the frequency:
freqVar = freqVar \2
```

Though count will give you limited success with a sound that's mostly one pitch, it won't work well for complex sounds like speech. Digital Signal Processing (DSP) processors are specially designed for the speed and math processing necessary for analyzing signals like these. These chips, like Motorola's MC56F8300DSK or Microchip's line of dsPICs, can also do some I/O like general-purpose microcontrollers, but they are more complex to program. As general processor speeds increase, however, you'll be able to get basic DSP-like functionality from general-purpose controllers. Already the dsPICs are designed to be similar to many of the general-purpose PIC families. The highest-level solutions for frequency analysis are devices like pitch-to-MIDI boxes or drum trigger modules. These will take input from a microphone, guitar pick-up, or piezo drum pad and send out MIDI to your microcontroller or multimedia computer describing the note. The cheaper ones will detect only one frequency and the better ones can detect chords. You could even use an electronic guitar tuner, if the tuner outputs a detectable electronic signal when the desired note is played.

Synthesizing Sound on a Microcontroller

The most basic way the microcontroller can synthesize sound is by turning a pin attached to an audio speaker on and off at different rates, causing the speaker to vibrate at different frequencies. This was covered using the freqout command in the section, "Analog Output," in Chapter 6. The freqout command doesn't give you the ability to synthesize complex sounds, however. There are a few methods for doing this using external chips. Chips like the 555 timer can also be attached to a speaker to create variable tones. A voltage-controlled oscillator such as the Texas Instruments 74LS628 (available from http://www.digikey.com) can produce voltages that change with a changing voltage signal. More recently, chips like the SpeakJet (available from http://www.acroname.com) have come on the market that can synthesize multifrequency sounds. There are also sound record/playback chips like the ISD4002 series from Winbond (http://www.winbond-usa.com), which allow you to record sounds and play them back sample by sample. Using these, you can create new sounds by combining bits of prerecorded sounds. The sound quality of these chips is the same as that of an answering machine, however, so you won't get high fidelity sound from them. Operating at the level of the sound wave often gives you more control than you

Sound

can tastefully use. The results will be satisfying for you and annoying for everyone else in the room. Creating your own synthesizers from individual oscillators is a lot of work. In contrast, controlling a MIDI synthesizer is easy work, and very easy on the ears. MIDI communication, which you need in order to do this, was covered in Chapter 12.

Speech

It is sometimes helpful to separate out language sounds from natural sounds and music sounds. Speech recognition tools make this possible on the input side, and text-to-speech synthesis modules make it possible on the output side. With both technologies, the promise is generally better than the delivery.

To synthesize speech, you have to break language down into prerecorded parts. If you break it down into larger parts, like words and sentences, it will sound better, but the range of possible utterances will be smaller. If you break speech all the way down to the phonemes of a language, you can theoretically synthesize any text, but the result always sounds artificial. By now, most speech synthesis tools are good enough to be understandable, but lack the ability to add intonation or character. There are a number of speech synthesis tools on the market. The SpeakJet mentioned above is one of the simplest and least expensive chip-based versions on the market, but there are others. There are also software-based speech synthesis tools for multimedia computers as well. The biggest weakness of most of these tools is that they tend to have well-developed libraries for synthesizing English speech, but they have little or no facilities for synthesizing speech in other languages.

Speech recognition has come a long way, but it still usually fails to live up to our high standards for understanding language. If a person hears only half of what is said, she can construct the rest from the context. Computers can't do this. Usually, speech recognition systems are good when trained for an individual speaker, okay for a limited set of words with little or no background noise, and otherwise dicey. Speech recognition is easier when the machine is queued before the speaker begins speaking. For example, many early speech recognition systems often missed the first syllable of a sentence because they needed to be triggered by the beginning of a new sound.

If you're looking for hardware modules for speech synthesis, Sensory, Inc. makes a speaker-dependent continuous voice recognition module, the Voice Direct II (available from http://www.jameco.com). After you train it for a specific individual, it can continually listen for 15 different words. It can communicate with your microcontroller with a simple parallel interface. They also make a higher-end product, the Voice Extreme, that will allow you to experiment with all types of IC based speech recognition. Images SI (http://www.imagesco.com/) has a similar kit with a bigger vocabulary that will also work without a microcontroller.

Multimedia computers have the advantage in both speech synthesis and speech recognition because of their greater speed and memory capacity. They also allow you to recognize and synthesize on the same platform. Of the environments covered in this book, Director has text-to-speech capabilities using the built-in Speech Xtra, and can be given speech recognition capabilities through the XtrAgent Xtra from DirectXtras (http://

www.directXtras.com). Java's speech API allows for both. Processing can be extended via the Java speech API as well.

Telephone Sounds

The telephone is a sound device so ubiquitous that it often gets overlooked. It's a valuable tool, though, because your microcontroller can communicate using a plain old telephone, either to exchange data or to communicate using analog sound. The increasing ubiquity of digital networks has upstaged the use of sending analog tones to communicate over telephones lines, but telephones are still more common than data connections. Maybe you want people to be able to call from the street on their cell phones and use their touch-tone keypad to change the sequence of your Christmas lights in your apartment window. Or maybe you are collecting data that needs to be posted immediately on the Internet about trains passing in a place where there is no broadband Internet connection, but where plain old telephone service (the technical term is *POTS*) is available. Or maybe you need to build a digital answering system to allow people to leave voice messages from different places around the city. If there are computers on both ends of the phone line and you are only sending digital data, it's easier to skip the circuitry that we are about to show you and use a modem as described in Chapter 12.

Phone Line Interface

The phone jack in your wall might have a lot of wires, but on standard telephone there are only two that matter (usually red and green in the US). The red wire is called the *ring* and the green is called the *tip*. The voltage on these wires when the phone rings is high enough to cause pain (typically 90 volts AC). To avoid getting shocked, make a connector and plug it into your phone line only after you've got the circuit completed. In our example, we used a female phone jack, called an RJ-11 jack. When the phone is sending audio on the phone line to or from your electronics, you need an interface circuit, as shown in Figure 13.4. The transformer is the essential component in this circuit, isolating your electronics from the phone network, and transforming the voltage to phone system levels. You might be able to get by without some of the other components. You use a relay to imitate the phone's switch hook. Figure 13.4 shows a double pole relay for switching both wires, but switching only the ring wire will do the job. The sidactor is a surge suppressor, used to protect the circuit against lightning strikes, and the zener diodes on the other side are to protect your electronics against surges in voltage, including the ring voltage. The resistors and capacitors help hold the line at the desired voltage for a connection and filter the signal to give you better sound quality. Putting a speaker across the red and green wires is a quick way to debug this circuit. You should hear all the normal sounds of a phone connection: the dial tone, the tones of dialing, and the pickup.

This circuit is a great way to annoy your friends. Make it dial their homes, then use the freqout command to make the microcontroller play "Funky Town" to them over the phone.

You can get the parts for this circuit at Radio Shack or any telephone parts store, but for reference, here are the Digi-Key part numbers for the specialty items used in our example circuit:

> ▶ *Transformer.* 600 ohm telephone coupling transformer, MT4134-ND
> ▶ *Sidactor.* P3002AB-ND

Sound

▶ *Zener diodes.* 3.9 volts, 1N5228BCT-ND

▶ *Relay.* 5V DPDT DIP relay with protection diode, 306-1034-ND

This circuit works for most ordinary phone lines, but if you find your transformer overheating, chances are you are connected to a non-standard phone system, which will not work with this circuit. If you will be using your microcontroller to field incoming calls, you need to build a sensor for detecting the ring. You can buy chips for this, but the easiest ring detector to use is a phone flasher. Radio Shack or any phone store will carry them. This is a device that connects a relay to turn on a light every time the phone rings. If you open it up and find the contacts to the relay, you can use the relay as a switch input into your microcontroller.

For one phone connection, this circuit is not very difficult to set up and manage. If you need more sophisticated call management, you can buy phone line interface boxes (from

Figure 13.4

A phone line interface circuit will allow your microcontroller to send data or sound over phone lines. With this interface in place you can start sending sound generated from your microcontroller or from out of your multimedia computer's sound port down the phone line.

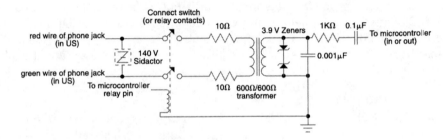

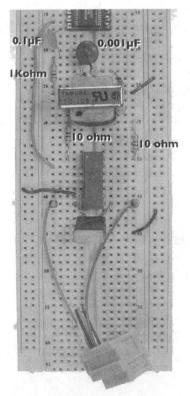

http://www.blackbox.com), modules (from http://www.micromint.com), or "DAA" modules (from http://www.xecom.com), which manage all the circuitry and connection status and also do "call progress," busy signal detection, and more. If your project involves many simultaneous users calling into a central server, you'll need multiple phone lines, each with its own interface. It can get quite expensive. As an alternative, consider call management services like Tellme (http://studio.tellme.com) that handle all the call management on an Internet-connected server, allowing interface with the phone management system using voice commands and standard Internet server-side CGI programming. You could also look at Asterisk (http://asterisk.org/), a tool that allows you to build a phone management system on your own computer.

DTMF

Using the phone to send data involves sending tones at different frequencies and having an agreement on both sides about what each frequency means. You could build your own protocol using the freqout commands, but there is a standard already in place: the tones that are produced whenever you press the keys on a touchtone phone. These are known as *DTMF* tones. Using DTMF is useful when one side of the line is a telephone or a telephone system. If there are computers on both sides of the telephone line, you might consider using modems (see Chapter 12), which make the whole process of encoding and decoding frequencies transparent to you.

Once you have a phone line interface in place, it's a snap to use DTMF tones to dial the phone or control a device with a DTMF decoder on the other end after you have connected. There are sixteen DTMF tones that are associated with touchtone telephones, though most phones only use twelve of them. Most of the microcontrollers we're using have a command, DTMFout, for generating them. The BX-24 is a notable exception to this, but Table 13.1 gives you the frequencies so you can generate them using the freqout command.

Table 13.1
DTMF Frequency Combinations

Freq.	1209	1336	1477	1633 Hz
697 Hz	1	2	3	A
770 Hz	4	5	6	B
852 Hz	7	8	9	C
941 Hz	*	0	#	D

Here's a snippet of code for dialing a phone number:

PBASIC

MBasic

PicBasic
Pro

```
'connect a relay attached to a pin to take the phone off the hook:
low relayPin
pause 500
High relayPin
Pause 500
' dial on a different pin:
DTMFOUT phonePin, 200,200, [1,2,1,2,5,5,5,1,2,1,2]
```

Sound

NOTE

On the PIC, you'll get much better results from this circuit using a 20Mhz clock. On the Basic Atom Pro24, there are DTMF commands, but we have not seen them function as of this writing.

It's a bit more complex on a BX-24:

BX-Basic

```
'connect a relay attached to a pin to take the phone off the hook:
call putPin(relayPin, 0)
call delay(0.5)
call putPin(relayPin, 1)
call delay(0.5)
' dial on a different pin:
call freqout(phonePin, 697,1209, 0.2)     '1
call freqout(phonePin, 697,1336, 0.2)     '2
call freqout(phonePin, 697,1209, 0.2)     '1
call freqout(phonePin, 697,1336, 0.2)     '2
call freqout(phonePin, 770,1336, 0.2)     '5
call freqout(phonePin, 770,1336, 0.2)     '5
call freqout(phonePin, 770,1336, 0.2)     '5
call freqout(phonePin, 697,1209, 0.2)     '1
call freqout(phonePin, 697,1336, 0.2)     '2
call freqout(phonePin, 697,1209, 0.2)     '1
call freqout(phonePin, 697,1336, 0.2)     '2
```

Decoding DTMF tones involves detecting both frequencies (the "D" is for *dual*) in an incoming sound. As you might have guessed, it's not easily done on a microcontroller. Unfortunately this is exactly the capability you will need in order to allow someone to control your project using a touchtone phone. You can use a DTMF decoder chip, such as the 75T204 (available from http://www.alphamicro.net and others), that requires only an external timing crystal and interfaces with your microcontroller using four pins in parallel to send the number of the DTMF tone detected. Many companies sell kits that detect DTMF tones as well (http://www.ramseyelectronics.com, http://www.kitsrus.com, and others), and any of the call management tools mentioned in the phone interface section will also work. You could also decode these frequencies on a multimedia computer with one of the FFT tools discussed earlier.

Light

Our sensory system is so prejudiced towards our eyes that light sensors are often the first thing people want to connect to a microcontroller. On the input side, there is a wide array of sensors, like the photocells that you have already used in Chapter 6, or the video camera covered in Chapter 9. Below, we'll cover some other sensors for light input, but we'll spend more time on the more difficult problem of controlling light output.

Light Sensors

Photocells (more precisely, photoresistors) are the easiest sensors to connect to a microcontroller. They can be a little slow for some applications, but overall they're the staple tools when it comes to light sensing. *Photodiodes* and *phototransistors* are similar to photocells in that they react to light. They are usually used as digital input sensors, but you can get an analog reading from them as well. The main difference between photodiodes or phototransistors and photoresistors is that the former react faster to changes in light. For example, to be able to communicate at serial data rates, a photoresistor wouldn't react fast enough. IR serial receivers typically use photodiodes or phototransistors to detect the changing pulses of data that they receive. Photodiodes usually require an operational amplifier (op amp) circuit to raise their voltage levels to those that a microcontroller can read. Phototransistors, on the other hand, are usually easily readable as digital switches. They work like normal transistors, except they have no base. The light source acts as a base, allowing current to flow from collector to emitter when enough light hits the lens of the phototransistor. Figure 13.5 shows a phototransistor used as a digital input. If you connect this same circuit to an analog-to-digital converter, you get good analog changes based on incoming light values as well. It won't work well using the RCTime circuit on the BS-2, however.

Figure 13.5
A phototransistor used as an input.

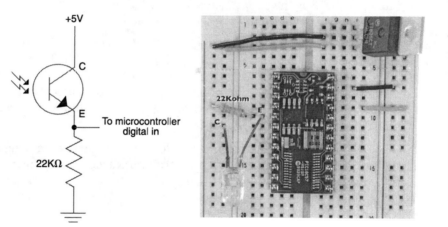

The TAOS light-to-voltage sensors (available from http://www.taosinc.com) incorporate a photodiode and op amp in one device, so you only have to supply power and ground to get an analog voltage in the 0 to 5 volt range. They offer a wider range of sensitivity than the circuit above.

If you need faster or more accurate light readings than you will get from your average photocell, you could use a photodiode array. The TAOS TSL230 sensor encloses an array of photodiodes and some analog circuitry. The chip converts light readings into frequencies, so you can get a reading using the count function (countTransistions on the BX-24) on your microcontroller. There is a variation on this chip (TCS230, available in a module from http://www.parallax.com) that uses multiple arrays, each with a different color filter. This allows you to detect the intensity of certain individual colors in addition to the general intensity of the light.

DC Lighting Control

LEDs, once relegated to feedback for power switches, are now used in large screen displays, light sculptures, and even household lighting. Super bright LEDs that are bright enough to read by are now common. You can get them from Digi-Key, Super Bright LEDs (http: //www.superbrightleds.com), LED Effects (http://www.ledeffects.com), and many other distributors. Anything above 1000 millicandelas is considered super bright, but nowadays you can find LEDs that can produce ten to 20 times that amount of light. You can also get super bright RGB LEDs that produce three colors (red, green, and blue). RGB LEDs have two extra legs (one for each color). Despite the increased output, they're still just diodes, controlled by sending current through them just like the LEDs you've been using from the beginning of this book. Super brights generally consume more current than regular LEDs, so you might find that you need to use a transistor to control them, depending on the LED. To dim them, you can pulsewidth modulate them just like regular LEDs. You can also use a digital potentiometer, as shown in Chapter 12. The PIC 18F452, the Basic Atom, and the BX-24 have pins that can produce a dedicated PWM signal (sometimes called *hardware PWM*, or *HPWM*). This signal will run smoothly while your microcontroller's processor does other things. If you need more than two channels of dedicated PWM, you can buy external chips to get more channels. The PAK-Vb PWM coprocessor, available from microEngineering Labs (http://www.melabs.com) offers eight channels of hardware PWM. It's controlled using asynchronous serial commands.

Eventually LEDs become so much fun you might find yourself wanting to control lots of them individually. Techniques for doing this are covered in Chapter 14, "Managing Multiple Inputs and Outputs." Ultimately, the high-level solution is to buy lighting devices made with LEDs that you can control from your microcontroller. For example, Color Kinetics (http://www.colorkinetics.com) sells a range of light fixtures controllable using the DMX512 serial protocol.

While LEDs are fun, they're not physically flexible. For flexible lighting materials, consider electroluminescent paper and electroluminescent wire. These are materials that glow in various colors when you apply current to them. They can also be shaped and cut. They are AC devices that operate at a very high voltage and very low amperage. In order to control them, you'll need an inverter, which converts DC current to AC and transforms the amperage and voltage into ranges that the EL-wire or EL-paper can use. There are countless electroluminescent kits on the market now, many of which come with an inverter. Sometimes they are a little fussy about power requirements, so you might start with a kit that includes a power supply. Elwire.com (http://www.elwire.com) has a wealth of information on controlling electroluminescent wire. There are many distributors of EL-wire and kits, including http://www.thatscoolwire.com. All Electronics (http://www.allcorp.com) has electroluminescent paper kits as well. Controlling electroluminescent sources is a bit different than controlling LEDs because the former are AC sources. In the next section, we will talk about some of the difficulties of controlling AC power. You may find it easier to look for inverter modules that have an enable pin on the DC side of the inverter. Pulsewidth modulating the enable pin is a simpler way to control electroluminescent wire, and safer, as you're dealing with the low-voltage side of the inverter instead of the high-voltage side.

AC Lighting Control

When you want to control lighting on an architectural scale, super bright LEDs are nice for subdued lighting, but they're no substitute for AC incandescent light sources. Yet. Until they are, it's worthwhile to know about AC lighting control.

In Chapter 6, we covered how to turn on and off an AC source using a relay. You have to be much more careful of electrocution and fire when using AC power, but don't be too paranoid. It's not that hard once you have some experience and caution. While turning on and off AC lights is relatively simple, however, dimming them is not.

AC Dimming Circuits

With DC power you can simulate an analog voltage by turning the power on and off at varying rates. With AC voltage there are more timing issues to worry about. To create a lower average voltage, you turn off the power for part of every AC cycle. To get half the voltage, you turn the power off for half of each cycle. In order to do this, you have to turn on the current at just the right moment in each cycle. Figure 13.6 illustrates this concept. To switch the AC on and off, you can use a triac. A *triac* is basically an electronic switch that's used to switch AC current. Triacs are a bit like relays, but operate at the speed of transistors. This makes them useful for switching high-frequency AC signals. The differences between the triac and the transistor are beyond the scope of this book. Dimming high voltage, high current AC is enough to kill you if you don't know what you're doing. Because it takes a lot of effort and experience to get a modest result, we strongly recommend the high-level approach when it comes to AC dimming.

CAUTION

One common mistake that people make when they first learn about AC dimmers is to try to control the speed of an AC motor, like a fan or a winch motor, using a dimmer. AC motors and other inductive loads should never be controlled using AC dimmers. The back voltage that a motor produces can damage the dimmer and the motor. If you're trying to control the speed of an AC motor, never use an AC lighting dimmer.

Figure 13.6
To dim an AC current, you have to turn off the current for part of each half-cycle of the AC wave. The top figure shows an AC current at 50 percent. The bottom figure shows it at 25 percent.

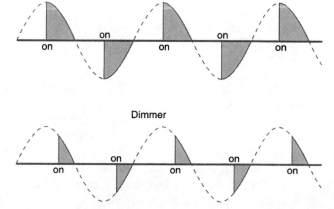

Light

MIDI Dimmers

It you have some cash and not much time, small MIDI dimmers (like the Light Master from Topaz, http://www.tpz.com) are a really great solution. At the low end, these look just like ordinary power strips with a MIDI input on the end. Each socket can be individually controlled by MIDI commands. Typically they can handle about 300 watts per channel. Most local lighting and sound rental houses will carry some lower end MIDI controllable dimmers like this. You can also get them from suppliers of DJ equipment. Moving up from there, most commercial dimmers used for high-wattage lighting communicate the DMX-512 serial protocol. DMX-512 is a much faster protocol than MIDI, operating at 250Kbps. Of the microcontrollers we're using, only the PIC can communicate directly at DMX speeds. However, there are several MIDI-to-DMX converters and RS-232-to-DMX converters on the market. These dimmers are essential when you're lighting professional performance events, where the lights are all much higher-powered than home lighting.

Hacking a Dimmer

If you've got time and not much money, but don't feel like getting intimate enough with electronics to build your own dimmers, there are some workarounds you can build by repurposing household dimmers. The quickest hack is to simply strap an RC servo motor to the knob of a standard rotary dimmer. These dimmers typically turn more than 180 degrees, so consider a stepper motor if a servo doesn't give you enough range. This isn't the prettiest solution, but it is relatively safe, quick, and inexpensive. It also prevents you from having to deal with the AC current directly.

A similar trick is to find an automatic dimmer that dims based on light. Many home and garden stores sell these for controlling outdoor lighting. Many of them will not work because they are simply switches that turn the lights on at dusk, but there are some dimmer modules available as well. You can place an LED over the built-in sensor and regulate the light coming out of the LED.

There are also remote-controlled dimmers that respond to infrared serial signals. You can program a microcontroller to simulate the remote control signals. First, you need to program the microcontroller to "learn" the remote's protocol by adding an IR receive circuit (see Chapter 12) and noting the codes when you press the remote's buttons. From there, you can reprogram the microcontroller to send the protocol using an IR transmitter.

All of these solutions may seem clunky, but when you have little money to spend on more elegant solutions, lay elegance aside and let ingenuity reign.

AC Dimming Using X10

For slower interactions, using X10 is very attractive. X10 is a serial protocol developed for home appliance control that operates over AC power lines. To use it you need an interface box for converting from RS-232/TTL serial to X10. Smarthome (http://www.smarthome.com) sells the TW523 interface module, as do many other home-automation vendors. This module is essentially a modem for X10. There are a number of X10 control modules, but they fall into two basic categories: dimmers and switches. An X10 dimmer can control resistive loads like incandescent light bulbs. It controls the voltage going to the load using methods discussed in the "AC Dimming Circuits" section.

An X10 switch doesn't change the voltage, it just turns it on or off. X10 switches are used for appliances that contain motors and other inductive loads. X10 dimmers, on the other hand, can dim resistive loads like incandescent light bulbs. Don't try to use any device with a motor or other inductive load on an X10 dimmer, or you'll destroy the dimmer and probably damage the motor. All the microcontrollers we cover in this book, except the Basic Atom Pro24, have built-in commands for communicating with X10 boxes. One big advantage X10 offers is that you can plug the interface box into an ordinary AC outlet in your home and it can control a dimmer plugged in anywhere within your AC system. This can save you a few long cable runs. The big disadvantage of X10 is that it's very slow. It can take up to a few seconds for a simple dimming command to take effect. The resolution of X10 dimmers is very coarse; they can only manage about ten different levels of brightness.

Figure 13.7
Pin connections for a TW523 X10 modem. The photo shows both a control module (right) and a light dimmer module (left).

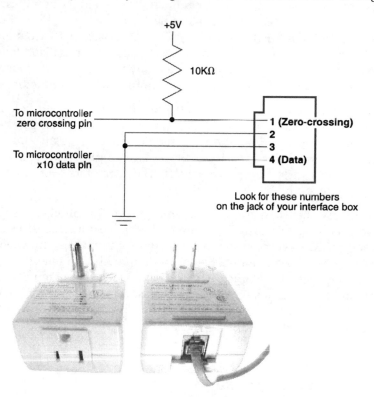

X10 works by sending bits over AC power lines when the voltage on the lines is zero. In order to do this, an X10 device needs to be able to detect when the voltage is crossing the zero point. As a result, an X10 modem like the TW523 has two control pins: a data pin (sometimes called a *modulation pin*, since the data is being modulated on the AC wave) and a zero-crossing detect pin. The TW523 has an RJ-11 phone-jack style connector with four wires. Figure 13.7 shows the pin connections. Consult the manual for your microcontroller and the manual for your individual X10 device for details on how to write the code. In pBasic, and PicBasic Pro, the X10 commands are called Xin and Xout. In BX-Basic, there's only an output command, called X10Cmd().

Screen Graphics

Though we're often working to expand computing beyond the screen in physical computing, we're not looking to eliminate the screen. We will talk here about some options for graphics produced by a microcontroller and some options for embedding graphics produced by a multimedia computer in a physical context.

Controlling Character Displays

Small-text LCD panels like the ones that you commonly see in watches and other consumer electronic devices are easily controlled by your microcontroller. They are useful for displaying short messages in text or for producing rudimentary graphics. As usual, the easier ones to use are a little more expensive because you can use serial communication to send your text to them. Modules like the serial backpack LCDs from Scott Edwards Electronics (http://www.seetron.com) or the serial displays from NetMedia (http://www.basicx.com) fall into this category. If you only need one LCD display, these are worth the extra expense because you will be up and running almost immediately.

If you are willing to work a little closer to the metal, you can buy much cheaper LCD panels without a serial interface. Many LCD panels are based on a parallel control interface from Hitachi, the 44780. PicBasic Pro has a set of commands, LCDin and LCDout, that allow you to control these modules as easily as the serial modules. For the Stamp-like controllers, you will have to do a little more work, sending the characters over one by one using a parallel interface, usually four bits at a time.

The most basic character display is the seven-segment LED number display. You see variations on this in microwaves, VCRs, and other home appliances. These are usually made from seven LEDs arranged so they look like the number eight when they're all turned on. With seven pins for every number, you would quickly run out of microcontroller pins if you tried to drive multiple digits directly. Fortunately, there are LED driver ICs that cut down on the number of pins required. A BCD-to-seven-segment driver like the CD4543B (available at Digi-Key, Radio Shack, and other distributors) has four inputs to control the seven outputs needed to drive one of these displays.[2] You can also apply some of the techniques in Chapter 14 for managing multiple outputs.

Controlling Video Displays

The volume of information in a video signal and the speed at which it can change is a worthy challenge to your body's perceptual system. There are a lot of interesting ways to integrate video into your physical installations.

Video Types

There are two main types of video signal you might use. Composite video is what is typically output by VCR and DVD players and viewed on a television screen. There are a

---

[2] BCD stands for *Binary-Coded Decimal*. These displays output a decimal digit (0 to 9) when you place the value of the digit in binary on the input pins. For example, the decimal digit 9 is 1001 in binary, 8 is 1000, and so forth. Since 9 is the highest decimal value that one display can show, and it's no larger than four bits in binary, there's never a need for more than four input pins on a BCD-to-seven-segment driver.

couple of different flavors of composite video (NTSC, PAL, SECAM), but they all use two-conductor cables, generally with RCA or BNC connectors.[3] We will call the second type of video *computer video*. The dominant flavor (for now) of computer video is called SVGA, and it usually uses a 15-pin connector. Computer video offers a much better picture, but composite video is a simpler signal that is easier to generate, manipulate, and transmit and can be displayed on cheaper monitors. To get these benefits, there are many converters for going from your multimedia computer's SGVA to composite (NTSC, PAL, or SECAM).

Generating Video

You would need a very fast microcontroller to generate a composite video signal. The PIC chip covered in this book could do it, and an SX chip (available from http://www.parallax.com) could do better. This resolution of control for a microcontroller is an exciting threshold, but it is a lot of work to squeak out even the simplest of graphics. However, modules like the BOB-II and BOB-3 video overlay boards from Decade Engineering (http://www.decadenet.com) take in ASCII text serially and output it to an NTSC monitor. The BOB boards also have an NTSC video input, so you can overlay your text on a video image from a camera or VCR. You have only limited control over the format of the text onscreen with the BOB boards, but they allow for larger displays than an LCD affords. Of course, all of these pale in comparison to what you can easily do on a multimedia computer.

Manipulating Video

There are many devices that allow you to control video devices, as opposed to actually generating your own video. For example, the AutoSwitch4 Lite from Nexus Controls (http://www.nexuscontrols.com) is an inexpensive, serially controlled NTSC video switcher. By sending it serial messages, you can switch any of four video inputs to its video output. You can also buy models for switching SVGA. Often, you want to send the same signal from one video input to two or more displays. Unfortunately you can't just split the signal using a Y-adaptor. You need a distribution amp, which repeats and amplifies the signal for multiple outputs.

Video switchers allow you to switch from one video source to another. Sometimes you need more control and want to combine two video images on the same screen. Video mixers allow you to do this kind of mixing. They also allow you to fade or wipe from one source to another, insert part of one image into another using a chroma-koy or luminance key, and add various effects. Video mixers aren't cheap. The cheapest ones we've used, like the Edirol V4 (http://www.edirol.com) or the Videonics MXPro (http://www.focusinfo.com) start at about $900. The professional workhorse models like the Panasonic WJ-MX50 are about $4000. They offer video mixing at a speed and fidelity you won't get any other way, and most of them are serially controllable in one form or another (the V4 is MIDI controlled; the others are RS-232/RS-485 controlled). They also offer a tangible physical interface for video mixing. This can make a significant difference if you're mixing video live. Multimedia computers offer functionality similar to dedicated video mixers, but if you want physical handles and buttons to grab when you're mixing, you'll need a dedicated mixer or you'll need to build your own interface. In performance, those physical handles can make all the difference between missing a cue and getting it just right.

---

[3] S-Video is a small variation on composite in which color and brightness are carried on separate wires. It gives a slightly better picture and uses a different connector.

If you are using a multimedia computer to mix video, the environments we've recommended can all do it to a limited degree, but Max/MSP using Jitter is hands down the best of them. Jitter gives you excellent control over video mixing and display. Isadora, by TroikaTronix (http://www.troikatronix.com) is another very good video mixing environment. Like Max/MSP, it's a visual programming environment, but it's dedicated specifically to video control. Its interface is more specifically tailored to performance work. It can take input from microcontrollers via MIDI and control video based on incoming sound levels as well.

Plugging and playing with composite video is so easy that you get used to keeping all the components and connections in your head. When you build an interactive system, though, the complexity can creep up on you. Draw a picture of your system at the outset. It will save you the catastrophe of overlooking a crucial element at a grave moment.

Transmitting Video

There are many suppliers of simple plug-and-play video transmitters for composite video (x10.com, Supercircuits.com). The picture quality is not very good, the transmission distances quoted are always overly optimistic, and they require a lot of wattage, so they go through batteries quickly. As with most wireless applications, we suggest you try it with a wire first. Quite often composite video signals are *frequency modulated* for transmission (just like the radio waves in RF serial transmission; see Chapter 12). This allows you to put more signals on a wire and to send it longer distances. A screw-on F-connector, as opposed to the pluggable RCA and BNC connectors, is a tipoff to a modulated signal. You would plug a modulated signal into the tuner (usually tuned to channel 3) rather than the line input on your monitor. You can buy converters for modulating and demodulating video. If you want to transmit over longer distances, you can use streaming video over the Internet. You will need a multimedia computer on the receiving side. On the transmitting side, you can use a multimedia computer with a camera attached or a standalone camera like the D-Link DCS2100+ wireless Internet camera.

LCDs

Once you've got control of video, whether you're generating it from analog sources or a multimedia computer, the next challenge you face is how to insert the video into the physical context of your project. There is something magical about objects appearing to move back and forth between the screen and physical space. Even for more functional projects, it's nice for the user to have a single focus instead of looking back and forth between the physical interface and the screen graphics. A CRT television or computer monitor can stand out like a sore thumb in the middle of a sculptural installation, and it's just too big if you're developing a handheld device. If you're trying to get the video embedded in a wall or floor, these monitors won't do the job. There are many different form factors for LCD displays, from eyepiece monitors to wall-sized televisions. It's possible to buy them without a case so you don't have a frame to contend with, and it's often less expensive. For a flat screen that is more easily embedded directly in your project, the simplest method is to just fold back the display on a tablet computer, unhinge a laptop computer, or take the casing off a desktop LCD monitor (be careful not to electrocute yourself), and run long VGA cable. You can also find cheaper surplus and specialty screens (for example, touch screens) online. EarthLCD (http://store.earthlcd.com) carries

LCD panels from 2.7 inches on up. AEI components (http://www.aeicomp.com) carries LCDs from 1.8 inches to 22 inches. Kopin's CyberDisplay is less than an inch across (http://www.kopin.com). These are just a few of thousands of display distributors. Keep in mind that you will need driver circuitry for any display you buy. All of the distributors mentioned here also sell NTSC, PAL, or SVGA driver circuitry for their displays.

Video Projectors

We've watched a long love affair between physical computing practitioners and video projectors. The size of an image really does matter in evoking a more emotional response from your user.[4] Video projectors can effortlessly scale and also give you easy flexibility about where and on what the image is displayed. The downside of projectors has always been the cost, but they've gone from untouchable to just expensive (don't forget the replacement lamps). Almost all LCD projectors on the market these days come with both analog video and SGVA inputs, so you can have your choice as to what devices you want to use to generate your image.

There are many artists and designers who use projection extensively in their work, but there are surprisingly few books on how to do it well. We can't treat the subject comprehensively here, but we can offer a few tips that will make life easier if this is your first time working with projections.

There are a few terms used in describing projection that are helpful to know in planning your work. Figure 13.8 illustrates these terms. The *throw distance* is the distance from the projector to the surface that it's projecting on. The *beam angle* of the projector refers to the angle of the beam that comes out of the projector. The wider the beam angle, the larger your image, and the less throw distance you need. Ideally, you should position your projector so that the beam is perpendicular to the surface. Otherwise, keystoning will result.

Figure 13.8
Projection basics. This projector's beam doesn't come out perpendicular from the projector, nor is it perpendicular to the screen. Many projectors are designed for ceiling or table mounting, and have built-in beam and keystone adjustment like this so that the image will come out square on the screen, even though the projector isn't centered on the screen.

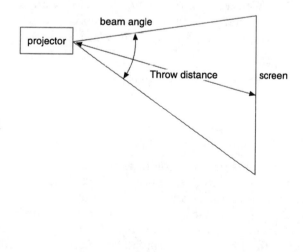

[4] *The Media Equation: How People Treat Computers, Television, and New Media like Real People and Places* (Cambridge University Press,1998), by Byron Reeves and Clifford Nass, describes tests that show people have much stronger reactions and better memories of larger images.

Keystoning refers to the distortion that makes the image look like a trapezoid instead of a rectangle. Some projectors have keystone correction built in, which allows you to reshape the image and gives you more flexibility in positioning the projector.

The brightness of an image decreases with the square of the distance. This means that if the projector is two feet from the screen, your image will only be one quarter as bright as it was when the projector was one foot from the screen. At three feet, it will be one ninth as bright as it was at one foot. By moving the projector closer, you gain brightness, but you lose size. Projector brightness is measured in *lumens*. A projector's lumen output is constant regardless of the distance or projection surface, but by changing the surface or the distance or the surrounding lighting, you can change the apparent brightness of the image.

In order to see an image from a projector you need a surface to project it on. To date, no one's perfected *Star Wars*-like projection in mid-air without a surface to reflect the projection, because it defies the laws of physics (though someone will probably prove us wrong by the time you're reading this). At the most ephemeral level, this means you need to generate a cloud of smoke or a haze of water or oil to reflect the light. On a more concrete level, you can buy special material for making projection surfaces, such as the rear projection material from Rose Brand Fabrics (http://www.rosebrand.com) in several colors, including the surprisingly bright black. Black actually works well as a projection surface because it makes the dark parts of your image appear darker, increasing the contrast with the bright parts of the image. Tracing paper or vellum will work well as a projection surface in a pinch. If you're looking for a more transparent image, you can use various scrims or semi-transparent fabrics. The more transparent the surface, the less bright your image will be, but in many cases, getting a projector bright enough is not a problem. Toshio Iwai's *Piano* installation makes use of a black scrim in a display space that's mostly dark in order to make the projection surface disappear so that the animations seem to float in air (http://www.iamas.ac.jp/~iwai/artworks/piano.html). Lighting an object behind the semi-transparent projection material is a key element in making the screen disappear. The viewer's eye, focusing past the screen to the object beyond, does not notice the screen itself, only the images on it.

In interactive projection systems, the viewer is often very close to the screen. Rear projection is commonly used in this case, so your user does not cast a shadow in the projection. Space behind the projected surface is too tight to get the throw distance to produce a large enough image. You might look for a projector with a wide-angle lens or adapter or use mirrors to increase the projected size of the image.

You don't have to project on a flat surface. Sometimes projections can be used to add texture or motion to an object on which they're projected. Sculptor Tony Oursler often projects on blank masks to give the appearance of three-dimensionality to his video, and to give animation to the masks. You don't have to use all of the projection's image space either. A small animation floating on a black background can appear as if it's floating free and unframed if you let the rest of the image fall on a black background. Soft black materials like velvet and duvetyn are particularly good for absorbing stray projection edges.

Almost all projectors have adjustments to flip the image for rear projection or upside down projection for ceiling mountings. Some projectors also have digital zooms, which are very handy for enlarging scenes that are too processor intensive for your computer to render full screen. If you point the projector directly at the screen, you will probably get a glare on the screen and some keystoning because they are designed to project as a slight angle above or below. Figure 13.8 shows a typical projector-to-screen offset relationship. To protect the life of the projector's lamp, try not to move the projector when it is hot. Try to work with a partner and leave a lot of time for positioning and securing your projector.

Sculptural Video Display

When video input is combined with physical output, interesting things happen. The artist Daniel Rozin, who is fascinated with the pixel, has made a series of sculptural displays in which each pixel is a moving object. His *Wooden Mirror* is shown in Figure 13.9. Rozin digitizes a video image and translates the brightness of each pixel to the angle of a servo motor. Over 800 servo motors in the mirror move pixels of wood to create a moving video image in wood. The camera lens is hidden at the center of the mirror. Rozin has done similar video mirrors using silver balls and pieces of trash as pixels as well. The artist Jim Campbell does similar work, depicting video using arrays of LEDs and light bulbs to absolutely stunning effect (http://www.jimcampbell.tv/). Campbell's images are large and low-resolution; up close, they appear to be simply blinking lights. At a distance, they resolve into coherent images. Artist Leo Villareal does similar work with more abstract images, sometimes on an architectural scale (http://www.villareal.net).

Sculpting with pixels is just one possibility for making physical video. Scanning is another option. Pendulum displays and fan clocks like Bob Blick's (http://www.bobblick.com/techref/projects/propclock/propclock.html) use a single line of lights moving rapidly in a line (or in Blick's case, a circle) to create an image in empty space. While moving, the lights or LEDs are turned on and off in particular patterns so that the viewer's eye creates a persistent image from the pattern of blinking lights.

Computational methods of drawing offer many other interesting sculptural possibilities. For example, programs like Adobe Illustrator and Macromedia Flash MX rely on vectorized drawing methods, in which a shape is represented by a series of points along its perimeter, and a description of the curves between the points. What would a vectorized video sculpture look like?

Figure 13.9
Daniel Rozin's *Wooden Mirror*. (Photo courtesy Israel Museum. Photographer, Yossi Glalanti).

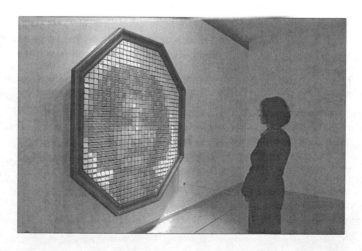

Screen Graphics

Linear Media on a Multimedia Computer

If you have long, high-quality sound or video files that need to be played back in response to a viewer's actions, consider the multimedia computer first. Dedicated media playback devices, like serially driven DVD players, samplers, and video servers might seem attractive: they tend to crash less than multimedia computers because they're dedicated to one task. In an industrial setting, this makes sense. But these devices will add up to a more expensive system and a much less flexible one. Playback of media is easily done natively in most multimedia programming environments. There is usually a single command for playing files of at least one format. Most commonly thought of as a video format, QuickTime has proven popular for sounds as well, because in addition to the usual controls for looping, volume, and speed (which affects pitch in a sound), it also gives you options for layering multiple tracks and selectively enabling and disabling tracks. Check your authoring environment for the file formats that it will accommodate. After you learn how to play a sound in your programming environment on the multimedia computer, see Chapter 7 to see how to get your microcontroller to trigger the playback serially.

Playback capabilities allow you to build something that resembles a jukebox, where the user picks from media that has been provided for them. If you want your user to leave something of herself as a result of the interaction, like a photo booth, you will need recording capabilities. This allows your project to grow as its database of media from past users grows. Recording a sound or video on the fly is a less common capability in an authoring environment, but possible with the addition of various plug-ins or Xtras. One catch in recording media on the fly is that you are potentially creating very large files, and you might fill up your storage space. These projects also present an interface challenge for prompting the user to start and stop at good times so that you can avoid a lot of hand editing later. Finally, but most important, they assume that people are willing and able to speak up. This is not always the case.

Linear Media on a Microcontroller

Microcontrollers do not have enough memory for storing and playing back large sound or video files. As we have mentioned, most people combine the sensors of their microcontroller with a multimedia computer, even a very cheap one. On the other hand, if your microcontroller is embedded in a small toy, then a multimedia computer is not going to be practical. There are smaller devices for storing linear media that can be controlled by the microcontroller.

Sound recorded onto chips is used in everything from greeting cards and toys to digital answering machines. The sound quality is not fantastic, and the clips cannot be too long. Radio Shack sells an easy-to-use module with instructions (part no. 276-1323). Find the Record button and the Playback button and bypass them with relays. You can then use your microcontroller to start and stop playback and record by turning on and off the relays. Figure 13.10 shows how to do this. Here's some pseudocode for a basic control application:

```
close the record switch relay (take the record pin high)
pause 20 seconds
open the record switch relay (take the record pin low)
```

```
pause 1 second
loop to play the message repeatedly:
    close the play switch relay (take the play pin high)
    pause 20 seconds
    open the play switch relay (take the play pin low
    pause half a second
end loop
```

Parallax sells a high-level module (QV306M4P) for more controlled playback of sounds and another module (QV430P) for programming sounds from .wav files. Winbond (http://www.winbond-usa.com) makes the ISD series of record-playback chips that offer a wide range of record times and playback control. All of them can interface with a microcontroller through asynchronous serial interface. The ISD chips are generally cheaper than the other solutions and offer more control, but they take more time to set up.

Figure 13.10
A simple sound record/playback module from Radio Shack. Replace the buttons with relays connected to your microcontroller, and you've got a controllable sound player.

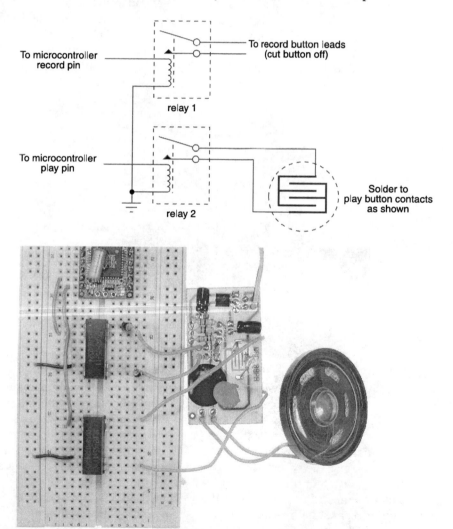

For longer and higher-quality sounds, your options are not as inexpensive. There are a few MP3 player modules on the market that are serially controllable, like the QV502 from Quadravox (http://www.tetraphon.com/ under "Audio Products"), or the yampp MP3 modules from Jelu (http://www.jelu.se/shop.php). Newer MP3 modules like these are coming on the market every day from professional engineering companies and hobbyists alike. Most of them cost a couple of hundred dollars by the time you've got all the parts together, though, so tread carefully.

Many consumer video cameras and some decks come with a control port in the form of a mini-jack that you might have seen and overlooked. A typical one is shown in Figure 13.11. This port gives you control over some of the device's functions, using a protocol developed by Sony called "Control-L" or "LANC." Most Sony devices and some non-Sony devices feature Control-L or LANC ports. The specifics of the protocol are unusual, but there are converters for it, like the 624P chip from Elm Electronics (http://www.elmelectronics.com). The Control-L protocol bytes are sent as ASCII-encoded hexadecimal values. You will need to learn the specific commands for your device. The datasheet for the 624P gives a good overview, however, and can get you started. Depending on your camera or deck, you can play, record, read time code, fast-forward, rewind, or do stop frame animation. Videotape is usually too slow for interactive playback of clips, but a DVD player with Control-L input offers many possibilities in this arena.

Figure 13.11
A Control-L connector on a Sony TRV-18 digital video camera.

For very simple needs, there is the time-honored tradition of hacking open a CD player, DVD, MP3 player, or VCR and bypassing the switches of their manual interface with relays. This will void your warranty, of course, but it's the most enjoyable way to do so. You can imitate any functionality offered by the buttons on the outside of the case by activating the relays with your microcontroller. The connectors behind these switches are usually mounted on circuit boards, and the connections are very small and delicate. Often there is a coating on these boards to protect the circuit traces. You might have to scrape off the coating to get a good solder connection at the base of the switches. Hacking these devices is delicate work, and you might consider sparing the device itself and operating first on the switches within a remote control for the device. A quicker and more non-intrusive hack is to strap a servo motor onto the case and have the microcontroller move the arm of the motor to imitate your finger pressing the button. The reaction time is slower than relay control, but it's usually faster than your finger would be, and it saves the device for future use.

Single-Board Computers

Throughout this chapter, we've mentioned several applications that work better on a multimedia computer. While a desktop tower is often too large to hide inside a project, laptops are smaller and easier to embed. Single-board computers are even smaller. A single-board computer contains the guts of a typical PC and not much else. Figure 13.12 shows a typical one. They offer the same basic functionality as a PC in a much smaller form factor. Most of them are about 6 to 8 inches square and 2 or 3 inches high. Many are smaller. They typically cost in the $150 to $300 range, which is a pretty good price if you need a computer you can dedicate to a project. If you're looking for something to run only a single program and accept connections from a serial or Ethernet port, which is the case in most physical computing applications, these can be very useful.

Figure 13.12
A VIA EPIA MII Mini-ITX single-board computer.

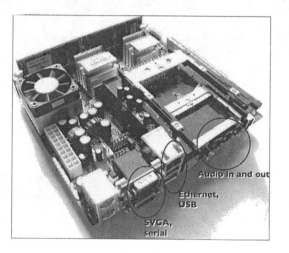

Single-board computers show up frequently in home appliances these days, from set-top boxes to game consoles. You have to add your own hard drive, power supply, keyboard, mouse, and screen if you need them. You also have to install an operating system. Most of the ones on the market can use Windows, Linux, or other Unix variations, but not the Macintosh OS. Some of the single-board computers are very basic and require you to build your own motherboard, add sockets for RAM, video ports, and more. These are lower-level than we recommend. However, devices like the VIA EPIA Mini-ITX boards (http://www.via.com.tw/en/VInternet/mini_itx.jsp) or the net4xxx boards from Soekris Engineering (http://www.soekris.com/) are reasonably simple to get started with. They have video, mouse, hard drive, USB, RAM, and power connections already on the board, so you only have to connect the devices and install the operating system to get started.

Single-board computers have some significant limitations. Not all of them have fast video processors, or sound outputs, so you need to check that the board you're buying has the outputs you need. You have to know your way around the insides of a computer reasonably well to get them connected. If you've never added RAM to a computer, or even looked inside, these are not for you. But if you're comfortable swapping RAM or hard drives, and you can install an operating system, you've got the level of expertise you need to get started with these.

Conclusion

In writing this book, we needed to come up with a name for computers that are not microcontrollers. We called them "multimedia computers" because the main advantage they have over microcontrollers is the ability to work with audio and video. However, many multimedia devices and lighting and sound control systems can be controlled from microcontrollers, making them multimedia computers as well. In fact, once you've got a taste of what a microcontroller can do, it's tempting to try to get it to do everything. Fight this temptation, because it can lead to more electrical engineering than you need to do. The increasing trend of single-board computers towards lower prices and more ease of use is worth watching because they can give you the best of both worlds. Use each type of computer for its natural strengths. To think broadly about light and sound interfaces, though, you will need skills on both sides.

14

Managing Multiple Inputs and Outputs

To keep things simple in our examples, we have been showing you how to turn on a single LED or how to listen to one switch. In practice, people tend to want lots of inputs and outputs. If you repeated our existing example multiple times, your code would get a little long, and you would certainly run out of pins on your microcontroller. In this chapter, we'll discuss coding techniques for managing several I/O pins in groups and for addressing multiple bits within a byte. We will also show you hardware techniques for getting past the limited number of pins on your microcontroller. As with other situations, you'll find that controlling many digital inputs and outputs is easier than controlling many analog inputs and outputs.

Setting Groups of Pins in Parallel

In Chapter 5, when we discussed variables, we described how variables were like DIP switches, where each bit is represented by a switch. In fact, this is not far from the reality of how the microcontroller manages its inputs and outputs. You may have noticed that the microcontrollers we're using have I/O pins in multiples of 8. These groups of eight pins are called *I/O ports*, and you can use them to manipulate several pins at once, in parallel. The I/O ports are connected to special addresses in the microcontroller's memory called *special function registers*. They're variables that you can use to manipulate many of the I/O pins at once.

For each set of digital I/O pins, there is one special function register that keeps track of the pins' direction—that is, whether the pins are inputs or outputs—and a second register that keeps track of what the actual state of each pin is. If you want to set all the pins of one port at once, for example, you set all the pins to be outputs, then set them high. This technique was used for stepper motors in Chapter 10. For a more illuminating display, try the following example. First, put eight LEDs on the following pins of your microcontroller. Make them normal LEDs, not superbrights, because eight superbrights could consume more than your chip's maximum output.

> BS-2 or Basic Atom Pro24: pins 8 – 15
>
> BX-24: pins 13 – 20
>
> PIC 18F452: pins RB0 – RB7

Next, run the following code:

```
' set pins 8 - 15 to all output:
DIRH = %11111111
Main:
        OUTH = %11111111
        Pause 1000
        OUTH = %10101010
        Pause 1000
        OUTH = %00000000
        Pause 1000
Goto main
```

PBASIC
MBasic

```
' set pins RB0 - RB7 to all output:

TRISB = %00000000
Main:
        PORTB = %11111111
        Pause 1000
        PORTB = %10101010
        Pause 1000
        PORTB = %00000000
        Pause 1000
Goto main
```

PicBasic Pro

```
sub Main()
        ' set pins 13 - 20 to all output:
        register.ddra = bx11111111
        do
                register.porta = bx11111111
                call delay(1.0)
                register.porta = bx10101010
                call delay(1.0)
                register.porta = bx00000000
                call delay(1.0)
        loop
end sub
```

BX-Basic

As you can see, this is a much quicker way to change all the outputs than having to set one pin at a time. You can also read switches on all the pins of a port at once. For this example, put a switch (digital input) on each of the pins you've currently got an LED on, as follows:

> BS-2 or Basic Atom Pro24: pins 8 – 15
>
> BX-24: pins 13 – 20
>
> PIC 18F452: pins RB0 – RB7

Then run this code:

PBASIC

```
' set pins 8 - 15 to all input:
DIRH = %00000000
Main:
     Debug BIN8 INH, 10, 13
Goto main
```

MBasic

```
' set pins 8 - 15 to all input:
DIRH = %00000000
Main:
     ' You'll see 16 digits, representing all 16 I/O pins
     ' when you run this on the Basic Atom Pro24:
     Debug [BIN INH, 10, 13]
Goto main
```

PicBasic Pro

```
' set pins RB0 - RB7 to all input:

TRISB = %11111111
Main:
     Serout2 portc.6, 16468, [BIN8 PORTB, 10, 13]
Goto main
```

BX-Basic

```
sub Main()
     ' set pins 13 - 20 to all input:
     register.ddra = bx11111111
     do
          ' note: the BX-24 has no modifier for debug.print
          ' that allows it to print a number in binary notation,
          ' like the BIN modifier does for the other microcontrollers.
          ' tough luck!
          debug.print cstr(register.pina)
     loop
End sub
```

Because these special function registers work just like variables, you can change the outputs or read the inputs the same way you read and write to variables. For example, any number you put into the output register (OUTH, PORTB, or register.porta depending on your microcontroller) shows up as a binary number on the LEDs. Likewise, if you have several switches connected to the I/O port, every combination of switches shows up as a unique number in the input register. What you're doing is controlling your I/O in parallel. It can save you a few lines of code for examples like these, but it becomes more useful when you see it applied in the examples below.

Setting Groups of Pins in Parallel

Tables 14.1–14.3 list a few more useful register names.

Table 14.1
BS-2, Basic Atom Pro24

PINS	FUNCTION	REGISTER	NOTE
0 – 7	Set as input or output (data direction register)	DIRL	
0 – 7	Set high or low (output register)	OUTL	Set DIRL appropriately first
0 – 7	Read all at once (input register)	INL	Set DIRL appropriately first
8 – 15	Set as input or output (data direction register)	DIRH	
8 – 15	Set high or low (output register)	OUTH	Set DIRH appropriately first
8 – 15	Read all at once (input register)	INH	Set DIRH appropriately first
0 – 15	Set as input or output (data direction register)	DIRS	A word variable; 16 bits
0 – 15	Set high or low (output register)	OUTS	A word variable (16 bits). Set DIRS appropriately first.
0 – 15	Read all at once (input register)	INS	A word variable (16 bits). Set DIRS appropriately first.

Table 14.2
PIC 18F452

PINS	FUNCTION	REGISTER	NOTE
RA0 – RA5	Set as input or output (data direction register)	TRISA	Set register ADCON1 to %10000110 first if using as digital I/O
RA0 – RA5	Set high or low (output register)	PORTA	Set TRISA appropriately first
RA0 – RA5	Read all at once (input register)	PORTA	Set TRISA appropriately first
RB0 – RB7	Set as input or output (data direction register)	TRISB	
RB0 – RB7	Set high or low (output register)	PORTB	Set TRISB appropriately first
RB0 – RB7	Read all at once (input register)	PORTB	Set TRISB appropriately first
RC0 – RC7	Set as input or output (data direction register)	TRISC	
RC0 – RC7	Set high or low (output register)	PORTC	Set TRISC appropriately first
RC0 – RC7	Read all at once (input register)	PORTC	Set TRISC appropriately first
RD0 – RD7	Set as input or output (data direction register)	TRISD	
RD0 – RD7	Set high or low (output register)	PORTC	Set TRISD appropriately first
RD0 – RD7	Read all at once (input register)	PORTC	Set TRISD appropriately first
RE0 – RE2	Set as input or output (data direction register)	TRISE	Set register ADCON1 to %10000110 first if using as digital I/O
RE0 – RE2	Set high or low (output register)	PORTC	Set TRISE appropriately first
RE0 – RE2	Read all at once (input register)	PORTC	Set TRISE appropriately first

Table 14.3
BX-24

PINS	FUNCTION	REGISTER	NOTE
5 – 12	Set as input or output (data direction register)	register.ddrc	
5 – 12	Set high or low (output register)	register.portc	Set register.ddrc appropriately first
5 – 12	Read all at once (input register)	register.pinc	Set register.ddrc appropriately first
13 – 20	Set as input or output (data direction register)	register.ddra	
13 – 20	Set high or low (output register)	register.porta	Set register.ddra appropriately first
13 – 20	Read all at once (input register)	register.pina	Set register.ddra appropriately first

*Note: the BX-24 relationship between pins and bits is a little counterintuitive. Register.portc bit 0 is actually pin 12, bit 1 is pin 11, and so on, until bit 7 is pin 5. Likewise on porta, bit 0 is pin 20, bit 1 is pin 19, and so forth up to bit 7, which is pin 13.

For more on the registers and their names, consult the manual for your processor.

Bitwise Operations

The smallest unit of data storage in your programs is usually a byte. As you've seen above, that byte might be the state of eight pins in an I/O port. Dealing with pins as a group is one time where you need *bitwise notation* in order to look down into a byte at the bits.

Before you get started, it is nice to be able to visualize the bits of the bytes in a binary format using zeros and ones. You can represent a number in binary form in your code in pBasic, MBasic, and PicBasic Pro using the prefix "%"; for example, 255 (decimal) is equal to %11111111 (binary). On the BX-24, the prefix is "bx." The BIN modifier for the debug command outputs a binary representation (there is no simple equivalent on the BX-24).

To address an individual bit in pBasic, MBasic, and PicBasic Pro, you can use dot notation. For example, to turn on pin 6 (the fifth bit of the OUTL register on the BS-2 or the Basic Atom Pro24), you could try:

```
OUTL.BIT5 = 1     ' BS-2 and Basic Atom Pro24
```

Or

```
PORTB.5 = 1   ' PicBasic Pro only
```

If you're using PicBasic Pro, you've already been doing this.

Having all your pins in one byte can also simplify communication. For example, if you wanted to communicate the state of eight switches from your microcontroller to your multimedia computer (a pretty common task), you could replace the debug statements in the input examples above with serout statements. The entire program is only four lines long. The software on your multimedia machine would then need bitwise access to the bytes it receives. If it has no commands for looking at the bits, here's some pseudocode to show you how:

```
Put the incoming byte in a variable called decimal
make an array called bits = [0,0,0,0,0,0,0,0]
make an array called weights = [128,64,32,16,8,4,2,1]
for i = 1 to 8
    weight = weights[i]
    if decimal/weight= 1 then
        bits [i] = 1
        decimal = decimal - weight
    else
        bits [i] = 0
    end if
next
' the bits array now contains the states of
' the 8 bits of the variable decimal
```

Logical or *bitwise operations* compare two values bit by bit and generate a third value from the comparison. The main logical operations are AND, OR, NOT, and XOR (exclusive or). Here's how they work:

▶ AND checks to see if both values are 1, and if so, returns a 1. Otherwise it returns 0.

▶ OR checks to see if either value is 1. If one or the other is, it returns a 1.

▶ NOT reverses the value.

▶ XOR checks to see that the two values are different. If they are, it returns a 1. Otherwise it returns a 0.

These tables will help you keep everything clear. To read them, read the digit in the left column, then the operation, then the head of the next two columns. The number in the row you're considering is the result. For example, in the AND table, row 1: 0 AND 1 gives 0. 0 AND 0 gives 0. In row 2, 1 AND 1 gives 1. 1 AND 0 gives 0. These are called *truth tables*. You'll see this format often when you have a matrix of inputs and outputs to compare for a result.

AND	1	0
0	0	0
1	1	0

OR	1	0
0	1	0
1	1	1

XOR	1	0
0	1	0
1	0	1

When you operate on two multiple-bit numbers, you compare each bit to the one in the same place in the other number, just like in regular math. For example

```
        10110100
AND  01010100
=    00010100
```

Bitwise operations are very handy for looking at a subset of the bits in a byte. For example, if you were looking at an input port, but only cared about the last pin of it, you could do this:

```
inputPort AND 10000000
```

The result of this is either **00000000** if bit 7 of inputPort is 0, and **10000000** if bit 7 is high. Hiding the other bits like this to check one is referred to as *bitmasking*, and the number you use to do it is called the *bitmask* (**10000000** in this case).

The logical operators are indicated by their names in BX basic, but are given symbols in the other Basics, as follows:

OPERATOR	PBASIC, MBASIC, PICBASIC PRO
AND	&
OR	|
NOT	~
XOR	^

It's also useful to be able to shift bits within a byte. You might have this pattern of bits (decimal value 5):

```
00000101
```

but you want this pattern of bits:

```
01010000
```

It would be nice to be able to just shift the first pattern over to the left by four bits. We saw why you might want to do this in the stepper motor example (Chapter 10) and in the synchronous serial example (Chapter 12). You can do this, using the shift operators in pBasic, MBasic, and PicBasic Pro.

```
SomeVar << x
```

shifts a SomeVar to the left x bits, and

```
SomeVar >> x
```

Bitwise Operations

shifts all the bits of SomeVar to the right *x* bits. There is no shift operator in BX-Basic, so you have to multiply by powers of 2. Multiplying by 2 to the power *x* shifts the value *x* bits left, and dividing by 2 to the power *x* shifts the value right *x* bits. You'll see many bitwise operations in the examples below.

Bit shifting and bitmasks are often used in combination when you want to put multiple values into a single variable. In this snippet of code, we store the values of several inputs in a single byte:

```
'just look at the bottom of the byte,
' this will always be a number between 0-16 (4 bits):
Value1 = inputPort AND 00001111

'just look at the top of the byte but not the bottom:
Value2 = inputPort AND 11110000

'the bits are in the top four positions of the byte.
' shift them down reduce it to a number between 0-16:
Value2 >> 4
```

Running Out of Pins

If you do enough physical computing, you will probably run out of pins on your microcontroller at some point. Often the simplest way to get multiple inputs or outputs is to combine several microcontrollers in a larger network of input and output. Increasingly, large-scale electronic displays and input arrays are using this method. Individual microcontrollers have gotten cheap enough that it can be as cost effective to put several PICs or their equivalent into a project as it is to spend time configuring and managing complex circuits like the ones we'll show below. This may not be cost-effective if you're using the mid-level microcontrollers, but as you migrate to the cheaper ones, it becomes easier to think about each as a building block in a larger whole, rather than the center of your physical computing universe. Throwing more microcontrollers at the problem also requires that you develop your own communication protocol and programming for all the chips. Below we will introduce some other techniques for getting more inputs and outputs from a single microcontroller.

Resistor Ladders as Analog Input

The cheapest trick in the book for reading many switches on a single pin is to use a single analog input. Each switch is connected from 5 volts to the analog input through a series of resistors. The first switch is connected through one resistor, the second through two, the third through three, and so forth. Figure 14.1 shows the schematic. You will get a different reading with an analog input for each button. This trick is called a *resistor ladder* because each switch is one rung higher on the ladder than the others. It will only work if you are sure only one switch at a time will be pressed. It's a variation on multiplexing, which we'll get to later in the chapter. When more than one switch is pressed, only the highest switch up the chain would register. You can buy resistor ladders as discrete components that are wired much like this schematic, for convenience. All you add is the switches.

NOTE

The examples in this chapter all involve multiples, and multiples mean lots of wire. That means a breadboard that you can't make sense of in a photo. So we'll only use schematics in this chapter to make things more comprehensible. To simplify your actual wiring, always be on the lookout for many wires that run back to the same place on your breadboard. For example, if you had 16 switches you might run 32 wires back to your breadboard, two from each switch. One side of every switch is running back to +5 volts, though, so you can reduce the number of wires by running one +5V wire out of the breadboard and have it hop from one switch to the next.

Figure 14.1

A resistor ladder and eight DIP switches as analog input.

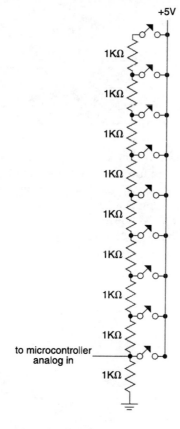

Row-Column Scanning

Controlling the I/O pins in parallel using registers makes your code neater and programs faster, but it doesn't get you any extra inputs or outputs. *Row-column scanning* is a simple method for increasing the number of digital inputs or outputs you can control from one microcontroller without adding any additional hardware. It relies on arranging (at least conceptually) the inputs or outputs in rows and columns. For example, let's say you're building a dance floor with switches underneath that trigger lighting effects. You want 16 switches, but you've only got eight I/O pins to work with. Imagine the switches are arranged in a grid, like the one in Figure 14.2.

Figure 14.2
A row-column arrangement of switches.

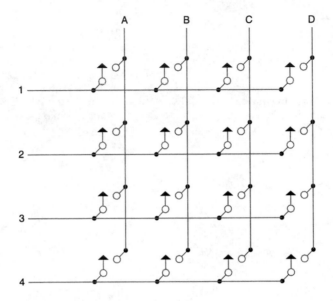

Each switch connects one column to one row. All the switches in one column are electrically in parallel with the others in that column, and all the switches in one row are electrically in parallel with the others in that row. If there's voltage on any column, and a switch on that column is closed, then the row that the switch is connected to will receive the voltage. This means that, by changing which column has voltage and by scanning over the rows for each column, you can read the state of all 16 switches. The advantage of this method is that for every $2x$ pins you need, you can read x^2 switches: eight pins gives 16 inputs, 16 pins gives 64 switches, and so forth.

To do it, you'd attach the columns to output pins, and the rows to input pins, and read them like this:

```
set up an array of 16 positions
loop:
loop from column 1 to column 4
        take this column high
        loop from row 1 to row 4
            if this row is high then
                This switch is closed.
                Put a 1 in this position in the array.
            End if
        End row loop
        Take this column low
    End column loop
```

```
          The array now contains the state of all 16 switches.
          Act on the data in the array.
    end loop
```

At the end of each main loop, you know the state of all 16 switches. To see this in action, connect 16 switches as follows:

BS-2 or Basic Atom Pro24: rows, pins 0 – 3; columns, pins 8 – 11

BX-24: columns, pins 5 – 8; rows, pins 13 - 16

PIC 18F452: columns, pins RC0 – RC3; rows, pins RB0 – RB3

Figure 14.3
A row-column
arrangement of
switches with
pulldown resistors and
diodes to control back
voltage.

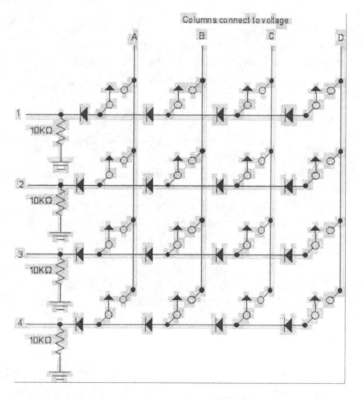

Note that the input pins of your microcontroller (the rows) need pulldown resistors, just like they do with a normal switch. The diodes going from each switch to ground prevent the circuit from giving false readings if more than one switch is pressed.

Wiring your rows and columns is always confusing. We find it easiest to make a chart of which pins are the rows and which are the columns, and then wire one switch at a time to the appropriate row or column.

The following code checks all the rows and columns and stores the states of the switches in an array. At the end of each cycle, you have the states of all the switches.

Row-Column Scanning

PBASIC

```
' set pins 0 - 3 to input:
DIRL = %11110000
' set pins 8 - 11 to output:
DIRH = %00001111
' set up constants to use in the code:
numRows con 4          ' total number of rows
numCols con 4      ' total number of columns
colOffset con 8   ' first pin number of the columns
' set up variables:
rows var byte      ' the row counter
cols var byte      ' the column counter
switchArray var bit(16)    ' the array of switch states
thisSwitch var byte    ' the switch we're dealing with
bitmask var byte ' used to look at one bit at a time

main:
    ' loop over the columns, turning one on at a time:
    for cols = 0 to 3
        ' set this column high to check the switches in it:
        high (cols + colOffset)
        ' loop over the rows, reading one switch at a time:
        for rows = 0 to 3
            ' calculate this switch's position in the array:
            thisSwitch = (cols * numCols) + rows
            ' isolate this switch in input port register:
            bitmask = 1 << rows
            ' if this switch is high,
            ' then set the bit in the array high too:
            if INL & bitmask = bitmask then
                switchArray(thisswitch) = 1
            else
                switchArray(thisSwitch) = 0
            endif
            ' print out the switch state:
            debug DEC switchArray(thisSwitch)
        next
        ' set this column low to prep for the next column loop:
        low (cols + colOffset)
    next
    debug 10, 13, "end of loop", 10, 13
goto main
```

MBasic

```
' set pins 0 - 3 to input:
DIRL = %11110000
```

```
' set pins 8 - 11 to output:
DIRH = %11111111
' set up constants to use in the code:
numRows con 4        ' total number of rows
numCols con 4      ' total number of columns
colOffset con 8  ' first pin number of the columns
' set up variables:
rows var byte      ' the row counter
cols var byte      ' the column counter
switchArray var bit(16)    ' the array of switch states
thisSwitch var byte    ' the switch we're dealing with
bitmask var byte ' used to look at one bit at a time
i var byte         ' loop counter

main:
    ' loop over the columns, turning one on at a time:
    for cols = 0 to 3
        ' set this column high to check the switches in it:
        high (cols + colOffset)
        ' loop over the rows, reading one switch at a time:
        for rows = 0 to 3
            ' calculate this switch's position in the array:
            thisSwitch = (cols * numCols) + rows
            ' isolate this switch in input port register:
            ' (shift functions don't work in mBasic,
            ' so we wrote our own here):
            bitmask = 1
            for i = 1 to rows
                bitmask = bitmask * 2
            next

            ' if this switch is high,
            ' then set the bit in the array high too:
            if (INA & bitmask) = bitmask then
                switchArray(thisswitch) = 1
            else
                switchArray(thisSwitch) = 0
            endif
            ' print out the switch state:
            debug [DEC switchArray(thisSwitch)]
        next
        ' set this column low to prep for the next column loop:
        low (cols + colOffset)
    next
    debug [10, 13, "end of loop", 10, 13]
goto main
```

PicBasic
Pro

```
' set pins RB0 - RB3 to input:
TRISB = %00001111
' set pins RC0 - RC3 to output (and RC6 to output for serial out):
TRISC = %10110000
' set up constants to use in the code:
numRows con 4        ' total number of rows
numCols con 4       ' total number of columns
colOffset con 0    ' first column pin in column port
' set up variables:
rows var byte      ' the row counter
cols var byte       ' the column counter
switchArray var bit(16)   ' the array of switch states
thisSwitch var byte    ' the switch we're dealing with
bitmask var byte ' used to look at one bit at a time

main:
    ' loop over the columns, turning one on at a time:
    for cols = 0 to 3
        ' set this column high to check the switches in it:
        PORTC = 1 << cols
        ' loop over the rows, reading one switch at a time:
        for rows = 0 to 3
            ' calculate this switch's position in the array:
            thisSwitch = (cols * numCols) + rows
            ' isolate this switch in input port register:
            bitmask = 1 << rows
            ' if this switch is high,
            ' then set the bit in the array high too:
            if (PORTB & bitmask) = bitmask then
                switchArray(thisswitch) = 1
            else
                switchArray(thisSwitch) = 0
            endif
            ' print out the switch state:
            serout2 portc.6, 16468, [DEC switchArray(thisSwitch)]
        next
        ' set this column low to prep for the next column loop:
        PORTC = 0
    next
    serout2 portc.6, 16468, [10, 13, "end of loop", 10, 13]
    pause 750
goto main
```

(BX-Basic)

```
' set up constants to use in the code:
const numRows as byte = 4     ' total number of rows
const numCols as byte = 4     ' total number of columns
const colOffset as byte = 13  ' first column pin
const rowOffset as byte = 5   ' first row pin
' set up variables:
dim switchArray(1 to 16) as byte    ' the array of switch states
dim thisSwitch as byte    ' the switch we're dealing with

Sub main()
    ' counters must be local variables in BX basic:
    dim rows as byte      ' the row counter
    dim cols as byte      ' the column counter
    do
        ' loop over the columns, turning one on at a time:
        for cols = 0 to 3
            ' set this column high to check the switches in it:
            call putPin(cols + colOffset, 1)
            ' loop over the rows, reading one switch at a time:
            for rows = 0 to 3
                ' calculate this switch's position in the array:
                thisSwitch = (cols * numCols) + rows
                ' if this switch is high,
                ' then set the bit in the array high too
                ' (simplified by BX-basic's getPin() function):
                if getPin(rows + rowOffset) = 1 then
                    switchArray(thisswitch) = 1
                else
                    switchArray(thisSwitch) = 0
                end if
                ' print out the switch state:
                debug print cstr(switchArray(thisSwitch));
            next
            ' set this column low to prep for the next column loop:
            call putPin(cols + colOffset, 0)
        next
        debug.print chr(10); chr(13); "end of loop"
    loop
end sub
```

Row-Column Scanning

Row–Column Scanning Analog Inputs

Row–column scanning can be used for analog input as well, to a limited extent. In order to do this, you'd replace the switches with analog input circuits with either potentiometers or variable resistors arranged as a voltage divider. You'd then use pseudocode like the following:

```
set up an array of 16 positions
loop:
    loop from column 1 to column 4
        take this column high
        loop from row 1 to row 4
            read analog in on this row
            store it in the array
        End row loop
        Take this column low
    End column loop
    The array now contains the state of all 16 analog inputs.
    Act on the data in the array.
end loop
```

This will only work for as many analog inputs as your microcontroller has, but that means that with eight analog input pins, you can read up to 64 analog inputs. It will be somewhat slower than the digital row–column input because each ADC reading takes a few microseconds or milliseconds.

Row–Column Scanning Outputs

Row–column scanning also works well for output control. In this case, you replace the switches with output devices. If you simply want LED control, an LED on each output will do. If you want to control something that uses more amperage than an LED, you'll need the base of an NPN transistor on each row-column junction. Figure 14.4 shows a typical arrangement of row–column scanned LEDs.

Figure 14.4
A row–column
arrangement of LEDs.

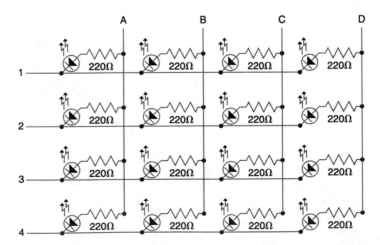

The pseudocode for controlling LEDs is slightly different than for reading inputs. In order to turn on the LED, you need to create a voltage difference across the LED, with the high end on the anode side. This means that if both sides of the LED are high, or if both sides are low, the LED is off. The same principle applies to a transistor in that a voltage difference between the base and the emitter is what causes it to turn on. Here's the pseudocode:

```
set up an array of 16 positions
Store the intended states of the LEDs in the array
loop:
    loop from column 1 to column 4
        take this column high
        take all the rows high
        loop from row 1 to row 4
            Read the LED's intended state from the array
            If this LED should be on, take this row low
        End row loop
        Take this column low
    End column loop
end loop
```

If the loop is running fast enough, the LEDs will appear to be on constantly because they're turning on and off faster than your eye can perceive the difference. This is the principle behind most digital displays, from LEDs to LCDs to plasma screens. This is also why you can perceive a slight flickering of the LEDs when you shake your head fast from side to side while looking at a digital LED display.

Analog control using row-column scanning is more tricky because the pulsewidth modulation necessary to create a pseudo-analog voltage takes time, and as a result you get a more flickery display. To make this happen using the example above, you pulsewidth modulate each row in the inner loop using the inverse of the analog value you want. For example, if your dimming range goes from 0 to 255, and you want to dim your LED to 100, then you pulse the row at 155. Remember, this means it's high for 155 of 255 counts and low for 100 counts. The row must be low in order to turn the LED on, so the LED will be on for 100 of 255 counts.

Shift Registers

There are other methods of controlling multiple inputs and outputs, if you're willing to add an extra IC or two. The *shift register* can take a serial stream from a single pin and create a parallel output to many pins. In the other direction, it can take many parallel inputs and place them in a serial stream that can be input on a single pin.

Shift registers work like a bucket brigade. A typical shift register has eight positions, lined up in a row. Data is pushed into or pulled out of first position and passed on from there. When the first position receives a new bit, it first shifts the bit that it's holding to the second position, then takes the new bit. The second position shifts to the third position, then takes from the first, and so on. Figure 14.5 illustrates how bits move through a shift register.

Figure 14.5
How a shift register
works.

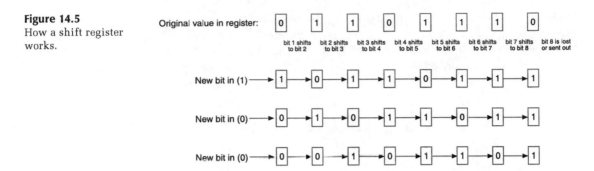

There are two basic types of shift registers: serial in, parallel out; and serial out, parallel in. The former are used for controlling multiple outputs, and the latter are used for reading multiple inputs. Both are asynchronous serial devices like the digital potentiometer discussed in Chapter 12. The shiftin and shiftout commands discussed in that chapter are used with shift registers as well. They operate by shifting bits every time they receive a clock pulse from a master device. The direction of the bits depends on the type of register. Serial in, parallel out shift registers receive bits from a serial input each clock pulse, then shift them to a set of output pins so that the bits can affect the pins all at once, in parallel. Parallel in, serial out shift registers read their inputs in parallel each time the clock is pulsed, then shift the values down the line to a serial output.

Both types of shift register usually have a pin that tells them to move data to or from an internal register to the I/O pins. It's called something different from one brand of shift register to the next. In some cases it's called a *latch*, or a *strobe*. Unlike other synchronous serial devices, they don't always have a chip select pin. To make a shift register ignore data, you turn the strobe or latch off. Many shift registers will also have an extra output pin so that they can send bits to another register. In this way, several shift registers can be cascaded to make one very large shift register. Shift registers come in a variety of sizes as well (in multiples of 8). Though 8-bit shift registers are the most common, you can get 16-bit, 32-bit, and more.

The process of using a serial in, parallel out shift register goes like this:

```
set up an array of 8 positions
Store the intended states of the outputs in the array
loop:
    take the strobe pin low to prepare for new data
    shift 8 bits out to the register
    take the strobe pin high to move the bits to the output pins
end loop
```

The example below uses a UCN5841 serial in, parallel out shift register from Allegro Micro to control eight LEDs. This is a useful shift register because it can handle higher voltages and currents, so it's good for controlling motors directly as well. It's generally used as a current sink rather than a current source (see the sidebar "Sources, Sinks, and Buffers"), which is why the LEDs attached to it are connected to +5 volts instead of to ground. Think of it a bit like the transistor example in Chapter 6; the LEDs are the load, the shift register acts as the transistor, and the emitter voltage pin on the shift register is the emitter pin, going to ground. Figure 14.6 shows the schematic.

Figure 14.6
A UCN5841 shift register controlling eight LEDs.

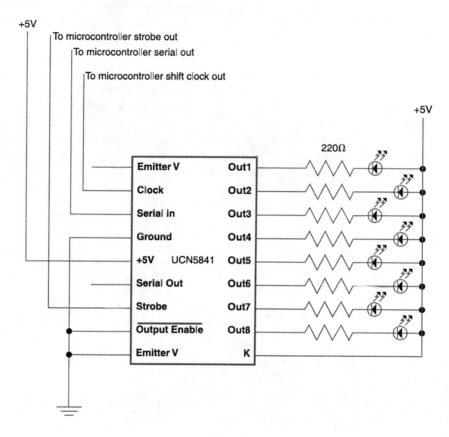

If you were controlling devices that operated on voltages other than +5 volts with this shift register, you'd change the input voltage to the devices, and in some cases, the emitter voltage as well. If you wanted to control 16 outputs on the same line, you'd connect the serial out pin to the serial in of a second shift register and the clock and strobe lines to the microcontroller, in parallel with the current shift register. Then you'd shift out 16 bits instead of eight.

The following code counts from 0 to 255 in binary on the shift register:

PBASIC

MBasic

```
' Serial in pin of shift register is connected to pin 6
' clock pin of shift register is connected to pin 7
' strobe pin of shift register is connected to pin 4

serialPin con 6
clockPin con 7
strobePin con 4
```

Shift Registers

```
        outByte var byte

    main:
        ' disconnect the output pins from the internal register:
        low strobePin
        ' set the clock pin low so it pulses high properly:
        low clockPin
        ' shift out 8 bits to control all the pins:
        shiftout serialPin, clockPin, MSBFIRST, [outByte\8]
        ' connect the output pins to the internal register:
        high strobePin
        ' add 1 to the data to be shifted next loop:
        outByte = outByte + 1
        ' hold long enough to see the result:
        pause 100
    goto main
```

PicBasic
Pro

```
    ' Serial in pin of shift register is connected to RC3
    ' clock pin of shift register is connected to pin RC2
    ' strobe pin of shift register is connected to pin RC1

    include "modedefs.bas"

    serialPin var PORTC.3
    clockPin var PORTC.2
    strobePin var PORTC.1
    outByte var byte

    main:
        ' disconnect the output pins from the internal register:
        low strobePin
        ' set the clock pin low so it pulses high properly:
        low clockPin
        ' shift out 8 bits to control all the pins:
        shiftout serialPin, clockPin, MSBFIRST, [outByte\8]
        ' connect the output pins to the internal register:
        high strobePin
        ' add one to the data to be shifted next loop:
        outByte = outByte + 1
        ' hold long enough to see the result:
        pause 100
    goto main
```

BX-Basic

```
    ' Serial in pin of shift register is connected to 11
    ' clock pin of shift register is connected to pin 12
```

```
' strobe pin of shift register is connected to pin 10

const serialPin as byte = 11
const clockPin as byte = 12
const strobePin as byte = 10
dim outByte as byte

sub main()
    do
        ' disconnect the output pins from the internal register:
        call putPin(strobePin, 0)
        ' set the clock pin low so it pulses high properly:
        call putPin(clockPin, 0)
        ' shift out 8 bits to control all the pins:
        call shiftOut(serialPin , clockPin , 8, outByte)
        ' connect the output pins to the internal register:
        call putPin(strobePin, 1)
        ' add 1 to the data to be shifted next loop:
        outByte = outByte + 1
        ' hold long enough to see the result:
        call delay(0.1)
    loop
end sub
```

Parallel in, serial out shift registers are useful for reading large numbers of switches. They work in the opposite direction as serial in, parallel out registers. They read a number of parallel inputs into a register, then shift the contents of that register out serially on a clock pulse. Like the parallel out registers, they usually have a strobe or latch pin that connects the inputs to the registers and a clock pin to shift the data out serially. Most of them can be daisy chained as well, using a separate serial in pin. The general control sequence goes like this:

```
set up an array of 8 positions
loop:
    take the strobe pin high to move bits from the inputs to the register
    take the strobe pin low to prepare to get the bits
    shift 8 bits in from the register
end loop
```

The example below uses a CD4021 8-bit parallel in, serial out shift register to read eight switches. Figure 14.7 shows the schematic. The CD4021 is similar to the 5841. It has a clock pin, a serial out pin, and eight parallel in pins, all equivalent to the 5841's clock, serial in, and parallel outs. It's got a latch pin (called a *serial/parallel control* in the datasheet) that moves the states of the switches into the shift register. To read the inputs, you take the latch pin high to load their states into the register, then low so that you can shift the data out the serial out pin. It also has a serial in pin, equivalent to the 5841's serial out pin, so that it can be daisy-chained to other CD4021s. If you wanted to read 16 switches, for example, you'd connect the serial in of the first register to the serial out of the second, and the clock and latch lines to the microcontroller, in parallel with the current shift register. Then you'd shift in 16 bits instead of 8.

The CD4021 shifts its data out before the clock, meaning that the state of the first switch is on the serial out line before you pulse the clock. For PBASIC, MBasic, and PicBasic Pro, this is not a problem, because their shiftin commands can read the serial line before or after the clock pulses. However, the BX-24 has no such option, so in the example below, you pulse the clock and read the bits manually rather than by using the shiftin() command.

Figure 14.7
A CD4021 shift register reading eight switches.

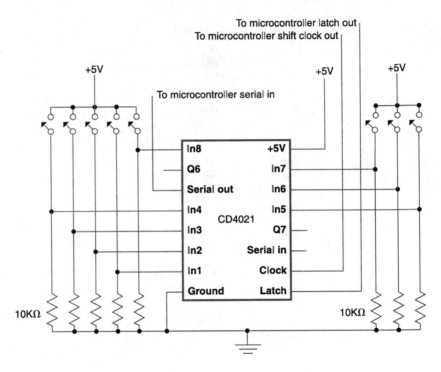

```
' serial data pin from shift register is on pin 5
' clock pin is on pin 6
' shift register latch pin is on pin 7
serialPin con 5
clockPin con 6
latchPin con 7

switchStates var byte

main:
        ' take the clock pin low to get ready to shift data:
        low clockPin
        ' pulse the latch pin to move the switch states into
        high latchPin
        pause 1
```

PBASIC

MBasic

```
          low latchPin
          ' shift the data into the microcontroller:
          shiftin serialPin, clockPin, MSBPRE, [switchStates\8]
          ' print out the states of the switches:
          ' note: for mBasic, put [] around the contents of the debug
          debug BIN switchStates, 10, 13
      goto main
```

PicBasic Pro

```
' serial data pin from shift register is on pin RB0
' clock pin is on pin RB1
' shift register latch pin is on pin RB2
INCLUDE "modedefs.bas"

serialPin var PORTB.0
clockPin VAR PORTB.1
latchPin VAR PORTB.2

switchStates var byte

main:
    ' take the clock pin low to get ready to shift data:
    low clockPin
    ' pulse the latch pin to move the switch states into
    high latchPin
    pause 1
    low latchPin
    ' shift the data into the microcontroller:
    shiftin serialPin, clockPin, MSBPRE, [switchStates\8]
    ' print out the states of the switches:
    serout2 portc.6, 16468, [BIN8 switchStates, 13,10]
goto main
```

BX-Basic

```
' serial data pin from shift register is on pin 10
' clock pin is on pin 11
' shift register latch pin is on pin 12

const serialPin as byte = 10
const clockPin as byte = 11
const latchPin as byte = 12

dim switchStates as byte

sub main()
    dim thisbit as byte
```

```
        do
            ' take the clock pin low to get ready to shift data:
            call putPin(clockPin, 0)
            ' pulse the latch pin to move the switch states into
            ' the shift register:
            call putPin(latchPin, 1)
            call delay(0.001)
            call putPin(latchPin,0)
            ' shift the data into the microcontroller:
            for thisBit = 0 to 7
                call putPin(clockPin,0)
                call delay(0.0001)
                call putBit(switchStates, thisBit, getPin(serialPin))
                call putPin(clockPin, 1)
            next     ' print out the states of the switches:
            for thisbit = 0 to 7
                debug.print cstr(getBit(switchStates, thisbit));
            next
            debug.print " "
        loop
    end sub
```

The shift registers shown here are only two of the many different ones on the market. While we find these ones handy for some applications, it's useful to know about others as well. For example, the 74F675A is a 16-bit serial in, parallel out shift register that you can find from many online retailers. Its cousin, the 74F676 is a 16-bit parallel in, serial out shift register. The 74ALS164A is an 8-bit parallel out, serial in shift register, and its cousin the 74ALS165 is an 8-bit parallel in, serial out shift register. The details of operating these chips will differ slightly from the examples here, but the general principles will be the same. Knowing a few different ones will make life easier when you can't get exactly the one you want.

Multiplexers

Shift registers are great for digital input and output, but they don't allow you to manage analog output. Multiplexers are useful for this because they can handle both digital and analog input and output. A *multiplexer* has several inputs and one output (or several outputs and one input). Any of the inputs can be routed to the output, one at a time. A multiplexer also has a series of address pins that set which input is routed to the output. Multiplexers come with banks of eight inputs. You can get 8-channel multiplexers, 16-channel multiplexers, and so forth.

To select the channel you want to route to the output of a multiplexer, you use address pins. The address of the channel you want to use is put on the pins as a binary number, as you've seen above. The channel selected and the output are then connected. Most

SOURCES, SINKS, AND BUFFERS

When you're working with external ICs of many types, you'll hear the terms "source" and "sink" frequently. A *current source* is a device that's supplying current for another device. For example, when you light an LED by connecting the LED's anode to one of your microcontroller's output pins and the cathode to ground, the pin is a source when you take the pin high. This is the way you've been building your output circuits because it's clear how the chip is turning on the LED. When you connect the LED's anode to voltage and the cathode to the microcontroller's output pin, the pin acts as a sink when you take it low. The pin is giving the current that's passing through the LED somewhere to go, like ground does in most of our circuits. Many driver devices can sink more current than they can source, so it's actually more common to connect the thing you're driving to a big current source and use the driver IC as a sink. In Chapter 6, we used a darlington transistor as a current sink for a motor. The UCN5841 above is a good example too. When you start shopping for shift registers, multiplexers, and other devices to drive I/O, it's useful to know whether the device is intended to be used as a *source driver*, meaning that it supplies the current, or a *sink driver*, meaning that it takes the current.

It's also useful to know about buffers. A *buffer* is basically a transistor or a collection of transistors. Buffers take input from a device and use it to turn on or off a different current. Buffers are useful when the device you're using can't source enough current to control another device, or when the current needs to be changed in some simple way. You've seen some buffers so far in this book. The 2004 darlington array in Chapter 10 used to drive a stepper motor is a buffer. The 7404 hex inverter used to invert serial signals is an *inverting buffer*. Many circuits you'll find on the Web and in other books will include buffers as a safety measure. If you ever find that your microcontroller can't send a strong enough signal to drive an external device, or if you're worried that the external device might damage your microcontroller with back voltage, put a buffer in between them.

multiplexers are bi-directional, meaning that electrical signals can pass from the input to the output or from the output to the input. This is handy, since it means you can use the same multiplexer to control inputs or outputs. The signals passed can be digital or analog.

Unlike shift registers, multiplexers can route to only one channel at a time. This means that when a multiplexer is being used as an output, no two pins can be on at the same time. Because of this, they're more often used to control input than to control output.

The example below uses a CD4067 16-bit multiplexer to read 16 analog inputs. This could be useful if you wanted to make the dance floor example from the row-column section above able to sense how hard people stomp on the floor. Figure 14.8 shows the schematic.

Figure 14.8
A CD4067 multiplexer reading 16 analog inputs. For the BS-2, you will need to use the R-C analog circuit instead of the potentiometer shown here. If you're not using all the input pins, attach the unused ones to ground with a 10-kilohm resistor.

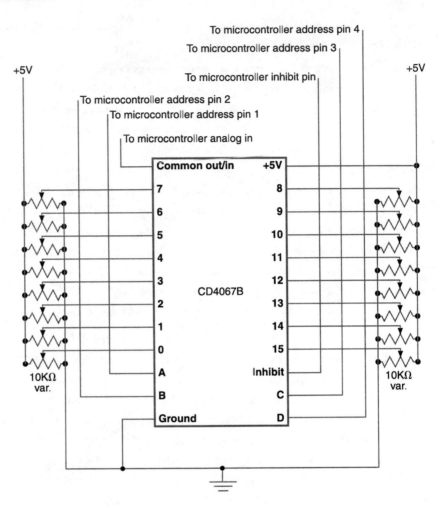

The general sequence goes like this:

```
set up an array of 16 positions
loop 16 times:
    take the inhibit pin high to turn off inputs
    set the address pins to the number of the loop we're on
    take the inhibit pin low to turn on input
    read the input into this position in the array
end loop
```

Here's the actual code:

PBASIC

```
' input pin is pin 7
' inhibit pin is pin 6
' channel pins A, B, C, D are pins 0, 1, 2, 3, respectively
```

```
        inhibitPin con 6
        inputPin con 7


        channelVar var byte
        inputVal var word(12)  ' note: the BS-2 does not have enough memory
                       ' for 16 word variables.


        'set pins 0 - 6 as output, 7 as input
        DIRL = %01111111

        main:
            for channelVar = 0 to 11
                ' Turn off inputs:
                high inhibitPin
                ' set the address you want to read:
                OUTL = channelVar
                ' turn on inputs:
                low inhibitPin
                ' read input into the array:
                high inputPin
                Pause 1
                Rctime inputPin, 1, inputVal(channelVar)

                ' print it out:
                debug "ch: ", DEC channelVar, 9, DEC inputVal(channelVar),10,13
            next
            debug 10, 13, "end of sequence", 10, 13
            pause 1000
        goto main
```

(MBasic)

```
        ' input pin is pin 0
        ' inhibit pin is pin 7
        ' channel pins A, B, C, D are pins 8, 9, 10, 11, respectively
        inhibitPin con 7
        inputPin con 0

        channelVar var byte
        inputVal var word(16)

        'set pins 8 - 11 as output
        DIRH = %00001111


        main:
            for channelVar = 0 to 16
                ' Turn off inputs:
                high inhibitPin
```

Multiplexers

```
                ' set the address you want to read:
                OUTH = channelVar
                ' turn on inputs:
                low inhibitPin
                ' read input into the array:
                ADin 0, inputVal(channelVar)

                ' print it out:
                debug ["ch: ", DEC channelVar, 9, DEC inputVal(channelVar),10,13]
            next
            debug [10, 13, "end of sequence", 10, 13]
            pause 1000
        goto main
```

PicBasic
Pro

```
    ' input pin is pin RA0
    ' inhibit pin is RD1
    ' channel pins A, B, C, D are RC0, RC1, RC2, RC3, respectively
    inhibitPin var PORTD.1
    inputPin con 0

    ' Define ADCIN parameters
    DEFINE ADC_BITS 10          ' Set number of bits in result
    DEFINE ADC_CLOCK 3     ' Set clock source (3=rc)
    DEFINE ADC_SAMPLEUS 20     ' Set sampling time in uS
    TRISA = %11111111     ' Set PORTA to all input
    ADCON1 = %10000010     ' Set PORTA analog and right justify result
    TRISC = %10110000     ' SET RC0 - RC3 and RC6 to output

    channelVar var byte          ' channel number counter:
    inputVal var word(16) ' array to hold values

    main:
        for channelVar = 0 to 15
            ' Turn off inputs:
            high inhibitPin
            ' set the address you want to read:
            PORTC = channelVar
            ' turn on inputs:
            low inhibitPin
            ' read input into the array:
            ADCin inputPin, inputVal(channelVar)

            ' print it out:
            serout2 PORTC.6, 16468, ["ch: ", DEC channelVar, 9]
            serout2 PORTC.6, 16468, [DEC inputVal(channelVar),10,13]
        next
```

```
          serout2 PORTC.6, 16468, [10, 13, "end of sequence", 10, 13]
          pause 1000
      goto main
```

BX-Basic
```
' input pin is pin 20
' inhibit pin is pin 12
' channel pins A, B, C, D are on pins 13, 14, 15, 16, respectively
const inhibitPin as byte = 12
const inputPin as byte = 20

' array for holding readings:
dim inputVal(1 to 16) as integer

Sub main()
    ' set pin 17 -20 as input, all others of porta as output:
    Register.ddra = bx11110000
    Dim channelVar as byte
    do
        for channelVar = 0 to 15
            ' Turn off inputs:
            call putPin(inhibitPin, 1)
            ' set the address you want to read:
            register.porta = flipbits(channelVar)
            ' turn on inputs:
            call putPin(inhibitPin, 0)
            ' read input into the array:
            inputVal(channelVar) = getADC(inputPin)

            ' print it out:
            debug.print "ch: "; cstr(channelVar); " = ";
            debug.print cstr(inputVal(channelVar))
        next
        call delay(0.5)
        debug.print "end of sequence"
    loop
end sub
```

Latches

Latches

Addressable latches are very useful for managing multiple outputs. They are like one-way multiplexers in that they have a single input that is routed to one of several outputs by setting a series of address pins. However, latches have an additional feature: once an output pin's level is set, it can be kept at that level so that the address pins can be changed to address another pin. This means that you can have several, or all, of the pins of a latch on at the same time. This makes them similar to shift registers as well, but you don't have to send out the data for all the pins in order to set only one.

Using a latch is very similar to using a multiplexer. First you set the inhibit or write disable pin to disconnect the input from the outputs. Then you set the address pins. Then you turn off the write disable pin to reconnect the input to the desired output. The previously addressed output will hold its value until it's addressed again. You also need to hold the clear pin on the latch low in order to enable the pins to latch.

Latches can also be used as demultiplexers. When you take the clear pin on a latch high, only one output pin at a time will be enabled. In this mode, you to set an address on the input pins, and only the output pin corresponding to that number will go high. This is useful when you have a large number of synchronous serial chips all sharing the same serial data line from your microcontroller, and you need to switch their chip select pins to control who should be listening at any time. With an 8-bit latch, you can control the chip select pins for eight chips with only four pins from your microcontroller. The example below demonstrates both latching and demultiplexing with the same latch.

Here's the sequence for addressing all eight pins of a latch:

```
loop 8 times:
        take the write disable pin high to turn off outputs
        set the address pins to the number of the loop we're on
        set the input pin to the state for this output pin
        take the write disable pin low to turn on outputs
    end loop
```

Figure 14.9 shows the schematic of the latch.

Figure 14.9
An 8-bit addressable
latch controlling eight
LEDs.

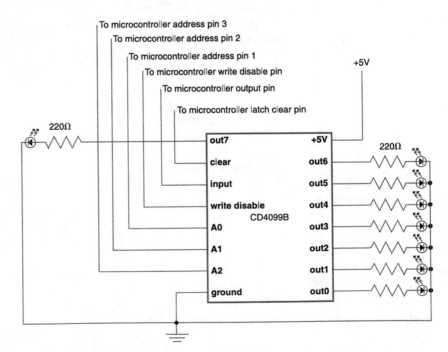

The following code controls eight LEDs from a single latch. It loops eight times, setting each output high, then loops another eight times, with the clear pin activated. In the second loop, only one LED will be on at a time.

PBASIC

MBasic

```
' the latch's input pin is connected to pin 7.
' the latch's write disable pin is attached to pin 6.
' the latch's clear pin is attached to pin 5.
' the latch's address pins are connected to pins 8 - 10.
clearPin con 5
writeDisablePin con 6
outputPin con 7

channelVar var byte
' set all pins 8 - 10 to output:
DIRH = %00000111

main:
    ' enable latching by turning off the clear pin:
    low clearPin
    ' loop over the channels, lighting each one:
    for channelVar = 0 to 7
        ' disable the outputs:
        high writeDisablePin
        ' set the address:
        OUTH = channelVar
        ' set the desired state:
        high outputPin
        ' enable the output:
        low writeDisablePin
        pause 500
    next

    ' disable latching by turning on the clear pin:
    high clearPin
    ' loop over the channels, lighting each one:
    for channelVar = 0 to 7
        ' disable the outputs:
        high writeDisablePin
        ' set the address:
        OUTH = channelVar
        ' set the desired state:
        high outputPin
        ' enable the output:
        low writeDisablePin
        pause 500
    next
goto main
```

Latches

PicBasic
Pro

```
' the latch's input pin is connected to pin RB0.
' the latch's write disable pin is attached to pin RB1.
' the latch's clear pin is attached to pin RB2.
' the latch's address pins are connected to pins RC0 - RC2.
clearPin var PORTB.2
writeDisablePin var PORTB.1
outputPin var PORTB.0

channelVar var byte
' set all pins RC0 to RC2 and RC6 to output:
TRISC = %10111000

main:
    ' enable latching by turning off the clear pin:
    low clearPin
    ' loop over the channels, lighting each one:
    for channelVar = 0 to 7
        ' disable the outputs:
        high writeDisablePin
        ' set the address:
        PORTC = channelVar
        ' set the desired state:
        high outputPin
        ' enable the output:
        low writeDisablePin
        pause 500
    next

    ' disable latching by turning on the clear pin:
    high clearPin
    ' loop over the channels, lighting each one:
    for channelVar = 0 to 7
        ' disable the outputs:
        high writeDisablePin
        ' set the address:
        PORTC = channelVar
        ' set the desired state:
        high outputPin
        ' enable the output:
        low writeDisablePin
        pause 500
    next
goto main
```

BX-Basic

```
' the latch's input pin is connected to pin 12.
' the latch's write disable pin is attached to pin 11.
' the latch's clear pin is attached to pin 10.
' the latch's address pins are connected to pins RC0 - RC2.
const clearPin as byte = 10
const writeDisablePin as byte = 11
const outputPin as byte = 12


Sub main()
Dim channelVar as byte

' set all pins 13 to 15 to output:
register.ddra = bx11100000

do
    ' enable latching by turning off the clear pin:
    call putPin(clearPin, 0)
    ' loop over the channels, lighting each one:
    for channelVar = 0 to 7
        ' disable the outputs:
        call putPin(writeDisablePin, 1)
        ' set the address:
        register.porta = flipBits(channelVar)
        ' set the desired state:
        call putPin(outputPin, 1)
        ' enable the output:
        call putPin(writeDisablePin, 0)
        call delay(0.5)
    next

    ' disable latching by turning on the clear pin:
    call putPin(clearPin, 1)
    ' loop over the channels, lighting each one:
    for channelVar = 0 to 7
        ' disable the outputs:
        call putPin(writeDisablePin, 1)
        ' set the address:
        register.porta = flipBits(channelVar)
        ' set the desired state:
        call putPin(outputPin, 1)
        ' enable the output:
        call putPin(writeDisablePin, 0)
        call delay(0.5)
    next
loop
end sub
```

Latches

Conclusion

This chapter has presented only a few of the ways to control multiple inputs and outputs. Nevertheless, if you use the methods presented here as building blocks, combining them with each other as needed, you'll find you can probably control more inputs and outputs than your pocketbook or your attention span can bear.

A
Choosing a Microcontroller

There are several different levels of microcontrollers and microcontroller systems. Some are very small, chip-sized devices, to which you have to connect your own electronics. Others are larger, composed of several components and ports for input and output, ready to plug right into other devices. If the terms in this appendix still seem daunting to you, we recommend that you just get started at a middle level with one of the Stamp-like microcontrollers that we cover in this book, like the BX-24, Basic Stamp, or the Basic Atom.

Higher-level microcontrollers will have a simple hardware interface to other devices (usually a plug or a couple of wires), and have a simpler programming language, if any at all. They will also usually be the most expensive microcontrollers because someone else has done the work for you. Lower-level microcontrollers will require more work, both in terms of hardware connections (you will have to build your own circuits to interface them to other devices), and in terms of programming (you will need to use a lower-level programming language like C or assembler for the lowest level chips). Lower-level processors usually have more expensive development environments, but the chips themselves are generally cheapest and most flexible in terms of what you can make them do.

There are a variety of factors to consider when picking a microcontroller. Not all of these may apply in your case.

Costs

How much do you want to spend? There are two costs to consider: the cost of the chip and the cost of the development environment. A PIC chip may only cost $10 (much less in quantities), but the compiler and a programmer will cost $300 or more. Mid-level chips cost more, but they often have development environments that are freely downloadable from the Web, so you will be pretty much ready to go on your first project for $50. High-level boxes cost in the hundreds of dollars before you add in their software, sensors, and other extensions. We recommend you stay away from them unless you are sure that your needs are extremely simple and your time and patience are extremely short. Low-level chips become more economical if you expect to use many chips in a project or in the long run, or if an organization is buying one development environment that many members can use on their own chips. For most beginners working alone, we recommend staying in the $50 range for a medium-level, Stamp-like microcontroller.

Time

How much work do you want to do? A higher-level controller will generally minimize the amount of work you do to build your interface to the world. Lower-level controllers will take more work before you have things working.

What programming languages, communications protocols, or electronics do you already know? All other things being equal, pick a system whose components you know something about.

What's the knowledge base like? Most microcontrollers have several Web sites and mailing lists dedicated to their use and programming. Quite often, the best ones are linked right off the manufacturer's or distributor's Web site. Check them out; look at the code samples and application notes. Read a few of the discussion threads. Do a few Web searches for the microcontroller environment you're considering. Is there a lot of collected knowledge available in a form you understand? This is a big factor to consider. Sometimes a particular processor may seem like the greatest thing in the world, but if nobody besides you is using it, you'll find it much harder to learn.

Expandability/Compatibility

What other components is the microcontroller compatible with? Can you add on modules to your microcontroller? For example, are there motor controllers compatible with it? Display controllers? Sensors or sensor modules? Often these modules are expensive, but they just snap into place without any special circuitry. If your time is worth a great deal, then these modules are a good buy. Sometimes, even if you know how to build it with a lower-level controller, a higher-level system is worth the cost because it saves building and maintenance time.

What do you have to connect to? Are you connecting to a MIDI synthesizer? A DMX-512 lighting board? A desktop computer? The phone system? The Internet? Different microcontrollers will have different interface capabilities. Make sure you can connect everything together. Sometimes this requires some creative combinations of controllers if no one controller can speak to all the devices you want it to speak to.

Physical and Electrical Characteristics

How many inputs/outputs do you need? Every system has a certain number of ins and outs. If you can, decide how many things you want to sense or control before you pick your controller.

What kinds of inputs and outputs do you need? Do you need analog inputs and outputs for sensing changing values, or do you only need digital ins and outs for sensing whether something is on or off? Will you need dedicated PWM (see Chapter 10)?

What kind of power is available to you? Does it need to be battery powered? Does it need to match the voltage of another device? Does it need to draw very little amperage?

How fast do you need to process data? Lower-level processors will generally give you more speed.

How much memory do you need? If you're planning some complex data processing or logging, you may need a microprocessor with lots memory or the ability to interface with external memory.

How small does it need to be? A lower-level controller generally lets you build your own circuitry, allowing you to reduce the size of the hardware you need.

The Microcontrollers Covered in This Book

The most obvious question that we haven't yet answered, of course, is why we chose the four microcontrollers covered in this book, and how you, the reader, can make your own choice. As we discussed in the Introduction, we believe in using the highest-level tool that gets the job done. Given an unlimited budget, this can mean using systems like Teleo, Infusion Systems' I-Cube, or other high-level solutions that require no programming or electronics. However, in practice, there's generally a limited budget. There are often physical and logistical limits that make systems like these impractical. To begin with, if you want to customize anything in ways they haven't thought of, if you want to use them with software other than that which they recommend, or if you want to use them without a PC (or MIDI controllers, in the case of the I-Cube), you're out of luck unless you know a few of the techniques covered in this book. For these reasons, we usually find the mid-level microcontrollers the easiest way to go, if we're doing a simple project that requires only one microcontroller.

Parallax Basic Stamp 2

Of the three mid-level modules we've chosen, Parallax's Basic Stamp 2 (BS-2) has been around the longest and probably has the biggest user base. We used it as the basis for our physical computing classes for years. It's simple to learn, reliable, and there are tons of examples available online. However, it has some limitations. Until recently, PBASIC was very limited in terms of control. Parallax has made some significant improvements in their control methods, though, and now PBASIC is on a par with the MBasic and PicBasic Pro for flexibility and ease of use. Unlike those languages, PBASIC is an interpreted language. This means that the text of your program is actually stored on the chip, and the chip interprets the program line by line as it's run. This makes it slower in execution speed than the other modules. For most physical computing projects this is not a problem, but occasionally, in complex projects, we've hit the speed limit on the BS-2. Finally, the BS-2 has no analog-to-digital converters on the module. Analog in must be done using a resistor-capacitor circuit, which measures the time a capacitor takes to discharge (rctime command). This is slower than an ADC, and limits you to sensors that can produce output that works with the RC circuit.

The Stamp programming environment is probably the simplest of all the controllers in this book. There's very little to it, and you'll be up and running with it in about a minute. The BS-2 is notable among the controllers in this book for being the only one that has a Macintosh-based programming environment. Though Parallax's development environment is Windows-based, a user in England has written a Mac compiler. It's a pretty good compiler, and we'd love to see an equivalent for all of the controllers in this book.

The Microcontrollers

NetMedia BX-24

Around 1998 or 1999, NetMedia introduced a competitor to the BS-2: the BX-24. This module was based on a more modern microcontroller from Atmel, and the programming environment produced compiled programs that ran without interpretation. As a result, it's faster in execution speed than the BS-2. In addition, the BX-24 has some useful features, such as eight analog-to-digital converters, onboard a built-in real time clock, and more EEPROM memory than the BS-2. The programming language, based on Microsoft's Visual Basic, is more complex than any of the other BASIC variants used in this book, which makes it harder for beginning programmers to learn. However, for advanced users, it allows for some powerful techniques, such as passing parameters from one subroutine to another, floating point math, and multitasking. There's a good knowledge base for the BX-24 online, but it hasn't been on the market long enough to establish as big a base as the BS-2.

Basic Micro Basic Atom Pro24

Basic Micro is the newcomer on the block, having been around less time than either NetMedia or Parallax. Their Basic Atom Pro24 offers advantages from both of its competitors. For example, code is compiled, making it reasonably fast in execution speed. The programming language, MBasic, is syntactically similar to pBasic and PicBasic Pro, meaning that examples for those platforms can be converted to MBasic very easily. However, it's got its own limitations. For one thing, there are only four analog-to-digital converters onboard, compared to the BX-24's eight. And as the newcomer, it's got a relatively small user base to compare notes with.

Though it's not on the market as of this writing, Basic Micro promises a Macintosh and a Linux development environment soon.

Microchip PIC

For those who feel they're ready to go to a lower level than the mid-level microcontrollers, we recommend Microchip's PIC family of microcontrollers. They make a wide range of controllers, some tiny ones with very few pins, some with large numbers of pins. They include a number of useful functions on the various PICs, such as multiple analog-to-digital converters, hardware PWM outputs, specialized synchronous serial control, and more. We recommend the 16F819, 18F252, or the 18F452. They're relatively cheap, once you've paid the development costs, and there's a decent amount of code and knowledge about them available on the Web in a number of programming languages.

Up until about 1998, most of the PIC family of microcontrollers were either UV-erasable, meaning that you had to expose them to ultraviolet light to erase them, or one-time programmable, meaning that if you didn't get it right the first time, you couldn't reprogram them. This made them cheap, but difficult for anyone without industrial support to use easily. In the past few years, Microchip has introduced a large number of *flash-programmable* PICs, meaning that, like the mid-level controllers, they can be reprogrammed electronically.

If you've got the basic electronics knowledge covered in Chapters 1 and 3, and you're comfortable with the programming concepts covered in Chapter 5, then you won't find the step to the PIC too hard. You will have higher up-front costs than you would for the mid-level microcontrollers, though, because you'll need to buy a programmer and a compiler. The code in this book for the PIC is written for microEngineering Labs' PicBasic Pro compiler (http://www.microengineeringlabs.com), which costs $249. They also make a less expensive compiler, PicBasic, but we find it too limiting in a number of ways, and prefer the Pro compiler. It's based on pBasic, which makes it very compatible with BS-2 example code.

There are a few other BASIC compilers on the market for the PIC as well, such as Basic Micro's MBasic compiler, and Crownhill's Proton+ compiler. The latter is notable in that it's the only one we've come across that has floating point math capability. The code looks syntactically similar to PicBasic Pro. However, we haven't used these compilers extensively, so you're on your own if you choose to use them.

If you really want to strike out on your own, and prefer programming in C, you should check out the C compilers for the PIC by Custom Computer Services (http://www.ccsinfo.com). They make a number of good libraries that make common functions on the PIC relatively easy for the experienced C programmer.

You'll need a hardware programmer too, and the range is wide on these. You can get professional-level programmers that cost hundreds of dollars, or you can get hobbyist ones that cost as low as $7. To a certain extent, you get what you pay for; the cheapest ones are the most limited, and the most expensive ones have many features you may never use. The ones we use most commonly are microEngineering Labs' EPIC programmers. They have a programmer that connects to your computer's parallel port for about $60. We've used them for years with good results. Recently, they came out with a serial programmer that's been getting good reviews as well. For these, you'll need both the 18-pin and 40-pin programming adaptors. Another programmer that we're relatively fond of is the K-150 from Dontronics (http://www.dontronics.com). It costs only about $35, but you have to solder some components on yourself. It's definitely not for the absolute beginner, and it doesn't cover all the same PIC models as the EPIC programmers; but it's the best thing we've seen in its price range, and it's USB-based.

So far, the programmers that we have talked about require you to remove your chip from the circuit in order to program it. *In-circuit serial programmers* are a convenience because they save you a little time every time you make a small change in code. Some programmers will allow you to run a simple extension cable from your programmer to the circuit board. The EPIC programmers mentioned have an in-circuit serial programming adaptor for 18-pin chips like the 16F819, and you can build your own for the larger chips. The K-150 programmer comes with an in-circuit serial programming cable that you only need to solder headers on to. Another technique is to program your chip once with a *boot loader* program that allows you to henceforth program it using a serial connection from your computer. This allows you to avoid using a programmer after you've loaded the boot loader, and feels very similar to higher level Stamp-like chips. This may seem like the best of all choices, but we find that they create some irritating limitations. We usually fall back to using the programmers instead.

The Microcontrollers

No matter which microcontroller environment you choose, you should get familiar with the user base, mailing lists, and online forums that support it. While this book can give you a good introduction, you'll learn far more from regular contact with other users and probably make a few friends along the way.

PIC Programmers

If you're working with the PIC microcontrollers, you need a programmer to get code into the chip. There are many programmers on the market. Following are a few we've had experience with, to give you an idea of the range of possible programmers. We recommend sticking with the EPIC if you can. It's still the one we prefer to use most of the time.

EPIC Plus Programmer from microEngineering Labs
http://www.melabs.com
$70 – $100

This is the programmer we use all the time. It's a no-frills parallel port programmer that works perfectly with Microcode Studio and PicBasic Pro. It comes with either a 40-pin or a 20-pin ZIF socket to mount the PIC on for programming. If you're using the PIC 18F452, you'll need the 40-pin socket. You can also get an 8–40 pin ZIF adaptor that lets you program almost any DIP-package PIC. You may need the smaller socket later, if you move to some of the other PICs. You can make your own in-circuit serial cable for it as well. Instructions can be found on the microEngineering Labs site.

There is a serial model of this programmer that's quite good, too. It's a bit more expensive, but we know many Macintosh users who swear by it, as it's easier to use under VirtualPC than the parallel programmer.

MPLAB ICD2 from Microchip
http://www.microchip.com
$150 – $180

This is a professional-level programmer made by Microchip, the company that makes the PIC. It has a lot of special features, including in-circuit debugging, which is the ability to run code line by line while the chip is in the circuit. It's also got a USB interface to the desktop. It's a higher-end tool than most individuals need, but it's the most affordable professional programmer.

K150 USB Programmer from Kits R Us
http://www.kitsrus.com
$35

This is a low-end programmer with a USB interface. You have to solder some parts on the circuit board yourself, and it doesn't cover all models of PIC, but it's a handy low-end programmer.

PIC-PG1 from Spark Fun
http://www.sparkfun.com
$9

This is the cheapest programmer we've found. It's as bare-bones as they come. It only works in-circuit, and it's not proven on laptop serial connections or USB-to-serial adaptors. It's not for beginners, but with some massaging, it will work reliably.

Spark Fun also sells some easier-to-use, more expensive programmers, including an ICD2-compatible programmer.

PIC Programmers

B

Recommended Suppliers

This is where you'll find specialty items, weird parts, and items that are specific to a particular application. This appendix is divided into two sections: staples and extras. The "Staples" section includes the microcontrollers, software, and basic electronic vendors needed for physical computing projects of all types. The "Extras" section includes all the vendors of sensors, motors, and other electronic systems and software. Both sections are divided up into hardware and software. The "Staples" section divides hardware into microcontrollers and electronic parts.

The Staples

These are the parts you'll need no matter what. The vendors here are ones that we use on a regular basis (sometimes weekly).

Microcontrollers

For more on choosing a microcontroller, see Appendix A and Chapter 2.

Basic Micro
http://www.basicmicro.com

They make and sell the Basic Atom Pro24 microcontroller module and several other modules. They're relatively new in the microcontroller market compared to Parallax and Microchip, but their products are promising.

Microchip
http://www.microchip.com

They make the PICmicro family of microcontrollers. PICs are found in all sorts of commercial and industrial applications and are the least expensive of the microcontrollers we recommend. That cost is offset by the cost of software and the extra time needed to learn the PIC. Nevertheless, it's the most flexible microcontroller platform in this book.

microEngineering Labs
http://www.melabs.com

They make PicBasic Pro, a very useful and simple programming environment for the PIC microcontroller. All of the PIC code in this book is written in PicBasic Pro.

NetMedia
http://www.netmedia.com

They make and sell the BX-24 microcontroller module. The BX-24 is a good competitor to Parallax's Basic Stamp 2, with some powerful additional features, like analog to digital converters, multitasking, and more.

Parallax
http://www.parallax.com

They sell the Basic Stamp 2 (BS-2) and a range of other microcontroller modules; a range of sensors and sensor modules; RF modules, IR modules, and Bluetooth modules; robotics parts; and much more. They also have some excellent tutorials for the Basic Stamp on their site.

Electronics Parts

The suppliers below can always be counted on to have the basic resistors, capacitors, transistors, switches, and other components you need on almost every project. For more exotic parts, see the second section of this appendix.

Digi-Key
http://www.digikey.com

They sell electronics components: resistors, capacitors, transistors, connectors, breadboards, and much more. They're one of our most regular and reliable suppliers of the staple components needed for every project.

Jameco
http://www.jameco.com

They sell electronics components: resistors, capacitors, transistors, connectors, breadboards, and much more. Along with Digi-Key, they're one of our most regular and reliable suppliers of the staple components. They also have pictures of nearly everything they sell on their Web site, which makes them attractive for beginners.

Software

The programming environments listed below are ones we've used regularly for developing interactive multimedia that interfaces with physical devices using a computer's serial port. There are many other packages out there, and you may already have one you love. If so, check if your environment has the capability to communicate via the computer's serial port, and you're good to go.

Cycling '74
http://www.cycling74.com

They make Max/MSP, a visually based multimedia programming environment that's very useful with MIDI systems and other physical computing projects. They also make Jitter, a real-time video manipulation and tracking tool.

Macromedia
http://www.macromedia.com

They make Flash MX and Director MX, two good multimedia authoring environments. Of the two, Director is the more powerful for physical computing, thanks to its Xtra expansion toolkit.

Miller Puckette
http://www-crca.ucsd.edu/~msp/software.html

He makes PD, an open-source Max-like programming tool for Windows computers, and a number of objects for both PD and Max/MSP. See also Ted Apel's externals for Max/MSP and PD at http://crca.ucsd.edu/~tapel/software.html.

Processing
http://www.processing.org

They make an excellent authoring environment that's Java-based. It's also free.

The Extras

Every project has its own specialized needs. This section contains some of the more exotic or specialized elements that you might need for different projects. It's also a good place to browse for ideas on what's technically possible that you may not have thought of before.

Hardware

This section is a delightful mix of sensors, materials, hardware, and other tangible things you might need to realize your work. It's impossible to categorize this mix effectively, so the suppliers are listed in alphabetical order.

3M
http://www.3M.com

If it's vinyl or glue, they probably make it. They're one of the leading suppliers of plastics, adhesives, and more. Their retroreflective tape reflects infrared light really well and is very easy to track using a video camera.

ABACOM
http://www.abacom-tech.com

They make RF-to-serial modules.

Acroname
http://www.acroname.com

Great for sensors and motors. They sell the best assortment of ranging sensors of anyone we know.

AEI Components
http://www.aeicomp.com

They sell small LCDs, cameras, DVD players, and other video accessories.

Allegro Micro
http://www.allegromicro.com

They make motor drivers, shift registers, and other useful integrated circuits.

All Electronics
http://www.allcorp.com

This is a surplus vendor of electronic parts. They sell lots of sensors, switches, and parts taken from junked items that are still very useful. They're often cheaper than the retail vendors.

Analog Devices
http://www.analog.com

They make accelerometers, digital potentiometers, analog-to-digital converters, and many other useful special-purpose ICs.

Ascension Tech
http://www.ascension-tech.com

They make and sell precision 6-degrees of freedom motion trackers for virtual reality systems.

ASCI
http://www.as-ci.net/asFFTXtra/

They make Xtras for Director MX, including the asFFT Xtra, which performs fast Fourier transformations on incoming live sound.

Black Box
http://www.blackbox.com

They make protocol converter boxes of all kinds.

Cermetek
http://www.cermetek.com

They make modem ICs and other network interface ICs.

Color Kinetics
http://www.colorkinetics.com

They make LED-based spotlights and architectural lighting.

D-Link
http://www.dlink.com

They sell commercial converters of all types: USB, Ethernet and wireless Ethernet, serial, Bluetooth, and more. They also sell various wireless Ethernet cameras and video phones.

Decade Engineering
http://www.decadenet.com

They sell text overlay boards for analog video.

EarthLCD
http://store.earthlcd.com

They sell LCD panels of all sizes and shapes.

Edirol
http://www.edirol.com

They make video mixers and other video control products.

Electronic Goldmine
http://www.goldmine-elec.com

A surplus supplier of electronic parts. Very cheap, and very useful for sensors, electronic components, kits, motors, and more.

Elm Electronics
http://www.elmelectronics.com

They make various specialty ICs, including a Control-L to RS-232 converter.

Elo TouchSystems
http://www.elotouch.com

They make computer touch screens.

Elwire
http://www.elwire.com

They sell electroluminescent wire and drivers.

FerretTronics
http://www.ferrettronics.com

They sell a number of motor control chips, including a servo motor controller chip and a two-stepper motor X-Y plotter chip.

Findchips.com
http://www.findchips.com

They don't sell anything themselves, but they link to over a dozen electronics vendors. You can search by a part number and get a list of vendors that sell that part, including links to data sheets.

The Extras

Focus Enhancements
http://www.focusinfo.com

They make video converters, projectors, video mixers, and many other analog and digital video products.

Happ Controls
http://www.happcontrols.com

They sell pushbuttons, joysticks, coin slots, and other devices for vending machines and arcade games. Their pushbutton selection is an excellent source for kiosk designers.

Highly Electric
http://www.highly.com

They sell photoelectric switches and other intrusion detection systems.

IBVA Technologies
http://www.ibva.com

They make brainwave sensors.

Images SI, Inc.
http://www.imagesco.com

They sell various sensors and actuators. They're a good source for flex sensors, FSRs, and many other common sensors.

Infusion Systems
http:// www.infusionsystems.com

They sell the I-Cube system, a high-level sensor system that reads sensors and sends the results out as MIDI messages. Their TapTiles floor sensors are very expensive and very reliable.

Interlink Electronics
http://www.interlinkelec.com

They make FSRs and sell them in large quantities only, along with touchpad systems.

Kits R Us
http://www.kitsrus.com

They make DIY electronic kits: DTMF decoders, strobe flashers, and more. They also make a number of inexpensive PIC programmers.

Kopin
http://www.kopin.com

They make very small LCDs.

Lantronix
http://www.lantronix.com

They make embedded net controllers. Their CoBox Micro and Xport serial-to-Ethernet converters are relatively easy to work with, and relatively inexpensive.

LED Effects
http://www.ledeffects.com

They sell super bright LEDs and LED products.

Lemos International
http://www.lemosint.com

They sell a range of RF modules, GPS modules, and many other radio-related communications parts. They also sell several Bluetooth modules.

Linx Technologies
http://www.linxtechnologies.com

They make a wide range of RF modules. They're more expensive than others, but incorporate error-checking and other useful features.

Mark of the Unicorn
http://www.motu.com

They make synthesizers, keyboards, and MIDI gear.

Marlon P. Jones Associates
http://www.mpja.com

They sell a variety of surplus electronics, including power supplies, motors, and miniature steppers dirt cheap.

Maxim
http://www.maxim-ic.com

They make a variety of signal conditioning ICs: analog-to-digital converters, digital potentiometers,TTL-to-RS-232 converters, and much more.

McMaster-Carr
http://www.mcmaster.com

If we had to single out one supplier for construction and mechanical parts, it would be McMaster-Carr. They carry a very wide variety of hardware and construction materials, and their catalog and Web site is very detailed and helpful. If you can't find what you're looking for locally, check out http://www.mcmaster.com.

Micromint
http://www.micromint.com

They make embedded controllers, phone line interfaces, and various other ICs.

Nexus Controls
http://www.nexuscontrols.com

They sell serially controlled switchers for analog video.

The Extras

Oncore
http://www.oncore.com

They make and sell GPS products of all sorts. Owned by Motorola, they're one of the leaders in this field.

Polhemus
http://www.polhemus.com

They make and sell precision 6-degrees of freedom motion trackers for virtual reality systems.

Quadravox
http://www.quadravox.com

They make MP3 modules and other sound record and playback devices.

Quantum Technologies
http://www.qprox.com

They make capacitive touch sensor ICs.

Ramsey Electronics
http://www.ramseyelectronics.com

They make electronic kits of all sorts: amplifiers, RF modules, DTMF decoders, and more. They're useful when you don't want to build a complex circuit yourself, as many of their kits are sensors or actuators that require a little extra circuitry.

Rentron
http://www.rentron.com

They sell RF modules, IR modules, home automation components, PIC programming accessories, and more. They also have a number of useful tutorials on their site.

Rose Brand Fabrics
http://www.rosebrand.com

They sell all kinds of fabrics for stage work: curtains, velour, muslin, projection screens, Mylar, and more. They will also custom make all kinds of curtains and drops.

Scott Edwards Electronics
http://www.seetron.com

They make and sell a number of useful motor control modules for servos, steppers, and DC motors, as well as some simple-to-use LCD and VFD display modules.

SkyeTek
http://www.skyetek.com

They make RFID products: readers, writers, and tags.

Smarthome
http://www.smarthome.com

They sell home automation products, including X10 interfaces.

Solarbotics
http://www.solarbotics.com

They sell motors, small sensors, solar cells, and other useful parts for making small solar-powered robots.

Spark Fun
http://www.sparkfun.com

They sell GPS modules, sensors, PIC programmers, and tools. A small company that makes some handy bits and pieces not found elsewhere, for relatively low prices.

Super Bright LEDs
http://www.superbrightleds.com

They sell super bright LEDs, of course.

Symbol Technologies
http://www.symbol.com

They make a number of electronic devices for sales, inventory, and manufacturing, including RFID products, barcode scanners, and more.

Tapeswitch
http://www.tapeswitch.com

They sell inexpensive floor switches in rolls.

Texas Advanced Optoelectronic Solutions
http://www.taosinc.com

They make color sensors and light-to-voltage and light-to-frequency converters.

VIA Technologies, Inc.
http://www.via.com.tw

They make single-board computers, including the Mini-ITX mainboards, which make good replacements for multimedia computers in physical computing projects.

Vicon
http://www.vicon.com

They make motion capture systems for film animation.

Winbond Electronics
http://www.winbond-usa.com

They sell sound record and playback devices and chips of all sorts.

Xecom, Inc.
http://www.xecom.com

They make phone line interface modules.

Heading 1

Software

The software listed here includes video and audio processing software and other extensions for the multimedia authoring environments listed above. These extensions will give you a greater range of possible hardware input devices.

Amit Pitaru
http://www.pitaru.com

Amit makes Sonia, an extension to Processing that allows for playback and manipulation of sound and control of live sound input.

David Rokeby
http://www.interlog.com/~drokeby/softVNS.html

David makes the Very Nervous System, a video tracking system for Max/MSP.

Direct Xtras
http://www.directXtras.com

They make Xtras for Director MX.

Eric Singer
http://www.ericsinger.com

Eric makes Cyclops, a video tracking system for Max/MSP, and a number of useful MIDI components.

Physical Bits
http://www.physicalbits.com

They make the best Serial Xtra for Director MX, and a number of useful Xtras for Director. Their bedtime reading list is also entertaining.

Smoothware Design
http://www.smoothware.com

They make a number of useful Xtras for Macromedia's Director MX programming environment, including TrackThemColors, a video tracking Xtra.

SoftSynth
http://www.softsynth.com

They make extensions for Java, including the JSyn libraries, which allow you to synthesize sounds in real time.

Tellme Networks, Inc.
http://www.tellme.com

They make voice menu software for automated calling systems.

TroikaTronix
http://www.troikatronix.com

They make software for live performance, including Isadora, a live video mixing tool, MIDI Xtras for Director MX, and more.

C
Schematic Glossary

Throughout this book, we've used a number of schematic diagrams. Following is a glossary of all the schematic symbols in the order in which they appear in this book, along with some common ones you may encounter in other schematic diagrams. For more thorough explanations of them, consult a more detailed electronics text like Paul Scherz's *Practical Electronics for Inventors* (McGraw-Hill/TAB Electronics, 2000).

Junctions

Not all the lines that cross in a schematic are meant to be connected. When crossing lines connect they are marked with a dot and are called *junctions*. The illustration below shows both junctions and three different ways to draw unconnected crossings.

Connected junctions   Unconnected junctions

Power and Ground

DC power sources always have a positive side and a negative side; AC power sources don't. The voltage of a power source should always be indicated. In addition to the standard symbols, we've also thrown in the schematic for a 7805 voltage regulator, which we use all the time in this book.

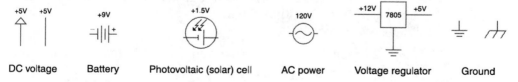

DC voltage   Battery   Photovoltaic (solar) cell   AC power   Voltage regulator   Ground

Every circuit should have a ground. Sometimes ground is indicated in several places, to keep the drawing uncluttered.

Switches

Switches are *either normally open (NO)* or *normally closed (NC)*. A normally open switch will conduct only when you activate it, and a normally closed switch will conduct only when not activated.

Switches can be *momentary* or *toggle* switches. Momentary switches (or pushbuttons) spring back to their normal position after you release them. Toggle switches stay in the last position to which they were set. Remote control buttons and keyboard keys are momentary switches, whereas household light switches are toggle switches.

A switch has a certain number of *poles*. Each pole can connect (or disconnect) two wires. In other words, each pole can control a separate circuit. A switch's *throw* describes how many possible closed positions it has. You'll see these two characteristics, pole and throw, listed together frequently and abbreviated as SPST (single-pole, single-throw—the most common and most basic switch), DPDT (double-pole, double-throw), DPST (double-pole, single-throw), and so forth.

| Single-pole, single throw (SPST) | Single-pole, double throw (SPDT) | Double pole, single throw (DPST) | Double pole, double throw (DPDT) | Normally closed (NC) |
| | | | | Normally open (NO) |

Resistors

Fixed resistors should always have the resistance value indicated. Variable resistors come in many different forms. Some variable resistors have their own symbols, like thermistors and photoresistors. Others don't. The generic variable resistor can stand in for any of them. A variable resistor's range should be indicated, and a variable resistor or potentiometer's range should be indicated.

Fixed Resistor   Variable Resistor   Potentiometer   Thermistor   Photoresistor

Fixed resistors' values are indicated by a standard color code, as follows: There are four color bands on a resistor. The fourth band is always either silver or gold, indicating the error tolerance of the resistor's value. Locate a band of this color first and hold the resistor so it is on the right. The first band indicates the first digit of the resistor's value, and the second band indicates the second digit. The third band indicates the order or magnitude, in powers of ten. This means that you multiply the first two numbers by ten to the power of the multiplier indicated by the third color.

For example, a resistor whose bands are red, red, brown, and gold has the following value:

Red = 2 (first digit)

Red = 2 (second digit)

Brown = $\times 10^1$ (or 10)

Gold = ±5%

That's a 220-ohm resistor ±5%

Refer to Table C.1 for color codes and their values.

Table C.1
Resistor Color Codes

COLOR	VALUE	MULTIPLIER
Black	0	x1
Brown	1	x10
Red	2	x100
Orange	3	x 1k
Yellow	4	x 10k
Green	5	x 100k
Blue	6	x 1M
Violet	7	x 10M
Grey	8	x100M
White	9	x1G
Fourth Band		
Gold	±5%	
Silver	±0%	

Capacitors

Capacitors can be polarized or unpolarized. Polarized caps will have the polarity indicated. There are variable capacitors as well, though we haven't used any in this book. A capacitor's capacitance or its range (if it's a variable cap) should be indicated.

Unpolarized capacitors   Polarized capacitor   Variable capacitor

Like resistors, capacitors have a standard code for their values, but it's numerical, not in colors. The first two digits are the first two digits of the value, and the third digit is the multiplier. The result is the value in picofarads. Most of the capacitors in this book are specified in microfarads. Move the decimal point six positions to the left to change the picofarads into microfarads. A small "u" or the Greek symbol μ are the most commonly used symbols for microfarads. Occasionally you might see "M" used, which might be confused for Mega or Milli, but in the context of capacitors usually means micro.

For example, a capacitor marked 104 is 10 with four more zeros, or 100,000 picofarads. That's 0.1 microfarads. Table C.2 lists some of the more common capacitor codes.

Table C.2
Common Capacitor Codes

CODE	VALUE
102	0.001 microfarads
103	0.01 microfarads
104	0.1 microfarads
105	1 microfarad

The letters after the number are tolerance codes, like the fourth band on the resistor. Refer to Table C.3 for what they mean.

Table C.3
Capacitor Tolerance Codes

LETTER	TOLERANCE
B	+/- 0.10%
C	+/- 0.25%
D	+/- 0.5%
E	+/- 0.5%
F	+/- 1%
G	+/- 2%
H	+/- 3%
J	+/- 5%
K	+/- 10%
M	+/- 20%
N	+/- 0.05%
P	+100%, -0%
Z	+80%, -20%

Diodes and Diode-Based Devices

Diodes allow the flow of current and stop the flow in the other.

Light-emitting diodes light up when current is passed through them in the forward direction.

Photodiodes allow current to pass from anode to cathode when a sufficient amount of light hits them.

Zener diodes block up to a certain breakdown voltage and allow it to pass above that voltage.

Silicon-Controlled Rectifiers allow current to flow from the anode to the cathode when a control voltage is applied to the gate. Once current is flowing, the gate has no effect until there's no voltage difference between the anode and cathode. They act like electronically controlled switches.

Triacs allow current to flow in either direction when a control voltage is applied to the gate. They act as electronically controlled switches for AC.

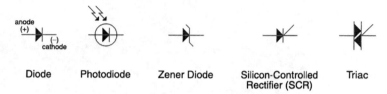

| Diode | Photodiode | Zener Diode | Silicon-Controlled Rectifier (SCR) | Triac |

Transistors

Bipolar NPN transistors allow current to pass from collector to emitter when a control voltage and current are applied to the base. They act as normally open electronic switches.

Bipolar PNP transistors prohibit the flow of current when a control voltage and current are applied to the base. They act as normally closed electronic switches.

Phototransistors act like normal transistors when enough light hits the base.

Field-Effect Transistors (FETs) and *Metal Oxide Semiconductor FETs* (MOSFETS) are variations on the transistor that you'll see in some circuits. They need almost no current on the base (which is called a *gate* in FETS and MOSFETS). They're used commonly as electronic switches.

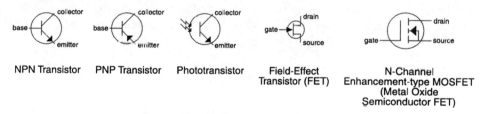

| NPN Transistor | PNP Transistor | Phototransistor | Field-Effect Transistor (FET) | N-Channel Enhancement-type MOSFET (Metal Oxide Semiconductor FET) |

Relays

Relays are electromechanical switches. They're slower than transistors, SCRs, or triacs, but they can control AC or DC sources. Like switches, relays can have multiple poles and throws.

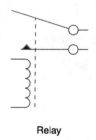

Relay

Opto-Isolators

Opto-isolators are electronic switches that combine an LED and a phototransistor. They allow you to electrically isolate your control circuit from the circuit it's controlling, because the only connection between the two is light. They generally don't carry as much current as relays.

Optoisolator

Sidactors

A sidac (sidactor) is a surge suppressing device mainly used in telephone equipment. It's much like a triac without a gate. It turns on with a voltage change and turns off with a current change.

SIDAC (Sidactor)

Solenoids and Inductors

Solenoids, like relays, are inductive loads. A charge applied to the coil of solenoid moves a mechanical shaft, just as a charge applied to the coil of a relay moves the switch contacts and closes the switch. Solenoids are used to create linear motion.

Inductors are coils of wire. When you put a current through an inductor, it induces a current in any nearby wire. We haven't used any in this book, but they're a staple of many electronic circuits. Inductors pass current when it's a steady DC current and resist it when it's an AC current.

Transformers are two coils of wire placed near each other. When current is passed through one, it generates a current in the other. The ratio of the voltage of the coils is the same as the ratio of the number of turns in each coil, so transformers are often used to transform one voltage into another. Below are the schematic symbols for inductors.

Inductor coil
(also used for a solenoid in this book)

Transformer

Crystal Oscillators

Crystals pulse at a specific frequency when triggered by a voltage or by mechanical force. They're used as timing oscillators for microcontrollers, or any other application where you need a precise, very fast pulse stream.

Crystal

Sound Devices

Piezoelectric devices generate a voltage when they're mechanically bent or reshaped. Conversely, a voltage passed through them causes them to change shape. They're used as the basis of many vibration sensors, and audio devices.

Speakers are coils of wire mounted to a paper cone. A magnet is mounted around the coil. When AC current is passed through the wire, the magnetic field that the current generates pushes the coil away from the magnet, and the cone vibrates. Sometimes a piezo cone is used, and the coil induces a voltage in the piezo, causing it to vibrate.

Microphones are devices convert movement from sound waves into electrical energy, generating a voltage.

The following illustration shows a range of audio devices:

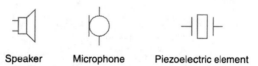

Speaker   Microphone   Piezoelectric element

Miscellaneous Devices

As we've discussed, when you pass an AC voltage through a wire, it induces a current in a nearby wire. *Antennas* are wires that you send AC voltages into in order to transmit the changes to another antenna. An antenna will transmit certain frequencies better than others, depending on its length. The signals from one antenna to another are very weak, and must be amplified.

Incandescent lamps (light bulbs) are thin wires placed in a vacuum or inert gas that resist the flow of current. In resisting, they generate heat and light.

Motors are coils of wire placed between two opposing magnetic fields. When you apply current to a motor's coil, it generates a magnetic field and causes the motor to move from one magnetic field to the other.

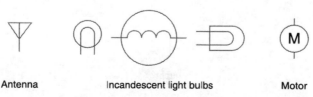

Antenna   Incandescent light bulbs   Motor

Schematic Glossary

Sockets

There are thousands of kinds of sockets available for a variety of purposes. We're only showing you three of the most common that are used in this book.

AC sockets have two AC terminals and a ground. The socket shown is the American standard 115-volt 15-amp socket.

Audio jacks typically have two or three connectors. If there are two, they're called the *tip* and the *sleeve*. If there are three, the middle conductor is called the *ring*.

AC socket   2-conductor audio jack   3-conductor audio or power jack

Logic Symbols

Schematics will often include logic symbols to indicate that the particular component used matters less than what it does. For example, if you want an inverter, which is basically a logic NOT gate, there are many possible components, and it may not matter which one you use. Logic schematics are used to give you an idea of what happens logically, not electrically, but sometimes they're mixed, as in the 7404 hex inverter you saw in the serial chapters.

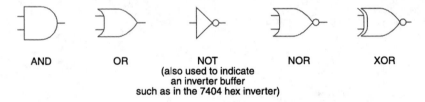

AND   OR   NOT   NOR   XOR
(also used to indicate
an inverter buffer
such as in the 7404 hex inverter)

Amplifiers

In our schematics, we've drawn the main ICs in a form that matches their physical packages. This is not always the case. Amplifiers are a notorious exception to this, and are hard to read if you've never seen a schematic of one. Every amplifier should have two inputs (usually called inverting and non-inverting, or negative and positive), an output, and two voltage supplies. A dual-supply amp has a positive and a negative voltage supply (not ground). A single-supply amp has only a positive supply and ground. Pin numbers are indicated by each connection.

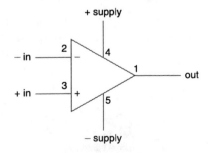

Common Schematic Terms and Abbreviations

There are a number of terms and abbreviations you'll see in schematics and pin diagrams that may not make sense at first glance. Below are some of the more common ones.

Voltage

Usually marked as V_{dd}, V_{in}, V_{cc}, or V^+. Some ICs will have a logic voltage input, which usually matches your microcontroller's voltage, and a supply voltage input, which matches the voltage and amperage of the motor or other device that the IC is meant to control.

Ground

Usually marked V_{SS}, V_{EE}, or Gnd.

RES, MCLR

Reset, or in the case of the PIC microcontrollers, master clear-reset (MCLR). Often you'll see a horizontal bar over the reset symbol, indicating that you connect the pin to ground to reset the chip (this is called an active low input).

CS

Chip select. This is common in synchronous serial slave chips, when you might have several devices sharing one serial line. Often you'll see a horizontal bar over this symbol, indicating that you connect the pin to ground to select the chip (this is called an active low input).

MOSI

Master out, slave in. This is the line that a synchronous serial master device uses to send data to a slave device.

MISO

Master in, slave out. This is the line that a synchronous serial slave device uses to send data to a master device.

CLK, SCLK, SCL

Clock (or serial clock). The clock line from a synchronous serial master device to the slave devices.

SDI

Serial data input. Synchronous serial input line (can be master or slave).

SDO

Serial data output. Synchronous serial output line (can be master or slave).

SDA

Serial data. In I2C synchronous serial communication, one data line is used for both input and output. Data goes from the master to the slave on the rising edge of the clock, and from the slave to the master on the falling edge of the clock.

TX

Transmit. This is the line that an asynchronous serial device sends data out on.

RX

Receive. This is the line that an asynchronous serial device receives data in on.

OSC

Oscillator. If the IC needs an external crystal oscillator, there will be pins to connect it.

Index

CPSIA information can be obtained
at www.ICGtesting.com
Printed in the USA
FFOW01n1358240617
37116FF